Society

D0583210

THE
THREE MESSIAHS

*The Historical Judas the Galilean, The Revelatory
Christ Jesus, and The Mythical Jesus of Nazareth*

DANIEL T. UNTERBRINK

iUniverse, Inc.
New York   Bloomington

The Three Messiahs
The Historical Judas the Galilean, The Revelatory Christ
Jesus, and The Mythical Jesus of Nazareth

iUniverse books may be ordered through booksellers or by contacting:

iUniverse
1663 Liberty Drive
Bloomington, IN 47403
www.iuniverse.com
1-800-Authors (1-800-288-4677)

ISBN: 978-1-4502-5946-0 (pbk)
ISBN: 978-1-4502-5947-7 (ebk)

Printed in the United States of America

iUniverse rev. date: 9/15/2010

Contents

PART II   CHRIST JESUS (THE REVELATORY MESSIAH)

PART III JESUS OF NAZARETH
(THE MYTHICAL MESSIAH)

INTRODUCTION

Two radically different interpretations exist concerning the possibility of an historical Jesus of Nazareth: the traditional or Orthodox Christian story and the Mythicist explanation of that traditional story. The traditional viewpoint, held by all Christian denominations, claims that Jesus existed in the flesh, his life and death described accurately in the New Testament. By adhering to the New Testament story, Orthodox Christianity also must accept the scientifically impossible notions of bodily resurrection and miracles which suspend the laws of nature, along with contradictions which arise from comparing the Old Testament to the New Testament. A few questions must be asked concerning this viewpoint:

1. Can any living organism be dead for days and then be brought back to life? Whether we like to believe it or not, dead people, rotting in the grave, do not come back to life. There are no such things as vampires or resurrected human beings.
2. Can any man walk on water? This feat can only be accomplished in winter months. Jesus, like you and me, would have been swimming, not walking.
3. Can any man control the weather? Even the weathermen, with all their modern equipment, cannot accurately predict weather events more than a few days in advance. To control the weather is science fiction at best.
4. Can food be produced out of thin air or can we actually create matter? We can certainly rearrange matter, but this feat is far different than creating matter out of nothing. Jesus, the man, could not produce this miracle.
5. Can water be changed into wine? Without grapes and fermentation, this too would be impossible. In the Middle Ages, scientists tried to change objects into gold, with little luck. This story of Jesus surely cannot be taken literally.
6. Why would God condemn human sacrifice in the Old Testament yet sacrifice his only son in the New Testament? If God condemned humans for sacrificing their sons and daughters, then would not God's sacrifice of his only son be a bit hypocritical?
7. Why would God need a human sacrifice in order to forgive sins if he already

had the power to forgive sins? An all-powerful God does not need human or animal sacrifices in order to forgive sins. John the Baptist understood God's forgiving power, preaching that the sinners needed to repent of their sins. With this repentance came forgiveness from God.

8. Why would God replace an Everlasting Covenant? Was it incorrectly termed Everlasting? This cannot be adequately explained by Orthodox Christianity. If God needed a New Covenant, then his Old Covenant must have been severely flawed. That would mean that God would not be perfect.

These questions, along with many others, have led some people to take a completely different approach to the existence of an historical Jesus. The second approach, represented by the Mythicists, denies the existence of an historical Jesus. Not only do the Mythicists see the futility in ignoring the obvious answers to the above questions, they also point to historical writings which do not mesh with the Gospel presentation of Jesus. Their conclusion: Jesus was a myth or possibly a composite of many historical figures. They do not see any one man as Jesus or the framework for this Jesus. Here is a list of items that these critics, the Mythicists, maintain in their opposition to a historical Jesus:

1. Since Jesus' life was not mentioned by Josephus, Jesus was either totally immaterial to society or he failed to exist. (The one passage in *Ant.* 18.63-64 was an interpolation, as it clearly portrayed the later Church's belief in Jesus, not the viewpoint of the cynical Josephus.) This omission of the Gospel Jesus by Josephus would be like compiling a list of the greatest basketball players and omitting Michael Jordan.

2. Paul may or may not have existed. If he did exist, he nevertheless did not champion the idea of a flesh and blood Jesus. He focused upon the Risen Christ. This, in and of itself, does not disprove an historical Jesus, but Paul's writings do little to support the Gospel Jesus.

3. The mention of James, the brother of Jesus, was an interpolation in Galatians, according to the Mythicists. If Jesus did not exist, they reason, he could not have had a brother. This is a circular argument. A James, the brother of Jesus, was mentioned by Paul and by Josephus. Instead of logically analyzing these passages, the Mythicists simply dismiss them as misinterpreted or interpolated.

4. The book of Acts also carried the story about James. This was merely to be consistent with the misinformation placed forward by the Pauline interpolation. However, the Mythicists do not explain why Acts presented a different James than the James of Paul or the James of Josephus. This would complicate their black and white scenario concerning James.

5. Consistent with 3 and 4 above, Josephus' mention of James, the brother of Jesus (*Ant.* 20.200), was really about James, the brother of Jesus, the son of Damneus (*Ant.* 20.203). This Mythicist interpretation is necessary to remove James and Jesus from the pages of actual history. You see, if you are a Mythicist, then you cannot accept anything which suggests a real history concerning Jesus.

6. The expulsion of Christians under Claudius, as reported by Suetonius, was really not about Christians but about followers of Chrestus. Thus, the Mythicists claim that this incident did not really confirm that Christians existed at this time in history (41 CE). They do not realize that Suetonius stated that the Jews, who were followers of a Chrestus, were removed from Rome because of disturbances. Jews would not have followed a pagan Chrestus but would have followed a Messiah (Christ).

7. The persecution of Christians by Nero, after the Great Fire of Rome (64 CE), was not true, and that Tacitus' record of this was invented by the later Church. Again, this is a circular argument. To the Mythicists, it is untrue because Jesus and Christians did not exist in the early and middle first century but were invented later.

8. The death and resurrection of Jesus mirrors other mystery religions and is not at all unique. This is true, but it does not disprove an historical Jesus. It just supports the notion that the Gospel Jesus did not exist.

There are many other criticisms put forth by the Mythicists, but the above list gives you an idea of their opposition to an historical Jesus. In short, outside of the Gospels, no reliable sources exist concerning the life of Jesus of Nazareth. They do have a good point concerning Jesus' absence from the pages of Josephus' histories. How could the Jewish historian miss the greatest story ever told?

I agree with the Mythicists on this: Jesus of Nazareth was invented. He did not really exist. But I also side with the traditionalists concerning the existence of a Messiah character. Was there any figure within the pages of Josephus who could have been the template for the Gospel "Jesus"? The answer is yes: a rabbi known as Judas the Galilean.

My premise is that Judas the Galilean was the original Messiah figure and that Jesus of Nazareth was based primarily upon Judas' life and death. Therefore, in this study, we will focus primarily upon the writings of Josephus, as he compiled the only complete account of this period in Jewish history. The Gospels and Acts also have many tidbits which help flesh out my thesis. In addition, I will also pay attention to the Slavonic Josephus, which paints a different story concerning John the Baptist, Barabbas, Judas Iscariot and Jesus. And most importantly, my thesis must be consistent with the writings of Paul and the histories of Suetonius and Tacitus. Judas the Galilean will become the bridge between the traditional and Mythicist viewpoints, a bridge that neither group will willingly want to cross.

This book attempts to construct a much different story concerning Jesus of Nazareth. Part I focuses upon Judas the Galilean, a first-century rabbi who helped shape the Jewish response to Rome's occupying power. He was the historical "Jesus". Much effort has been expended in connecting his actions to that of the Gospel Jesus. Yet, there are strong differences between Judas the Galilean and Jesus of Nazareth. For example, Judas preached a nationalism which demanded the elimination of Roman influence, while Jesus remained amazingly quiet on this issue. How then can I possibly claim that Judas the Galilean, a revolutionary, was the historical framework for Jesus of Nazareth, a pacifist?

Is it possible that the story of "Jesus" evolved during the first century? The Gospels were written several generations after the fateful events in Jerusalem, anywhere from 70 CE to 140 CE. The audience for these Gospels was also quite different from those who witnessed "Jesus" in the flesh: the Gospels were written for Gentile consumption, and their Jesus was meant to identify with Gentile notions concerning God. Therefore, the human sacrifice of Jesus became central to this Gospel, something abhorrent to the Jewish God of the Old Testament. Part II deals with Paul, the individual who bridged these two very different cultures. Paul's Christ Jesus was different from the Jews' avenging Messiah. Paul's Christ Jesus became the prism through which we interpret the Gospel's Jesus of Nazareth.

In Part III, a further examination of the New Testament has been undertaken. Every passage which questions the established storyline has been tackled. The result is startling: behind the traditional Jesus of Nazareth stands the historical Judas the Galilean. A thorough explanation will show how a revolutionary rabbi became the Gospel's pacific Messiah.

The thesis that Judas the Galilean was the historical Jesus is original to me, but others have clearly paved the way for my analysis. In the 1960s, S. G. F. Brandon wrote a book entitled, *Jesus and the Zealots,* where similarities were drawn between the Jesus movement and the Zealot movement. He stated: "The 'gospel' of Paul, so signally rescued from oblivion by the Jewish overthrow, became the source of Catholic Christianity, in which the Messiah Jesus was metamorphosed into the Divine Saviour God of all mankind." (1) In short, Brandon also adhered to the concept of three Messiahs: the original Jewish Messiah, the revelatory Christ Jesus espoused by Paul and the man-god presented in the Gospels.

In the 1980s, Hyam Maccoby published two books which also painted a different picture of Jesus. (2) Maccoby's Jesus lived the life of a devout Pharisee while Paul pretended to have such credentials. Maccoby attempted to prove that Paul was not a Pharisee but rather a Herodian. This revised framework also was consistent with the writings of Josephus and my own thesis. Josephus stated that Judas the Galilean held to the Pharisaic beliefs and that Saul (Paul) was a member of the royal family, a Herodian.

In the 1990s, Robert Eisenman wrote *James, the Brother of Jesus*. He clearly demonstrated that James was a devout Jew and popular among the Jewish people. If that were so, he reasoned, Jesus should be interpreted in light of his brother, James, not through the prism created by Paul and the later Church. His writings, full of insights, led me towards my Judas the Galilean thesis.

And finally, the contribution of Robert Graves cannot be ignored. Graves wrote two historical novels, titled, *I Claudius* and *Claudius the God*. He developed ideas about King Agrippa I and Claudius which were instrumental in the shaping of my own theory concerning Paul.

To these four scholars, along with others who have poured their hearts and souls into finding the historical Jesus, I offer my thanks. For my work, though original, has clearly been built upon these scholarly efforts.

PART I
JUDAS THE GALILEAN
(THE HISTORICAL MESSIAH)

Under his administration [Coponius] it was that a certain Galilean, whose name was Judas, prevailed with his countrymen to revolt; and said they were cowards if they would endure to pay a tax to the Romans, and would, after God, submit to mortal men as their lords. **This man was a teacher of a peculiar sect of his own, and was not at all like the rest of those their leaders**. (Josephus, *War* 2.118) (Emphasis mine)

But of the fourth sect of Jewish philosophy, Judas the Galilean was the author. These men agree in all things with the Pharisaic notions; but they have an inviolable attachment to liberty; and say that God is to be their only Ruler and Lord. They also do not value dying any kind of death, nor indeed do they heed the deaths of their relations and friends, **nor can any such fear make them call any man Lord**. (Josephus, *Antiquities* 18.23) (Emphasis mine)

The Jews he [Claudius] expelled from Rome, since they were constantly in rebellion, at the instigation of Chrestus. (Suetonius, *The Twelve Caesars*, Claudius 25)

We may therefore presume to imagine some probable cause which could direct the cruelty of Nero against the Christians at Rome, **whose obscurity, as well as innocence**, should have shielded them from his indignation, and **even from his notice**. The Jews, who were numerous in the capitol, and oppressed in their own country, were a much fitter object for the suspicions of the emperor and of the people. …although the genuine followers of Moses were innocent of the fire of Rome, there had arisen among them a new and **pernicious sect of Galilaeans**, which was capable of the most horrid crimes. Under the appellation of Galilaeans, two distinctions of men were confounded, the most opposite to each other in their manners and principles; the disciples who had embraced the faith of Jesus of Nazareth, and the zealots who had followed the standard of Judas the Gaulonite. …How natural was it for Tacitus, in the time of Hadrian, to appropriate to the Christians, the guilt and the sufferings, which he might, with far greater truth and justice, have attributed to a sect whose odious memory was almost extinguished! (conjecture of Gibbon, *The History of the Decline and Fall of the Roman Empire*) (Emphasis mine)

CHAPTER 1

TIME MARKERS

Time markers are important in determining the order of events in any historical period. Recent United States time markers include the bombing of Pearl Harbor on December 7, 1941, the assassination of JFK on November 22, 1963 and the twin tower disaster on September 11, 2001. By knowing certain dates, historians can order events based upon what is known about the time markers. For example, the United States did not officially declare war on Germany and Japan until after Pearl Harbor. Therefore, any reports of U.S. fighting in the war would be after the attack on Pearl Harbor. In the case of JFK, we know that his vice president, Johnson, became president in 1963, even though the scheduled elections were not until 1964. And the increased airport security, which we must all now endure, came after the September 11, 2001 plane attack.

These same time marker principles are also used in New Testament studies. Due to 2000 years of Church influence, scholars have given the Gospels' and Acts' dates a higher priority than other documents. Usually, when a discrepancy between the New Testament account and that of Josephus occurs, scholars generally side with the New Testament. This is understandable since the bulk of scholars in the past have had ties to religious organizations. But that is not good historical methodology. The time markers must make good historical sense. If they do not, then serious questions must be asked. That is what we shall do.

JOHN THE BAPTIST

The dating of Jesus' ministry, as described by the Gospels, was dependent on several time markers. The most important of these time markers concerned the coming of John the Baptist.

In the fifteenth year of the reign of Tiberius Caesar - when Pontius Pilate was governor of Judea, Herod Tetrarch of Galilee, his brother Philip tetrarch of Iturea and Trachonitis, and Lysanias tetrarch of Abilene - during the high priesthood of Annas and Caiaphas, the word of God came to John son of Zechariah in the desert. (Luke 3:1-2)

The definitive date of 28-29 CE can be calculated by adding fifteen years to the beginning of Tiberius' reign, which began in 14 CE. The other people mentioned reigned for a number of years and therefore cannot be used to pinpoint a specific date. For example, Annus acted as high priest from 6-15 CE and held much power during the high priesthood of Caiaphas (19-37 CE). This date range for Annas covers thirty-one years and cannot be considered as accurate as the Tiberius date.

From this "rock solid" date of 28-29 CE, scholars have calculated the approximate date of Jesus' birth and the approximate date of Jesus' death. According to Luke 3:23, Jesus was about thirty years old when he began preaching, after being baptized by John. This would make Jesus' birth at about 2 BCE. This is in the middle of two other birth dates given for Jesus in Matthew and Luke. In Matthew chapter 2, Jesus was born just before the death of Herod the Great, around 6-4 BCE. In Luke 2:1-3, Jesus was born at the census of Cyrenius or about 6 CE. So even though none of the dates for Jesus' birth agree, scholars, on the whole, hold to this approximate time period for Jesus' birth.

The duration of Jesus' ministry has been estimated at one to three years. If that were true, then the death of Jesus must have occurred somewhere between 30-32 CE. This crucifixion date falls within the reign of Pilate and is nearly universally accepted by scholars. (Note that the traditional dating for Pilate is 26-37 CE while I have assigned a reign of 18-37 CE (1)). Therefore, from the dating of John the Baptist's ministry, the lifespan of Jesus can be placed at 4 BCE to 32 CE, give or take a few years on either side. In this span of years, New Testament scholars have searched for the historical Jesus. Unfortunately, during this particular timeframe, no corroboration can be taken from Josephus, the Jewish historian who chronicled the history of the Jews. This omission of the "Greatest Story Ever Told" has largely been brushed under the table by most scholars.

PROBLEMS WITH THE TRADITIONAL DATING OF JOHN

The greatest problem with the traditional timeline concerns the relationship between Jesus and John the Baptist. According to the Gospel of Luke, John came preaching repentance in 28-29 CE and shortly thereafter baptized Jesus. John was then arrested and summarily executed by Herod Antipas, documented by Mark 6:14-16, Matt. 11:2-3 and Matt. 14:1-12. This last reference by Matthew explained why John was put to death: he criticized Herod for marrying Herodias, his brother Philip's wife. The Gospels all agree that John the Baptist died during the ministry of Jesus, around 29-32 CE. However, this dating does not agree with two other important sources.

The first and most authoritative source comes from the Jewish historian, Josephus. His account about John the Baptist can be dated at 35-36 CE, several years **after** the traditional dating for Jesus' crucifixion. He wrote:

"Now, some of the Jews thought that the destruction of Herod's army came from God, and that very justly, as a punishment of what he did against John, that was called the Baptist; for Herod slew him, who was a good man, and commanded the Jews to exercise virtue, both as to righteousness towards one another, and piety towards God, and so to come to baptism; for that the washing [with water] would be acceptable to him, if they made use of it, not in order to the putting away [or the remission] of some sins [only], but for the purification of the body; supposing still that the soul was thoroughly purified beforehand by righteousness. Now, when [many] others came in crowds about him, for they were greatly moved [or pleased] by hearing his words, Herod, who feared lest the great influence John had over the people might put it into his power and inclination to raise a rebellion (for they seemed ready to do anything he should advise), thought it best, by putting him to death, to prevent any mischief he might cause, and not bring himself into difficulties, by sparing a man who might make him repent of it when it should be too late. Accordingly, he was sent a prisoner, out of Herod's suspicious temper, to Macherus, the castle I before mentioned, and was there put to death." (*Ant.* 18.116-119)

Consistent with the Gospel account, Josephus mentioned that Herod Antipas had fallen in love with his brother's wife, Herodias. This may have been one reason for John the Baptist's imprisonment. But the above account about John stressed another reason for the imprisonment and execution of John: John was incredibly popular among the people, and they would do whatever he wished. Herod Antipas feared that John would call upon his followers to revolt. In order to prevent such an act, Antipas executed John. This scenario differs from the Gospel account, where Herodias asked for the head of John the Baptist, much to the chagrin of Antipas. (Matt 14:1-12) The Gospel version does not explain the great influence that John held over the people. In fact, in Matt. 11:1-7, John and his disciples wanted to confirm that Jesus was the Messiah. If they were then convinced, it would follow that they too would become disciples of Jesus. This is even more confusing when considering the introduction of John in the Gospels. In Mark chapter 1, John acknowledged that the baptism of Jesus would be more powerful than his own water baptism. Why then did John and his disciples not become full members of the Jesus movement? Why did Herod Antipas fear John's sway over the people if Jesus were more popular and powerful? Could it be that John outlived Jesus, contrary to the Gospel accounts?

In Mark 1:14, Jesus began his ministry **after** John was put into prison. Matthew chapter 14 confirmed that John was executed before Jesus fed the five thousand. If John were put to death in 35-36 CE, then the traditional timeline must be wrong. The second source to describe John's last days is called the Slavonic Josephus. This source is a slightly different version of Josephus' *Jewish War*. There are two separate accounts of John's last days in the Slavonic Josephus. The first details John's prediction of Philip's death, which occurred in 34 CE. (2) The second is another version of the Antipas and Herodias affair. It states: "But he accused Herod incessantly wherever he found him, and right up to the time when [Herod] put him under arrest and gave orders to slay him." (3) This followed the death of Philip in 34 CE and confirms the *Antiquities* dating of 35-36 CE for John's execution.

There is only one solution to this jumbled Jesus and John timeline. If Jesus died after John, then he must have died in 36-37 CE, not the traditional 30-32 CE as detailed above. But this later date for Jesus' death causes other problems. If Jesus were crucified in 37 CE, under Pilate, then he would have been forty years old, not thirty as claimed by Luke. In addition, Paul would not have been converted until around 39 CE. Paul claimed that the Jerusalem Council took place seventeen years after his conversion (Gal. 1:18-2:1). If Paul converted in 39 CE, then the Jerusalem Council did not meet until 56 CE, during the reign of Nero. But this later date for the Jerusalem Council (Acts 15) does not jibe with Acts 18:2, where Priscilla and Aquila had just been forced to leave Rome with other Jews during the reign of Claudius (41-54 CE). So, the later date for Jesus' crucifixion cannot be trusted.

Under the traditional timeline there are insurmountable difficulties with the dating of Jesus' death. If he were crucified in 30-32 CE, then he died **before** John the Baptist. If Jesus died after John as claimed by the Gospels, then the Pauline timeline is plainly affected. **Neither scenario works**. So we must ask: is there any other source which dates the ministry of John the Baptist, from beginning to end? The answer is yes, that source being the Slavonic Josephus.

Now at that time a man went about among the Jews in strange garments for he had put pelts on his body everywhere it was not covered with his own hair; indeed to look at, he was like a wild man. He came to the Jews and summoned them to freedom, saying: "God hath sent me, that I may show you the way of the Law, wherein ye may free yourselves from many holders of power. And there will be no mortal ruling over you, only the Highest who hath sent me." And when the people heard this, they were joyful. And there went after him all Judea, that lies in the region around Jerusalem. And he did nothing else to them save that he plunged them into the stream of the Jordan and dismissed them, instructing them that they should cease from evil works, and [promising] that there would [then] be given them a ruler who would set them free. ...And when he had been brought to Archelaus and the doctors of the Law had assembled, they asked him who he [was] and where he [had] been until then. And to this he made answer and spoke: "I am pure; [for] the Spirit of God hath led me on, and [I live on] cane and roots and tree-food." But when they threatened to put him to torture if he would not cease from those words and deeds, he nevertheless said: "It is meet for you [rather] to cease from your heinous works and cleave unto the Lord your God." (4)

The Slavonic description of John the Baptist agrees with the Gospels concerning John's dietary requirements and his mode of dress. However, everything else is much different. This John was much more political that the Gospel Baptist. In the Slavonic, John said: "God hath sent me, that I may show you the way of the Law, wherein ye may free yourselves from many holders of power. And there will be no mortal ruling over you, only the Highest who hath sent me." In short, John preached that the Jews would be freed from the earthly powers (Herodians and Rome) if they properly followed God's Law. This message was identical to that of Judas the Galilean. Josephus wrote this about Judas and his movement: "But the fourth sect of Jewish Philosophy, Judas the Galilean was the author. These men agree in all things with the Pharisaic notions; but they have an inviolable attachment to liberty; and say that God is to be their only Ruler and Lord." (*Ant.* 18.23) Both the Baptist and Judas the Galilean wanted to free the land from its earthly rulers.

It is also interesting that the above John passage was inserted into the *War* immediately before the introduction of Judas the Galilean. Josephus described Judas in a way that would remind the present day reader of Jesus. "Under his [Archelaus] administration it was that a certain Galilean, whose name was

Judas, prevailed with his countrymen to revolt; and said they were cowards if they would endure to pay a tax to the Romans, and would, after God, submit to mortal men as their lords. This man was a teacher of a peculiar sect of his own, and was **not at all like the rest of those their leaders**." (*War* 2.118) So the order of the Slavonic version of the *War* had John announcing Judas the Galilean, just as John announced Jesus in the Gospels.

The date when John was inserted into the story can be easily determined. He introduced Judas the Galilean, right before the census revolt, during the shaky reign of Archelaus. This can be accurately dated at 6 CE, a good twenty-two years before the Gospel arrival of John the Baptist. Thus, we have an alternate dating for the arrival of John the Baptist. The Gospel account had John introducing Jesus in 28-29 CE, but no information in Josephus supports this date. In fact, there was no Jesus in Josephus. (The supposed "Jesus" passage in *Ant.* 18.63-64 was an obvious interpolation.) (5) The Slavonic version placed John the Baptist in 6 CE where a great rabbi also preached a message of revolution, namely Judas the Galilean.

THE STAR OF BETHLEHEM

The Gospel of Matthew is the only Gospel which detailed the Star of Bethlehem story. Mark does not mention anything about the birth of Jesus, starting instead with the Baptism of John. Luke placed his birth story at the time of the Census, or at 6 CE, a good eleven years after the Star of Bethlehem. And John simply did not deal with the birth of the earthly Jesus, but rather equated Jesus with God (John 1:1-5).

The exact date of the Star of Bethlehem has been debated over the centuries. It definitely occurred during the reign of Herod the Great (37 - 4 BCE). According to Matthew 2:19-20, Jesus was a young child when Herod died. If Herod died in 4 BCE, then Matthew's date for Jesus' birth can be approximated at 6 BCE, eleven years earlier than the Census of Cyrenius (Luke 2:1-7). Scholars have tried in vain to find a celestial event which corresponds to this date. Some have even pushed the birth back to 12 BCE so that Haley's comet would coincide with Jesus' birth. The important point concerning this particular time marker, however, would be the end of Herod the Great's reign or 4 BCE.

In Matthew's story, Magi from the east came to Herod in Jerusalem and asked: "Where is the one who has been born king of the Jews?" Herod inquired of his priests and determined that Bethlehem was the city of Scripture. Herod sent the Magi to Bethlehem, instructing them to return to him after locating the child. Herod wanted to kill the baby as this new king would be a threat to his own rule. Being warned in a dream, the Magi returned to their own country by another route, bypassing Herod. Herod was furious and ordered that all boys under the age of two, in and around Bethlehem, should be killed. The massacre took place but Jesus had been taken away by Joseph, who had been forewarned by a dream.

Matthew's version is not the only version of the Star of Bethlehem. The Slavonic Josephus also boasted an account which gave greater detail to the story. This version had Persian astrologers, who had traveled for a year and a half, meet with Herod the Great. They, too, did not return to Herod after finding the Messiah. Herod asked his advisors if they knew the meaning of the star. They replied: "It is written: 'A star shall shine forth from Jacob and a man shall arise from Judah'. ...It is written that the Anointed One is [to be] born in Bethlehem. Even if you have no mercy on your servants, kill those infants of Bethlehem and let the others go." Herod thus spared all the infants except those around Bethlehem.

There are two major differences between the Slavonic Josephus and the account given by Matthew. The first concerns the meaning of the Star of Bethlehem. Matthew did not broach the subject but the Slavonic Josephus tied the star to the "Star Prophecy", which promised the Messiah. Herod had good reason to be so upset, wishing to kill the young king. The second difference concerns the dating of events. In Matthew, the Star of Bethlehem came in 6-4 BCE. In the Slavonic Josephus, the story date was approximately 25 BCE (6). Thus, there is a one generation difference between the two accounts.

It should not be missed that this generation gap was also present in the John the Baptist accounts. In the Gospels, Jesus was born in 6 BCE and began his ministry around 29 CE, at the age of 34. In the Slavonic Josephus, the Messiah was born around 25 BCE and followed John the Baptist in 6 CE, at the age of 30. These are the two choices we can make: the traditional Jesus of Nazareth or the radical rabbi, Judas the Galilean.

One coincidence is worth noting. The two birth stories of Jesus, at the end of Herod the Great's rule (6-4 BCE) and at the Census of Cyrenius (6 CE), correspond to the major episodes of Judas the Galilean's ministry. In 4 BCE, right before the death of Herod, Judas and Matthias engineered the Golden Eagle Temple Cleansing. Josephus detailed this episode in *War* 1.648-655 and *Antiquities* 17.148-167. The Census uprising of Judas the Galilean occurred in 6 CE and was recorded by Josephus in *War* 2.117-118 and *Antiquities* 18.4-25. It is also curious that the Slavonic Josephus added its own history to these Judas the Galilean events. Additional passages in the Slavonic version of the *War* relate to the Messiah, John the Baptist and the later Church. Why would additional information be added to the Judas passages if he were not part of the original Messianic movement, later ascribed to Jesus of Nazareth?

PONTIUS PILATE

It is generally agreed that Jesus was crucified under Pontius Pilate. Tacitus wrote the following:

Nero set up as the culprits and punished with the utmost refinement of cruelty a class hated for their abominations, who are commonly called Christians. Christus, from whom their name is derived, was executed at the hands of the procurator Pontius Pilate in the reign of Tiberius. (Tacitus, *Annals,* xv.44)

Tacitus wrote about the Great Fire of Rome (64 CE) around 120 CE. Surely, the legend of the Christ was well known by those who had investigated the cult. Note that the above passage appears genuine as a later Christian apologist would not have denigrated the Christians in such a manner. From the passage we can tell that Pilate was procurator during the reign of Tiberius, somewhere between the years 14-37 CE.

According to our current version of *Antiquities*, Pontius Pilate became procurator of Judea in 26 CE. As noted earlier, the traditional dating for Jesus' crucifixion is between 30-32 CE. Thus, the traditional crucifixion occurred near the middle of Pilate's career. However, the text of Josephus suggests that Pilate arrived in 18 CE. The timeline of Josephus as detailed in *Antiquities* 18.26-84 is as follows:

6 CE	Joazar - High Priest
6-9 CE	Coponius - Roman Governor
6 CE	Judas the Galilean - Tax Revolt
6-15 CE	Annas - Appointed High Priest by Coponius
9-12 CE	Ambivulus - Roman Governor
12-15 CE	Rufus - Roman Governor
15-26(18) CE	Gratus - Roman Governor **(11 or 3 years)**
15 CE	Ishmael - Appointed High Priest by Gratus
15-16 CE	Eleazar - Appointed High Priest by Gratus
16-17 CE	Simon - Appointed High Priest by Gratus
18-37 CE	Caiaphas - Appointed High Priest by Gratus
26(18)-37 CE	Pilate - Roman Governor
18 CE	City of Tiberius Built
19 CE	Germanicus Poisoned
26(19) CE	Pilate - Roman Effigies; Sacred Money for Aqueducts
26(19) CE	Jesus Passage (Replaced Judas the Galilean's Death)
19 CE	Paulina Affair - corroborated by Tacitus

The following points should be noted. First, the text of Josephus described only three years for Gratus instead of eleven years. This eleven year stretch is crucial to the traditional dating. Second, Caiaphas was appointed High Priest by Gratus in 18 CE. He then served 19 consecutive years as High Priest. According to John 18:13, Jesus was brought before Caiaphas, "the high priest that year." Such wording only makes sense after the merry-go-round of High Priests from 15-18 CE. In addition, Tiberius liked his procurators to stay in the provinces for extended periods of time, to cut down on corruption. The High Priesthood of Caiaphas would agree with Pilate's tenure if Pilate came in 18 and not in 26 CE. Third, after both mentions of Pilate (supposedly 26 CE), Josephus described events occurring in 18-19 CE. If Pilate were really procurator from 26-37 CE, then the whole rhythm of the timeline is disrupted. However, if Pilate came in 18 CE, then everything flows perfectly.

Why would anyone change the tenure of Gratus from three to eleven years, thus delaying Pilate's governorship until 26 CE? This was done to distance Jesus from Judas the Galilean. Note that the spurious Jesus passage is where we would expect to see Judas' death. Thus, not only was the death of Judas the Galilean replaced with the death of Jesus, but the beginning of Pilate's career was also a victim of tampering.

There is one other source which supports the earlier timeline for Pilate. Eusebius, the fourth century historian of the early church wrote the following concerning Pilate:

In "Antiquities" Book XVIII, the same writer [Josephus] informs us that in the twelfth year of Tiberius, who had mounted the imperial throne after the fifty-seven-year reign of Augustus, Judea was entrusted to Pontius Pilate, and that Pilate remained there ten years, almost until Tiberius's death. This clearly proves the forged character of the "Memoranda" so recently published, blackening our savior; at the very start the note of time proves the dishonesty of the forgers. If they are to be believed the crime of the Savior's Passion must be referred to Tiberius's fourth consulship, i.e. the seventh year of his reign, but at that time it is clear that Pilate was not yet in charge of Judea, if we may accept the testimony of Josephus, who explicitly declares, in the passage already quoted, that it was in the twelfth year of his reign that Tiberius appointed Pilate procurator of Judea. (7)

The *Memoranda* claimed that the Messiah was crucified in 21 CE. This is very close to the actual text of Josephus as chronicled above. Note that I claim that Pilate came to Judea in 18 CE and that the spurious Jesus passage fits into the 18-19 CE flow of events. It is very possible that the arrest could have taken place in 19 CE and the actual crucifixion occurred in 21 CE. Prisoners were often kept on ice for the most opportune time to carry out their sentence.

Why is it so important to pinpoint Pilate's career and the crucifixion of the Messiah? It has everything to do with the time markers. This will become clear when the Pauline time markers are examined.

CEPHAS AND PAUL AT ANTIOCH

The time markers already examined about John the Baptist and Jesus are actually important in exploring Paul's career. The traditional timeline has Jesus being crucified somewhere between 30-32 CE. If that were the case, then Paul could not have been converted before 31 CE. In fact, most scholars place Paul's conversion between 31-35 CE.

There is one set of years that no scholar disputes. According to Galatians, Paul spent 17 years in the movement, between his conversion and the Council of Jerusalem. (Gal. 1:18-2:1) That means that the Council took place between 48-52 CE. Galatians then goes on to describe a confrontation between Cephas and Paul at Antioch, concerning table fellowship and circumcision. This was shortly after the Council, possibly one year or even longer. There is no way to know for sure. So at the earliest, the confrontation occurred in 49 CE and by 55 CE at the latest. This confrontation between Cephas and Paul does have a corresponding story recorded by Josephus.

Now, during the time Izates abode at Charax-Spasini, a certain Jewish merchant, whose name was Ananias, got among the women that belonged to the king, and taught them to worship God according to the Jewish religion. … and he said [to Izates], that he might worship God without being circumcised, even though he did resolve to follow the Jewish law entirely; **which worship of God was of a superior nature to circumcision**. …So the king at that time complied with these persuasions of Ananias. But afterwards, as he had not quite left off his desire of doing this thing, a certain other Jew that came out of Galilee, whose name was Eleazar, and who was esteemed very skillful in the learning of his country, persuaded him to do the thing; for as he entered into his palace to salute him, and found him reading the law of Moses, he said to him, "Thou dost not consider, O king! that thou unjustly break the principal of those laws, and art injurious to God himself, [by omitting to be circumcised]; for thou ought not only to read them, but chiefly to practice what they enjoin thee. How long wilt thou continue uncircumcised? But, if thou hast not yet read the law about circumcision, and does not know how great impiety that thou art guilty of by neglecting it, read it now." When the king had heard what he said, he delayed the thing no longer, but retired to another room, and sent for a surgeon, and did what he was commanded to do. (*Ant.* 20.34-48) (Emphasis mine)

This clash of ideas between Ananias and Eleazar over circumcision was the very same argument that Paul described in Galatians. Note that Eleazar was sent from Galilee to push the circumcision line. In Galatians 2:11-13, Paul wrote: "When Peter came to Antioch, I opposed him to his face, because he was in the wrong. Before certain men came from James, he used to eat with the gentiles. But when they arrived, he began to draw back and separate himself from the Gentiles because he was afraid of those who belonged to the circumcision group." In the Josephus passage, Eleazar was sent from Galilee while members of the circumcision group were sent by James. It can be argued that James was based out of Galilee at this time. In fact, James no doubt sent Eleazar as well. The timing of this is interesting. The Ananias and Eleazar exchange occurred in 44 CE. The Antioch dispute between Cephas and Paul also can be assigned to this time, 44 CE. Of course, this is at least five to ten years earlier than the traditional timeline will allow. My point is this: the Messiah figure was crucified somewhere between 19-21 CE and Paul converted in the early 20's. The 44 CE confrontation makes sense only if Paul joined the movement in the early 20's.

The Ananias and Eleazar story is also present in the book of Acts. Acts often incorporated Josephus' history in its representation of early Church history. This Church history is patently fraudulent. Note that the instructor who took Saul by the hand in Acts 9:10-19 was named Ananias. This may be a coincidence, but the Philip story in Acts 8:26-39 also uses much of the King Izates story. Philip instructed a Eunuch while Ananias gained access through the King's harem. The eunuch then was persuaded by Philip to be baptized just as King Izates was persuaded by Eleazar to be circumcised. Both the eunuch and the king were reading the Scriptures prior to being persuaded. In short, the miraculous Philip story was just a fanciful retelling of the King Izates circumcision. This proves that the King Izates conversion was an important moment in the movement's history. Otherwise, the author of Acts would not have twisted it into his own perverted history.

THE EXPULSION OF JEWS UNDER CLAUDIUS

Suetonius supplied information about the early Messianic movement which proved that the person referred to as the Christ was real, thus angering the Mythicists. This victory for the traditionalists has been somewhat tempered by the message implied by the passage, which does not agree with what we know of the pacifist Christ taught throughout the ages. The passage is as follows:

The Jews he [Claudius] expelled from Rome, since they were constantly in rebellion, at the instigation of Chrestus. (8)

From this passage, we can assume that the Jews were following a Christ or Messiah figure. This Christ, however, incited the rebellious nature of the Jews. This is definitely a different picture of Jesus of Nazareth. In fact, it is a picture of Judas the Galilean. But is this passage about "Chrestus" really referring to the Jewish Messiah? The answer can be gleaned from Acts 18:2, where Aquila and Priscilla had just been ordered to leave Rome during the reign of Claudius. According to the traditional timeline, this order by Claudius was post Council and post Antioch argument, thus being around 49-54 CE. (Note that Claudius reigned from 41-54 CE.) Thus, the traditional timeline at least falls within the reign of Claudius. It is also interesting that the author of Acts felt that the expulsion of Jews was an important part of the early "Christian" movement. The question is this: Is the traditional timeline consistent with other data concerning the expulsion of Jews from Rome under Claudius. The above passage from Suetonius does not tell us when the event occurred, but two other passages from other historians may answer our question. First, Tacitus wrote:

It is true that the Jews had shown symptoms of commotion in a seditious outbreak, and when they heard of the assassination of Caius [Caligula], there was no hearty submission, as a fear still lingered that any of the emperors might impose the same orders. (9)

Although not pinpointing the date of the expulsion from Rome, Tacitus did lean towards the early years in Claudius' reign. Caligula had ordered a statue of himself be placed inside the Temple in Jerusalem. This order, had it been successfully carried out, would have caused war between the Roman Empire and the Jewish state. Only the assassination of Caligula saved the day, as the order was rescinded. The Jews, however, did not trust Claudius either and this mistrust probably resulted in the disturbances which Suetonius blamed upon the Jews who were followers of a "Chrestus". Thus, the dating of this event was in the early years of Claudius.

There is one other historian who sheds greater light upon this inquiry. Dio Cassius wrote:

As for the Jews, who had again increased so greatly that by reason of their multitude it would have been hard without raising a tumult to bar them from the city, he did not drive them out, but ordered them, while continuing their traditional mode of life, not to hold meetings. He also disbanded the clubs, which had been reintroduced by Gaius (10)

This passage is consistent with that of Tacitus and points to the early years of Claudius' reign, around 41 CE. However, according to Dio Cassius, the Jews were not expelled from the city but their actions were being monitored and curtailed. This would be consistent with keeping a close eye upon the trouble-makers, the followers of "Chrestus".

THE FAMINE

In Acts 11:27-30, a great famine spread across the entire Roman Empire. This passage was inserted between the Peter and Cornelius episode (Simon and Agrippa I, 43 CE) and the imprisonment of Peter and James (the crucifixion of Simon and James, the sons of Judas the Galilean, 46-48 CE). Thus, this must have occurred sometime in the mid 40's. According to *Antiquities* 20.101, a great famine occurred during the reign of two procurators, Fadus and Tiberius Alexander, dated at 44-48 CE. This is interesting because Josephus mentioned the famine right before writing about the crucifixions of Judas' two sons, Simon and James. Perfectly corresponding to this is the Acts' chronology where the famine was introduced right before the imprisonment of Simon Peter and James. Certainly, the author of Acts was simply rewriting the history of Josephus.

Not only does the famine help confirm Acts' usage of *Antiquities* (post 93 CE), it also exposes lies concerning Paul. In Acts, Paul visited Jerusalem 4 times: after his conversion, at the famine, at the Council of Jerusalem and before his exile to Rome. When Paul wrote to the Galatians, he stated that he went to Jerusalem twice: 3 years after his conversion and 14 years later at the Council of Jerusalem. There is no way that Paul could have known about the last visit because it had not yet occurred. But Paul should have known about the famine-relief visit. The reason why Paul did not acknowledge it was because it also had not yet occurred. Could Paul have forgotten the famine? Considering Paul was comparing his credentials to the Pillars, he would not have failed to place this famine relief on his scorecard. Thus, the famine occurred after the Council of Jerusalem, not before as Acts suggests. Once again, if the Council was before the famine, which can be dated at 44 CE, then the New Testament chronology cannot work.

TIMELINES

The traditional timeline is an anachronistic nightmare. Perhaps the most damning evidence against this timeline is the sequence of events concerning John the Baptist. The New Testament claims that John the Baptist came onto the scene in 28-29 CE and was executed a few years later, approximately 30-32 CE. From this dating springs forth the dating of Jesus' birth and the later ministry of Paul. Most scholars reluctantly buy into the timeline because they see no alternative. My purpose is to supply an alternative, one that is consistent with Josephus and other early writers. For example, both Josephus and the Slavonic Josephus dated the death of John the Baptist at 36 CE, much later than the Gospel death of Jesus. In addition, the Slavonic Josephus introduced John in 6 CE, not 28 CE. These alternatives dates for John make sense and will be shown to be more accurate than the Gospel dates. Below are both the traditional and my Judas the Galilean timelines concerning the time markers.

MATTHEW, LUKE and GALATIANS

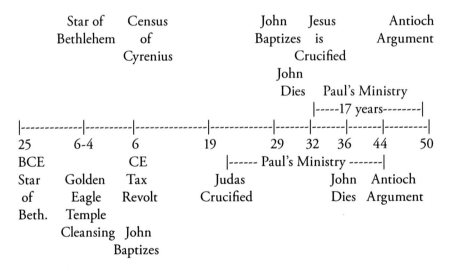

JOSEPHUS AND THE SLAVONIC JOSEPHUS

As each chapter unfolds, this basic comparison of events will be the centerpiece. The reader must ask if the traditional timeline can be trusted. And the reader must determine if that timeline should be replaced with my Judas the Galilean timeline.

CHAPTER 2

THEUDAS AND JUDAS THE GALILEAN

The handling of Theudas and Judas the Galilean by the author of Acts is perhaps the most confusing, most illogical and most dishonest literature one will ever come across. Its purpose was to mislead, so one must admire the desired effects over the past two thousand years. It has worked brilliantly: the histories of both Theudas and Judas the Galilean have been suppressed to the point that these two Jewish revolutionaries are insignificant footnotes, never even considered in the Jesus story.

But were they really only bit players in a much larger drama, or did Luke distort their true contributions to Jewish history by his own unflattering account? After all, their very mention means that some people still remembered them. Is it possible that both Theudas and Judas the Galilean were much more important than we can even imagine? Luke's take on the two is reproduced below.

Having brought the apostles, they made them appear before the Sanhedrin to be questioned by the high priest. "We gave you strict orders not to teach in this name," he said, "yet you have filled Jerusalem with your teachings and are determined to make us guilty of this man's blood."

Peter and the other apostles replied, "**We must obey God rather than men!** The God of our fathers raised Jesus from the dead -- whom you had killed by hanging him on a tree."...

When they heard this, they were furious and wanted to put them to death. But a Pharisee named Gamaliel, a teacher of the law, who was honored by all the people, stood up in the Sanhedrin and ordered that the men be put outside for a little while. Then he addressed them: "Some time ago Theudas appeared, claiming to be somebody, and about four hundred men rallied to him. He was killed, all his followers were dispersed, and it **all came to nothing**. After him, Judas the Galilean appeared in the days of the census and led a band of people in revolt. He too was killed, and **all his followers were scattered**. Therefore, in the present case I advise you: Leave these men alone [Peter and the apostles]! Let them go! For if their purpose or activity is of **human origin, it will fail**. But if it is from God, you will not be able to stop these men; you will only find yourselves fighting against God." His speech persuaded them. (Acts 5:27-40) (Emphasis mine)

In this story, Peter and the apostles were arrested for preaching in the name of Jesus of Nazareth. It is quite revealing that the author of Acts had Peter and his followers say, "We must obey God rather than men!" That was the philosophy of Judas the Galilean as expressed by Josephus. He wrote: "But of the fourth sect of Jewish philosophy, Judas the Galilean was the author. These men agree in all other things with the Pharisaic notions; but they have an inviolable attachment to liberty; and say that God is to be their only Ruler and Lord." (*Ant.* 18.23) Note that the Fourth Philosophy, like Peter and the apostles, had only one ruler and that was God. The statement by Peter was very serious. He and his brethren were challenging the rule of Rome and their hirelings. Most scholars miss this point because they are convinced that the Jesus movement had no connections to the Fourth Philosophy. This proves the power of this Acts' passage.

The supposed author of this passage on Theudas and Judas the Galilean was Gamaliel, a renowned teacher of the law. He came to Peter's and the other apostles' rescue after they had been detained by the religious authorities for preaching the message of Jesus of Nazareth. The apostles were brought to the Sanhedrin by the Sadducees and were being questioned by the High Priest. This part of the Sanhedrin wanted to put the apostles to death. Their opinion of the Jewish Christians had not changed since the crucifixion of Jesus. The same Sadducees and High Priest had arrested and condemned Jesus. (This trial of Jesus was at night and was not conducted in front of the whole Sanhedrin.) Luckily for the apostles, this arrest was brought to the Sanhedrin which consisted of Sadducees and Pharisees. Gamaliel, a leader of the Pharisees, convinced the whole Sanhedrin that the apostles should be freed. Unlike the trial of Jesus, the Sanhedrin was ruled by majority vote. Gamaliel had the full support of the Pharisees and thus saved the apostles.

This act by a Pharisee contradicts the traditional teachings concerning the Pharisees. In the Gospels, we are led to believe that the Pharisees hounded Jesus and were responsible for his capture and crucifixion. However, on the night of Jesus' arrest, Jesus was taken to Annas and Caiaphas and was then handed over (the same Greek word as applied to Judas Iscariot's supposed betrayal) to Pilate for crucifixion. The Pharisees had nothing to do with Jesus' arrest! That the Pharisees were not opposed to Jesus' movement can also be supported by Josephus. In *Ant.* 20.197-203, James, the brother of Jesus, was stoned to death by the illegal actions of the High Priest, Annas. (This was the son of the Annas responsible for Jesus' arrest and crucifixion.) In response to the police action against James, the Pharisees petitioned to have Annas removed as High Priest. Thus, the friendly relations between Jesus and the Pharisees existed over several generations. (The Gospels occasionally portrayed the Pharisees in a positive light, such as when they warned Jesus about Herod's plans to kill him. (Luke 13:31)) It is also illuminating that Judas the Galilean and his movement "agreed in all other things with the Pharisaic notions." (*Ant.* 18.23) Also, the Sadduc, Judas' co-teacher and second-in-command, was a Pharisee. (*Ant.* 18.4)

Gamaliel's reasoning for rescue was simple: these men would fail miserably if they were not from God, and the converse, nothing could be done to stop them if God were on their side. Obviously, there was nothing in the apostles' message which was deemed blasphemous. The claims for the Messiah and for resurrection were both acceptable to the Pharisees. This was not true for the Sadducees. Jesus' claim for kingship (Messiah) and his cleansing of the Temple were political attacks on the power structure, and they (Sadducees and High Priest) were the ones with the most to lose. The authorities agreed with Gamaliel only because the majority of the Sanhedrin sided with him. The apostles were set free after an obligatory flogging and a warning to stop preaching about Jesus. The use of Theudas and Judas the Galilean by Gamaliel was meant to show how unholy men failed who were not from God. The Pharisees were willing to take a wait and see attitude towards the Jesus movement.

According to the traditional timeline of the Gospels, this event took place shortly after the crucifixion, between 30-35 CE. If that were true, then how could Gamaliel have known about Theudas? In *Ant.* 20.97-99, Josephus wrote that Theudas persuaded many people to follow him to the river Jordan, where he promised to divide the river as Moses had parted the Red Sea. This failed spectacle occurred during the reign of Cuspius Fadus, procurator from 44-46 CE. Theudas' attempt to alter the elements fizzled, and he was captured and beheaded with the sword, an unfortunate ending for an apocalyptic leader. Theudas' attempt at the miraculous was the first of many who tried to coax God into action. He was no doubt a member of Judas the Galilean's Fourth Philosophy, but his methods were different than the wait and see disciples. Like Jesus on the Mount of Olives, Theudas wanted God to intervene into history. If only God would part the Jordan as he had done in the time of Moses and Joshua, then people would know and believe that the Kingdom of God was returning to earth. In short, this may have been a desperate plea for Jesus to return in power and glory.

How different was Theudas' attempt to that of Jesus on the Mount of Olives? Jesus expected God to fulfill the oracle of Zechariah by defeating the enemies of Israel. Theudas was simply following the examples of Moses and Joshua. Moses parted the Red Sea and Joshua led his followers into the promised land. Like other apocalyptical preachers of the time, these men trusted in the Scriptures. If God worked miracles in the past, then He could work miracles in the present. It never dawned upon them that the Old Testament Scriptures were exaggerated or flat out inventions. Like Jesus, these miracle workers were true believers. So we must not judge them strictly on our knowledge but on what they truly believed.

The first unraveling of Luke's cover-up concerns the dating: if Theudas were killed between 44-46 CE, then how could Gamaliel have known about this in 30-35 CE, ten to fifteen years prior? Talk about a prophet! In reality, Gamaliel could not have known about Theudas. But Luke knew about Theudas from the works of Josephus. *Antiquities* was written in 93 CE, so Luke's history must have been written after this date. This confusion between the author's knowledge and a character's knowledge is revealing: Luke was a terrible historian but a very capable fiction writer.

After noting that Theudas' efforts "came to nothing," Luke introduced Judas the Galilean, a rebel leader who appeared in the days of the census. Gamaliel would have known about Judas the Galilean, who led a tax revolt against Rome in 6 CE. This Judas was the most influential rabbi of the first century, so it is inconceivable that Gamaliel would have considered him a onetime wonder with no existing following. In fact, the Jewish war was started by Judas' later followers, sixty years after the census. Is it possible for a respected religious leader to be so out of touch with current events? Gamaliel would not have been so blatantly ignorant of current religious and political affairs.

According to Luke's convoluted history, this Judas arrived on the scene a short time **after** Theudas. This error by the author of Acts is simply shoddy history work. Most Christians refuse to believe that the Bible contains errors so they hopelessly try to find a Theudas that lived and died prior to 6 CE. Josephus must have forgotten about this Theudas, they "reason." But Josephus did not write about any other Theudas other than the one in 45 CE; so the hypothesis that an unknown Theudas roamed the countryside before the census is extremely unlikely.

In *Ant.* 20.101-102, Josephus followed the story of Theudas with the grim tale of Judas the Galilean's sons, who were crucified during the governorship of Tiberius Alexander, between 46-48 CE. Could Luke have confused Judas the Galilean with his sons? It certainly appears so. This at least restores the order of the passage. But again, we have the same problem: Gamaliel (35 CE) was foretelling the future (45-48 CE) and ascribing it to the past.

The Slavonic Josephus may hold the truth to the whole situation.

But when those noble governors [Fadus and Alexander, 44-48 CE] saw the misleading of the people, they deliberated with the scribes to seize and put them [Jewish Christians] to death, for fear lest the little be not little if it have ended in the great. But they shrank back and were alarmed over the signs, saying: **"In the plain course such wonders do not occur. But if they do not issue from the counsel of God, they will quickly be convicted." And they gave them [the Christians] authority to act as they would.** But afterwards, becoming pestered by them, they had them sent away, some to the Emperor, but others to Antioch, others again to distant lands, - for the testing of the matter. But Claudius removed two governors, [and] sent Cumanus [48-52 CE] (1) (Emphasis mine)

This passage was inserted into the *War* after the death of Agrippa I (44 CE) and before the appointment of Agrippa II (49-93 CE) and the arrival of the new Roman governor, Cumanus. During the governorships of Fadus and Alexander, the Jewish Christians were causing problems for the ruling elites. There was talk of seizing the Christians and putting them to death. This no doubt happened as the sons of Judas the Galilean were captured and crucified as reported in *Ant.* 20.101-102. But after this period of persecution, the Pharisees used the same reasoning to spare the Christians as was reported in Acts 5:37-39. Essentially, if the wonders were not from God, then the Christians would be convicted. "And they gave them authority to act as they would," at least for a little while. The passage then suggests that the persecutions began anew after the arrival of Cumanus. In both Acts and the Slavonic Josephus, the Jewish Christians were given the benefit of the doubt for a short period of time. It seems quite obvious that Luke took his material from the same source as the Slavonic Josephus. But once again, the dating was between 44-48 CE. There is little doubt that the Gamaliel story was fictitious. The events did occur, but not in or before 35 CE.

Eusebius, the "Father of Ecclesiastical History", adds to the confusion with his own take on the passage. He compared Theudas with the Theudas of Josephus, the one who was put to death by the sword in 45 CE. Eusebius then stated: "Immediately after this he [Josephus] mentions the famine that took place in Claudius's time." This he then compared to the account in Acts 11:27-

30, where Paul and Barnabas accompanied famine relief to Jerusalem. (2) Note that Eusebius did not deal with the time discrepancies. In his history, the death of Theudas and the famine happened in close proximity to each other. And this agreed with Josephus (*Ant.* 20.97-102). However, Eusebius never explained how the conversion of Paul (Acts 9), which supposedly occurred in the early 30's, could be sandwiched by two events in the mid 40's (Acts 5 and Acts 11). Possibly understanding his dilemma, Eusebius then skipped the part of the passage concerning Judas the Galilean. Bringing a 6 CE figure into the equation may have been too much even for the great apologist. But this can be explained by an earlier section in his history. When describing the birth of Jesus, Eusebius quoted Luke in Acts 5:37: "After **him** came the rising of Judas the Galilean at the time of the registration. He persuaded a number of people to revolt under his leadership; but he too perished, and all his followers were dispersed." (3) The reference to "him" was none other than Theudas, the person who Eusebius claimed to have died in 45 CE. In addition to these shenanigans, Eusebius created one other problem: he claimed that Jesus was born at the Census of Cyrenius in 6 CE, at the time of Judas the Galilean's tax revolt. This in no way can be reconciled with the birth of Jesus according to Matthew, who had Jesus born right before the death of Herod the Great, in 6-4 BCE. In an attempt to tie Acts to Josephus, Eusebius unwittingly uncovered some major errors in New Testament chronology. This was simply a repeat of the same error by Justin, who also regurgitated Luke's timeline in 150 CE. (4)

Many scholars have recognized the impossible situation of the dating and have come up with a mediocre solution. As noted above, they simply argue that there was another Theudas who lived a short time before Judas the Galilean, approximately 1-5 CE. They claim that the silence of Josephus on such a figure does not prove that a Theudas did not live at this time. Thus, the Scriptures have been saved from error.

This "scholarly" explanation requires a stretch of the imagination. But even if it were true, then the description of Judas the Galilean can be shown to be maliciously misleading. According to Acts chapter 5, Judas was killed, his followers were scattered, and his movement failed because it was not from God. Is that what really happened?

Josephus wrote this about Judas the Galilean at the time of the Census of Cyrenius:

...there was one Judas, ...[who] became zealous to draw them to a revolt, [who] said that this taxation was no better than an introduction to slavery, and exhorted the nation to assert their liberty. [6 CE]... for Judas and Sadduc, who excited a fourth philosophic sect among us, and had a **great many**

followers therein, filled our civil government with tumults at present, and **laid the foundation of our future miseries,** by this system of philosophy, ...because the **infection** which spread thence among the younger sort, who were zealous for it, brought the public to destruction. [66-70 CE] (*Ant.* 18.4-10) (Emphasis mine)

This passage assures us that Judas the Galilean founded a new philosophy and this new teaching infected the nation for the next sixty years. (Josephus' use of infected was similar to Tacitus' description of Christianity as a "pernicious superstition" (5) and Pliny's description as "the contagion of this superstition." (6)) In fact, this philosophy led the Jewish nation to war with Rome, the greatest power on earth. So it is obvious that the death of Judas, mysteriously missing from Josephus, did not stop or even slow his movement. Eerily, like the movement of Jesus, it flourished to a great extent after his death.

So why did the author of Acts feel it necessary to lie to the reader? The confusion or poor history concerning Theudas can be innocently explained away, but the unfair characterization of Judas the Galilean cannot. Luke purposely belittled Judas with the intent of minimizing him in the eyes of second-century Christians. He also wanted to forever cut the ties between Judas and the mythical Jesus. Surely, Jesus could never be associated with such an apparent loser. This misleading history has been working well to the present day.

However, the statement that the movement was scattered after Judas' death may have some truth to it. If the Romans captured Judas, then it would have been a prudent move to scatter or to hide. Eventually, these individuals reorganized as the Fourth Philosophy coalesced and expanded. But how was this scattering of Judas' movement any different from Jesus' disciples' reaction after the arrest and crucifixion of Jesus? After Jesus was arrested, "then everyone (all the disciples) deserted him and fled." (Mark 14:50 and Matt. 26:56) The non-canonical Gospel of Peter stated: "But we, the twelve disciples of the Lord, wept and grieved; and each one returned to his home, grieving for what had happened." (vs. 59) The disciples of Jesus fled from the scene of his arrest, denied Jesus when questioned and hid in fear from the authorities. Jesus' followers acted exactly the same as Luke's portrayal of Judas' followers (Acts 5:37). It is interesting to note that Luke did not report that Jesus' followers had fled, unlike Mark and Matthew. Instead, Luke reserved his scattering of disciples to the movement of Judas the Galilean. This, like so many other events, ties Jesus to Judas.

Judas the Galilean may have been the historical Jesus. The mythical Jesus of the Gospels was framed from the theology of Paul, and the life of the Jewish revolutionary, Judas the Galilean. The great number of coincidences between Jesus and Judas shows how much of Judas' history was incorporated into Jesus of Nazareth. Therefore, it was necessary to color the history of Judas with failure. With one stroke of the pen, Christians and scholars alike have forfeited reason in favor of misguided faith. Unfortunately, Judas the Galilean has been long forgotten. As of the writing of this book, only two other books have been written about Judas the Galilean, and those books were penned by this author. (See Bibliography)

A TIMELINE

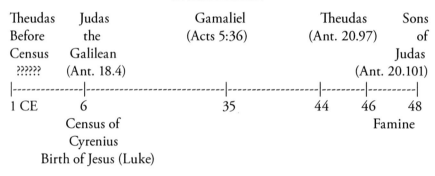

Theudas	Judas	Gamaliel	Theudas	Sons
Before	the	(Acts 5:36)	(Ant. 20.97)	of
Census	Galilean			Judas
??????	(Ant. 18.4)			(Ant. 20.101)

1 CE	6	35	44	46	48
	Census of				Famine
	Cyrenius				
	Birth of Jesus (Luke)				

According to Gamaliel, Theudas preceded Judas the Galilean and both were "some time ago." We are given the impression that both individuals were one-hit wonders. And if they were insignificant footnotes to history, then would anyone even remember their names, thirty to thirty-five years after their deaths?

Josephus never mentioned a Theudas before Judas the Galilean. His only Theudas in *Antiquities* was beheaded during the governorship of Fadus, between 44-46 CE, some ten years after Gamaliel spoke of his death. If this were **the** Theudas, then Gamaliel was surely a prophet, predicting the future using past references such as "some time ago."

After Theudas, Josephus wrote that the sons of Judas the Galilean were crucified. Luke was a poor historian as he mistook the sons of Judas the Galilean for Judas the Galilean. In addition, Luke's treatment of Judas the Galilean is misleading, as Gamaliel supposedly said that Judas was killed and his followers scattered. Per Josephus, this minimizing of Judas and his movement was totally unjustified. In short, Luke lied about the whole episode.

One other point should be noted. Theudas may have been an apostle. In the Gospels, there was a Judas (not Iscariot), a Thomas (twin) and a Thaddeus. It is likely that this Judas was a twin and nicknamed Thomas. The combination would yield Theudas or Thaddeus. There was a Judas Barsabbas in Acts 15:22, a leader in Jerusalem, and a Joseph Barsabbas in Acts 1:23, also a main player in the early church. Could these two have been twins? (Jesus' sons (brothers) were Simon, James, Judas and Joseph). It may be that Theudas was a son of Judas the Galilean/Jesus. And considering that Simon and James were captured and crucified a few years later, three sons may have been lost in a short period of time. This would have been a painful time for the early Jewish movement. (It also corresponds with the time of Paul's dismissal from the Jewish church and the attack upon James, the brother of Jesus, reported in the Pseudoclementine *Recognitions*.) (7) Could Paul have been behind this rash of persecutions? (This will be answered in Part Two - Christ Jesus.)

CHAPTER 3

JUDAS THE GALILEAN

In the first two chapters, I have endeavored to challenge the traditional timeline by exposing obvious errors in the New Testament chronology. In so doing, I hope to engage the reader in an historical quest for the real Jesus. Certainly, some may be confused while others have a hazy understanding of my arguments concerning Jesus and Judas the Galilean. Therefore, I deem it necessary to chronologically recount the life of Judas the Galilean and his movement, the Fourth Philosophy. This is done to tie together any loose ends which may be troubling the reader. This history will focus primarily upon the writings of Josephus (*Antiquities* and *War*) and the Slavonic Josephus. How close this corresponds to the story of Jesus as revealed in the Gospels is left up to your good judgment.

WHAT REALLY HAPPENED

In the year 4 BCE, two learned teachers of the law gazed out upon their students, an army of young men thirsting for righteousness. Every day this throng of Israel's future sat and listened to the wizened Matthias and his younger partner, Judas, preach the Kingdom of Heaven. The relationship between the two wise men can be argued as well as their ages, but the pattern of the Maccabees suggests that Matthias was the older father figure (or literal father) and Judas, the son. How they came to the Temple, to this point in the history of Israel can be deduced from what preceded them.

A generation earlier, according to the Slavonic Josephus, the priests argued among themselves concerning the promised Messiah. This passage was placed into the text of the *War* shortly after the discussion on Actium, dating this episode at approximately 31-30 BCE.

"The Law forbids us to have a foreigner [as] king, but we are expecting the Anointed, the Meek one, of David's line. Yet we know that Herod is an Arab, uncircumcised... What is this? Or did the prophets somehow lie? They wrote that we shall never lack a prince of Judah until there comes the One whom it is given back; in him the nations will hope. But is this [King Herod] the hope of nations? We detest his misdeeds; are the nations going to hope in him?" (After *War* 1.369)

Surely, this negative feeling by the priests was shared by the common man. The Jews were looking for a King from their own line, from the promised line of David. A little further into the Slavonic text was inserted a variant form of the "Star of Bethlehem". This can be dated to the early years of Herod the Great, or to about 25 BCE. The details are slightly different from the account in Matthew, but the meaning of the "Star" is explained.

And after waiting a year for them [Persian astrologers], they did not come to [see] him [Herod the Great]. And he [Herod] was furious and summoned the priests [who were his] advisors and asked if any of them understood [the meaning of] the star. And they answered him: "It is written: '**A star shall shine forth from Jacob and a man shall arise from Judah**'."... "It is written that the Anointed One is [to be] born in Bethlehem. Even if you have no mercy on your servants, kill those infants of Bethlehem and let the others go." And he [Herod] gave the order and they killed all the infants of Bethlehem. (After *War* 1.400) (Emphasis mine)

According to Balaam's fourth oracle, as predicted in Numbers 24:17-19, "a star will come out of Jacob; a scepter will rise out of Israel... A ruler will come out of Jacob and destroy the survivors of the city." The religious leaders pointed to this passage as proof that God would send a ruler from Jacob. That is why the Jews detested Herod. Herod was an interloper, an outsider. He would never command the respect of the Jewish people. The Slavonic passage also detailed that this Anointed One was born in Bethlehem, but not in 6-4 BCE as reported by Matthew's Gospel, but rather in 25 BCE, a good generation earlier.

Herod the Great may have been a good ruler in that he built fine cities and restored the Temple itself, but his introduction of pagan ways (athletic events, the theater and images within the Temple) alienated a portion of the populace. Surely, to these religious fanatics, the reign of Herod was inconsistent with the Scriptures and the Reign of God. In 25 BCE, a group of ten men planned to assassinate Herod, using short knives hidden within their garments. The plot was exposed, and the ten were put to death. But the struggle against Herod and pagan influences had just begun. A movement was forming that was based upon the distant exploits of Mattathias and his son Judas Maccabee (170 BCE). In this new Jewish sect. a leader named Matthias taught about the true meaning of God's promises, freedom from pagan influences and the equality of all Jews. Whether or not Matthias began in Jerusalem or among the cities of Galilee, we will never know. But his teachings did bring him to Jerusalem by 4 BCE, along with his son, Judas.

The Slavonic Josephus includes many passages about the "Christian" movement, including three about John the Baptist and one on the "wonder worker", or the Messiah. It is revealing that this source also expands upon the Golden Eagle Temple Cleansing. (This suggests that this Temple Cleansing was part of the early movement's most famous stories.) According to the Slavonic Josephus, Matthias and Judas said this to their followers:

"Come, men of Judaea, **now is the time for men to behave like men, to show what reverence we have for the Law of Moses.** Let not our race be shamed, let us not bring disgrace on our Law-giver. Let us take as the model for [our] exploits Eleazar first and the **seven Maccabee brothers** and the mother who made men [of them]. For, when Antiochus had conquered and subjugated our land and was ruling over us, he was defeated by these seven youths and [their] old teacher and an old woman. Let us also be worthy of them, let us not prove weaker than a woman. **But even if we are to be tortured for our zeal for God, a greater wreath has been plaited for us.** And if they kill us, our souls as it leaves [this] dark abode will return to [our] forefathers, where Abraham and his offspring [dwell]." (After *War* 1.650) (Emphasis mine)

The passage emphasizes that the current freedom movement should be modeled upon the Maccabee uprising. Note that there is also an emphasis on family: a father, a mother and seven brothers. It is quite probable that Matthias was the father and Judas the son. However, it also implies that there were other brothers involved. This would be consistent with what is known about Jesus and his brothers from Paul (1 Cor. 9:5 and Galatians) and from a few passages in Acts. It is clear that Judas the Galilean had sons because Josephus mentioned the crucifixion of two sons, James and Simon, in *Ant.* 20.102 and the stoning of another son, Menahem, in *War* 2.433-434. It is quite probable that Judas also had brothers who helped carry on the movement when he himself was killed.

The Slavonic Josephus also ties the Temple-cleansing Judas to Judas the Galilean, mentioned by Josephus in 6 CE, at the Census of Cyrenius. The

Temple-cleansing Judas preached a great reverence for the law and zeal in the face of torture. This is exactly equal to the teachings of Judas the Galilean. So this lone passage tells us that Judas was Judas the Galilean, that he came from a large family with several brothers, and the placement of the text at the Golden Eagle Temple Cleansing brings the "Jesus" movement back a generation, to 4 BCE.

To Matthias and Judas, the Temple was dedicated to the unseen God, the God of Abraham, Isaac and Jacob. But Herod had purposely adorned the Temple with the Golden Eagle, an image of beauty to Herod and his followers, a sign of fealty to Rome and a slap in the face to those who strictly interpreted the Scriptures. After all, did not God command His followers to abstain from idols (Deut. 5:8-9), and did He not punish the children of Israel who fashioned a calf from gold while Moses received the Ten Commandments (Ex. 32). To Matthias, the Golden Eagle was no different than the calf authorized by Aaron. God would surly reward those who destroyed such idols.

The young impressionable students were whipped into frenzy by the seditious teachers. They were convinced that God expected them to rise up against Herod and his graven image of homage to Rome. Such a show of devotion would be richly rewarded not only in this life but in the life to come. In this life each would be remembered as a martyr, bringing fame upon the household. In the life to come, God would honor them with eternal happiness. So, like the martyrs of today, these followers of Matthias and Judas were all too willing to attack the power structure, that being Herod the Great.

In broad daylight, the students brought down the Golden Eagle, crashing it to the ground. But in their enthusiasm, the students were oblivious to Herod's guards, who quickly brought an end to the uprising and imprisoned those caught at the Temple. Included among the prisoners were the authors of the sedition, Matthias and Judas.

A trial of sorts was arranged, but the sentence had already been passed. The prisoners were bound and sent to Jericho awaiting Herod's final decision. Herod was bitter about the whole affair. After all, had he not provided the Jews with a beautiful Temple and the Golden Eagle. This act against the Golden Eagle was no different than an attack upon himself. So there was no doubt in the matter; the prisoners were guilty and deserved death. In a related matter, the high priest with the same name, Matthias, was also punished as a result of this sedition. Reminiscent of Pilate relinquishing power to the mob due to his wife's dream, this Matthias had once before stepped down from his office for a day because of a dream involving sexual relations with his wife. But now he was being permanently replaced by Joazar, who was his wife's brother.

The sentence of death was the expected outcome. Herod had Matthias and his followers burnt alive. Josephus stated in the *War* that both rabbis were killed, but in *Antiquities* mentioned only the death of Matthias. What most likely occurred was the execution of the movement's leader, Matthias, and a number of his followers. Those remaining, including Judas, were imprisoned in order to dangle their fate in the face of the seditious. In short, Judas was an insurance policy against any other rebellious acts against Herod. A second powerful motive in imprisoning Judas involved Herod's desire for true mourning at his own death. Josephus stated that Herod planned to kill a great number of people at the time of his death so that there would be mourning throughout Israel. Judas and his followers may have been part of this plan. Either way, it was just a matter of time until Judas would meet the same fate as Matthias.

Judas and his fellow prisoners were spared an eventual death for only one reason: Herod the Great had died (4 BCE), and his insane orders of mass murder were not obeyed. In terms of stability, the death of this tyrannical yet able administrator rocked the country. But it also presented a great opportunity for those who had been persecuted and oppressed for so many years. Herod's death coincided with the Passover feast, a time when pilgrims flocked to Jerusalem to celebrate Israel's deliverance from Egypt. This left Herod's son, Archelaus, with a dilemma: how could he gain firm control of the government without offending the masses?

The crowds sensed that Archelaus was not dealing from strength and that he might be swayed by their desires. They asked if he would ease their annual taxes and remove all taxes related to sales and purchases. These were very serious requests, for a king must have revenues to rule effectively. Even so, Archelaus assented to their will, pretending to agree to these requests. And a segment of the people, those who mourned the death of Matthias, asked one other favor: release those who had been imprisoned by Herod. And once again, Archelaus agreed. Judas was now a free man. (Some argue that Archelaus did not release prisoners as he promised. That may be true for his tax promises, for these promises could only be realized sometime in the future. But the release of prisoners could be made **now**. Josephus also mentioned that Archelaus replaced the High Priest upon the requests of the crowd. This plea, too, could be accomplished at the present and was therefore acted upon.)

Archelaus soon realized that any concession to the followers of Matthias and Judas was fruitless, for these fanatics could never be won over by friendly intentions. In this, he was correct, for this new movement had no intention of meekly following the Herodian dynasty. In fact, they wished to upset this structure in order to fully implement their theocracy. Predictably, tensions arose and the military slaughter began. Judas escaped with a group of disciples and headed to Galilee, to the city of Sepphoris.

Judas had witnessed the execution of Matthias and many of their students and had just fled from a massacre in Jerusalem. His thoughts must have been upon the security of the small group he now led. In a bold move, he attacked the armory with its large cache of weapons. His followers were now well armed and could defend themselves from all except the army of Archelaus. His reliance upon these weapons of man diminished as he witnessed the awesome power of Rome. Consistent with guerrilla warfare, Judas and his bandit followers blended into the countryside as the Roman army marched upon Sepphoris, burning it to the ground, enslaving all its inhabitants. Surely, this sight hardened Judas against Rome and the Herodian sycophants.

But safety depended upon guile and resourcefulness. The message of fealty to God and refusing to be a slave to human masters (Rome) was transmitted to eager ears throughout Galilee on a small-scale basis. Judas did not draw too much attention to himself by setting up base in any city. Instead, he moved throughout the countryside, always prepared for a quick getaway.

As his popularity grew in Galilee, Judas may have asked his disciples this question: "Who do people think I am?" A teacher, a prophet and the Messiah were the answers. Unlike our heavenly vision of the Messiah, the Jews held that the king or Anointed One was the Messiah. In fact, in this particular era (shortly after the death of Herod the Great in 4 BCE), many warlords and popular teachers were crowned King by their disciples. In this way, Judas was no different. His disciples led the way to Mount Tabor where they anointed Judas King and Messiah. This probably occurred some short time after his release from prison, between 4-2 BCE. Thus, Judas' tenure as Messiah in Galilee lasted anywhere from eight to ten years, depending on his anointment. During this time, Judas widened his appeal among the downtrodden in Galilee, always being careful not to directly engage the authorities.

But an event stirred the pot, where all Jews were affected. The Census of Cyrenius (6 CE) was a means for Rome to separate Judea from its wealth. The Roman Governor, Coponius, was appointed to lend the power of Rome to this taxing situation. At first, the population was outraged. But this opposition soon melted away as the High Priest, Joazar, convinced the people that such a tax was for their own good. In this he may have been correct as the Romans were adept at building and improving the means of transportation throughout the Empire. But to Judas the Galilean, this taxation was nothing other than support for another king, another power. Judas preached that only God was their master, and that the foreigners were merely slave masters. Thus, his opposition to this taxation was direct and to the point. "Whom do you support, God or Rome?"

Judas the Galilean was a clever rabbi, as ascribed by Josephus (*War* 2.433). In conjunction with his census revolt, Judas sent out a holy man to introduce him to the Jewish nation. In Luke 3:1-3, John the Baptist introduced Jesus to the world. In the Slavonic Josephus, the holy man passage was placed right before this description of Judas the Galilean:

Under his administration [Coponius] it was that a certain Galilean, whose name was Judas, prevailed with his countrymen to revolt; and said they were cowards if they would endure to pay a tax to the Romans, and would, after God, submit to mortal men as their lords. **This man was a teacher of a peculiar sect of his own, and was not at all like the rest of those their leaders.** (*War* 2.118) (Emphasis mine)

To Josephus, Judas the Galilean was unlike any other teacher. This same sentiment is evident throughout the Gospel portrayal of Jesus. Note the charge against Jesus in Luke 23:2-5: "And they began to accuse him, saying, 'We have found this man subverting our nation. He opposes payment of taxes to Caesar and claims to be Christ (Messiah), a king... He stirs up the people all over Judea by his teaching. He started in Galilee and has come all the way here.'" This passage about Jesus of Nazareth was surely a rewrite of Judas the Galilean's ministry.

This was the radical rebel who John the Baptist introduced in 6 CE. The Slavonic Josephus described John as "wild of visage", and his message mirrored that of Judas the Galilean. John called the Jews to freedom stating: "God hath sent me to show you the lawful way, by which you will be rid of [your] many rulers. But there will be no mortal ruling [over you], only the Most High, who hath sent me." (After *War* 2.110) This was a call for freedom, a warning signal to the ruling elites. John was brought before Archelaus (6 CE), where he was questioned before the experts in the law, and threatened with torture if he did not refrain from his activities. John simply replied: "It is you who should cease from your foul deeds and adhere to the Lord, your God."

Unlike the Gospels, John appeared in 6 CE, before the tax revolt of Judas the Galilean. The Gospel of Luke placed John in 29 CE, many years after Archelaus and the census. Why would there be two completely different chronologies for the introduction of John? The historical story of Judas the Galilean confirms the 6 CE date while the later date of 29 CE is fraught with contradictions, per Chapter 1. The reason is clear for the displacement of John: the early church had to distance itself from the "Jesus" of history or Judas the Galilean. In his place was inserted the Gospel Jesus of Nazareth.

The census was the launching pad for Judas' nationwide campaign. His Kingship in Galilee had been solid, and his reputation was beyond reproach, but not since his brush with death in the Golden Eagle Temple Cleansing had Judas returned to Jerusalem. How long did the tax revolt last and when did Judas once again march on Jerusalem? According to Acts 5:37, Judas' tax revolt was crushed and his followers were scattered. However, this does not square with history or common sense. Josephus never mentioned Judas' death although he did relate the deaths of Judas' sons, Simon and James, by crucifixion, another son's stoning (Menahem) and the death of a grandson at Masada. It is inconceivable that Josephus would have omitted the death of his main character, Judas. This, too, was probably overwritten by early Christians. The lone passage of Jesus in the *Antiquities* (18.63-64) is an obvious interpolation and comes right when we would expect to read of Judas' death. Thus, my hypothesis is that Judas led his tax revolt from 6-19 CE. (This explains how the movement flourished!) Assuming that Judas was born in 25 BCE (Slavonic Josephus version of the Star of Bethlehem), he would have been captured at the age of 43. This is very interesting considering the Gospel of John said this about Jesus: "You are not yet fifty years old." (John 8:57) This implies that "Jesus" was in his forties, not his thirties as claimed by the traditional timeline. Being in his forties is consistent with Judas the Galilean but not the traditional Jesus of Nazareth.

In 19 CE, the time must have seemed right for action. Judas' popularity soared, and the call against Rome was a strong rallying cry. God would deliver the Jews from the hands of the invaders just as He had done in the days of Judas Maccabee. At this fateful time in history, Judas the Galilean was a middle-aged man, somewhere in his early forties. His ministry had begun at the side of an older mentor and possibly father, Matthias. Like his teacher Matthias, Judas also worked with a lieutenant. He was named Sadduc according to Josephus (*Ant.* 18.4) and was probably nearly the same age as Judas or even a few years younger. Although age and wisdom went hand-in-hand in Jewish culture, the second-in-command could have been a younger, more vigorous man. Moses chose Joshua, a much younger man, to lead the nation of Israel into the Promised Land. But since Judas was relatively young, a major difference in age would be unlikely.

This question of age is very important as one other figure must also be counted in the equation. James the Just, or the brother of the Lord, would have been between 38-53 years old in 19 CE, most likely the younger brother of Judas. (Tradition says that James was ninety-six years old at his death in 62 CE. Based upon that, James may have been born as early as 35 BCE. This extremely old age of ninety-six may have been an exaggeration, but James was probably an old man at his death, between eighty and ninety-six.) Regardless, the age of James comes much closer to the age of Judas the Galilean than to that of the Gospel Jesus.

The age of Judas is also necessary to compute the approximate ages of his sons and grandsons. If Judas were married at age twenty (4 BCE) and had sons every third year for twelve years, then the ages of Judas' sons in 19 CE would have been twenty-two, nineteen, sixteen and thirteen. The elder two (Simon and James) were crucified under Tiberius Alexander in 47 CE. Their approximate ages would have been fifty and forty-seven. Menahem, the youngest son, was stoned to death in 66 CE, making him approximately fifty to fifty-five years old. A grandson, Eleazar, committed suicide at Masada in 73 CE, making him nearly fifty years old as well. Thus, the dating for the life and times of Judas the Galilean fits perfectly well within the 4 BCE to 19 CE timeframe.

Josephus did not record anything else about Judas directly. But much more can be deduced from other materials about his grandson, Menahem. This Menahem overtook the king's armory at Masada in the same way that Judas had captured the armory at Sepphoris, some seventy years earlier. After the capture of Masada, Menahem marched as king (Messiah) to Jerusalem, where he assumed control for a short while before being murdered. Menahem's actions closely followed the pattern set by Judas. After Judas captured Sepphoris, his disciples proclaimed him king or Messiah. This title he kept, but his influence was centered primarily in Galilee. It was the nationwide census and the arrival of the Roman governors which eventually drove Judas to Jerusalem.

The exact date of Judas' triumphal entry into Jerusalem may be forever a mystery. His nationwide ministry began with the census in 6 CE, but his actions at that point are not so certain. He may have rallied the troops and headed straight to Jerusalem. However, that does not appear to be the modus operandi of that "clever rabbi". He most likely built a large opposition to the census tax by traveling from town to town. This would have taken many years to accomplish. In addition, his movement may have gone beyond the bounds of Israel, even to Rome itself. The history of Josephus is curiously missing data between 7-37 CE, as if someone had purposely expunged his information. But the Roman historian, Tacitus, may help in identifying the date of Judas' death. Between 16-18 CE, in the reign of Tiberius, he wrote: "The provinces too of Syria and Judaea, exhausted by their burdens, implored a reduction of tribute." (1) It appears likely that Judas' movement was having an impact on the nation's attitude towards Roman taxation. Whether or not Judas was still alive at this point may be answered by what was happening in Rome in 19 CE.

There was a debate too about expelling the Egyptian and Jewish worship, and a resolution of the Senate was passed that four thousand of the freedman class who were infected with those superstitions and were of military age should be transported to the island of Sardinia, to quell the brigandage of the place, a cheap sacrifice should they die from the pestilential climate. The rest were to quit Italy, unless before a certain day they repudiated their impious rites. (Tacitus, *The Annals* ii.85)

For some reason, the Jews were being expelled from Rome, especially those of military age. It is quite probable that the crucifixion of Judas the Galilean had started riots throughout the Roman Empire where Jewish settlements had been infiltrated by those of the Fourth Philosophy. If this were the case, then Judas died in 19 CE. This date also conforms to the dating of the spurious Jesus passage in *Antiquities* 18.63-64. This may explain why the Fourth Philosophy spread so far. In the New Testament account, Jesus died in 30-33 CE with only 120 disciples remaining (Acts 1:15). From that pathetic beginning, we are to believe that the movement spread throughout the Roman Empire in only a few short years. If, however, Judas the Galilean were active in spreading his message afar from 6-19 CE, either personally or through surrogates, the overall reach of the movement makes sense.

The march into Jerusalem for Judas and his disciples would have been exciting yet foreboding. The belief that God would deliver them from the powerful grip of Rome was a centerpiece of their religion. Josephus plainly stated that these followers of Judas willingly gave their lives rather than worship anyone or anything other than the one true God. Yet, even with this firm system of beliefs, doubts must have entered their minds in those times when silence reigned, in the nighttime or when negative thoughts pervaded their consciousness.

But such thoughts of failure were not uttered aloud. Judas' mission as Messiah would not fail. And it was not at the Passover when Judas entered the city but at the Feast of Tabernacles. Maccoby presents a convincing case that Jesus entered Jerusalem in the fall, at the Feast of Tabernacles. The conflict prophesied by Zechariah (14:16) was to take place at the Feast of Tabernacles. (2) As Jesus supposedly rode into Jerusalem on a donkey, he and his disciples must have been fully aware of the time predicted by Zechariah. It was also at this time that the king was to read a portion of the law relating to his duties at the Temple. Thus, a Temple Cleansing was necessary. So when Judas entered Jerusalem as King, or Messiah, he at once went to the Temple in order to prepare it. This was the second Temple Cleansing by Judas. The first was in 4 BCE in the Golden Eagle Temple Cleansing. This second cleansing was in preparation of the new Kingdom, where God would govern His people. The time for Rome was short.

After this second Temple cleansing, Judas readied himself for the fateful clash with Rome, on the Mount of Olives, as prophesied by Zechariah. Never did Judas believe that God would abandon him. But on the Mount of

Olives, Judas and some of his followers were captured. These individuals were crucified under the governorship of Pontius Pilate. Giving their approval were the High Priest, Caiaphas, and his father-in-law, Annas, both active in the crucifixion of Jesus in the Gospels.

It is quite interesting to note that Judas led a Temple Cleansing at the beginning of his mission as did Jesus according to the Gospel of John. The Synoptic Gospels talk of a second Temple Cleansing, of which Judas would have performed as well upon entering Jerusalem, consistent with the actions of his son, Menahem, who cleansed the Temple in 66 CE. In 4 BCE, there was a prisoner release. These prisoners were no doubt associated with the Golden Eagle Temple Cleansing, which was an insurrection in the city. In addition, this prisoner release occurred at the Passover. This is perfectly in-sync with the Gospel account of Barabbas. After this, Judas was proclaimed Messiah in Galilee, just as the Gospels portrayed the ministry of Jesus. Judas' march to Jerusalem was predicated by the census, which was convincingly sold to the masses by the High Priest, Joazar. This Joazar was replaced by Annas in 6 CE, who would then be the major opponent of Judas until Judas' death. That is why the Gospel Jesus was taken first to Annas after the arrest in the Gospel of John. For his efforts, Judas was crucified under Pilate for his refusal to pay taxes to Rome and for being hailed as King. These were the two main charges leveled against the Gospel Jesus.

Even with the death of Judas the Galilean, the Fourth Philosophy grew in number and power. Led by his second-in-command, Sadduc, the movement strengthened. (Sadduc will be examined in Chapter 4.) In Acts chapter 1, the Jesus movement replaced Judas Iscariot with a Matthias, who was never heard from again. In reality, the one who was replaced was Judas the Galilean, not Judas Iscariot. (There was no Judas Iscariot as will be explained in Chapter 17). The person who replaced Judas was his brother, James the Just. This James led the movement until his death by stoning in 62 CE. (See Chapter 5.)

JUDAS, JUDAS THE BANDIT, and JUDAS THE GALILEAN

Many scholars do not believe that Judas the Galilean was the same Judas as was described in the Golden Eagle Temple Cleansing or the Judas who raided the armory at Sepphoris. In *War* 1.655, Josephus claimed that the rabbis (Matthias and Judas) were put to death, although not mentioning them by name. However, in *Ant.* 17.167, only Matthias died and it appears as if Judas was imprisoned under Herod and awaited final sentencing. If Judas languished in prison, he was undoubtedly released by Archelaus as part of the Barabbas-style prisoner release in 4 BCE (*War* 2.4). Once released, Judas went to Sepphoris with his disciples and raided the armory. Later, he was proclaimed Messiah and claimed the nationwide stage at the census in 6 CE. Eventually, he rode into Jerusalem as Messiah and was summarily crucified by Pontius Pilate (19-21 CE) for his refusal to pay taxes to Rome and his claim of being Messiah, or King of the Jews.

There is one scholar who believes that the Golden Eagle Judas may well have been Judas the Galilean. Robert Eisenman, author of *James, the Brother of Jesus*, writes:

This rabbi [Golden Eagle Judas] is hardly to be distinguished from Judas the Galilean subsequently, even though for Josephus Judas Sepphoraeus, together with another 'rabbi' he calls Matthias (again note the Maccabean names), are burned alive ('being guilty of sacrilege under the pretence of zeal for the law'), while Judas the Galilean goes on functioning and Josephus never does delineate his fate. Josephus (or his sources - this is forty years before Josephus was born), may have been mistaken about this detail, as later in the *Antiquities* he says only Matthias was burned. Here, Josephus portrays the people as preferring the burning of the rabbis and their followers rather than having 'a great number prosecuted', a point of view echoed in John 11:50's picture of Caiaphas' famous explanation to his fellow Chief Priests about Jesus: 'it profits us more that one man die for the people, rather than the whole nation perish.' (3)

The following passages from Josephus and the Gospels will bring the Temple-Cleansing Judas, the armory-raiding Judas and Judas the Galilean together. This is important because the traditionalist and Mythicist theories of Christianity both see Judas as a one-act wonder. Tying Josephus' three Judas' together gives a fuller picture of this great rabbi, extending his ministry from before 4 BCE through the armory raid in Sepphoris to the census uprising in 6 CE and to Jerusalem and his death in 19-21 CE.

1. Two Gospel references may describe Jesus fleeing from Herod Antipas. "At that time some Pharisees came to Jesus and said to him, 'Leave this place and go somewhere else. Herod wants to kill you.'" (Luke 13:31) And in Matt. 12:1-8, Jesus and his disciples picked heads of grain and ate them on the Sabbath, thus working on the Sabbath. As a defense, Jesus referred his critics to David, who ate consecrated bread while being chased by Saul. Jesus' argument seems to place him in the same position as David, fleeing from the authorities. These two passages may hearken back to Judas escaping his death sentence imposed upon Matthias and forty others. (*Ant.* 17.149-167) In fact, Judas was probably imprisoned by Herod the Great and then later released in the Barabbas scenario noted earlier. (*War* 2.4)

Since Herod Antipas was Tetrarch of Galilee from 4 BCE to 39 CE, the references to this Herod do not necessarily put Jesus in a later time frame. The above passages may also describe the efforts put forth by Herod Antipas to capture Judas after his release and retreat from Jerusalem. After all, Judas did break into the armory at Sepphoris, supplying his followers with weapons and whatever money was there. (*Ant.* 17.271-272) Therefore, Herod Antipas would have been after Judas as well.

2. Josephus mentioned a bandit leader named Judas, who led a rebel group at **Sepphoris** in Galilee, around 4-2 BCE. This Judas attacked the royal armory and equipped his followers. (*Ant.* 17.271; *War* 2.56) The Temple-Cleansing Judas was the son of **Sepphoris**, per the account in *War* 1.648. In one instance, Sepphoris was a city, in another, a name. It is quite possible that Josephus mistook a place for a name. This error does link the released prisoner to the bandit, through the city name. Also note that Archelaus released political prisoners to the populace, hoping to atone for his father, Herod the Great. (*War* 2.4) Judas had been captured with Matthias and was no doubt placed in prison and later released. Shortly after this prison release, Josephus wrote about Judas the bandit. This proximity of events is not clear cut proof but it is circumstantial evidence.

3. The teachings of Matthias and Judas were similar to those of Judas the Galilean. Both were obsessed with following the Law and keeping the Temple pure. They also would gladly die rather than worship idols or Caesars. (*Ant.* 17.151; *Ant.* 18.23) Note also that Matthias and Judas cleansed the Temple of an idol, the Golden Eagle, thereby confronting Herod the Great with sedition. In 41 CE, the Jewish fanatics were willing to go to war with Rome if Caligula placed a statue of himself in the Temple. (Tacitus, *Histories*, v.9) The followers of Hezekiah, Judas the bandit's father or grandfather, also had a presence at the Temple. (*Ant.* 14.168)

The tie between Judas and Judas the Galilean is assured when we consider the symbolism of the Golden Eagle. Not only did this represent the power of Herod the Great, but its placement in the Temple area was a not too subtle way of paying homage to Rome. (The Eagle was the symbol of Rome.) By tearing down the Golden Eagle, Judas and Matthias were proclaiming war upon Rome. This same mentality was present at the Census of Cyrenius, where Judas the Galilean and Sadduc opposed Roman taxation.

This secure connection is further cemented by the Slavonic Josephus. Additional data concerning the Golden Eagle Temple Cleansing was included in this account. The Golden Eagle was placed in the Temple as an honor to Caesar. In addition, Judas and Matthias patterned themselves after the

Maccabees in resistance against a foreign power and in their willingness to die for their cause. (4) This is identical to the Fourth Philosophy of Judas the Galilean.

4. Joazar was the High Priest in 4 BCE during the Golden Eagle Temple Cleansing. (*Ant.* 17.164) Joazar persuaded the people to accept the Roman taxation of 6 CE which was opposed by Judas the Galilean. (*Ant.* 18.3) In both cases, the High Priest supported the Roman presence in Judea. Joazar could be considered the Evil Priest of the Dead Sea Scrolls. However, his replacement, Annas (6-15 CE) makes an even better Evil Priest.

5. Matthias and Judas worked as a team. Judas the Galilean also had a second-in-command, Sadduc. (*Ant.* 17.149; *Ant.* 18.4) This organizational structure was modeled after the Maccabees. Mattathias and Judas led rebels against the Greek occupiers beginning around 195 BCE. When Mattathias died, his son Simon replaced him. Thus, Judas Maccabee and his brother, Simon, were the leaders of the movement. In the New Testament, Jesus appointed Peter as his second-in-command, although a closer reading of Paul's letters shows that James was the leader and Cephas (Peter) was second-in-command to James. (See Galatians) Sometime after Jesus' death, James and Peter led the Jewish Christian movement. (The Sadduc may have been leading the movement after the death of Judas. Chapter 5 will attempt to identify this shadowy historical figure.) In all the above cases, the movements were led by two men. When one died, the other became leader and a replacement was added to the team.

6. Matthias and Judas were referred to as wise men by Josephus, a high honor indeed. (*Ant.* 17.155) Judas the Galilean was called a clever rabbi by Josephus in *War* 2.433. These words of honor are especially important because Josephus opposed Judas the Galilean. Josephus wrote his history for the Romans. However, even though he did not agree with the politics of Judas, he did understand Judas' great influence throughout first-century Judea. There even may have been a touch of admiration for the rebel leader.

7. Judas the Galilean's son, Menahem, broke into King Herod's armory in Masada (66 CE) just as Judas, the bandit, had done in Sepphoris (4-3 BCE). (*War* 2.433; *War* 2.56) This definitely links the 4 BCE Judas with the 6 CE Judas the Galilean. And this also proves that Judas the Galilean would have been active at the time of the Golden Eagle Temple Cleansing of 4 BCE.

8. The father, or most likely grandfather, of Judas the bandit, was Hezekias (Ezekias). This Hezekias was put to death by Herod the Great. Hezekias'

followers petitioned at the Temple for justice in regards to Herod's actions. Hezekias' followers had a presence in Galilee and in Jerusalem, just as Matthias and Judas in 4 BCE and Judas and Sadduc in 6 CE. In addition, King Hezekiah purified the Temple, so the name Hezekias may hearken back to this as well.

9. Matthias and Judas resembled Mattathias and Judas Maccabee in that both pairs cleansed the Temple and the names were identical. Judas the bandit and Judas Maccabee were both terrible to all men. (*Ant.* 12.314; *Ant.* 17.272) And Judas the Galilean and Sadduc were also based upon the Maccabean precedent of a leader and second-in-command.

10. After the death of Matthias and the imprisonment of Judas, their followers petitioned Archelaus for the release of Judas (Barabbas) and for **tax** relief. (*Ant.* 17.204-205) Judas the Galilean led his followers in opposing the **census tax** of Cyrenius. (*Ant.* 18.1-10) This concern for tax relief is very important. It was one of the cornerstones of the movement. Note also that Jesus was crucified for his refusal to pay taxes to Rome.

CONCLUSION

This short section on Judas the Galilean is based primarily upon the writings of Josephus, the only Jewish historian of the time. The Slavonic Josephus also contributes to the overall picture of this man and his movement. The picture that emerges is quite different from the accepted storyline of Judas as represented in Acts chapter 5. (See Chapter 2 for an analysis of Acts chapter 5.) Judas the Galilean was not a one-hit wonder. His movement lasted from before the Golden Eagle Temple Cleansing in 4 BCE to the last gasp at Masada in 73 CE. His fight against Rome was legendary. How could this history have been lost for two thousand years? How could this powerful rabbi have been reduced to a mere footnote in the history of first-century Judea? These questions will be answered in Part III, but now we will attempt to further explore the history of Judas' movement, starting with the Sadduc.

CHAPTER 4

THE SADDUC

Very little attention has been given to Judas the Galilean's second-in-command. This omission stems from the paucity of information concerning him. That being said, three individuals have characteristics consistent with the Sadduc. But before introducing them, the Sadduc must be fully defined, and this from the writings of Josephus.

...yet there was one Judas, a Gaulonite, of a city whose name was Gamala, who, taking with him **Sadduc, a Pharisee**, became zealous to draw them to a revolt, who **both** said that this taxation was no better than an introduction to slavery, and exhorted the nation to assert their liberty. ...For Judas and **Sadduc**, who excited a fourth philosophical sect among us, and had a **great many followers** therein, filled our civil governments with tumults at present, and laid the foundation of our future miseries, by this system of philosophy, which we were before unacquainted withal; concerning which I shall discourse a little, and this the rather, because the **infection** which spread thence among the younger sort, who were zealous for it, brought the public to destruction. (*Ant.* 18.4; 9-10) (Emphasis mine)

This is the only mention of the Sadduc in Josephus, the only Jewish historian of his time. It would seem a daunting task to identify this Sadduc, but with our knowledge of Judas the Galilean, it may be quite possible. From the above passage, we can glean three bits of pertinent information concerning Sadduc: the name Sadduc itself, that he was a Pharisee and the fact that he preached the same message as Judas the Galilean, that is, freedom from earthly rulers. Josephus also added his own commentary concerning Judas

41

and the Sadduc and their movement, calling it an **infection**. This, too, will be examined.

The followers of Judas and Sadduc were said to be **infected** with the Fourth Philosophy. This derogatory statement by Josephus is similar to other negative comments about the early Christians. Tacitus wrote the following concerning the fire at Rome which occurred in 64 CE.

Nero set up as culprits and punished with the utmost refinement of cruelty a class hated for their **abominations**, who are commonly called Christians. Christus, from whom their name is derived, was executed at the hands of the procurator Pontius Pilate in the reign of Tiberius. Checked for the moment, this **pernicious superstition** again broke out, not only in Judea, the source of the evil, but even in Rome... (*Annals*, xv. 44) (Emphasis mine)

This sentiment by Tacitus is supported by Suetonius, who wrote that the Jews who followed "Chrestus" caused disturbances in the city of Rome. This disturbance can be dated at approximately the rise of Claudius, or 41 CE. (1) Thus, the Jewish Christians were reviled by a large section of the Gentile population in Rome. This revulsion of Jewish Christianity was not limited to just Judea and Rome. Pliny the Younger wrote about the Jewish Christians in Bithynia, around the year 112 CE.

The **contagion of this superstition** has spread not only in the cities, but in the villages and rural districts as well; yet it seems capable of being checked and set right. (Pliny. Epp. X (ad Traj.), xcvi) (Emphasis mine)

This infection ascribed to the Fourth Philosophy was mirrored in the descriptions of the early Jewish Christians in Rome and beyond. (Pliny's Christians were probably Gentile because they generally recanted, an act Jewish Christians did not do.) And it should be noted that both Tacitus and Pliny commented on how the true Christians would undergo torture as opposed to betraying God. This same virtue was also attached to the Fourth Philosophy.

Josephus also wrote that the infection had spread to the younger generation who were zealous for it. This passage may have been used by the author of Acts to describe the followers of James.

Then they [James and the elders] said to Paul, "You see, brother, **how many thousands of Jews have believed, and all of them are zealous for the law.** They have been informed that you [Paul] teach all the Jews who live among the Gentiles to turn away from Moses, telling them not to circumcise their children or live according to our customs." (Acts 21:20-21) (Emphasis mine)

Although the whole of Acts is an attempt to misdirect, there are some passages which appear genuine. This dialogue between James and Paul did not actually happen as Paul had been removed from the movement in 44 CE (See Part II), but the description of James' disciples is consistent with Paul's dreaded "circumcision group" (Gal. 2:11-13). In essence, the Jewish Christians and the Fourth Philosophy were one in the same group. This realization will help us in our quest for the Sadduc's true identification.

Now we will entertain the three pertinent pieces of information Josephus wrote concerning the Sadduc. First, the name Sadduc is a very powerful clue. According to Eisenman, Sadduc or Saddok is a "term linguistically related both to the word 'Sadducee' in Greek and the 'Zaddik' in Hebrew." (2) This Zaddik terminology is associated with the idea of Righteousness.

'Kabbalah' means that which is received, the received tradition. It is the Jewish mystical tradition. One of its better known tenets is the idea of 'the Zaddik' or 'the Righteous One'. James is known in almost all early Christian texts as 'the Just' or 'Just One', and this eponym is, in fact, equivalent to that of the 'Zaddik' in Jewish Kabbalah. (3)

In a sense, Eisenman is tying the Zaddik definition to James, the brother of Jesus. Indirectly, although he never claims it, Eisenman is also comparing James to the Sadduc. James, for sure, is one of three individuals who qualify for examination concerning the Sadduc, but it must be remembered that other people in first-century Judea would have been considered Righteous or even be labeled as the "Righteous One". For now, let us just be assured that the Sadduc had a reputation for being Righteous.

Second, Josephus stated that Sadduc was a Pharisee. In describing the Fourth Philosophy, Josephus also wrote that "these men agree in all other things with the Pharisaic notions; but they have an inviolable attachment to liberty; and say that God is to be their only Ruler and Lord." (*Ant.* 18.23) The only thing that separated Judas and Sadduc from the other Pharisees was a political desire for autonomy. Most Pharisees had learned to live with Herodian and Roman political rule as long as such rule did not hinder their religious life. So the average Pharisee divided the political from the religious. Judas and the Sadduc could not divorce the realities of everyday life from the commands of God. In fact, to them, the Roman rule was intolerable. They could only follow God.

The other Pharisees, outside of Judas' Fourth Philosophy, would have questioned the wisdom of tackling the Roman Empire, but there was probably also a bit of admiration thrown in as well. In the Gospels, Jesus was often invited into the Pharisees' homes and was warned by them on at least one occasion about Herod's intentions to kill him (Luke 13:31). Thus, even the Gospels show that there was a relationship between Jesus and the Pharisees. How then did the Pharisees get such a bad rap? The answer to that question concerns a rewrite of Judas' life (the Gospels) and the identification of Paul as a Pharisee in Philippians 3:5. Philippians has been attributed to Paul by many scholars, but the claim attesting to his imprisonment is patently false (Phil. 1:12-14). As will be delineated in Part II, Paul never was placed in chains in Rome as described by Acts chapter 28. Thus, the claim of him being a Pharisee must also be questioned as too convenient. The early Church tried to place all evil intents upon the Pharisees. For example, Jesus was constantly being hounded by the Pharisees while Paul persecuted the Church while associated with the Pharisees. This picture completely misrepresented the actual situation as will be proved throughout this book. For now, let us just be content in knowing that Judas and Sadduc were radical Pharisees and that the Gospel Jesus was on good terms with many Pharisees.

Third, Josephus confirmed that the Sadduc had a very close tie to Judas the Galilean. Josephus wrote that both preached against the Roman taxation and both "exhorted the nation to assert their liberty." Therefore, Sadduc was much more than a religious figure to back the radical message of Judas. Sadduc was standing right beside Judas, preaching the same brand of radical Judaism. This makes sense as the entire movement combined the political with the religious. Even though they were all zealous for God's Law, they also preached a revolution against the earthly powers. Righteousness and freedom were entwined.

That is the sum of Josephus' comment concerning Sadduc. And very little has been written about him by scholars. Knowing what we do about the relationship between the historical Judas the Galilean and the Gospel Jesus of Nazareth, a list of three candidates must be examined in our search for the historical Sadduc. The three are all figures from the pages of the New Testament, all quite familiar to the average reader. They are: Cephas (Peter), James the Just or the brother of the Lord, and John the Baptist. Each will be considered below.

CEPHAS OR PETER

In my first book, *Judas the Galilean: the Flesh and Blood Jesus*, I associated Cephas with Sadduc. On the surface, this was the obvious choice as Peter was the lead apostle throughout the Gospels. Certainly, if Jesus had a second-in-command, it had to be Peter. In Matthew 16:16-19, Jesus praised Peter for the identification of himself as the Christ:

Jesus replied, "Blessed are you, Simon son of Jonah, for this was **not revealed to you by man, but by my Father in heaven**. And I tell you that you are Peter [Rock], and on this rock I will build my church, and the gates of Hades will not overcome it. I will give you the keys of the kingdom of heaven; whatever you bind on earth will be bound in heaven, and whatever you loose on earth will be loosed in heaven." (Emphasis mine)

This seems quite straightforward. Jesus was giving Peter power after his own death. Therefore, Peter must have been the second-in-command or Sadduc. However, since we know that the Gospels and Acts were a rewrite of Judas and the Fourth Philosophy, it may be wise to further examine this relationship between Jesus and Peter. From the above passage, Jesus claimed that Peter's faith in him was not taught by man but by God. This sounds an awful lot like Paul's own praise concerning his Gospel. In Galatians 1:11-12, Paul distinguished his Gospel from that of the Pillar apostles (Cephas, James and John).

I want you to know, brothers, that the gospel I preached is not something that man made up. I did not receive it from any man, nor was I taught it; rather, I received it by revelation from Jesus Christ.

In both cases, the message to Peter and Paul was not derived from any man but was given by revelation by God. In Paul's case, it came from Christ Jesus, who resided in heaven. This Pauline message was no doubt placed into the Gospel story to make Peter's faith stand out. It is interesting to note that the Galatians' declaration was made to distinguish Paul from Cephas and James. Paul claimed a superior message to that of the Pillars as his message came directly from the Risen Christ. And if that were the case, then it can be assumed that Peter's message from the earthly Jesus never really occurred.

Cephas' age must also be examined in relation to Sadduc. Josephus wrote that Sadduc teamed up with Judas the Galilean in 6 CE. We also know that Cephas' quarrel with Paul as described in Galatians, occurred around 44 CE. Could Cephas have been roaming the Mediterranean world for that long? It is possible but not likely. If Sadduc were 30 years old in 6 CE, then he would have been 68 years old in 44 CE. Travel today is exhausting. Travel in those days was certainly not for the physically impaired. An aged man around 70 would not have been the first choice for missionary travels. Therefore, the age question does not favor Cephas.

But why would the Gospel writer invent the successor story? Why would Peter be placed in this situation if Sadduc was someone else? This will be answered as we explore James and John the Baptist.

JAMES THE JUST, THE BROTHER OF THE LORD

Was James the Just the true successor to Jesus? To determine this, we must go back to the oldest known document concerning James. That document is the letter to the Galatians, written approximately 45 CE by Paul. In that letter, Paul stated that three years after his conversion, he met privately in Jerusalem with Cephas and James, the brother of the Lord. Fourteen years later, Paul once again traveled to Jerusalem and met with the Pillar apostles: James, Cephas and John. From this, we know that James was one of the top three leaders. In an earlier letter to the Corinthians, Paul said that the resurrected Jesus appeared to Cephas, the Twelve and then to James. All this proves is that James was important, not necessarily the leader or the Sadduc.

However, after discussing the Jerusalem Council, Paul revealed the true role of James in the Church.

When Peter came to Antioch, I opposed him to his face, because he was in the wrong. Before **certain men came from James**, he used to eat with the Gentiles. But when they arrived, he began to draw back and separate himself from the Gentiles because he was afraid of those who belonged to the circumcision group. The other Jews joined him in his hypocrisy, so that by their hypocrisy even Barnabas was led astray. (Gal. 2:11-13) (Emphasis mine)

Paul's take on this event may be very skewed and self-serving. He called Peter a hypocrite and a coward because he followed the instructions of James. First of all, the instructions from James must have included information concerning Paul's true teachings, of which Peter was unaware. Paul boasted in how he shaped his message when with Jews or with Gentiles. "To the Jews, I became like a Jew, to win the Jews. To those under the law, I became like one under the law (though I myself am not under the law), so as to win those under the law." (1 Cor. 9:19-23) It is very likely that Cephas (Peter) did not realize what Paul was preaching to his Gentile followers. Cephas and his Jewish friends turned their backs upon Paul when informed of his true teachings by James' ambassadors. This not only shows that Paul's gospel was alien to the Jerusalem leaders but that James led the movement at this time, in 44 CE. Josephus wrote of a similar event, where Eleazar was sent from Galilee in 44 CE to correct the teachings of Ananias. (*Ant.* 20.34-48) Eleazar was no doubt also sent out by James to combat this Pauline-style philosophy (Judaism without the law and circumcision).

In fact, James also certified teaching credentials in the early Church. Paul bitterly complained about this certification in 2 Cor. 3:1-3:

Are we beginning to commend ourselves again? Or do we need, like some people, letters of recommendation to you or from you? You yourselves are our letters, written on our hearts, known and read by everyone. You show that you are a letter from Christ, the result of our ministry, written not with ink but with the Spirit of the living God, not on tablets of stone but on tablets of human hearts.

Paul had a way of buttering up his audience. He told his congregation that they were his letter from Christ. Therefore, he did not need a letter from the Jerusalem Church or from James. The Corinthians may have bought this line, but the Jerusalem apostles would not have approved. In fact, this section of Corinthians proves that Paul's name did not appear on the approved teachers list.

From Paul, we know that James led the Church, at least from the Jerusalem Council (38-39 CE?) to the argument at Antioch (44 CE). Yet James' role in the early Church is somewhat hidden in the book of Acts. But even this document has to eventually admit his preeminence. In the Jerusalem Council, after hearing all the facts, James, not Peter, decided the issue concerning the Gentiles. "It is my [James] judgment, therefore, that we should not make it difficult for the Gentiles who are turning to God." (Acts 15:19) This has been misconstrued by Christians throughout the ages to mean that James approved of Paul's methods. That is not true as James did not fully understand Paul's gospel at this time. James wanted circumcision and the entire law **presented** to the Gentiles, but he also could accept God-fearing Gentiles, those who did not follow the entire law. However, it is obvious that James preferred full conversion. (Paul's gospel dissuaded Gentiles from circumcision and the law.)

James led the Jerusalem Church in Acts Chapter 15, but he was not introduced until Acts chapter 12. Robert Eisenman convincingly proves that James was actually written out of the early chapters of Acts, the early history of the Church. The election of Matthias to replace the mythical Judas Iscariot was simply a rewrite of James replacing Jesus (Judas the Galilean). The stoning of Stephen was actually a worked over version of the stoning of James. (Note that Saul was mentioned right after Stephen in Acts and was in action shortly after the stoning of James, per *Ant.* 20.214.) In addition, the early chapters of Acts had Peter and John preaching at the Temple, but never mentioned James.

In short, the book of Acts very successfully minimized the role of James in the early Church. However, by reading between the lines, James' preeminence becomes obvious.

Many other early documents point towards the leadership of James. Robert Eisenman presents a compelling case for the supremacy of James in his book, *James, the Brother of Jesus*. A few of his proofs will be reproduced below. The first comes from Eusebius, who quotes Hegesippus, an early Church historian who lived from 90-180 CE.

But James, the brother of the Lord, who, as there were many of this name, was surnamed the Just by all of his days of our Lord until now, received the Government of the Church with [from] the Apostles. (4)

Eusebius then quotes Clement of Alexandria, who lived from 150-215 CE. Note that even though Clement followed the Gospel script for the Central Three (as opposed to Paul's Central Three), he still did not deny that another James, surnamed the Just, was chosen as the leader.

Peter, James and John after the Ascension of the Savior, did not contend for the Glory, even though they had previously been honored by the Savior, but chose James the Just as Bishop of Jerusalem. (5)

These early Christian historians readily admitted that James occupied the most important position in the early Church. They do seem to imply that the office was voted upon by the Apostles as opposed to have been given by the earthly Jesus. However, the following passage from the Gospel of Thomas overtly states that Jesus directly honored James with the leadership role.

The disciples said to Jesus: "We know that you will depart from us. Who is it that shall be great over us [after you are gone]?"
Jesus replied to them: "In the place where you are to go [Jerusalem], go to James the Just for whose sake Heaven and Earth came into existence." (Logion 12)

In the Gospel of Thomas, Jesus directly appointed James. Regardless of whether James was directly appointed by Jesus or was voted upon by the Apostles, the point is clear: James was the undisputed leader of the early Church. This is very important as James was the brother of Jesus. Like the Maccabean dynasty, brothers served after brothers. In this respect, the Jesus movement mirrored the Maccabees. And it should be noted that the Fourth Philosophy also had relatives of Judas in important positions. Judas' own two sons (Simon and James) were crucified and another son, Menahem, marched into Jerusalem as a Messiah and cleansed the Temple. Judas' grandson, Eleazar, led the Sicarii in their last stand against Rome at Masada.

In my second book, *New Testament Lies*, I associated James with Sadduc, based upon the righteousness concept and James' age. According to Epiphanius, James died at the age of ninety-six in 62 CE. This would bring his birth date to 35 BCE. By the time Sadduc joined Judas the Galilean in 6 CE (maybe earlier), James would have been approximately forty years old. This was certainly old enough to be taken as a Righteous Teacher or a Holy Man.

So it is obvious that James was a follower of Judas from the census and was elected the movement's leader after the death of Jesus (Judas the Galilean). But does that make him Sadduc? James was elected to replace Judas, not Sadduc. The Sadduc was still alive and in charge. James played second fiddle to Sadduc until the Sadduc's death. It was at this time that Cephas replaced Sadduc. Thus, by 40 CE, James and Cephas were the leaders of the Jewish Christian movement. It is our task to determine who guided the movement after Judas the Galilean's death in 19-21 CE.

JOHN THE BAPTIST

Only one other credible candidate exists for the role as Sadduc: John the Baptist, the man who introduced the Gospel Jesus to the world. I had extreme difficulty identifying John as the Sadduc (my third book!) due to the clever way the Gospels separated Jesus from his true past by a generation. The same held true for Sadduc. For two thousand years, historians have incorrectly assigned John the Baptist's introduction to 28-29 CE. We will reassign him to 6 CE. According to the Slavonic Josephus, John came baptizing during the later years of Archelaus, right before the census of Cyrenius.

And at that time a certain man was going about Judaea, [dressed] in strange garments. He donned the hair of cattle on those parts of his body which were not covered with his own hair. And he was wild of visage. **And he came to the Jews and called them to freedom, saying, "God hath sent me to show you the lawful way, by which you will be rid of [your] many rulers. But there will be no mortal ruling [over you], only the Most High, who hath sent me."**

And when they heard this, the people were joyful. And all Judaea and the environs of Jerusalem were following him. And he did nothing else for them, except to immerse them in Jordan's stream, and dismiss them, **bidding them refrain from their wicked deeds, and a king would be given to them,** saving them and humbling all the unsubmissive, while he himself would be humbled by no one. Some mocked his voices, others believed them. And when he was brought before Archelaus and the experts of the Law were assembled, they asked him **who he was and where he had been up till then**. In answer he said, "I am a man. Where the divine spark leads me, I feed on the roots of reeds and the shoots of trees." **When those [men] threatened him with torture if he did not cease those words and deeds, he said, "It is you who should cease from your foul deeds and adhere to the Lord, your God."**

And arising in fury, Simon, an Essene by origin [and] a scribe, said, "We read the divine scriptures every day, and **you have [just] now come in like a beast from the woods** dare to teach us and to lead people astray with your impious words." And he rushed forward to tear his body apart.

But he, reproaching them, said, "I am not revealing to you the mystery which is [here] among you, because you have not wished it. Therefore, there will come [down] on you an unutterable calamity, because of you and your people." Thus he spoke and left for the other side of the Jordan. And as no one dared to prevent him, he was doing just what he had done before. (After *War* 2.110) (Emphasis mine)

Many striking similarities exist between this Baptist, who was inserted into the *War*, and the description of the Fourth Philosophy as detailed in the *Antiquities*. It is interesting that the *War* does not include this mention of the Baptist and also omits the Sadduc, while *Antiquities* mentions the Sadduc as being Judas the Galilean's co-teacher. It seems as though the Slavonic *War* is supplementing the *War* with its own version of the Sadduc, one which fits perfectly with the *Antiquities'* version.

The Baptist called the people to freedom while the Sadduc "exhorted the nation to assert their liberty." (*Ant.* 18.4) The Baptist taught that only God, not mortals, should rule over you. This is echoed in *Antiquities* where Judas and the Sadduc "say that God is to be their only Ruler and Lord." (*Ant.* 18.23) In the Slavonic Version, the Baptist played second fiddle to the king who was to come while the Sadduc was the second to the Messiah figure, Judas the Galilean. (*Ant.* 18.4) This Baptist also was new to the political arena as he was not familiar to the experts in the Law. This would have made the Baptist a younger man, approximately the same age as Judas the Galilean, or about thirty years of age in 6 CE. In addition, like the Fourth Philosophy, the Baptist was willing to undergo torture. (*Ant.* 18.23-24) And finally, he was attacked by an Essene and others who supported Archelaus (Sadducees). This would most likely make the Baptist a Pharisee, just like the Sadduc. (*Ant.* 18.4) In every way, the Slavonic version of the *War* likens the Baptist to the Sadduc.

In addition, the placement of the Slavonic version of the Baptist is right before the introduction of Judas the Galilean. Eight verses after the Baptist section, Josephus wrote:

Under his [Coponius] administration it was that a certain Galilean, whose name was Judas, prevailed with his countrymen to revolt; and said they were cowards if they would endure to pay a tax to the Romans, and would, after God, **submit to mortal men as their lords.** This man was a **teacher of a peculiar sect of his own, and was not at all like the rest of those their leaders.** (*War* 2.118) (Emphasis mine)

In this passage about Judas the Galilean, it must be noted that he, like the Baptist, preached that mortal men should not replace God as their Lord. This was a hallmark belief of the Fourth Philosophy. The description of Judas does remind us of the Gospel Jesus, in that Judas was so different from all the other teachers. In *Antiquities*, Josephus goes as far as attributing a philosophy to Judas and Sadduc, the Fourth Philosophy. (*Ant.* 18.9) (The other three were the Pharisees, Sadducees and Essenes.) Thus, Judas and Sadduc stood out from all other teachers. From the above, I think it is obvious that John the Baptist and Jesus were really the Sadduc and Judas the Galilean.

The Slavonic Josephus placed the Baptist's introduction at 6 CE, but it also devoted two other passages to him. One was about the death of Philip (34 CE) and the other mirrored the Gospel John story and the John of *Antiquities*. This would date the death of the Slavonic Baptist at 35-36 CE, the same dating as the passage in *Antiquities*. The *Antiquities'* passage will be reproduced below.

Now, some of the Jews thought that the destruction of Herod's army came from God, and that very justly, as a punishment of what he did against **John, that was called the Baptist**; for Herod slew him, who was a good man, and commanded the **Jews to exercise virtue, both as to righteousness towards one another, and piety towards God**, and so to come to baptism; for that the washing [with water] would be acceptable to him, if they made use of it, not in order to the putting away [or the remission] of some sins [only], but for the purification of the body; supposing still that the **soul was thoroughly purified beforehand by righteousness**. Now, when [many] others came in crowds about him, for they were greatly moved [or pleased] by hearing his words, **Herod, who feared lest the great influence John had over the people might put it into his power and inclination to raise a rebellion (for they seemed ready to do anything he should advise), thought it best, by putting him to death**, to prevent any mischief he might cause, and not bring himself into any difficulties, by sparing a man who might make him repent of it when it should be too late. Accordingly, he was sent a prisoner, out of Herod's suspicious temper, to Macherus, the castle I before mentioned, and was there put to death. Now the Jews had an opinion that the destruction of this army was sent as a punishment upon Herod, and a mark of God's displeasure against him. (*Ant.* 18.116-119) (Emphasis mine)

Josephus does recognize that John was referred to as the Baptist by the people. This Baptist exhorted the Jews to "exercise virtue" both towards themselves and to God. His baptism was with water and this water represented cleansing, but there was nothing miraculous about the liquid. The baptism was purely for purification of the body; the soul was purified beforehand by repentance and by acting right or by righteousness. This is a far cry from the Christian concept of justification by faith alone. To the Baptist, one was only justified by walking right before God, and this included following the law.

It is interesting that John had great influence over the crowds in 35-36 CE. According to the Gospels, John was put to death before Jesus, somewhere from 30-32 CE. Obviously, the Gospel story does not tell the truth concerning John. John the Baptist was the most popular teacher in Judea at this time (35-36 CE), and the crowds would do anything he wished. Where was Jesus? Where was James?

In answer to the above questions, Judas the Galilean (Jesus) had been put to death under Pilate many years earlier, around 19-21 CE. This means that John the Baptist (Sadduc) ruled in his place for about fifteen years, until John's own death around 36 CE. After Judas (Jesus) suffered crucifixion, James took his place, but James would have been the second-in-command to John the Baptist until John's death. Only at that time did James become the movement's leader. His second-in-command would have been Cephas. This will be detailed below.

THE LEADERSHIP OF THE EARLY JEWISH CHRISTIANS

The following pairings will show the approximate dates of each leadership pair.

4 BCE and earlier - Matthias and Judas led their students in the Golden Eagle Temple Cleansing, an awakening for the movement. It is my contention that Matthias or the event may have been associated with the Root of Planting, a term taken from the Dead Sea Scrolls. (The Fourth Philosophy did not write the Scrolls but they did use them to their own advantage. Some Scrolls were found at Masada and the heaviest coin usage at Qumran occurred during the

heyday of the Fourth Philosophy, from 4 BCE to 68 CE.) (6) With the death of Matthias, Judas headed to Galilee. Matthias was replaced by the Sadduc, anywhere from 4 BCE to 6 CE.

6 - 19 or 21 CE - This period of the Jewish Christian movement brimmed with excitement as both Judas (Jesus) and Sadduc (John the Baptist) roamed the countryside. They preached the Kingdom of Heaven on earth. In 19 CE, Judas marched to Jerusalem and was hailed as Messiah by the crowds. However, the Kingdom on earth did not prevail and Jesus was crucified.

19 or 21 - 36 CE - After Judas' (Jesus') death by crucifixion, James became second-in-command to John the Baptist. Acts chapter 1 obscured the election of James by reporting that a Matthias (a playful usage of the above Matthias) replaced Judas Iscariot. In Chapter 17, I will prove that a Judas Iscariot never lived but was purely an invention of the Gospel writers as a way to hide Judas the Galilean and James. Robert Eisenman proves that the election of James was the real event, not the election of a Matthias. (7)

Even though James replaced Judas (Jesus), the movement was still headed by John the Baptist. This is hard to accept considering the Gospels insist that John died before Jesus. But history does not jibe with the Gospel account. John lasted until 36 CE, many years after the Gospel story and many more years after the real crucifixion as outlined above, around 19-21 CE. Even within the pages of Acts, the truth emerges. Peter preached a strong sermon after the death of Jesus.

When the people heard this [sermon], they were cut to the heart and said to Peter and the other apostles, "Brothers, what shall we do."

Peter replied, **"Repent and be baptized, every one of you, in the name of Jesus Christ so that your sins may be forgiven. And you will receive the gift of the Holy Spirit.** The promise is for you and your children and for all who are far off - for all whom the Lord our God will call."

With many other words he warned them; and he pleaded with them, "Save yourselves from this corrupt generation." Those who accepted his message were baptized, and about three thousand were added to their number that day. (Acts 2:37-41) (Emphasis mine)

The above passage combines some truth with some Pauline teachings. Since John was the leader, it only makes sense that the cornerstone practice of the movement would be baptism. This water baptism was in reality just a purification of the body as the soul was cleansed through righteousness (repentance). The author of Acts does try to combine this water baptism with Paul's Holy Spirit baptism, but this was never part of the early Jewish Christian movement. This too can be explained using the New Testament.

In the first letter to the Corinthians, written somewhere around 40 CE, Paul complained that his followers were split among several factions.

My brothers, some from Chloe's household have informed me that there are quarrels among you. What I mean is this: One of you says, "I follow Paul"; another, "I follow Apollos"; another, "I follow Cephas"; still another, "I follow Christ." ...What, after all, is Apollos? And what is Paul? Only servants, through whom you came to believe - as the Lord has assigned to each his task. I planted the seed, Apollos watered it, but God made it grow. (1 Cor. 1:11-12; 3:5-6)

This passage was written by Paul probably after the Jerusalem Council (38-39 CE) and before his removal from the movement in 44 CE. During this period, Paul was careful to hide his true feelings and thoughts concerning the Fourth Philosophy. Therefore, his words seemed conciliatory. After all, Paul desired that his congregations follow his preaching. This becomes crystal clear when reading Corinthians, where four different factions vied for converts. Paul had his followers, Christ (the original Judas the Galilean) had his, as did Cephas (representing James), but Apollos has never been adequately explained before. With his name, Paul used water baptism. Acts 18:24-25 stated that Apollos was "a learned man, with a thorough knowledge of Scriptures. He had been instructed in the way of the Lord, and he spoke with great fervor and taught about Jesus accurately, though he knew only the baptism of John." From this passage we can infer that Apollos knew of John's water baptism but had never heard of the Holy Spirit baptism, even though he knew of Jesus' teachings. This shows that the Jewish Christians did not practice the Holy Spirit baptism. Thus Acts 2:38 incorrectly attributed Paul's Holy Spirit baptism to Peter's preaching.

It should also be noted that around 40 CE, the cult of John was still quite powerful. That is why some still followed his teachings. Remember, Paul complained of the factions who followed Cephas and Apollos. At 40 CE, there was not a universal leader of the movement. Even though John was dead, many of his disciples did not want to follow anyone else. That is why there was such a strong emphasis on the death of John the Baptist before Jesus in the Gospels. This disunity within the Fourth Philosophy had to be hidden. This disunity also explains the Pseudoclementine *Recognitions*, where John's movement was criticized. "Yea, some even of the disciples of John, who seemed to be great ones, have separated themselves from the people, and proclaimed their own master as Christ. (Chapter LIV - Jewish Sects) This second-century document recognized a group which still considered John the Baptist as Messiah. This further strengthens the point that John lived much beyond the lifetime of Jesus. The Sadduc outlived Judas the Galilean.

36 - 38 CE - This was a time for consolidation of power. When one reads Paul's letter to the Galatians, it appears as if the Council of Jerusalem was called simply to decide Paul's place in the church. Paul stated that he went to Jerusalem in "response to a revelation" and presented his Gospel before the Pillar apostles. (Gal. 2:2) In Jerusalem, Paul claimed that he was "given the task of preaching the gospel to the Gentiles, just as Peter [Cephas] had been given the task of preaching the gospel to the Jews." (Gal. 2:7) It is quite possible that the most important part of the so-called council of Jerusalem was to install Cephas as the second-in-command. Any dealings with Paul would have been secondary in nature. Besides, at this point in Paul's relationship with James, Paul was still hiding his own gospel. In 1 Corinthians 9:20, Paul made it quite clear that he told the Jews what they wanted to hear, not his own unique gospel.

So is it possible that the Council of Jerusalem was used by James as a way to consolidate power. John the Baptist had just been put to death and his fervent followers may have been clinging to his memory. It was James' task to place all emphasis back upon the resurrected Jesus, making himself a caretaker leader until the Messiah's return in power and glory. It is interesting to note that the fourth-century Church historian, Epiphanius, stated that James ruled the Church for 24 years until his death in 62 CE. (8) This would have made James leader of the Church from 38 CE until 62 CE. This is generally the time period covered by the book of Acts, although the Acts' version is a twisted jumble of time and events.

I had previously overlooked the Epiphanius claim of 24 years as this did not jibe with the death of Jesus and the rise of James. Even in the traditional timeline, Jesus died in 30-33 CE and James would have been appointed leader shortly thereafter. The 38 CE date seemed way too late. And this dating is even further away from my timeline, where Judas the Galilean (Jesus) suffered crucifixion around 19-21 CE. The one thing that I and all others missed was the Sadduc, or John the Baptist. John led the movement until his death in 35-36 CE.

If the Council of Jerusalem were used by James as a way to consolidate power, then it occurred around 38-39 CE. It was here that the new more intense mission was launched. Under John the Baptist, the emphasis was upon repentance. The new strategy would be for the return of Jesus in power and glory. That is why the passages about John the Baptist in the Gospels appear to talk about the return of the resurrected Jesus. (See Matt. 3:11-12, where Jesus will come to separate the wheat from the chaff.)

Using this more exact time for the Council of Jerusalem at 38-39 CE, we can therefore calculate Paul's conversion into the movement. If Paul converted 17 years before the Council, then he became a member around 21-22 CE. Paul also would have had five to six years in the movement after the Council, as he was thrown out in 44 CE, per the argument with Cephas over Paul's Gentile gospel. In all, Paul was a member of the Fourth Philosophy for 22 to 23 years. (This will be further examined in Part II.)

38 - 62 CE - The Fourth Philosophy was guided by James and Cephas. As the years rolled on, it was more difficult to keep the young disciples under control. It was not easy to wait for the coming of a dead Messiah. Many, like Theudas, tried to prod God into action, but this simply led to their own deaths. In time, the movement would splinter and at the death of James in 62 CE, all hell would soon break loose.

CHAPTER 5

THE STONING OF JAMES THE JUST

One of the most important and controversial passages in Josephus concerns the stoning of James, the brother of Jesus. Two distinct viewpoints exist today, from the Mythicists and from the Traditionalists. The existence of a family member is tantamount to proving the reality of the Jesus figure in history. That is why there are such radically different views on this subject.

Before examining the two viewpoints, it would be wise to look at Josephus' passage concerning James.

...Ananus was of this disposition, he thought he had now a proper opportunity [to exercise his authority]. Festus was now dead, and Albinus was but upon the road; so he [Ananus] assembled the sanhedrin of judges, and brought before them **the brother of Jesus, who was called Christ, whose name was James,** and some others, [or, some of his companions]; and when he had formed an accusation against them as breakers of the law, he delivered them to be stoned. (*Ant.* 20.200) (Emphasis mine)

It would be beneficial to have some background of the circumstances surrounding James' death. The high priest at the time was Ananus, the son of the famous high priest Annas, who served from 6-15 CE, being the first person who examined Jesus after the arrest, per John 18:12-14. Thus, there was a historical link between the deaths of Jesus and this James. The authenticity of the highlighted section of the passage has been questioned by many over the years. Was "the brother of Jesus" added, or was "who was called Christ" added, or was the passage simply as stated? Considering that Josephus never mentioned a Messiah figure named Jesus, "the brother of Jesus" was probably a later interpolation. Josephus obviously did not consider this "Jesus" as the Messiah, so the passage "who was called Christ" may very well be genuine. Now if the passage read "who was the Christ", then we would be assured that this was counterfeit, as Josephus attributed the "Star Prophecy" to Vespasian, not to any Jewish leader. My solution for this passage would read as such: "the brother of Judas the Galilean, who was called Christ." Note that Josephus always referred back to Judas the Galilean when mentioning a son or grandson. (*Ant.* 20.102; *War* 2.433; *War* 7.253) It is not wild speculation to assume that Josephus was referring back to James' brother, Judas, as he had done in the cases mentioned above.

THE MYTHICIST INTERPRETATION

As mentioned earlier, the Mythicists believe that this passage does not refer to the brother of the Lord, the brother of Jesus or the brother of Judas the Galilean. Some claim that the interpolation was the phrase "who was called Christ." They also claim that the "Jesus" referred to was Jesus, the son of Damneus. This revelation of pure genius rests on the position of the two names. In the above passage about James, there is a reference to a Jesus. After the removal of Ananus from the high priesthood due to complaints about his unholy actions, the newly arrived governor, Albinus, appointed Jesus, son of Damneus to the high priesthood. This strained interpretation has James being the brother of the high priest Jesus and the son of Damneus. There are several reasons to doubt that the James of *Ant.* 20.200 was the brother of Jesus, the son of Damneus (*Ant.* 20.203).

First, this James and his companions were put to death on the orders of Ananus, who was the son of the former high priest, Annas. The former high priest ruled from 6-15 CE and had five sons who enjoyed the high priest position. The elder Annas held the position during the lifetime of Judas the Galilean, being mentioned in the Gospel of John, concerning the interrogation of Jesus. It seems that there is more of a connection between the brother of Judas/Jesus and Ananus than with the brother of another Jesus, the son of Damneus. In addition, the name Jesus in connection to James may be a later interpolation as Josephus never wrote about Jesus, the Christ. (The spurious "Jesus passage" (*Ant.* 18.63-64) is undoubtedly a later Christian interpolation).

James and his companions were accused of having broken the Law. Josephus often referred to the Fourth Philosophy as bandits and breakers of the law. (It seems as if Ananus was attacking a group as opposed to a single individual.) In addition, many of the citizens did not approve of Ananus' actions and petitioned Albinus, which resulted in Agrippa removing the high priesthood from Ananus. If this were simply a quarrel gone wrong between two upper class families, the outcry from the citizens would not have been so vehement.

After being removed from the high priesthood, Ananus "cultivated the friendship of Albinus, and the high priest [Jesus], by making them presents." (*Ant.* 20.205) If Ananus had murdered the son of Damneus, then the making of friends with another son of Damneus seems absurd. In addition, Ananus later worked with the other wealthy families and high priests to cheat the lower priests of their meager tithes, so that the poor priests "died from want of food." (*Ant.* 20.207) This being the case, there is no way that Ananus would have condemned another wealthy individual; he would have just bought him off, just like he did everyone else.

Shortly after Jesus, the son of Damneus, was made high priest, he was removed and replaced by Jesus, the son of Gamaliel. (*Ant.* 20.213) Since the name Jesus is the only thing tying James to Damneus, why should James not be tied to Gamaliel as well? Or is the name Jesus just a coincidence between James and Damneus? (Jesus was not an uncommon name.)

After Ananus put James and his companions to death, the Sicarii began kidnapping relatives of Ananus for trade. (*Ant.* 20.208-211) In short, not only had Ananus put James to death, he also held other Sicarii in prison. Note that Ananus not only arrested James but some of his companions as well. It is my contention that James was part of the Fourth Philosophy, part of the Sicarii. In this, he was no different than Menahem (son of Judas the Galilean) or Eleazar (leader at Masada and a grandson of Judas). Thus, James had no connection to a priestly party, no connection to Damneus!

The stoning of James was part of the early Church tradition. The book of Acts rewrites the story in its account of Stephen (Acts 7). Shortly after the death of Stephen, Saul began to persecute the church. It should not be missed that Saul persecuted those weaker than himself shortly after the stoning of James. (*Ant.* 20.214) So even though the Acts' version is fiction, it was based upon an historical event. This may be the strongest piece of evidence against the Mythicist theory. Certainly, this James was an important part of the "Jesus" story or it would not have been reshaped and placed in the book of Acts.

THE TRADITIONAL VIEW

James, the brother of Jesus, holds a strange position in the history of the Church. On the one hand, Acts downplayed and even ignored James. On the other hand, James' earthly relationship to Jesus was the only real proof that a flesh and blood Jesus ever lived. Paul, of course, mentioned James in his letter to the Galatians. In this letter, James was honored as one of the Pillars of the Church and was the one responsible for Paul's removal from the movement. James was leader of the circumcision group. (Gal. 2:9-12) So there was real motive for the author of Acts to downplay James' role in the Church while elevating Paul's role.

Most Christian scholars and historians claim that the stoning of James was not recorded in the book of Acts. They claim that the New Testament Church history ended with Paul's imprisonment in Rome, somewhere between 60-62 CE, conveniently before the death of James (62 CE). First, we must ask ourselves: why would the author of Acts stop his history right before the death of James, the undisputed leader of the movement from the time of Paul to 62 CE? It makes no sense whatsoever, unless of course, the stoning of James was purposely ignored or more ingeniously, hidden from clear view.

In his book, *James the Brother of Jesus*, Robert Eisenman writes that the stoning of Stephen was simply a rewrite of the stoning of James. (1) In essence, the death of James was included in Acts' convoluted history, although placed in the late 30's opposed to the proper date of 62 CE. In both accounts, Saul persecuted those weaker than himself after the respective deaths of Stephen and James. If it were not for many other rewrites in Acts, it would be easy to say that the deaths of Stephen and James were just coincidental. However, with one rewrite after another, this argument becomes quite weak. (See Chapter 14 for an analysis of Acts).

Not only was the death of James hidden from view in Acts, but his role in the early Church was obscured in the Gospels and Acts. In the Gospels, the brothers of Jesus were no better than the brothers of Joseph, who sold Joseph into slavery. In the Synoptic Gospels, Jesus' family was often associated with those who did not believe in Jesus. (Mk. 3:20-21; 3:31-35) In fact, they said, "He is out of his mind." In John 7:1-10, Jesus' brothers urged him to go to Jerusalem, to a certain death. This was done out of jealousy and unbelief. James fared no better in the book of Acts. When Jesus (Judas the Galilean) had just been crucified, the apostles picked a replacement. According to later traditions, this replacement was James the Just. However, according to Acts, Matthias replaced the mythical Judas Iscariot. (Judas Iscariot will be examined in Part III - Chapter 17). Later, in Acts 15, at the Council of Jerusalem, James miraculously became the leader of the movement. If it were not for the letter of Galatians, the author of Acts would have no doubt created another leader. The acknowledgment of James in Acts 15 was grudgingly given, but even his role was overshadowed by Paul, who would have been an inconsequential part of the Jerusalem Council.

The reason that James was discounted in the Gospels and Acts stems from the persecutions that the early Christians were undergoing in the late first and early second centuries. The main purpose of the Gospels was to show Jesus in an acceptable light to a pro-Roman audience. Therefore, the familial ties between Jesus and his family had to be broken. (This will be fully explained in Part III.). The brother connection had a close parallel with the Maccabees, those brothers who fought an occupying force between two and three centuries earlier. Thus, James was given only the slightest credit for his role in the early church.

But James was afforded much more credit in other sources. Here is a sample from Eusebius, who quoted the fifth book of Hegesippus. (Hegesippus was a second-century Christian historian while Eusebius wrote in the first half of the fourth century.)

Control of the Church passed to the apostles, together with the Lord's brother, James, whom everyone from the Lord's time till our own has called the Righteous, …So they went up and threw down the Righteous one. Then they said to each other, "Let us stone James the Righteous", and began to stone him, as in spite of his fall he was still alive. But he turned and knelt, uttering the words: I beseech Thee, Lord God and Father, forgive them; they do not know what they are doing. (*Eusebius*, Tiberius to Nero, Book 2.23.4,17)

Note that James was accorded special recognition by Hegisippus, in that he stressed the term Righteous in relation to James. He said that everyone knew him as "Righteous". It is also quite revealing that James forgave his own murderers, saying, "…Father, forgive them; they do not know what they are doing." This same act of forgiveness was placed into the mouth of Stephen, the stand-in for James in the book of Acts. This Stephen said, "Lord, do not hold this sin against them." (Acts 7:60) The early Church historians did not quite understand that the even earlier Gospel and Acts writers had hidden James in their text. Time certainly can hide many misdeeds.

The New Testament discounted James the Just, but early Church historians knew of his legendary status in the movement. If he had been restored, then why do so many current Christians have so little knowledge of James? The answer is two-fold. First, the Catholic Church attached itself to Peter, giving him preeminence due to the passage in Matthew 16:18 where Jesus said to Peter: "And I tell you that you are Peter [rock], and on this rock I will build my church." The Papacy was developed through this passage and James the Just was lowered a level. The second reason has to do with the Protestant movement's reverence for the New Testament. Most liberal and conservative Protestant churches preach the infallibility of the Scriptures. This being the case, James the Just became a nonentity. Thus, both the Catholic and Protestant churches discount James today.

MY VIEWPOINT

Of the above two scenarios for James, the Tradition viewpoint, which supports the familial relationship between "Jesus" and James, appears the more reasonable. The Mythicist argument is extremely weak and is made simply because any familial relationship between the two men, Jesus and James, destroys their theory concerning the nature of Jesus: that he never really existed. This, I believe, is utter nonsense. The connection between James and "Jesus" is confirmed by the rewriting of the story in the book of Acts (Stephen's stoning). But the Traditional viewpoint also has its own problems. The greatest weakness has to do with the lack of information anywhere in Josephus describing the traditional Christian movement. The one passage about Jesus, in *Ant.* 18.63-64, is an obvious interpolation, according to a majority of scholars. However, I am the only one who insists that the "Jesus" interpolation is really a replacement passage for the death of Judas the Galilean.

If I am right concerning the "Jesus" passage, then Josephus never mentioned the Gospel Jesus in his history. This is extraordinary, considering that a major religion supposedly sprang from the Gospel Jesus. And if Josephus never mentioned Jesus, then he did not refer back to Jesus when describing the stoning of James. I believe that the original passage about James referred back to Judas the Galilean. This makes much more sense since Josephus always referred back to Judas when writing about his relatives. A few examples are as follows:

...the sons of Judas the Galilean were now slain; I mean of that Judas who caused the people to revolt, when Cyrenius came to take an account of the estates of the Jews, as we have shown in a foregoing book. The names of those sons were James and Simon, whom Alexander commanded to be crucified. (*Ant.* 20.102)

Meanwhile one Menahem, son of Judas the Galilean, the very clever rabbi who in the time of Quirinius [Cyrenius] had once reproached the Jews for submitting to the Romans after serving God alone, took his friends with him and went off to Masada, where he broke open King Herod's armory and distributed weapons to his fellow-townsmen and bandits. With these as bodyguards he returned like a king to Jerusalem, put himself at the head of the insurgents and took charge of the siege. (*War* 2.433-434)

It was one Eleazar, a potent man, and the commander of these Sicarii, that had seized upon it [Masada]. He was a descendant [grandson in Slavonic Josephus] from that Judas who had persuaded abundance of the Jews, as we have formerly related, not to submit to the taxation when Cyrenius was sent into Judea to make one... (*War* 7.253)

Josephus constantly referred back to Judas when introducing his sons and grandsons. The same was no doubt true for any brother who was important enough to be part of the history. The passage about James stated: "and brought before them the brother of Jesus, who was called Christ, whose name was James and some others..." This reference back to Jesus, who was called Christ could have really been "Judas, who claimed to be the Messiah." At least, this makes sense when viewing the above passages about Josephus' treatment of Judas.

If James were the brother of Judas the Galilean, then he was the uncle of Menahem, a leader of the Sicarii in 66 CE. This would make James the leader of the Sicarii in 62 CE, at the time of his death. This would ensure that my Judas the Galilean theory is correct. Is there anything which ties James to the Sicarii? Before answering this question, it should be noted that there is nothing in the passage which connects James to the Gospel Jesus. So what does Josephus really say about the whole issue of James?

There must have been a strong motive for Ananus, the high priest, to take the opportunity to have James killed. As noted above, Ananus was the son of the famous high priest Annas. Josephus tells us that this elder Annas had five sons who performed the high priest duties. The New Testament also states that Caiaphas was the son-in-law of Annas. Thus, it is quite plain that Annas and his family were well connected and very powerful. Annas had been appointed high priest in 6 CE, roughly the same time as Judas the Galilean's tax revolt. Surely, the animosity between Annas and his family and Judas' movement started very early. But is this the only reason for Ananus to attack James?

A few years before the stoning of James, under the governorship of Felix, Jonathan, another son of Annas, was high priest. Jonathon often criticized Felix on his unjust administration of Jewish affairs, giving Felix reason to hate the high priest. Felix planned the murder of Jonathon, using the Sicarii as assassins. Josephus even went as far as blaming this assassination for the reason why Jerusalem was eventually destroyed. (*Ant.* 20.160-166) Needless to say, the murder of Jonathan by the Sicarii may have added to the hatred of Ananus towards James, the leader of the Sicarii.

Motive for murder existed on the family level for Ananus. But were there any other reasons behind his actions? Agrippa II appointed Ananus as high priest after the death of Festus (62 CE). Thus, Agrippa II gave Ananus the position while the new governor, Albinus, was still on the road to Jerusalem.

Did this appointment of Ananus have any strings attached to it? It should be noted that Agrippa's father, Agrippa I, had died in 44 CE, most likely from poison. (In Part II, we will examine Agrippa I more closely.) But for now, let us assume that the Fourth Philosophy was responsible for the poisoning. This murder of Agrippa I would have been reason enough for Agrippa II to take revenge upon James.

Agrippa II may have had even more reason to kill James. Agrippa built himself a large dining room which overlooked the Temple. While reclining and eating, Agrippa could observe the Temple machinations. This joy was taken away by the Jews who built a wall which disrupted the view. Agrippa and Festus were both displeased by the wall and sought to have it torn down. However, the Jews petitioned Nero and he ruled on their part as a favor to his wife, Poppea, herself a religious woman. (*Ant.* 20.189-197) Upon hearing the verdict, Agrippa II appointed Joseph high priest. This Joseph was subsequently replaced by Ananus upon the death of Festus.

One other clue may tie Agrippa II to the stoning of James. This concerns the person known as Saul in both the *Antiquities* and in Acts. After the stoning of Stephen, Acts 8:1 stated: "And Saul was there, giving approval to his death." As noted earlier, the stoning of Stephen was merely a rewrite of the stoning of James. If this is true, then Saul approved of the stoning of James. After the stoning of James, as recorded in *Antiquities*, Josephus had this to say about Saul:

> ...a sedition arose between the high priests, with regard to one another: for they got together bodies of the boldest sort of the people, and frequently came, from reproaches, to throwing of stones at each other; but **Ananus was too hard for the rest, by his riches**, - which enabled him to gain those that were most ready to receive. Costobarus also, and **Saulus**, did themselves get together a multitude of wicked wretches, and this because **they were of the royal family**; and so they obtained favor among them, because of their **kindred to Agrippa**, but still they used violence with the people, and were very ready to plunder those that were weaker than themselves. (*Ant.* 20.214) (Emphasis mine)

This action by Saul against the lower level priests was a plain money grab. Saul aligned himself with Ananus and his kinsman, Agrippa II. It should be noted that the Fourth Philosophy was aligned with the poor and the lower priesthood. Thus, the stoning of James, the leader of the Fourth Philosophy, was the beginning of the war by the wealthy priests against the poorer ones. (*Ant.* 20.206-207) This case for Saul's complicity with James' murder can be further strengthened by using the rewrite in Acts.

Meanwhile, Saul was still breathing out murderous threats against the Lord's disciples. He went to the high priest and asked him for letters to the synagogues in Damascus, so that if he found any there who belonged to the Way, whether men or women, he might take them as prisoners to Jerusalem. (Acts 9:1-2)

This part of history from 62 CE was transported back to 35 CE to make Saul's unholy actions appear as a pre-conversion tirade against the disciples. In fact, this hatred for James and the Jewish Christian movement (Fourth Philosophy) had been growing steadily after Saul's/Paul's removal from the movement at Antioch (See Galatians). This incredible deception by the author of Acts has worked well throughout the centuries. Saul is now viewed as a young man who finally saw the light. In reality, he was a bitter old man who exacted revenge against those who had much earlier rejected his own Gospel.

One question which has always been asked is this: how could the young Saul have so much sway with the high priest? The answer is very simple. Saul was not young and he had aligned himself to Ananus and his kinsman, Agrippa. This alliance with the power structure armed Saul with power to do as he wished. Acts' version of history has once again proved to be inaccurate, but it does leave behind snippets of truth. Saul did persecute the Way, just as Josephus said that he and his followers persecuted "those that were weaker than themselves." (*Ant.* 20.214) In Part II, we will determine that Saul/Paul was not only the Liar and Enemy but the Traitor as well.

Before ending this section, we should look at the overall flow of Josephus' account, before and after the stoning of James. As described above, Agrippa II had a history of bad relations with the Fourth Philosophy, starting with the poisoning of his father. The wall affair was perhaps the last straw; someone would pay for this insult. But how did Agrippa II assign blame for this insult? How did he know to blame James? The answer to this question may be quite surprising. Saul, the kinsman of Agrippa, had many quarrels of his own with James (See 1 and 2 Corinthians and Galatians). As it turned out, James and his circumcision party had severed Saul/Paul from the Jewish Christian movement. This did not sit well with Saul, and his revenge came at the expense of James' life. Saul, no doubt, was instrumental in convincing Agrippa to eliminate James. The opportunity for action soon arrived; the death of Festus created a power vacuum which would last until the arrival of Albinus. Perhaps Agrippa asked the high priest, Joseph, to eliminate James. When this did not return dividends, a new high priest was appointed, that being Ananus, who "was a bold man in his temper, and very insolent." (*Ant.* 20.199) It was this

Ananus who carried out the orders of Agrippa, and James was stoned. Shortly after this death sentence, the Sicarii began kidnapping members of Ananus' family and household, demanding that Ananus persuade Albinus to release members of their own party, the release of Sicarii members. (*Ant.* 20.208-210) This shows that the Sicarii blamed Ananus for the death of James and would make him pay as long as possible.

CONCLUSION

The unholy alliance of Agrippa II, Ananus and Saul helped seal the fate of James the Just, brother of Judas the Galilean, who himself was known as the Messiah or Christ. This James was a powerful figure in the early Jewish Christian movement (Fourth Philosophy). James' association with "Jesus" was known to all early Christian historians, although none knew of his relationship with the Sicarii, or the Fourth Philosophy. But a simple reading of Josephus places this James in the midst of conflicts between the wealthy rulers (Agrippa, Ananus and Saul) and the poor and downtrodden. These poor were members of a revolutionary party called the Fourth Philosophy by Josephus and later derisively labeled as the Sicarii (assassins who carried a short curved knife or sica). It is not surprising that James was killed but how difficult it was to kill him. It took a king (Agrippa II), a high priest (Ananus), an informer (Saul) and good fortune (the death of Festus) to set up the opportunity to silence James. Until now, nobody has ever implicated Agrippa or Saul in the death of James. But I think that the evidence is too strong to ignore any longer.

CHAPTER 6

THE FOURTH PHILOSOPHY

We have mentioned the Fourth Philosophy in relationship to Judas the Galilean and Sadduc, but further analysis is needed to sort out various problems, such as the incompatibility between the love of God as espoused by Jesus and the assassinations carried out by the Sicarii, whose leader was James, the brother of Jesus (Judas the Galilean). Using Josephus as a roadmap, we will trace the Fourth Philosophy from its beginnings to its tragic ending. This movement was evolving, even during the lifetime of Judas and surely afterwards. But every movement changes, primarily to meet new challenges or to bend to the whims of new leadership. The classic description of the Fourth Philosophy by Josephus may be confusing because the movement is described from the Census of Cyrenius (6 CE) to the year 70 CE, where the "followers" of Judas helped destroy Jerusalem and bring down the Temple itself. The telescoping of sixty-five years does not let us appreciate the Fourth Philosophy as it developed during the first century.

But perhaps this can be better understood by studying a more recent philosophical movement: communism. In 1848, Karl Marx published *The Communist Manifesto*, believing that the final crisis of capitalism was at hand. Marx preached an economic communism based upon the workers owning the "means of production". With all ownership in the hands of the workers, Marx envisioned a utopian society with economic equality, where the state itself would eventually wither away. This revolution was to occur in the industrialized Western world, not in Russia's backward agrarian society.

Marx had expected the final [economic] crisis in 1848. When it failed to happen, he continued to hope that the next crisis would do the trick. An economic crisis duly occurred in 1857. It had no political consequences at all. (1)

And capitalism continued on, with power becoming more and more entrenched in the hands of the few.

The followers of Marx came to believe that communism would be ushered in with a great war between the industrial powers. In this, they were partly correct. The First World War helped create the Russian communist experiment. However, this was inconsistent with Marxist economic doctrine. Marx had pinned his hopes upon the industrialized nations. According to the Gospel of Marx, Russia had no chance of becoming communist as its industrial production was meager at best. But even this contradiction was explained away by Lenin, who saw Russia as the fuse to a great explosion; he believed that the rest of Europe would soon fall. In this, he was dead wrong.

By the 1920's, Stalin had replaced Lenin, and it was through this madman that all nations suffered. He purged his own country of anyone remotely opposed to him. Millions died in the purges and millions more during the Second World War, where Stalin and Hitler combined to reduce the world's population by at least 40 million.

So the dream of equality in 1848 became a nightmare of persecution and death seventy years later. The name communism was attached to both Marx and Stalin. The economic system of communism was tossed aside in favor of a totalitarian political communism, with no freedoms and no real equality. Is it accurate to paint Marx and Stalin with the same brush? After all, Marx wanted equality for the workers while Stalin desired power at the expense of these same workers. In the same way, we must not sully Judas the Galilean with all that happened forty to sixty years after his death: times change, new leaders emerge, and movements evolve.

THE BELIEF SYSTEM

The Fourth Philosophy did not create new beliefs but merged existing ones. Other philosophies predated it in Jewish society: the Essenes, the Pharisees and the Sadducees. Judas the Galilean showed his genius by combining the best of competing movements to his own advantage. Of the three earlier philosophies mentioned above, Judas intertwined the beliefs of the Pharisees with the practices of the Essenes. Since the Sadducees were few in number, opposed the belief system of the Pharisees and supported foreign invaders (Rome), they were left out of this strange mixture, termed the Fourth Philosophy by Josephus.

Such a combination of beliefs, though not standard practice, can be found in other movements as well. The New Democrats, headed by Bill Clinton, combined the economic policies of the Republican Party (welfare reform and trade policies) with social programs spearheaded by the most liberal of the Democratic Party (gay rights and abortion rights). Thus, Clinton was tolerated by the middle and had some support from the old Republican right and the far Democratic left. If it were not for his personal life, the New Democrats would have been landslide winners in 2000 and 2004. However, his affairs turned off more people than his policies recruited.

The new philosophy of Judas the Galilean may have had its beginnings before the Golden Eagle Temple Cleansing (4 BCE). For Judas and Matthias exhibited behavior which could have been associated with either Essenes or Pharisees. And the later passage by Josephus concerning the Census of Cyrenius (6-7 CE) also leaves us with a mixed picture of Judas' movement. To pinpoint the exact date of the Fourth Philosophy's birth may be impossible, but to examine the beliefs and practices is well within our abilities.

The Essenes had several practices which were also common to the Fourth Philosophy. Josephus claimed that the Essenes were "contemptuous of wealth [and] communists to perfection." (*War* 2.122) This fits in perfectly with the picture of Judas fighting Roman taxation and with later Sicarii burning the debt records to "enable the poor to rise with impunity against the rich." (*War* 2.427) This love of perfect communism is also found in the Dead Sea Scrolls (*Community Rule*). Jesus preached the same message and his disciples practiced this in Acts 2:44: "All the believers were together and had everything in common."

Although the Essenes were not a majority party, having only four thousand men (*Ant.* 18.20), they had colonies in every city. (*War* 2.124) This seems to be a contradiction, as the number of Essenes in the *War* appears much larger than the mere four thousand quoted from *Antiquities*. Josephus possibly conflated the Essene and Fourth Philosophy movements, attributing the popularity of Judas' movement to the Essenes. But even if the Essenes did have colonies in every city, this would have supplied the Fourth Philosophy with a pool of possible adherents throughout Israel. When Jesus sent the seventy-two out to proclaim his kingdom, surely each city had an Essene or Fourth Philosophy community which either supported him or had great sympathy for him. So the spread of the Fourth Philosophy may have been made possible by an existing network of like-minded communities.

Joining the Essenes was no easy task. In the first year, the initiate was excluded from the group, his temperance tested. If he passed the test, two more years of character testing occurred within the community. Only when deemed worthy, was he then accepted into the fold (*War* 2.137-138). This was consistent with the *Community Rule,* which also had some similarities to early Christian practice. In addition, Paul claimed a three year gap between his conversion and his first meeting with the Pillar Apostles. This three year absence may have been his testing period. (Gal. 1:18)

To the Essenes, "Obedience to older men and to the majority is a matter of principle: if ten sit down together one will not speak against the wish of the nine." (*War* 2.146) I mention this point because it emphasizes the place of elders in Jewish society. Unlike our own society, where the elderly are often ignored or shipped away to nursing homes, apart from the everyday troubles of this world, the elders of Jewish society were the teachers and well-respected by all. That is why I think it very unlikely that Jesus (Judas) was only thirty-three by the end of his career. He may have been the junior partner with Matthias, but this coupling with an older, wiser mentor would have added to Judas' resume. By the time of his final push to Jerusalem, Judas would have been in his mid forties, respected by the masses for his long fight against Rome.

Josephus stated: "They neglect wedlock, but choose out other person's children, while they are pliable, and fit for learning; and esteem them to be of their kindred, and from them according to their own manners." (*War* 2.120) The Essenes were so dedicated to following the Law that they viewed sex and marriage as a stumbling block. However, to perpetuate their own views, they had to indoctrinate other people's children and raise them up to be Essenes. This may explain why Judas and Matthias taught young men at the Temple. These men, Judas and Matthias, were "well beloved by the people, because of their education of their youth; for all those that were studious of virtue frequented their lectures every day." (*Ant.* 17.149) These students were eventually convinced to help tear down the Golden Eagle. So while Judas and Matthias taught other people's children, these children were not young and pliable but rather, pliable young men. This may be a case where the Fourth Philosophy copied a trait from the Essenes but for a different agenda. They wished to build an army of followers.

In many ways, the Fourth Philosophy appears similar to the Essenes. However, in describing the Fourth Philosophy, Josephus compared them with the Pharisees.

But the fourth sect of Jewish philosophy, Judas the Galilean was the author. These men agree in all other things with the **Pharisaic notions**; but they have an inviolable attachment to liberty; and they say that God is to be their only Ruler and Lord. (*Ant.* 18.23)

...yet there was one Judas, a Gaulonite, of a city whose name was Gamala, who, taking with him a **Sadduc, a Pharisee**, became zealous to draw them to a revolt, who both said that this taxation was no better than an introduction to slavery, and exhorted the nation to assert their liberty. (*Ant.* 18.4) (Emphasis mine)

The main thrust of Josephus' description of the Fourth Philosophy was their insistence on freedom from Roman rule. This thirst for liberty was not the sole possession of any one group. Members of both the Pharisees and Essenes could have been attracted to this freedom message. So, in that sense, Judas may have played quite well with both groups. But Josephus was clear in his identification of Judas and Sadduc with the Pharisaic notions. What exactly does that mean?

[The Pharisees were] esteemed most skillful in the exact explication of their laws. ...[They] ascribe all to fate, and to God, and yet allow, that to act what is right, or the contrary, is principally in the power of men, although fate does cooperate in every action... [and] the souls of good men are only removed into other bodies, - but that the souls of bad men are subject to eternal punishment. (*War* 2.162-163)

When Jesus prayed in the Garden, he believed it was within the power of men to assist God in His triumph over Rome. Although God was the ultimate force in the universe, men were not mere pawns to be moved against their free will. For example, if Jesus believed that man could not assist God, then he and his disciples would not have been fervently praying in the Garden. Certainly, Moses believed that he could bargain with God. After the people had cast a golden calf and angered God, Moses said, "But now I will go up to the Lord; perhaps I can make atonement for your sin." (Ex. 32:30) In addition, Jesus taught that the evil man would be punished forever in the fires of hell. (Matt. 5:27-30 and 7:15-23). Certainly, the Fourth Philosophy (Jewish Christianity) owed much to the Pharisees concerning these beliefs.

[The Pharisees] live meanly, and despise delicacies in diet; ...and what they prescribe to them as good for them, they do. ... They also pay respect to such as are in years; nor are they so bold as to contradict them in anything which they have introduced. ...[They believe that] souls have an immortal vigor in them, and that under the earth there will be rewards and punishments, according as they have lived virtuously or viciously in this life, and the latter are to be detained in an everlasting prison, but the former shall have power to revive and live again. (*Ant.* 18.12-14)

The diet prescribed by James and his followers was very strict, as noted by Paul in 1 Corinthians, chapter eight. In this respect, Jesus' followers adhered to the dietary laws, opposed to Paul's more liberal (non-Jewish) stance. So we have specific teachings which tie together the Fourth Philosophy, Pharisaic teachings and Jewish Christianity. In addition, these groups all respected their elders and had similar views concerning the rewards and punishments accorded to the good and bad. Unlike Paul's concept of Grace, Pharisees and the Fourth Philosophy counted heavily upon one's righteousness. As James wrote, "Faith without deeds is dead." (James 2:26) To top it off, the early disciples of Jesus were known as the "Way" (Acts 24:14) or the "Way of Righteousness".

So there was a solid link connecting the Pharisees, the Fourth Philosophy and Jewish Christianity. Note that both Judas the Galilean and Jesus were called rabbi or teacher, a Pharisaic designation. Josephus called Judas the Galilean a "clever rabbi" (*War* 2.433) and Peter referred to Jesus as rabbi in Mark 9:5 (the Transfiguration) and Mark 11:21 (the withered fig tree). We also know that Jesus taught through the use of parables, as did many other Pharisees. And Judas the Galilean's second-in-command (Sadduc) was denoted as a Pharisee by Josephus. Thus, the tie between the teachings of Judas and Jesus becomes more evident.

An interesting New Testament passage may help solidify this strange mixture of beliefs and practices.

"Master," said John, "we saw a man driving out demons in your name and we tried to stop him, because he is not one of us."

"Do not stop him," Jesus said, "for whoever is not against you is for you." (Luke 9:45-50)

Such a saying by Jesus is **not** consistent with traditional Christian beliefs espoused by Paul. "But even if we or an angel from heaven should preach a gospel other than the one we preached to you, let him be eternally condemned." (Gal. 1:18) Yet the attitude by Jesus fits perfectly with Judas the Galilean, that teacher who brought all types of men together. In terms of the Fourth Philosophy, the desire for freedom from Rome constituted an ally.

The unifying factor of foreign occupation made the Fourth Philosophy powerful and widespread. Both Essenes and Pharisees were drawn to this belief system because it took the best of their practices and added a touch of hatred for Rome, popular to the masses and to the teachers as well. Judas the Galilean must have been a very charismatic teacher to keep disparate groups together, but he was helped in this cause by continual Herodian and Roman oppression. Every time the Romans stepped near the Temple or displayed their standards, Judas had a ready-made disturbance at hand. And these unifying actions helped solidify his new philosophy amongst the masses. In Acts 21:20,

James and the elders said, "You see, brother, how many thousands of Jews have believed, and all of them are zealous for the law." These followers of James belonged to the Fourth Philosophy. This will be further proved in the following sections describing the movement's growth through the writings of Josephus.

THE DEAD SEA SCROLLS

Several credible explanations exist concerning the authorship of the Dead Sea Scrolls. The most popular is called the Standard model, where the Scrolls are credited to the Essenes. Josephus included the Essenes as one of his three philosophies in the *War*. In the *Antiquities*, Josephus added the Fourth Philosophy to those already noted in the *War*: the Sadducees, the Pharisees and the Essenes. It is quite possible that some of the attributes given to the Essenes in the *War* really belonged to Judas the Galilean's Fourth Philosophy. The two attributes in question are marrying and the willingness to undergo torture for their God.

In the *War*, Josephus mentioned another order of Essenes, who lived according to the customs and laws of the other Essenes but were allowed to marry. They reasoned that "by not marrying they cut off the principal part of the human life, which is the prospect of succession." (*War* 2.160) This marrying Essene was not included in the shorter version of the Essenes in *Antiquities*, but we know that the Fourth Philosophy of Judas practiced marriage, as Judas himself had several sons as noted by Josephus. Thus, it is very likely that Josephus might have combined some of Judas' practices with those of the Essenes in the *War*.

This merging of movements by Josephus can be best illustrated by the willingness to die. In the *War*, the Essenes underwent all types of torture during the Jewish and Roman war.

...although they [Essenes] were tortured and distorted, burnt and torn to pieces, and went through all kinds of instruments of torment, that they might be forced either to blaspheme their legislator, or to eat what was forbidden them, yet could they not be made to do either of them, no, nor once to flatter their tormentors, or to shed a tear; but they smiled in their very pains, and laughed those to scorn who inflicted the torments upon them, and resigned up their souls with great alacrity, as expecting to receive them again. (*War* 2.152-153)

Surprisingly, in *Antiquities*, Josephus failed to attribute this willingness to die to the Essenes. This trait was instead assigned to the Fourth Philosophy of Judas the Galilean.

> They [Fourth Philosophy] also do not value dying any kind of death, nor indeed do they heed the deaths of their relations or friends, nor can any such fear make them call any man Lord; and since this immovable resolution of theirs is **well known to a great many**, I shall speak no further about that matter; nor am I afraid that anything I have said of them should be disbelieved, but rather fear, that what I have said is beneath the resolution they show when they undergo pain. (*Ant.* 18.23-24) (Emphasis mine)

The possibility exists that both the Essenes and members of Judas' movement underwent torture during the Roman war. But it is fascinating that Josephus would give this unusual trait to both groups in his two histories. Josephus may have hidden the truth concerning torture in the *War*, for possible political reasons. The *War* was written shortly after the conflict (75 CE) while *Antiquities* was not published until 93 CE. Josephus may have felt more at ease with relating the true nature of things at this later date.

Thus, our understanding of the Essenes may be a bit distorted, in that we attribute to the Essenes marrying and the willingness to undergo torture. Regardless of the attribution to the Essenes, these two traits definitely belonged to the Fourth Philosophy. This is the more interesting as Pliny and the Jewish philosopher, Philo, described the Essenes as celibate, but many passages in the Scrolls presuppose that the members were married. (2) If the Essenes were truly celibate, then the passages must be talking about some other group, possibly the Fourth Philosophy. In addition, the Scrolls also contain other information not consistent with the Essenes but in conformity with the Fourth Philosophy. Philo stated that the Essenes were peaceful in nature, but the *War Scroll* warned of a future armed conflict with the forces of darkness. (3) Again, this appears to be more in line with Judas' movement, with the forces of darkness being represented by Rome and their hirelings, the Herodians.

So, the Essene Standard model may have some very real weaknesses. According to Michael Wise, many of the Scrolls have pro-Hasmonean leanings, pointing to a later dating of some of the Scrolls. He cites *In Praise of King Jonathon* as an example where Hasmoneans were highly regarded, unlike the picture painted by the Standard model. (4) This is important, as I have argued that the Fourth Philosophy modeled itself after the Maccabees. It appears as if those who followed the Scrolls also respected the Maccabees.

Although the Dead Sea Scrolls were mostly written before the Fourth Philosophy, it is almost certain that members of the Fourth Philosophy utilized the documents. The DSS documents detail certain characters who may have been perfect models for later movements. These characters include the Righteous Teacher, the Wicked Priest, the Liar and the Root of Planting. A movement which envisioned itself at war against an evil power could easily adopt these characters into their own teachings. According to Wise, these types of user groups are termed "carrier groups" by sociologists. (5) The Fourth Philosophy of Judas was a carrier group, where the Righteous Teacher was Judas and later James; the Wicked Priest could have been Annas; the Liar was no doubt Paul and the Root of Planting could have been Matthias. (6)

There is positive proof that the Fourth Philosophy did use the Scrolls. According to Wise:

The Dead Sea Scroll we have called *A List of Buried Treasure* is a list of treasures from Herod's Temple, compiled as part of an effort to hide the gold, silver, and other valuables from the Romans, should the Temple fall. Logically, the compilers of the list must have been in control of the treasures they wanted to save. According to Josephus, it was freedom fighters and Zealots who seized the Temple when the war broke out in 66, and they never relinquished control during the subsequent years of war against Rome and against other Jewish groups. Who but they could have drawn up this list? Thus, when it is found in Cave 3 among other Dead Sea Scrolls, we cannot but conclude that not only the *List*, but the other scrolls as well, may have been hidden by the same people. (7)

Thus, the Fourth Philosophy adopted the Scrolls as a carrier group. This claim is further cemented by the find of DSS type materials at Masada, where Judas the Galilean's grandson, Eleazar, led the Sicarii in their last stand against the Roman army in 73 CE. These Jews committed mass suicide, leaving behind the Scrolls as a testament to their use in the first century CE. Josephus named only the Sicarii when relating the story of Masada. The Scrolls belonged to them. (8)

This brings us to the Dead Sea Scroll theory as proposed by Robert Eisenman. Eisenman asserts that the internal evidence of the Scrolls points towards the first century CE, and that the Righteous Teacher was none other than James the Just, the brother of Jesus. He also presents a solid case which connects the Liar to Paul. This theory has been criticized by mainstream scholars as the external evidence, carbon dating and paleography, points towards the second and first century BCE. Since the external evidence does not coincide with first century CE dating, the mainstream confidently dismisses Eisenman. However, the above "carrier group" dynamic has not been adequately addressed by either Eisenman or the mainstream.

In Chapter 5, I have classified James the Just as leader of the Sicarii (Fourth Philosophy). If this is the case, then Eisenman may be right about the internal evidence pointing towards James as Righteous Teacher and Paul as the Liar. This only makes sense if James was a Sicarii leader. After all, the Sicarii held Masada and left the DSS type materials as evidence. They also would have been responsible for the *List of Buried Treasures*. Thus, Eisenman might very well have the last laugh after all.

STAGES OF THE FOURTH PHILOSOPHY
STAGE 1 - THE BEGINNINGS

The Fourth Philosophy did not mystically arise from a vacuum. The enemies were in place long before the movement officially began. A hatred of Herod the Great helped formulate the resistance, but although people yearned for freedom, there was no unified opposition. In *Ant.* 14.159-177, Josephus mentioned Hezekias, a captain of robbers who was hunted down and executed by Herod. Mothers of those slain went to the Temple and mourned, and charges were brought against Herod because he by-passed the Sanhedrin in his efforts to arrest and sentence the "robbers". Instead of standing trial, Herod fled to Damascus. This occurred around 48 BCE. (It should be noted that Hezekias might have been the father, or more likely the grandfather, of Judas the Galilean. (*Ant.* 17.271)) A decade later (40-37 BCE), Herod tracked down the robbers who lived in caves in Galilee. Some of the robbers "underwent death [suicide] rather than slavery [to Herod]." (*Ant.* 14.415-430) This unusual behavior or zeal for freedom was no doubt a precursor to the Fourth Philosophy. And finally, when Herod introduced foreign practices to Judea around 24 BCE (athletic events and theater productions), the zealous Jews were outraged and even tried to assassinate him. (*Ant.* 15.267-289)

This sporadic resistance against Herod the Great was to change with the Golden Eagle Temple Cleansing, where Matthias and forty students were put to death for their actions in the sedition. This event can be linked to the Root of Planting as described in the Dead Sea Scrolls (see above). This slaughter by Herod galvanized the resistance just as the cry "Alamo" did for Texan independence.

Shortly after the Temple Cleansing, Herod the Great died (4 BCE). His son, Archelaus, replaced him as Ethnarch of Judea (4 BCE - 7 CE).

This promise [of Archelaus to be kinder than his father, Herod the Great] delighted the crowds, who at once tested his sincerity by making large demands. Some clamored for a lightening of direct taxation, some for the abolition of purchase-tax, others for the release of prisoners. He promptly said Yes to every demand in his anxiety to appease the mob. (*War* 2.4) (See also *Ant.* 17.204-205)

Archelaus sensed that he had a potential disaster on his hands as the mob's hatred of his father was being transferred to him. To avoid a bloody coup, he attempted to appease the crowd by reducing their tax burden and by releasing political prisoners jailed by his father. (This may have been the genesis of the Barabbas story as Judas the Galilean was released by Archelaus). This short-term effort may have placated some, but the followers of Matthias and Judas were not going to stop their protests.

After the release of prisoners, the followers of Matthias and Judas insisted on the removal of the High Priest. This interest with the Temple workings was a consistent theme with the Fourth Philosophy. Archelaus granted their wish and appointed a new High Priest. (*Ant.* 17.206-208) This is important because it shows that Archelaus did more than just promise things; he delivered on those promises. If Archelaus actually appointed a new High Priest, he also actually released prisoners. (Some have argued that Archelaus only promised the release of prisoners but that he never did. I argue that the release of prisoners could have been done within minutes and was used to immediately gain support from the crowds. Archelaus may well have reneged on his promise to reduce taxes. The point is that the Barabbas episode did occur and Judas the Galilean was Barabbas, or son of the father.)

Within the year, at the Passover, another disturbance began (4-3 BCE), the first physical confrontation between the followers of Matthias and Judas and the soldiers of Archelaus. (*Ant.* 17.216) It seems as though the initial strategy of direct frontal warfare was not a well conceived program but rather one emotionally guided by revenge. After stoning Archelaus' soldiers, the insurgents returned to their Temple sacrifices. To them, the soldiers' deaths were seen as a victory for God, and that all such clashes would be viewed as the Good verses the evil of Herod and Rome. This viewpoint was consistent with the *War Scroll*, one of the Dead Sea Scrolls. This *War Scroll* detailed a future conflict of the Righteous versus the powers of evil. (9)

As they sacrificed at the Passover, another army of Archelaus arrived at the Temple and killed three thousand pilgrims in response to the earlier confrontation. (*War* 2.13) This stopped the Jews momentarily, but they regrouped at Pentecost (50 days after Passover) and organized a much larger army at Jerusalem. (Note that the Acts 2 version had three thousand being baptized on Pentecost.) At this time, the Romans became directly involved. In Jerusalem, great numbers opposed the Romans while the same occurred in the countryside. At Sepphoris, in Galilee, Judas (Judas the Galilean) "collected a considerable force, broke into the royal armory, equipped his followers, and attacked the other seekers after power," (*War* 2.56) So a full scale war was under way, the forces of the innovators (those aligned against the foreign domination of Rome and their vassals - the Herodians) versus the power of Rome.

Within a short period of time, the outcome was secure in favor of Rome. Gaius captured the city of Sepphoris and burnt it, enslaving the inhabitants. (*War* 2.68) Varus then marched upon Jerusalem with his Roman army. The sight of this power crushed the spirit of the Jewish armies and they fled to the countryside. Varus chased many down and crucified two thousand. (*War* 2.72-75) So it would seem that the uprising was finished or at least temporarily halted. For the fanatical Jews, or the "robbers" as Josephus called them, the Roman military actions, as well as their avaricious management of the Jewish affairs, actually inflamed their passions even more. (*Ant.* 17.277) The brute force of Rome helped consolidate the Jewish forces opposed to foreign intervention. The more the Romans mingled in Jewish affairs, the more the Jews hatred grew, as a fire grows with more dry kindling. The presence of Rome united the innovators with a tie stronger than life itself.

But one lesson was learned by Judas the Galilean as he watched the city of Sepphoris being destroyed: Rome could not be defeated by a poorly equipped Jewish army. From that time on, the opposition led by Judas the Galilean relied upon the power of God. Only God could destroy such a powerful foe as Rome. And according to the Scriptures, God had delivered Israel from Egypt, the Assyrians and the Babylonians. God could and would deliver His people once more. So Judas the Galilean set about to mold his followers in the ways of God. As in the past, he reasoned, God would respond favorably to those who followed His laws.

The Fourth Philosophy was a reawakening. Judas centered his opposition forces in the caves and in all areas where Rome could not easily attack. (Thus, it should be no surprise that the coin data from Qumran is primarily from 4 BCE to 68 CE.) The message was this: Israel must gain independence from their oppressors, both Rome and their Herodian hirelings. And to do this, Judas' disciples were taught to zealously follow God and His Law with all their hearts, minds, souls and strength. In this, Judas the Galilean was following the words of Mattathias, father of Judas Maccabee:

"If," said he, "anyone be zealous for the laws of his country, and for the worship of God, let him follow me," and when he said this, he made haste into the desert with his sons, and left all his substance in the village. (*Ant.* 12.271)

STAGE 2 - THE KINGDOM OF HEAVEN

To the disciples of Judas (Jesus), the eradication of Roman influence and the accompanying taxation would have been a move towards the Kingdom of Heaven, where the Jewish nation would be free to follow God and His Law. This is consistent with the Maccabean principle passed down by Mattathias to his sons: "recover your ancient form of government." (*Ant.* 12.280) But as long as Rome and their Herodian puppets ruled, this expression of freedom could not be realized. The chief priests were appointed by the Herodians, from Herod the Great to Agrippa junior. And these priests were often more concerned with politics and wealth than with the Temple's ministry.

To combat Roman influence and military power, Judas understood that weapons alone could not succeed. He had witnessed the slaughters of Jerusalem and Sepphoris, noting the military superiority of Roman forces. The only way to fight Rome was through the power of God. Had not Moses led Israel from the clutches of Egypt, and surely it was not Joshua's hand which stopped the sun from setting. But to accomplish what had been done in the far distant past would not come without effort on their part. Judas and his disciples planned to prepare the peoples for the coming of the Lord.

Two distinct commandments required obedience: to love God and to love thy neighbor as thyself. To love God involved following the Law to perfection. "Anyone who breaks one of the least of these commandments and teaches others to do the same will be called least in the kingdom of heaven, but whoever practices and teaches these commands will be called great in the kingdom of heaven." (Matt. 5:19) Here Jesus stressed the importance of each word of the Law and the necessity of following it. This included not only circumcision and food purity laws but the Tempe upkeep as well. When Jesus cleansed the Temple, he quoted Scripture saying, "My house will be called a house of prayer, but you are making it a den of robbers." (Matt. 21:13) The cynical money-making machine of the Herodians was temporarily shut down by Jesus. To Jesus (Judas the Galilean) and his disciples, Temple purity was absolutely necessary for the Kingdom of Heaven to be realized.

As for love of neighbor, the Essenes and the Fourth Philosophy (Jewish Christianity) practiced pure communism, where each looked out for everyone else's needs. This was a poor lot, and the idea of sharing would have been heavenly to these hard-pressed Jews. The more one accumulates, the harder it is to relinquish any wealth, as was noted in the story of the rich young ruler (Matt. 19:16-24). Thus, there was a very powerful social aspect to this impending Kingdom of God. That is why the taxation issue was so important.

Judas the Galilean was propelled to the national limelight by his stance against Rome and the High Priest, Joazar, during the Census of Cyrenius. Josephus said Judas "tried to stir the natives to revolt, saying that they would be cowards if they submitted to paying taxes to the Romans, and after serving God alone accepted human masters." (*War* 2.118) Note that this was not just a matter of money but religion as well. Judas plainly linked obeying Rome with obeying another master, and he had only one master, God. This is similar to the saying in Matt. 6:24: "No one can serve two masters. Either he will hate the one and love the other, or he will be devoted to the one and despise the other. You cannot serve both God and Money." In the same way, Judas would have said, "You cannot serve both God and Rome." (Note that Paul preached the exact opposite message, per Romans 13:1-7).

Judas patterned his movement after the Maccabees, those rebels who overthrew the Greek rule nearly two centuries earlier. After Matthias was killed by Herod the Great (4 BCE), Judas became the movement's leader and his second-in-command was the Sadduc. In Chapter 4, I identified John the Baptist as the Sadduc. This identification comes from the Slavonic Josephus, where John held the exact beliefs as Judas and was introduced into the story at 6 CE, right before the census uprising of Judas. This Sadduc, or John the Baptist, also stressed the importance of repentance and baptism. Josephus explained that the baptism itself was not magical but rather a "purification of the body; supposing still that the soul was thoroughly purified beforehand by righteousness." (*Ant.* 18.117) Thus, the Baptist prepared his followers for the coming of the Messiah, or rather, the nationwide tax revolt campaign by Judas the Galilean.

The book of Acts (5:33-39) gives us the impression that Judas was killed at the census or around 6 CE. In Chapter 2, I thoroughly debunked the Acts' account. Without this bogus claim by Acts, no information exists concerning Judas the Galilean's death. Josephus did not mention Judas' death even though Judas was the most important figure in first-century Israel. This is extraordinary considering Josephus did write about Judas' sons being crucified in 46-48 CE, another son being stoned in 66 CE, a grandson committing suicide at Masada in 73 CE and his brother, James, being stoned in 62 CE (see chapter 5 for James the Just's death). I hold to the position that Josephus originally wrote about the death of Judas but this death was replaced by the spurious Jesus passage in *Ant.* 18.63-64. This out-of-place passage may explain why Judas' death is missing from the historian's account. However, even though we do not know the exact date of Judas' death, we do know why he was put to death: Judas claimed to be Messiah and he had led a tax revolt against Rome. These were the same two charges leveled against Jesus in Luke 23:2:

And they [chief priests and teachers] began to accuse him, saying, "We have found this man subverting our nation. He **opposes payment of taxes to Caesar** and **claims to be Christ**, a king." (Emphasis mine)

The Gospel account had the chief priests accusing Jesus but asserted that Pilate and Herod both saw no harm in the man. (Luke 23:14-15) This claim is incredible considering the chief priests were appointed by Herod and Rome. They all worked together, not against one another. In short, the arrest and crucifixion of Jesus was just a rewrite of the charges brought against Judas the Galilean. I believe that Judas was arrested around 19 CE, near the beginning of Pilate's reign, per my timeline. (See chapter 1 for a reworking of Pilate's tenure using the information of Josephus.) Judas may have lingered in prison for a short time, but was certainly crucified by 21 CE, the date the supposed Roman forgery, the *Memoranda*, claimed for the death of Jesus. (10)

With the crucifixion of their leader, Judas, the Fourth Philosophy had a dilemma on its hands. If Judas were the Messiah, then how could a crucified Messiah still lead? The answer was ingenious: Judas (Jesus) would rise from the dead and reign from the sky until the day of wrath. This was a powerful message, as it assured present and future members of Rome's ultimate defeat. Jesus would lead the Jews in battle (see Revelation). This idea of the resurrection was probably cooked up by Judas as he awaited crucifixion. After all, Josephus did call Judas that "very clever rabbi." (*War* 2.433)

STAGE 3 - THE IMMINENT RETURN OF JESUS

As Judas (Jesus) hung dying on the cross, it is probable that John the Baptist, James and Cephas already knew of the resurrection. They had planned it all along, undoubtedly with the blessings of Judas. Without the resurrection, the movement was finished. Would you follow a leader who led you straight to the cross, or would you follow one who not only could conquer death but return as a super-human Messiah? The answer was obvious: Judas must be resurrected and then return in the near future to lead the Jews against Rome.

It was important to identify a scapegoat for Judas' failure. The answer was simple enough: the Jews were not yet ready for salvation. A period of repentance and soul searching was necessary in order for Judas to return. In the Garden of Gethsemane, the Pillar Apostles let Jesus and the Jewish nation down by falling asleep, certainly an act which did not merit any rewards from God. So it was very important to convey this message to all Jews: "Repent and be baptized, every one of you, in the name of Jesus Christ [Messiah] so that your sins may be forgiven." (Acts 2:38) Many believed and three thousand were added to their number that day. (Acts 2:41) Thus, the new recruiting tool was Jesus, the Messiah whose time had not yet arrived. When the numbers were complete, Jesus would return in glory and all disciples would partake in the victory. (Note that Jesus (Joshua) was a title given to Judas when he became Messiah and surely used by his disciples when referring to the resurrected Messiah. Just as Joshua conquered the land of Israel, Jesus would rid the land of the Roman presence.)

How did this waiting affect the movement? Remember, the Fourth Philosophy started as an opposition movement to Rome and continued under the leadership of Judas the Galilean. Now, the Fourth Philosophy would be reactive instead of proactive. Under Judas (Jesus), they marched into Jerusalem on a mission and expected victory in a few short days. Surely the creator of the heavens and earth could do quick work with the Romans. But God did not show up and a new strategy was needed. After the crucifixion of Jesus, the leaders could only react to events, hoping that Jesus would return as world conqueror. They themselves could not lead armed revolts, because they preached a message of prayer and forgiveness. This message was designed to prepare the people for the return of Jesus; and only Jesus could lead them to victory over Rome.

In the analysis of Josephus from 19 CE (the probable arrest and crucifixion of Judas (Jesus)) to 62 CE (the death of James, the brother of Jesus), one would expect to see little violence but great attention to the Law and the Temple. From 19-37 CE, very little was recorded by Josephus. These would have been the early years of the movement without Judas. According to the book of Acts, the Apostles preached baptism, repentance and the resurrection of Jesus. There is no need to doubt this, but the "Church" would have begun in 19-21 CE, not 30-33 CE as claimed by orthodox tradition. This may have been an era of peace, considering Josephus passed over it without relaying much information. After all, Tacitus stated that in Judea under Tiberius, all was quiet. (11) However, Tacitus' definition of all quiet included the provocative actions by Pilate and the crucifixion of Judas. In a much more likely scenario, information about the early Church may have been expunged from the record. Either way, from the death of Judas (19-21 CE) to the mention of John the Baptist (35-36 CE), little else was reported.

John the Baptist had charged onto the scene in 6 CE, baptizing in the Jordan, proclaiming the same message as Judas. In fact, John was the Sadduc or holy man, the second-in-command to Judas the Galilean. When Judas was put to death, John assumed control of the movement. The above description of the movement, where they emphasized repentance and baptism, was the result of John's leadership. It is no coincidence that Acts 2:38 had the disciples preaching this message: "Repent and be baptized for the forgiveness of sins."

The era of John was one of movement building and self evaluation. The emphasis on Righteousness would be the hallmark of the movement and John's popularity began to eclipse his former leader, Judas.

Josephus related the death of John the Baptist in *Antiquities*.

Now, some of the Jews thought that the destruction of Herod's army came from God and that very justly, as a punishment of what he did against John, that was called the Baptist; for Herod slew him, who was a good man, and **commanded the Jews to exercise virtue, both as to righteousness towards one another, and piety towards God**. ...Now, when [many] others **came in crowds** about him, for they were greatly moved [or pleased] by hearing his words, Herod, who feared lest the great influence John had over the people might put it into **his power and inclination to raise a rebellion** (for they seemed ready to do anything he should advise), thought it best, by putting him to death, to prevent any mischief he might cause, and not bring himself into difficulties, by sparing a man who might make him repent of it when it should be too late. (*Ant.* 18.116-119) (Emphasis mine)

As noted above, John preached righteousness towards one another and piety towards God. This was the same message he and Judas had preached from the time of the Census of Cyrenius in 6 CE. It is interesting that Josephus wrote that John had large crowds following him and that he could call upon them to revolt. This power over the masses defined a leader, the leader. According to the traditional timeline, John accepted Jesus as the Messiah and then went to his death **before** the crucifixion of Jesus. Interestingly, Josephus had John being put to death in 35-36 CE, many years **after** the death of Jesus. This is important because the early Gentile Church downplayed John's role in the movement, just as they marginalized the role of Jesus' brother, James. John's great popularity also explains why the John movement lasted so many years after his death. If John had really died when Judas (Jesus) lived then his following would have been absorbed into the Judas camp. But since he lived beyond the lifetime of Judas, John developed a popularity which may have been eclipsing the dead Messiah. Even in the second century, John's cult was thriving. The Pseudoclementine *Recognitions* 1.54 state: "Yea, some even of the disciples of John, who seemed to be great ones, have separated themselves from the people, and proclaimed their own master as the Christ."

The death of John the Baptist (the Sadduc) occurred in 35-36 CE. James the Just, the brother of Jesus, then became the movement's leader. As noted in Chapter 4, James may have been the number one man from 38-62 CE. The council of Jerusalem was probably an effort to consolidate James' control over the movement. This may not have been entirely successful as the John movement was still going strong into the second century and a reference to disunity was made by Paul in 1 Corinthians 1:10-12:

I appeal to you, brothers, in the name of our Lord Jesus Christ, that all of you agree with one another so that there may be no divisions among you and that you may be perfectly united in mind and thought. My brothers, some from Chloe's household have informed me that there are quarrels among you. What I mean is this: One of you says: "I follow Paul"; another, "I follow Apollos"; another, "I follow Cephas"; still another, "I follow Christ."

Note that four different factions competed in the Church at Corinth. Paul represented his own system, not yet fully developed but certainly beginning to pull away from James and Cephas (See Galatians for the final break between James and Paul.) Apollos led the Baptist branch of the movement. This is confirmed by Acts 18:24-26, where Apollos knew only of the baptism of John. This Acts' explanation was probably derived from 1 Corinthians 1:13, where Paul mentioned water baptism. In all likelihood, Apollos was still preaching John's baptism even though John had been put to death a few years earlier. This would date the 1 Corinthian letter to about 36-38 CE, far earlier than the traditional timeline would allow. The third faction followed Cephas, who was the second-in-command to James. This is deduced from the letter to the Galatians where James' letter dictated Cephas' behavior. The fourth group followed Christ or Judas the Galilean, the original leader of the movement. If this scenario is true, then the early Christian movement was much more fragmented than previously believed. The Jerusalem Council may well have been an effort to unite all these different factions. This would date the Council at around 38-39 CE and thus moves Paul's conversion to the movement to around 21-22 CE. This 21-22 CE date approximates the date that the *Memoranda* claimed for the crucifixion of Jesus under Pilate.

The next disturbance emanated from Rome in the mad wishes of the Emperor Gaius (Caligula), around the years 40-41 CE. Caligula ordered a statue of himself to be erected in the Temple. On hearing this, the Jews "threw themselves down upon their faces, and stretched out their throats, and said they were ready to be slain...rather than to see the dedication of the statue. ...[They] were ready to die with pleasure, rather than to suffer their laws to be transgressed." (*Ant.* 18.271-274) Again, the response of the most zealous of the Jews was peaceful protest, even to the point of their own deaths. They were not yet taking up arms against Rome but they were showing their devotion to God. In their minds, Jesus would return if they only stood up for God's Law.

If Caligula had lived and his orders followed, there would have been an insurrection in Jerusalem, verging on war. This statue would have been torn down just as Matthias and Judas had brought down the Golden Eagle of Herod the Great. Tacitus recorded the attitudes of the Jews during this period.

Under Tiberius all was quiet. But when the Jews were ordered by Caligula to set up his statue in the temple, they preferred the alternative of war. The death of the Emperor put an end to the disturbance. (*The Histories*, v.9)

This passage from Tacitus has several important points. First, he said that under Tiberius (14-37 CE), all had been quiet in Judea. The only conflict recorded by Tacitus was in 19 CE, and that in Rome. If Judas the Galilean had been crucified for his bloodless rebellion (two swords on the Mount of Olives), then it is likely that such an action would not seem worthy of notice by the **Roman** historian. This quiet of Tiberius follows Josephus' account of the Jews' **reaction** to events. This is consistent with the repentance phase of the Fourth Philosophy. Secondly, Tacitus stated that the death of Caligula (41 CE) put an end to the disturbance. Certainly, the Jews saw God's power in this. They had offered their lives for God and the Law, and He had answered their prayers. No statue to a divine Caesar would ever pollute their Temple. However, many Jews kept a keen eye upon Rome. Tacitus wrote:

It is true that the Jews had shown symptoms of commotion in a seditious outbreak, and when they heard of the assassination of Caius [Caligula in 41 CE], there was no hearty submission, as a fear lingered that any of the emperors might impose the same orders [setting up statues in the Temple]. (*Annals*, vii.54)

It is generally believed that Suetonius' account of Christians trouble-makers occurred around 51-52 CE, based primarily on the flawed chronology of Acts. However, per Chapter 1, the more likely scenario had the followers of Christ being removed from Rome around 41 CE. Note that Suetonius wrote: "because the Jews at Rome caused continuous disturbances at the **instigation of Chrestus**, he [Claudius] expelled them from the city." (12) So in the very early years of Claudius, the Jewish Christians (Fourth Philosophy) was being watched very closely by the Roman state. It should be noted that King Agrippa I was influential in placing Claudius on the throne after the assassination of Caligula in 41 CE. Agrippa I would have known firsthand the beliefs and goals of the Fourth Philosophy. This group was his main opposition in Judea and he wanted nothing less than to cause them grief throughout the Roman Empire. (This will be examined in detail in Part II.)

Back in Jerusalem (43-44 CE), a certain Simon, who "appeared to be very accurate in the knowledge of the Law… [accused Agrippa I as] not living holily, and he might justly be excluded out of the temple, since it belonged only to native Jews." (*Ant.* 19.332) To say the least, Agrippa was not pleased by this development and had Simon brought to Caesarea for questioning. (Note that the Gospel writers copied this behavior in their treatment of Jesus before Pilate, and used this story as a template for Acts 10, where Peter met Cornelius in Caesarea. However, while the meeting between Agrippa and Simon concerned non-Jewish exclusion the Acts' story championed inclusion of Gentiles.) Like Jesus before Pilate, Simon sat quietly before Agrippa. Since Simon had raised no armies or made threats, Agrippa decided to let him go. Once again, the zealous followers of the Law were more concerned with perfectly obeying the Law than with any armed revolts.

Concerning the Kingdom of Adiabene, Josephus wrote this very telling story about Queen Helena and her son, King Izates. King Izates was brought over to the Jewish religion by a Jewish merchant named Ananias, who had convinced the King's women (wives and concubines) to worship God according to the Jewish religion. At the same time, Helena was being instructed by another Jew. This Jew, along with Ananias, convinced Helena to persuade Izates to forgo circumcision.

[Ananias said that Izates] might worship God without being circumcised, even though he did resolve to follow the Jewish law entirely; which worship of God was of a **superior nature to circumcision**. …[however] a certain Jew that **came out of Galilee**, whose name was Eleazar, and who was esteemed very skillful in the learning of his country, persuaded him [Izates] to do the thing [circumcision]. (*Ant.* 20.34-43)

This event preceded the famine and the dating can be estimated at 44 CE. The broad gist of the story centers upon conversion to Judaism. Note that two sets of Jewish teachers instructed King Izates in his interpretation of the Law. Ananias told him that circumcision was unnecessary while the Jew from Galilee insisted upon circumcision. It should not be missed that this struggle for Izates' soul corresponds perfectly with the argument recorded in Galatians, where Cephas and James turned their backs upon Paul for teaching against circumcision and the Law. (This no doubt places many of Paul's letters before 44 CE, not in the 50's as traditionally believed.) Josephus did state that Eleazar was "very skillful in the learning of his country." This language echoes his treatment of Simon in the Agrippa episode mentioned earlier. Concerning Simon, Josephus wrote: "[Simon] appeared to be very accurate in the knowledge of the law." (*Ant.* 19.332) And Josephus wrote this about

Matthias and Judas the Galilean: "[They were] two of the most eloquent men among the Jews, and the most celebrated interpreters of the Jewish laws." (*Ant.* 17.149) Certainly, leaders of the Fourth Philosophy were deemed skillful and knowledgeable concerning the details of the Law. Thus, it is without a doubt that Eleazar was part of the Fourth Philosophy. This also helps confirm that James and Cephas were also part of that movement as their cause mirrored that of Eleazar.

After the conversion to full Judaism, King Izates and his mother, Helena, sent food and money to Jerusalem to help those facing serious famine. Josephus wrote that the famine stretched out during the terms of Fadus and Titus Alexander (44-48 CE). (*Ant.* 20.101) Note that in Paul's letters, he asked the Galatians and Corinthians to send money to the poor in Jerusalem. Such a request rings true considering the famine. In addition, Acts recorded four trips by Paul to Jerusalem. The first was after his conversion (supposedly around 35 CE) (Acts 9); the second during the famine (44 CE) (Acts 11); the third at the Council of Jerusalem (52 CE) (Acts 15); and the fourth in 58 CE, where he was arrested and imprisoned (Acts 21-28). In the letter to the Galatians, Paul stated that he was in Jerusalem twice, once three years after his conversion and the second, fourteen years later at the Council of Jerusalem. The last trip can be accounted for, as Paul could not have known about his arrest and imprisonment. But what about the trip concerning the famine?

It is my contention that the trip to Jerusalem with the money from the churches was in connection with the famine. Therefore, Paul could not have written about this second trip to Jerusalem for it had not yet occurred. Again, this would place the last years of Paul's association with the Fourth Philosophy in the early 40's. The Jews from Galilee were now following Paul and his disciples everywhere, preaching the necessity of circumcision. (Note that the Ananias of the King Izates story was probably a disciple of Paul's). Little doubt remains that Paul was at odds with the Jewish Christian movement, having been removed from fellowship at Antioch in 44 CE (Galatians 2:11-13) His only hope in retaining disciples came in trashing the apostles. This strategy was employed in Galatians and 2 Corinthians. (See Gal. 1:6-10; 2:9 (James, Cephas and John were reputed to be Pillars); 2 Cor. 11:3-15 (the super-apostles were servants of Satan!))

The story of Queen Helena and King Izates has also been used heavily in the creation of the "Church" mythology. The Ananias of Acts 9:10-19 was a reworking of the Ananias in the King Izates story. By Paul's own account, he went immediately into Arabia before going on to Damascus. (Gal. 1:17) Thus, the three different accounts of Paul's conversion in Acts cannot be believed. However, there may have been a real connection between Ananias and Paul; Ananias preached Paul's message concerning the law and circumcision to King

Izates. This Ananias was simply cast in a different role in Acts. In addition, Acts 8:26-40 related the story of Philip and the Ethiopian Eunuch. This Eunuch corresponded to Ananias, who "got among the women that belonged to the king." (*Ant.* 20.34) The Ethiopian Eunuch read Scripture which was then interpreted by Philip, and the Eunuch summarily underwent baptized. In Josephus, Izates read Scripture in front of Eleazar (from Galilee), and he was convinced to undergo circumcision. (*Ant.* 20.44-45) These conspicuous coincidences must give pause to even the most ardent traditionalists.

About this time, things became much more interesting. First, Agrippa I died in 44 CE, probably from poisoning. (*Ant.* 19.350) Who poisoned him? That will never be known with certainty, but the Fourth Philosophy had the most to gain from his demise. After all, as King (Messiah), Agrippa I was a serious rival to the resurrected Jesus. In addition, Agrippa had been a close friend and advisor to both Caligula and Claudius. The book of Acts may give a hint as to why Agrippa died.

On the appointed day Herod [Agrippa I], wearing his royal robes, sat on his throne and delivered a public address to the people. They shouted, "This is the voice of God, not of a man." Immediately, because Herod did not give praise to God, an angel of the Lord struck him down, and he was eaten by worms and died. (Acts 12:21-23)

Agrippa was a popular King, and he might have had a following in Judea and in surrounding countries. Note that Agrippa was struck down because he did not give praise to God after being compared to God by the people. This same story was also told by Josephus in *Ant.* 19.343-352. Here the praises came from his own flatterers, and he did not deny the exaltations. He immediately saw an owl (ill omen) and was taken ill. Five days later he died of a stomach ailment (poison?), and Judea was thrown into a bit of confusion. (Poison often killed without leaving a trace as to the perpetrator. Germanicus was poisoned over a lengthy period of time and the whole royal family at Rome experienced the horrors of knowing family poisoned by Livia.)

Since Agrippa's son, Agrippa II, was too young to assume control, Rome sent a new procurator, Fadus (44-46 CE). This must have seemed like a step backwards to some within the ranks of the Fourth Philosophy. However, to the leaders, the meddling of Rome may have been a great recruiting tool. The evil empire was once again front and center. Since the death of Judas the Galilean (Jesus), those zealous for the Law had waited patiently for the return of Jesus, resisting affronts to their religion with prayer and repentance. Surely it was time for Jesus to return in power and glory. A generation had passed since the death of Judas, and many of the younger followers may have been losing their patience with the policy of reaction. Perhaps, they argued, they should follow in Judas' footsteps. Just as Judas (Jesus) had stridden confidently to the Mount of Olives with two swords, awaiting the power of God, so too they would act. This change in policy was the result of Agrippa's assassination and the control exerted by Rome through Fadus. Under Fadus, a member of the Fourth Philosophy named Theudas tried to prod God into action.

A certain magician, whose name was Theudas, persuaded a great part of the people to take their effects with him, and follow him to the river Jordan; for he told them he was a prophet, and that he would, by his own command, divide the river, and afford them an easy passage over it; and many were **deluded** by his words. …[The Romans] took Theudas alive, and cut off his head, and carried it off to Jerusalem. (*Ant.* 20.97-98) (Emphasis mine)

Three important points should be noted about this passage. First, Josephus exhibits his utter contempt for Theudas by calling him a magician and claiming that he deluded the people. This, of course, was Josephus' attitude. This merely cements the argument that Josephus did not write the famous passage about Jesus, because Jesus was also a magician (healer) who led a band of rebels in a hopeless cause against Rome (on the Mount of Olives). Second, Theudas tried to recreate the miracle of Moses, by dividing the river Jordan, and of Joshua, by leading the people across the river. This was a mad attempt to gain God's attention. Maybe it was time for Jesus to return, and such an action would prove the faith of the masses. Unfortunately, Jesus did not return and Theudas forfeited his own life. The third point concerns the name, Theudas. This Theudas may have been the son of Judas the Galilean. In the Gospels, a Judas, a Thaddeus and a Thomas were listed as apostles. Thomas is merely a nickname for twin. This Judas may have been known as Judas Thomas. (13) In addition, both Judas and his brother Joseph were surnamed Barsabbas in Acts (Acts 1:23 and 15:22), clearly showing a close relationship between the two. It should also be noted that two of the supposed brothers of Jesus were named Judas and Joseph (Mark 6:3; Matt. 13:55). In Part III, I will support the claim that these supposed brothers were actually the sons of Jesus (Judas the Galilean). In any event, this Theudas was undoubtedly a member of the Fourth Philosophy.

The Fourth Philosophy (Jewish Christianity) was still practicing the restraint taught by Judas the Galilean, in that any attempt to resist Rome came from the hope in Godly miracles. Remember, Judas had witnessed the power of Rome and knew only too well that the Jews could not defeat Rome without the power of God. However, this mind-set could not last forever. Events and impatience could lead any movement in a different direction.

Under the administration of Tiberius Alexander (46-48 CE), during the famine, sparks of resistance were now seen.

...the sons of Judas the Galilean were now slain; I mean of that Judas who caused the people to revolt, when Cyrenius came to take an account of the estates of the Jews. ...The names of those sons were James and Simon, whom Alexander commanded to be **crucified**. (*Ant.* 20.102) (Emphasis mine)

The famine must have been a very stressful time for the inhabitants of Judea. Josephus mentioned the famine and the help which Queen Helen doled out to the people. Also at this time, the Romans moved against the sons of Judas the Galilean. Rome probably still remembered their father, Judas, and wanted to rid the land of such troublemakers. Josephus did not mention anything else, so we are left to our own imaginations as to why these two suffered crucifixion. One thing is certain: the situation in Judea was becoming tense.

The passage in Matthew 20:20-23 involved the two sons of Zebedee, who with their mother's approval, asked if they could sit at the right and left hands of Jesus in his kingdom. To this unusual request Jesus replied that they would drink the same cup as he, meaning crucifixion. The only brothers to be crucified were James and Simon, the sons of Judas the Galilean (Jesus). Note that the mother of the two brothers would have been the wife of Judas (Jesus). That is why she had easy access to this Messiah figure. James and Simon were crucified approximately 27 years after Judas (19-21 CE). Maybe the time had come for them to mount an attack against Rome, using the same tactics as their father: initiate the confrontation and wait for God to finish the battle. But once again, Rome triumphed and the radical Jews were slaughtered. This defeat may have been the genesis of a split within the Fourth Philosophy, as the leaders were being killed and Jesus still had not returned. The reason for the Gospel story is now clear: like the story of the Pillar Apostles sleeping in the Garden of Gethsemane, where all blame was taken away from Jesus and placed squarely on the shoulders of the unprepared, the deaths of James and Simon were not a failure on Jesus' part but a prophecy realized. Thus, Jesus was again vindicated, and the movement should go on as before. Some bought this line while others began plotting their own little war against Rome.

I believe that the Fourth Philosophy was being wrenched in half, one group following James and the other following those advocating open warfare against Rome. Both groups still had the same goal: the liberation of Israel. But the methods were clearly different. James and Cephas still recruited among the Jews, but as every year passed, their arguments grew weaker. Where was Jesus when Theudas called upon God? Why did Jesus ignore the pleas of his own two sons, James and Simon? How long would it be until he returned in glory to fight Rome? Time and circumstances were working against the movement's wing led by James. Those calling for direct confrontation could point to the failures of the miracle workers as proof that a better way existed. And their way might also trigger the return of Jesus. Remember that Jesus said that two swords were enough. It is possible that the more extreme elements were calling for hundreds or thousands of swords.

However, during the reign of the next procurator, Cumanus (48-52 CE), the Jamesian wing still prevailed. Two events clearly show that the Jews still waited for deliverance. In the Temple, a Roman soldier lifted "his garment and bent over indecently, turning his backside towards the Jews and making a noise as indecent as his attitude. This infuriated the whole crowd, who noisily appealed to Cumanus to punish the soldier." (*War* 2.224-225) (See also *Ant.* 20.105-112) Shortly after this episode, another event had the Jews howling. "In one village a soldier found a copy of the sacred Law, tore it in two and threw it into the fire. The Jews, as if their whole country was in flames, assembled in frantic haste, religious fervor drawing them together irresistibly, and on a single summons ran in their thousands from all directions to Caesarea" to petition Cumanus to punish the soldier. (*War* 2.229-230) (See also *Ant.* 20.115-117) Although the populace had not taken up arms, it appears as if tensions had grown and that a conflict brewed on the horizon. In both the above cases, the Romans incited the Jews to action. Such actions by the "enemy" moved the Fourth Philosophy closer and closer to open rebellion.

The Fourth Philosophy's split became more pronounced during the 50's and 60's, under the procurators Cumanus (48-52 CE), Felix (52-60 CE) and Festus (60-62 CE). In the latter years of Cumanus (51-52 CE), to avenge a Galilean murder, "the bandit and revolutionary elements among them was led by one Eleazar, son of Dinaeus, and Alexander." This element took to arms instead of petitioning the governor. (*War* 2.234-235) (*Ant.* 20.118-124) This change in methodology is significant because it shows that the old guard (James, Cephas and John) was losing its influence over the movement. Under Felix, Eleazar and his followers were captured and crucified. This Felix was a favorite of Claudius (14), who "indulging in every kind of barbarity and lust, exercised the power of a king in the spirit of a slave." (15)

In the early 50's, a new subgroup was introduced by Josephus.

When the countryside had been cleared of them [robbers], another type of bandit sprang up in Jerusalem, known as "Sicarii." These men committed numerous murders in broad daylight and in the middle of the City. Their favorite trick was to mingle with festival crowds, concealing under their garments small daggers with which they stabbed their opponents. (*War* 2.254-255)

The Sicarii were religious assassins who used the element of surprise to their advantage, like Pilate had done some twenty years earlier. They may have also patterned themselves after the ten men who conspired to kill Herod the Great by concealing daggers in their garments. These ten considered this "a holy and pious action" for Herod had introduced practices contrary to the Jewish laws and customs. (*Ant.* 15.267-289)

Josephus clearly painted an unfavorable picture of the Sicarii, saying they murdered others for money and political power, even unknowingly aligning itself with Rome if profitable. Josephus' account of the assassination of Jonathan makes the reader question the Sicarii's actual religious zeal. He made it seem as though the Sicarii were more interested in money than in anything else.

Felix persuaded one of Jonathan's most faithful friends ...to bring the robbers upon Jonathan [high priest and son of Annas, the high priest during the lifetime of Judas (Jesus)] in order to kill him [for money]. ...Certain of these robbers went up to the city, as if they were going to worship God, while they had daggers under their garments; and by thus mingling among the multitude, they slew Jonathan. (*Ant.* 20.162-164)

The religious goal of the Sicarii should not be missed. Their target was an unpopular high priest and the money gained could be used for recruitment against Rome, a win-win situation. As previously mentioned in the chapter on James, Jonathan was the target of these religious fanatics. This Jonathan was the son of Annas, the high priest most responsible for the crucifixion of Judas (Jesus). Jonathan was also the brother of Ananus, the high priest behind the stoning of James the Just, the brother of Jesus (Judas). In addition to the money given by Felix, revenge cannot be ruled out as a real motive in Jonathan's death.

The Gospel writers also mentioned the Sicarii under the guise of Judas Iscariot. Continuing where Josephus left off, they created Judas, the ultimate evil antagonist. Judas betrayed Jesus just as the Sicarii had betrayed Israel. Judas Iscariot stole from the money purse just as the Sicarii robbed its enemies. And Judas Iscariot ended his life by suicide, just as the Sicarii had done at Masada in 73 CE. That the Sicarii were named by Josephus as arising in the 50's did not deter the Gospel writers from creating Judas Iscariot and placing him in the 20's.

By this time, James, the brother of Judas (Jesus), was an old man. Although well respected by the masses, circumstances had complicated matters. Not only had a separatist wing deserted his campaign for Jesus (wait and see approach), but other more friendly elements were out of control.

In addition to these [the Sicarii] there was formed another group of scoundrels, in act less criminal but in intention more evil, who did as much damage as the murderers to the well-being of the City. Cheats and deceivers claiming inspiration, they schemed to bring about revolutionary changes by inducing the mob to act as if possessed, and by leading them out into the desert on the pretence that there God would show them signs of approaching freedom. (*War* 2.258-260)

Using the same methods as Jesus, who claimed inspiration and led his followers to an unsuccessful confrontation on the Mount of Olives, these "imposters" hoped to incite revolutionary changes. Like Jesus, they too were captured and punished. This flurry of activity must have been extremely damning to James and his disciples. With all the attempts to contact God and Jesus, not one had proved successful. This may explain the forward looking prophecy put into the mouth of Jesus in Matthew chapter 24.

Watch out that no one deceives you. For many will come in my name, claiming, "I am the Christ," and will deceive many. ...Then you will be handed over to be persecuted and put to death, and you will be hated by all nations because of me. ...So if anyone tells you, "there he is, out in the desert," do not go out ... For as the lightening comes from the east and flashes to the west, so will be the coming of the Son of Man.

Once again, the failures of those emulating Jesus were explained away by prophecy, placed in the mouth of Jesus. In fact, these miracle workers were part of the Fourth Philosophy, that particular wing that had lost patience. The movement led by James still waited upon the return of Jesus and these failures generated poor public relations.

One other "imposter" must be mentioned. Out of Egypt came a man who called himself a prophet. He led "the multitude of the common people" to the Mount of Olives and said by his command, the walls would fall down. (*Ant.* 20.169-172) The Egyptian, as he was called in Acts 21:38, was again trying to conjure up the same power that allowed Joshua to crumble the walls of Jericho. Like Jesus, he fully believed in the Scriptures. It may be from this episode that we get the infancy story where Jesus returned from Egypt and the quote, "Out of Egypt, I call my Son." (Hosea 11:1) Philo of Alexandria (20 BCE - 45 CE) claimed that a large following of the Therapuetae was located in Alexandria and throughout all areas of the Jewish Diaspora. According to Alvar Ellegard, this Therapuetae was a branch of the Essenes and closely resembled the Jewish Christian movement. (16) That a "Jewish Christian" traveled from Egypt to Jerusalem to stage a miracle should not surprise us, for followers of the Fourth Philosophy were throughout the Empire. This may show, however, the extended power of the movement and how worrisome it had become to Rome.

By the beginnings of the 60's, the rifts among the Fourth Philosophy factions were growing deeper. A wild debate raged within the movement: to take up arms or to wait patiently for the return of "Jesus". James, the venerated old holy man, still held considerable influence upon the masses, yet an uneasiness surely gripped the entire Jewish nation. Would Jesus return soon or would there be war between tiny Israel and the might of Rome? Surely James and his close followers understood that open revolt was simply suicide. Had they not witnessed the death of Judas the Galilean (Jesus), his two sons (James and Simon) and the many miracle workers who called upon God for salvation? And had not every armed revolt against Rome ended in mass destruction and certain crucifixion? The only solution for James was the return of Jesus. No other path to victory seemed possible.

STAGE 4 - DISINTEGRATION

Before Albinus (62-64 CE) arrived to assume control of Judea, the Sadducean High Priest, Ananus, illegally assembled the Sanhedrin and accused James, the brother of Jesus, as being a breaker of the law and had James stoned. (*Ant.* 20.200) This illegal trial should remind us of Jesus' trial. In fact, the trial of James may have been the basis for the trial of Jesus, as the actual trial of Judas (Jesus) before Pilate escaped mention by Josephus, at least by his writings that we possess today. (17) In any event, the murder of James was the last straw. No one could stand against those who insisted upon armed rebellion. Only James the Just could have persuaded the masses from going wild, from committing suicide as a nation.

This sentiment was echoed in a deleted passage from Josephus. In the early third century, Origen paraphrased Josephus concerning James:

This James was of so shining a character among the people, on account of his righteousness, that Flavius Josephus, when, in his twentieth book of the *Jewish Antiquities*, he had a mind to set down what was the cause, why the people suffered such miseries, till the very holy house was demolished, he said, that these things befell them by the anger of God, on account of what they had dared to do to James, the brother of Jesus, who was called Christ;

and wonderful it is, that while **he did not receive Jesus for Christ**, he did nevertheless bear witness that James was so righteous a man. He says further, that the **people thought they had suffered these things for the sake of James**. (18) (Emphasis mine)

The above passage contains three important points. First, Josephus did not consider Jesus as the Messiah. Thus, the passage in *Ant.* 18.63-64 about Jesus was a fourth century forgery, either a completely new passage or an alteration of material originally concerning Judas the Galilean. Note that the death of Judas is curiously missing from *Antiquities*. This is truly amazing considering Judas was the most influential rabbi of first-century Israel. I strongly believe that the passage about Jesus was initially an account of Judas' crucifixion at the hands of Pilate. Second, Josephus considered James a righteous man and that the downfall of Jerusalem was due to his death, not to the death of Jesus. That is why this part of the above passage was deleted by later Christians, who believed it unthinkable that the death of Jesus was not the direct cause of the Jewish downfall. Third, the peoples' belief that the death of James was the reason why God had forsaken the Jews rings true, considering the people also believed that Herod Antipas' army was destroyed because of John the Baptist's execution.

Although the split among the Fourth Philosophy had begun in the early 50's, the final blow was the murder of James. If James were simply a leader of an other-worldly pacifist movement and not a member of the Fourth Philosophy, then his death would have had little impact upon Jerusalem and its eventual destruction. However, if James controlled the "wait for Jesus wing" of the Fourth Philosophy movement, then his death would have been the cause of the increased hostilities. Though thoroughly anti-Roman, the "wait for Jesus wing" held that the overthrow of Rome would occur upon the return of the resurrected Messiah. They had nothing against fighting, but their leader had to be Jesus, armed with the power of God. Note that the book of Revelation is based upon this "wait for Jesus" approach. (Rev. 19:11-16) However, with each passing year and each failure, the "wait for Jesus wing" began losing its grip upon the masses. This murder of James would have given other branches of the Zealots and Sicarii ample ammunition to recruit among the thousands disillusioned by this particular gory chain of events. In fact, James, at the grizzled age of ninety-six, may have been the last surviving member of the **original** movement started by Matthias and Judas in 4 BCE. Without James to guide the masses, the ensuing chaos was inevitable.

During this time, the Sicarii and Zealots (another war party) occupied all of Josephus' accounts. Under the procurator Albinus, and with his express approval, the High Priest, Ananus, profited by stealing tithes from the lower priests. (*Ant.* 20.204-207) The lower priests were influenced heavily by the Fourth Philosophy and the above murder of James may have been the result of James' relationship with these priests. (19) James may have been their leader. In any case, this move by the wealthy priests against the lower priests accelerated the class struggle. This is suggested by the following passage:

Now too the revolutionary party in Jerusalem cast off all restraint, and its leaders bribed Albinus to shut his eyes to their subversive activities. …Every scoundrel, surrounded by his own gang, stood out from his followers like a bandit chief or dictator and used his henchmen to rob respectable citizens. (*War* 2.274-275)

In other words, the gangs were robbing the rich and giving to the poor. Josephus viewed these bandits as selfish brutes who kept all the gain to themselves. Undoubtedly, interspersed amongst the "honest" robbers were those who selfishly kept the booty for themselves. However, the class warfare should not be missed: the rich were being assaulted by an ever growing group of rebels. By Josephus' description, there does seem to be some chaos in the organization of the robbers. Again, this may have been due to the death of James, the one unifying force left to the insurgents.

In this general period (64 CE), a great fire destroyed five-sevenths of Rome, that city referred to as the harlot in the book of Revelation (Rev. 17 and 18). Tacitus reported that Nero used the Christians as scapegoats, to deflect criticism from himself. Some historians now see a more sinister past concerning these "Christians." It is my contention that these "Christians" were really members of the radical Jewish sect known as the Fourth Philosophy. Could it be that without James at the helm, members were taking this war directly to Rome, with swords or even fire? It is possible that the fire was propagated by these Jewish Christians. Such an action would have been consistent with the Jews growing hatred of Rome in Judea and in other parts of the Empire. So what was Nero's motive for persecuting the Jews: was he just an able administrator, who punished the guilty or did he persecute the Jewish Christians to simply cover his own actions? This will never be answered without doubt. But at least we should consider that the Jewish Christians were behind the great fire.

Tacitus described the torture of Christians at the hands of Nero, but he never positively assigned the blame for the fire on Nero. "A disaster followed [fire], whether accidental or treacherously contrived by the emperor, is uncertain, as authors have given both accounts." (20) In his famous passage about the persecution of Christians, Tacitus stated that the Christians had been arrested "not so much on the charge of arson as because of hatred of the human race." (21) Tacitus had nothing positive to say about the Christians, yet he could not declare them guilty of the fire. The following passage may further cloud the picture as to responsibility.

And no one dared to stop the mischief, because of incessant menaces from a number of persons who forbade the extinguishing of the flames, because again others openly hurled brands, and kept shouting that there was one who gave them authority, either seeking to plunder more freely, or obeying orders. (Tacitus, *The Annals*, xv. 38)

Considering the fact that James had been murdered in 62 CE and Saul was once again persecuting the Fourth Philosophy (*Ant.* 20.214), the anger of Jews throughout the Empire must have reached a fever pitch. The above passage seems to be describing actions of the most radical wing of the Fourth Philosophy, not paid henchmen of Nero. Why would a henchman risk the ire of Nero, and certain death, by proclaiming his boss was responsible for the fire? On the other hand, would not the Jewish Christians proudly proclaim the "One" who gave them authority to burn the harlot, Rome.

In any event, Nero blamed the Christians for the fire. By now, the reader should be aware that the Christians were **not pacifist Gentiles** but members of the Fourth Philosophy. In Josephus' description of the Fourth Philosophy, he stated that they would undergo any type of torture and fear rather than submit to Caesar as Lord. (*Ant.* 18.23-25) According to Tacitus, those who confessed to being Christian were convicted and put to death. "They were clad in the hides of beasts and torn to death by dogs; others were crucified, others set on fire to serve to illuminate the night when daylight failed." (22) Suetonius' assessment of the situation was much muted: "Punishments were also inflicted on the Christians, a sect professing a new and mischievous religious belief." (23) This new belief was undoubtedly the resurrection of Christ.

It is interesting to note that the 18th century English historian Edward Gibbon, author of *The History of the Decline and Fall of the Roman Empire*, agreed with my interpretation that the Fourth Philosophy was really the group that Nero blamed for the fire. Although Gibbon held the 18th century belief that Christianity was all good and that the Zealots were mostly evil, he did use pure logic to determine that the Christians were not on the scene at this time. (Gibbons refers to Christians in the traditional timeline, where Jesus was crucified in 33 CE and the small movement would have only been around for thirty years at the time of the fire.) He stated:

We may therefore presume to imagine some probable cause which could direct the cruelty of Nero against the Christians at Rome, **whose obscurity, as well as innocence**, should have shielded them from his indignation, and **even from his notice**. The Jews, who were numerous in the capitol, and oppressed in their own country, were a much fitter object for the suspicions of the emperor and of the people. ...although the genuine followers of Moses were innocent of the fire of Rome, there had arisen among them a new and **pernicious sect of Galilaeans**, which was capable of the most horrid crimes. Under the appellation of Galilaeans, two distinctions of men were confounded, the most opposite to each other in their manners and principles; the disciples who had embraced the faith of Jesus of Nazareth, and the zealots who had followed the standard of Judas the Gaulonite. ...How natural was it for Tacitus, in the time of Hadrian, to appropriate to the Christians, the guilt and the sufferings, which he might, with far greater truth and justice, have attributed to a sect whose odious memory was almost extinguished! (24) (Emphasis mine)

Gibbon stated that this was merely his conjecture, but his logic was much better than most Christian historians who preceded him. Eusebius quoted Tertullian, who used the complete opposite logic in describing Nero's persecution of the Christians. "For anyone who knows him [Nero] can understand that anything not supremely good would never have been condemned by Nero." (25) Gibbon argued that the Christians' obscurity and innocence would have shielded them from Nero's attention. They would have flown under the radar; Nero would not have known about them. On the other hand, Nero and all of Rome would have known about the followers of Judas the Gaulonite, "a pernicious sect of Galilaeans." Gibbon realized that the Christian sect as described in Acts could not have become such a major force in Rome a mere thirty years after the crucifixion of Jesus. In Acts 1:15, there were only a hundred and twenty disciples. From such a meager beginning, Gibbon reasoned that they could not have been a major player in Rome by 64 CE. This is very logical and speaks strongly against the traditional timeline. However, if the movement of Jesus (Judas the Galilean) had begun at least forty years earlier, then the Christians could easily have been the ones to blame for the fire.

Back in Jerusalem, around 66 CE, Eleazar, the son of Ananias the high priest, persuaded the Temple ministers to accept "no gift or offering from a foreigner. This is what made war with Rome inevitable for they abolished the sacrifices offered for Rome and Caesar himself. ...Their numbers made them supremely confident, backed as they were by the toughest of the revolutionaries..." (*War* 2.409-410) Note that even members of other parties were now being caught up in the war fervor. The revolutionary parties were now being led by individuals no longer holding onto the Jamesian philosophy to wait for Jesus. It does appear strange that in the case of Eleazar, he was the son of the high priest. Either Eleazar was caught up in the excitement, or he was a plant to turn the movement on itself.

[Soon after this], their opponents [Eleazar and the Sicarii] rushed in and burnt down the house of Ananias the high priest and the palace of Agrippa and Berenice; then they took their fire to the Record Office, eager to destroy the money-lenders bonds and so make impossible the recovery of debts, in order to secure the support of an army of debtors and enable the poor to rise with impunity against the rich. (*War* 2.426-427)

Two points must be made from the above passage. First, this was the ultimate in class warfare. Remember those passages in the New Testament where Jesus supported the poor against the rich. The letter attributed to James also sided with the poor over the wealthy. "Now listen, you rich people, weep and wail because of the misery that is coming upon you. ...You have fattened yourselves in the day of slaughter." (James 5:1-6) This passage by James says that the Lord Almighty, not the poor, will judge the rich. While the attitude about the rich was the same for James and this war party, the actions would have been different. James would have waited on God. The second interesting point concerns Eleazar. He is represented as leading the Sicarii in burning down his own father's house as well as King Agrippa's palace. This is extremely strange behavior for a son. Again, Eleazar was either fully against the wealthy elites (his father and Agrippa) or he was building more credit with the revolutionaries.

Meanwhile one Menahem, son of Judas the Galilean, the very clever rabbi who in the time of Quirinius [Cyrenius] had once reproached the Jews for submitting to the Romans after serving God alone, took his friends with him and went off to Masada, where he broke open King Herod's armory and distributed weapons to his fellow-townsmen and other bandits. With these as bodyguards he returned like a king to Jerusalem, put himself at the head of the insurgents and took charge of the siege. (*War* 2.433-434)

Once again we encounter the name Judas the Galilean. Not only had Josephus called him a wise man but now he was a very clever rabbi as well. It is noteworthy that Judas' son used the same strategy that his father had used seventy years earlier. Surely, the stories of Judas' exploits had been told and retold, especially by family members. Like Judas, Menahem broke into Herod's armory and distributed weapons to his followers. (See *War* 2.56)

After that, Menahem marched to Jerusalem and set himself up as a king, similar to the march by Jesus. Menahem and his men killed the high priest Ananias, and Josephus wrote that Menahem then became a tyrant. (*War* 2.442) According to Josephus, this behavior drove Eleazar and his men to kill Menahem. (*War* 2.445-447) Was Eleazar driven to kill Menahem as revenge for his father's death? If that is so, then why did Eleazar participate in the burning of his father's house? Was Eleazar simply jealous of Menahem's new position of authority? That is entirely possible, but it does not jibe with his initial actions. Originally, Eleazar led the lower priests in revolt against the ruling class, which included his own family. One would think that the arrival of Menahem would have strengthened Eleazar's position. Together, he and Menahem could have ruled without any other interference. But what if Eleazar had been commissioned by his father and other wealthy families to co-opt the revolutionary feelings of the priests? This would have seemed a prudent thing to do by the wealthy, as the priests were ready to revolt anyway. The murder, then, of Menahem might have been the end play to rob the kingship from a descendant of Judas the Galilean's family. Without the unifying power of Judas' name, the various revolutionary factions were doomed to fight amongst themselves. This seems to be the most reasonable explanation for the strange career of Eleazar, son of Ananias the high priest.

The remnant of Menahem's party retreated to Masada and eventually committed suicide there in 73 CE as one last act of resistance against Rome. The leader at Masada was also named Eleazar, and he was the grandson of Judas the Galilean. (*War* 7.253) (Slavonic Josephus, After *War* 7.253) How fitting that the last members of the Fourth Philosophy were led by a descendent of its original author, Judas the Galilean. (It should not be missed that the mythical Judas Iscariot also committed suicide in the Gospel accounts.) As for Masada, the Jewish nation today reveres the bravery of those valiant Jews who struggled against the greatest military power of their day, Rome.

A few other passages from Josephus must be quoted to further cement the argument tying Judas the Galilean to Jesus. The first passage regards religious practices: the Jews attacked the Romans near Jerusalem "utterly disregarding the seventh day's rest, although this was the Sabbath, which they usually observed most carefully." (*War* 2.517) These men, zealous for the Law, broke the Sabbath rest. However, a reading of the New Testament reveals that Jesus' attitude of the Sabbath was the same. He definitely kept the Sabbath unless there was a need to break it, such as in healing or in helping someone or in his flight from Herod. To attack the Romans on the Sabbath was in keeping with this philosophy and with a Maccabean precedent. Mattathias "taught them to fight even on the Sabbath day...and this rule continues among us to this day, that if there be a necessity, we may fight on Sabbath days." (*Ant.* 12.276-277) (See also *Ant.* 13.12-13)

Several other passages show that the movement that once valued experience and wisdom now placed its future in the hands of the reckless youth. In Jerusalem and in the countryside, "factions reigned everywhere, the revolutionaries and jingoes with the boldness of youth silencing the old and sensible." (*War* 4.133) And a little later, "[Ananus the high priest] roused the populace against the Zealots, though well aware that they would be most difficult to suppress now, numerous, young, and intrepid as they were..." (*War* 4.186)

This was Josephus' attitude towards the Zealots. "The dregs, the scum of the whole country, they have squandered their own property and practiced their lunacy upon the towns and villages around, and finally have poured in a stealthy stream into the Holy City..." (*War* 4.241) In his hatred for the Zealots, Josephus did tie them to a type of communism, in that they did not value private property. One must remember that Josephus represented those who highly valued private property, and this revolt against Rome was no different than that of Spartacus, one hundred and fifty years earlier. And the results would be the same: as Spartacus and his followers were crucified along the Appian Way, so too would all Judea suffer because of the ideals of one group, the Way of Righteousness or the Fourth Philosophy.

Suffering extended beyond Judea and Galilee. As already noted, the Jewish Christians (Fourth Philosophy) were persecuted by Nero in Rome. At the very end of the Jewish war against Rome, stragglers from the Sicarii escaped to Alexandria in an attempt to rouse the large Jewish population there to rise up against Rome. Undoubtedly, there were a great number of sympathizers in Alexandria. Remember, the Egyptian (58 CE) traveled to Judea to try his own hand in hastening the Day of Judgment against Rome. These Sicarii were not successful in persuading the Alexandrian Jews to revolt, and were summarily rounded up and executed. In one last chilling testimony to their will, Josephus wrote:

"...they could not get anyone of them to comply so far as to confess or seem to confess, that Caesar was their lord; but they preserved their own opinion, in spite of all the distress they were brought to, as if they received these torments and the fire itself with bodies insensible of pain, and with a soul that in a manner rejoiced under them. But what was most of all astonishing to the beholders, was the courage of the children; for not one of these children was so far overcome by these torments as to name Caesar for their lord." (*War* 7.418-419)

CONCLUSION

Josephus went into great detail describing the final battles between the revolutionaries and the Roman army. It is not necessary to go any further in our search because the pattern has already been exposed. The Fourth Philosophy movement had one thing in common with the economic theory of Karl Marx: they both began as a way to liberate and they both became a system to destroy.

Judas the Galilean, that wise man and clever rabbi, preached the kingdom of heaven and the eventual overthrow of Roman rule. His followers placed their trust in God, believing that righteousness could bring about a new era, one where God reigned on earth. However, each defeat brought doubts: first, Judas was crucified, then John the Baptist was slain, then the crucifixions of Judas' sons and finally the stoning of James the Just. These doubts helped splinter the movement, and this lack of cohesion brought utter destruction.

The Roman historians Tacitus and Suetonius wrote sparingly about the Jews, but their input only supports the picture left by Josephus. Their three accounts of Jews being expelled or persecuted in Rome occurred in 19, 41 and 64 CE, paralleling the death of Judas the Galilean (Jesus), the near revolt due to Caligula's designs for the Temple and the murder of James, the brother of Jesus. With these three historians, we are left with a coherent picture of the Fourth Philosophy and its amazing correlation to the "Christian" movement.

After Judas the Galilean was arrested and put to death (19-21 CE), John the Baptist (the Sadduc) assumed control and emphasized repentance and righteousness. For his efforts, Herod Antipas had him beheaded around 35-36 CE. Over the next three decades (36-62 CE), James the Just and Cephas guided the movement against Rome. But time was not on their side; every year the memory of Judas dimmed. Impatient youths, not familiar with the early movement, were not willing to wait for the return of Jesus. They wanted freedom, whatever the cost. And the cost was dear.

The Zealots and Sicarii were completely destroyed by the Roman army. However, tradition tells us that the Jewish Christians escaped the City and the destruction. Considering what we have learned, it seems probable that the most ardent supporters of Jesus would not have fought without him. By the year 70 CE, this Jewish Christian movement was very insignificant. All its original leaders were now dead and most of the youth were killed by the Romans. They became outcasts to their own people and were not accepted by the Gentile Christians either. In the early second century, Irenaeus described these Jewish followers, these Ebionites, so named for their poverty.

Those who are called Ebionites…use only the Gospel according to Matthew; they reject the Apostle Paul, calling him an apostate from the law. The prophetic writings they strive to expound with especial exactness; they are circumcised, and persevere in the customs according to the Law, and in the Jewish mode of life, even to the extent of worshipping Jerusalem, as if it were the abode of God. (26)

By the fifth century, the Ebionites were lost from recorded history.

For the past two thousand years, the truth concerning the Fourth Philosophy has been hidden behind false assumptions. Very few have searched the New Testament writings and Josephus trying to explain this Fourth Philosophy. But it is there. Using a slightly different timeline, it is quite easy to tie Jesus of Nazareth to Judas the Galilean and Jewish Christianity to the Fourth Philosophy. But for this theory to be taken seriously, the life and teachings of Paul must be somehow explained. In the next section, Paul and his relationship to the Fourth Philosophy will be explored.

PART II
CHRIST JESUS
(THE REVELATORY MESSIAH)

I am astonished that you are so quickly deserting the one [Paul] who called you by the grace of Christ and are turning to a different gospel – which is really no gospel at all. Evidently some people [followers of James and Cephas] are throwing you into confusion and are trying to pervert the gospel of Christ. **But even if we or an angel from heaven should preach a gospel other than the one we preached to you, let him be eternally condemned!** As we have already said, so now I say again: if anybody is preaching to you a gospel other than what you accepted [from Paul], let him be eternally condemned. (Galatians 1:6-9) (Emphasis mine)

I want you to know, brothers, that the gospel I [Paul] preached is not something that man made up. **I did not receive it from any man, nor was I taught it; rather, I received it by revelation from Jesus Christ**. (Galatians 1:11-12) (Emphasis mine)

Now that faith has come, we are no longer under the supervision of the law. (Galatians 3:25)

To the Jews I became like a Jew, to win the Jews. To those under the law I became like one under the law (though I myself am not under the law), so as to win those under the law. To those not having the law I became like one not having the law (though I am not free from God's law but am under Christ's law), so as to win those not having the law. (1 Cor. 9:20-21) (Emphasis mine) (Paul's double game)

Faith by itself, if it is not accompanied by action is dead. ...Show me your faith without deeds, and I will show you my faith by what I do. You believe that there is one God. Good! Even the demons believe that – and shudder. (Paul's gospel of grace under attack, James 2:17-19)

CHAPTER 7

PAUL, ACTS, AND JOSEPHUS

The book of Acts is sometimes referred to as the Acts of the Apostles, an obviously misleading title considering the main character was Paul, an outsider who had no contact with the earthly Jesus. In fact, only a few of the original apostles had any coverage in its pages. James and John, the sons of Zebedee, were shadowy characters, mentioned only to further the story line. Peter (Cephas) did have an important role in that he eventually sided with Paul's interpretation of the Gospel. In Acts chapter 10, Peter had a vision which convinced him to treat Gentiles differently, to accept them as members of the movement, in line with Paul's theology. This implies that the earthly Jesus had not taught him to respect the Gentiles in such a way. Of the other twelve Apostles, only Philip and Matthias were even named. The one great stunning omission concerns James the Just, the brother of Jesus. According to Church tradition, this James became the leader of the movement, the successor to Jesus. He was not introduced until chapter 12. He then, to the reader's surprise, led the Council of Jerusalem in chapter 15. If James was so important to the early Church, then why did the author of Acts downplay James' role and then stop his history without relating James' death? Acts ended with Paul in Rome between 60-62 CE, while the stoning of James occurred in 62 CE. Why did Acts not relate one of the most important stories in Christian tradition?

This chapter will introduce some interesting information which most historians ignore because of the traditional timeline. In Part I, a case was made for Judas the Galilean being the actual model for Jesus of Nazareth. This Judas was born approximately 25 BCE, cleansed the Temple in 4 BCE, started a tax rebellion against Rome in 6 CE and was probably crucified sometime between

19-21 CE. His second-in-command, Sadduc (John the Baptist), controlled the movement until his death in 36 CE and was then replaced by James. So, how does Paul fit within this new timeline?

According to the traditional timeline, Paul converted shortly after the death of Jesus, sometime between 31-35 CE. However, if Jesus (Judas) actually was crucified in 21 CE, the conversion of Paul could have been as early as 21-25 CE. From the letter to the Galatians, we know that Paul spent seventeen years in the movement, from his conversion to the Council of Jerusalem. This being the case, the Council took place between 38-42 CE. We also know that the conflict between Cephas and Paul at Antioch was similar to the King Izates conversion, where Eleazar and Ananias played the same roles as Cephas and Paul. This occurred in 44 CE. Thus, it is safe to assume that the Antioch conflict took place in 44 CE, a few years after the Council of Jerusalem. This new timeline, however, assumes that Paul was removed from the movement. A close reading of Galatians and 2 Corinthians indeed shows that Paul no longer kept fellowship with the Jerusalem Jewish Christian movement. A few passages illustrate this break in relations between Paul and James.

I am astonished that you are so quickly deserting the one who called you by the grace of Christ and are turning to a different gospel - which is really no gospel at all. Evidently some people are throwing you into confusion and are trying to pervert the gospel of Christ. **But even if we or an angel from heaven should preach a gospel other than the one we preached to you, let him be eternally condemned!** As we have already said, so now I say again: If anybody is preaching to you a gospel other than what you accepted, let him be eternally condemned!

Am I now trying to win the approval of men, or of God? Or am I trying to please men? If I were still trying to please men, I would not be a servant of Christ.

I want you to know, brothers, that the gospel I preached is not something that man made up. **I did not receive it from any man, nor was I taught it; rather, I received it by revelation from Jesus Christ.** (Gal. 1:6-12) (Emphasis mine)

…For if someone comes to you and preaches a Jesus other than the Jesus we preached, or if you receive a different spirit from the one you received, or a **different gospel** from the one you accepted, you put up with it easily enough. But I do not think I am in the least inferior to those "super-apostles." …For such men are false apostles, deceitful workmen, masquerading as apostles of Christ. And no wonder, for Satan himself masquerades as an angel of light. It is not surprising, then, if **his servants masquerade as servants of**

righteousness. Their end will be what their actions deserve. (2 Cor. 11:4-5; 13-15) (Emphasis mine)

While the book of Acts tried to downplay the rift between Paul and the Jerusalem Church, Paul's own language concerning this conflict cannot be ignored. In Galatians, Paul stated that his gospel was received by revelation from Jesus Christ. He also went so far as to distance himself from that lower form of Gospel, taught by James and Cephas. "I [Paul] did not receive it from any man, nor was I taught it." Thus, according to Paul, his Gospel was much superior to the gospel of mere mortals. In fact, Paul also asserted that anyone who preached a different gospel than his own would be eternally condemned. By this, he was condemning the Jerusalem apostles, including James and Cephas. This same attitude towards the leaders of Jewish Christianity can also be found in 2 Corinthians. In that letter, Paul wrote that the "super-apostles" were preaching a "different gospel". He then denigrated these apostles, calling them the servants of Satan.

The above passages contain very strong and condemning language. Could Paul have been allowed to stay within the movement after he denounced the original Gospel of Jesus? After all, the Jerusalem apostles had been preaching their message to the people for over twenty years. It should be noted that the Galatians passage as well as the one in 2 Corinthians can be dated to around 44 CE, to the time of King Izates conversion, per *Ant.* 20.34-38. This is important since it dates the time when Paul was removed from fellowship with other Jewish Christians. If Paul were removed from the movement in 44 CE, then what are we to make of the history of Acts? Acts claimed that Paul stayed within the movement, even up to his imprisonment in Rome, or to 62 CE. This difference in dating can be argued just upon the passages listed. But I will go much further in proving that Paul was not a member of the Jewish Christian movement after 44 CE. With the help of Josephus, a much more sinister picture of Paul will emerge.

ACTS AND JOSEPHUS

Several passages in the *War* and *Antiquities* compare to accounts in the book of Acts. If just one similarity in accounts existed, then an argument could be made against my conclusions based upon sheer coincidence. However, as the evidence mounts, a new evaluation of Paul should be considered.

The first mention of Paul in the book of Acts comes immediately after the stoning of Stephen. It is interesting that Paul was referred to as Saul in this initial introduction, with Saul being his Jewish name, and Paul, the later nickname.

And Saul was there, giving approval to his death. On that day a great persecution broke out against the church at Jerusalem, and all except the apostles were scattered throughout Judea and Samaria. Godly men buried Stephen and mourned deeply for him. But Saul began to destroy the church. Going from house to house, he dragged off men and women and put them in prison. ...Meanwhile, Saul was still breathing out murderous threats against the Lord's disciples. He went to the high priest and asked him for letters to the synagogues in Damascus, so that if he found any there who belonged to the **Way**, whether men or women, he might take them as prisoners to Jerusalem. (Acts 8:1-3 and 9:1-2) (Emphasis mine)

Although Saul was not physically involved in the murder, he surely approved. This passage suggests that Saul was more of an authority figure as he gave "approval to his death." This is at odds with the tradition of Saul being a very young man at this time. Would such a young man wield such power, considering he was from Tarsus? This, in and of itself, has been a difficult question to answer by Christian commentators. Regardless of Saul's age, he then began to persecute the church or the Way. This Way or Way of Righteousness was certainly another designation for the Fourth Philosophy of Judas and Sadduc. All in all, this young Saul was one hateful individual.

How does the above account of a young Saul compare to the parallel passage in Josephus? The following account of Saul occurred right after the stoning of James the Just in 62 CE:

Costobarus also, and Saulus, did themselves get together a multitude of wicked wretches, and this because they were of the royal family; and so they obtained favor among them, because of their kindred to Agrippa: but still they used violence with the people, and were very ready to plunder those that were weaker than themselves. (*Ant.* 20.214)

First, it must be emphasized that a Saul was introduced after the stoning of Stephen in Acts and after the stoning of James in *Antiquities*. Is this just some coincidence? According to Robert Eisenman, the stoning of Stephen was simply a rewrite of the stoning of James. (1) He builds his case by using the above passages as well as early Christian writings about James. This explains why the Acts' storyline ends with Paul in Rome in 62 CE without mentioning the stoning of James, the most influential member of the movement after the deaths of Judas and Sadduc (John the Baptist). Certainly, the story of James was legendary. That is why there are accounts of his death independent of Acts. The author of Acts did not want to relate the facts as they actually occurred.

Besides the stoning, the one common thread between the two above accounts was the involvement of a Saul. In both cases, this Saul persecuted those weaker than himself: in Acts, Saul persecuted the Church while in *Antiquities* he followed up on the attack of the lower priesthood, those represented by James. The great difference concerns the timing. In Acts, the persecution happened before Saul joined the movement, around 31-35 CE. In Josephus, Saul was in Jerusalem in 62 CE, involved in the murder of James.

If Saul were in Jerusalem in 62 CE, then the rest of the Acts' story must be invented as Acts had Paul in Rome between 60-62 CE. The reason for this rewrite is clear: the author of Acts wanted to distance Paul far from the scene of the crime. How would it look if the Apostle to the Gentiles approved of the murder of James, the Jewish Christian leader? Are there any other clues which may shed light upon this remarkable revelation?

In Acts, Saul was a young man, yet he wielded extraordinary power for one so young and outside of the power structure. After all, according to the New Testament, Paul came from Tarsus. However, the passage from Josephus answers these questions. Saul was an older man of around sixty, and he had connections within the power structure: Saul and his brother were members of the royal family. This connection with Agrippa II certainly persuaded many of the "wretches" to throw in their lot with him. This also explains the power of Saul with the high priest as described in Acts.

So, the persecution by Saul after the murder of James was used to portray Saul's hateful beginnings in Acts. This was how Saul behaved **before** his conversion to Christianity. In fact, Saul hated the Jewish Christians **after** his removal from the movement in 44 CE. His actions in 62 CE were those of a vengeful opponent. James had won the day in 44 CE at Antioch (see Galatians), but Saul claimed victory in 62 CE in Jerusalem. This awful picture of Paul also comes from another source. In the *Recognitions of Clement* 1.70,71, the "Enemy" attacked James at the Temple, nearly killing him. This "Enemy" then received letters from the high priest and proceeded to go to Damascus, to where he thought Peter had escaped. This second century story of the "Enemy," or Saul, was inserted into the Acts' story as well. Why would the author of Acts include this telling information?

This leads us to a very probable scenario. Perhaps the Acts' version of the Stephen episode was really a composite of two different persecutions by Saul. When Paul was removed from the movement, he was seething mad. This is evident from his own letters (quoted above). The first attack on James, as recorded by the *Recognitions,* did not kill James. This very well may have occurred in the mid 40's. It is interesting that two of Judas the Galilean's sons were also crucified about this time. Could Saul have had a hand in the attack on James and the crucifixions of Simon and James, the sons of Judas the

Galilean? The later stoning of James was the second attack, and it too found a place in the contorted history of Acts.

One other point must be made. In Acts chapter 6, hellenized Christians assumed some of the Church's responsibilities. Stephen, Philip and a few others have been a cherished scholarly explanation for the spread of Christianity. Now, if the Stephen story was a rewrite of the stoning of James, then is it possible that there was never a hellenized Christian group in Jerusalem? In addition, Philip's evangelization of the Eunuch (Acts 8:26-40) was also a rewrite of the King Izates conversion. Thus, the two stories behind this hellenized Christian wing never really happened. Using our common sense and knowing what we do about the Fourth Philosophy, a hellenized Christian group would not have been tolerated in Jerusalem. So why was this group introduced in Acts? The answer once again comes back to Paul. The author of Acts needed to predate Paul's ideas. The baptism of the Holy Spirit and the substitution of water baptism for circumcision needed to be established so that future worshippers would not give such credit to a later apostle. However, according to Paul's own words, his Gospel came through revelation, not from any man. Thus, we know that the earlier accounts in Acts about Philip and Stephen were not true.

The beginning of Paul's career within the Jewish Christian movement, as described by Acts, was shown to be lacking in truth. The same can be proved about his latter days. The second passage concerning Saul comes from Josephus' *Jewish War*, where Saul was a member of the Peace Party, around 66 CE.

So seeing that the insurrection was now beyond their control and that the vengeance of Rome would fall upon them first, the most influential citizens determined to establish their own innocence and sent delegations to Florus and Agrippa, the former led by Simon, son of Ananias, the other distinguished by the inclusion of **Saul, Antipas, and Costobar, kinsmen of the king.** They begged both to come to the City [Jerusalem] with large forces and suppress the insurrection before it got beyond control. (*War* 2.418-419) (Emphasis mine)

Once again, Saul teamed up with Costabar and another relative named Antipas. They were sent to their kinsman, Agrippa II, to petition for an army to help suppress the insurrection. This request had nothing to do with spiritual matters, but was simply an attempt to combat the more radical elements of the Fourth Philosophy. How was Saul viewed by the insurgents? If he were once a member of their movement, then they would have viewed him as a traitor. This type of treachery followed his earlier approval of James' stoning in 62 CE. Surely, this Saul was developing a strong negative tradition. According to

Eisenman, Saul was the "Liar" of the Dead Sea Scrolls and he certainly could be equated with the *Recognition's* "Enemy." I will go them one better: the life of Saul or Paul was also the foundation for the traitor story, later attached to Judas Iscariot. (Judas Iscariot was a fictional character as will be proved in Part III – Chapter 17.)

The rewrite of Acts 25:13 - 26:32 had Paul also meeting with Agrippa II. In this account, Festus discussed Paul's case with Agrippa, and Agrippa agreed to hear Paul's plea. Instead of the above mentioned call for arms against the insurgents, Paul's defense before Agrippa recalled his conversion to the Way and his hope for Agrippa's acceptance of his version of Christianity. This is truly amazing considering we have already proved that the Acts' version of Saul's conversion was simply a combination of later persecutions by Saul. And it is safe to say that Paul's Christianity was diametrically opposed to the movement once led by James. So, in both accounts, Saul/Paul was trying to convince Agrippa of his own personal viewpoint. The Acts' version of events does conveniently hide the fact that Paul and Agrippa were kinsmen. This sleight-of-hand was necessary to remove Paul from the petty politics of the time, and to remove him from the actual history of Saul as related by Josephus.

Thus, the meeting with Agrippa was turned into a spiritual discussion. It also set the stage for Paul's alleged trip to Rome and his appeal to Caesar. According to Acts, Agrippa told Festus: "This man is not doing anything that deserves death or imprisonment. ...[He] could have been set free if he had not appealed to Caesar." (Acts 26:31-32) This concocted statement had two main goals: first, Paul was deemed innocent of any crimes which the Jews had lodged against him, and second, this appeal to Caesar was necessary to get Paul out of town. Remember, Saul (Paul) was viewed by the Jewish Christians (Fourth Philosophy) as a liar, an enemy and as a traitor, in that he supported the death of James. It was paramount in importance to remove Paul from the scene of the crime. That is why the author of Acts sent Paul to Rome. But as we shall soon see, Paul never went to Rome.

In another interesting story related by Josephus, the ambassadors that had been sent to Agrippa returned to Jerusalem, where they hid from the insurgents, taking cover in the Upper Palace. (*War* 2.425-429) They later fled the city around 66 CE.

After this calamity had befallen Cestius, many of the most eminent of the Jews swam away from the city, as from a ship when it is going to sink; **Costobarus, therefore, and Saul, who were brethren**, together with Philip, the son of Jacimus, whom was the commander of King Agrippa's forces, **ran away from the city, and went to Cestius**. But then how Antipas, who had been besieged with them in the king's palace, but would not fly away with them, was afterwards slain by the seditious. (*War* 2.556-557) (Emphasis mine)

Saul and his brother escaped from Jerusalem with their lives while Antipas stayed and perished. That Saul was besieged by the Jews should not surprise us. He had been the Fourth Philosophy's thorn in the flesh for over twenty years. (Paul was removed from the movement in 44 CE.) Saul's protector, after he fled the city, was the Roman commander Cestius. So, in Josephus' version of events, Saul escaped from the murderous Jews and found refuge with the Romans.

In the book of Acts, Paul had been mobbed at the Temple and sought protection from the Jews. In a dramatic speech to the Jews, Paul explained his earliest contact with the Way; how he had persecuted them with great zeal. He then related his conversion experience on the road to Damascus, at which time he received instruction in the Way by Ananias. Later, he returned to Jerusalem but was told in a vision to leave the city and go to the Gentiles, who would listen to him (and God). (Acts 22:1-21) (It should be noted that the three conversion stories in Acts do not reconcile to Paul's own account in Galatians.) This statement that Paul was sent to the Gentiles drove the Jews mad; they intended to kill him. Paul's ally in his escape from the Jews was the Roman commander, who had just learned that Paul possessed Roman citizenship. This revelation saved Paul from the mob and into the protective arms of the Roman procurator, Felix (58-60 CE). It is interesting to note that Paul's nephew helped uncover an assassination plot against Paul (Acts 23:16). Two points tie this to Josephus' account. First, a family member was aiding Paul just as Costobar had done in the actual escape from Jerusalem. Second, an assassination would have been carried out by the Sicarii, members of the Fourth Philosophy, the same people that killed Antipas and would have killed Saul and Costobar if they had caught them stealing out of the city.

Both Saul and Paul escaped into the arms of the Romans. Josephus had Saul fleeing from the Fourth Philosophy (**Jewish Christians**) from the **Upper Palace**, while Acts had Paul escaping from the **Jews** at the **Temple**. Acts always put a spiritual spin to Paul's actions; the Jewish Christians became the Jews while the place of refuge was transformed from the unspiritual Upper Palace to the Holy Temple. One thing is perfectly clear: the Acts account never happened! Consider these two points. First, Paul supposedly went to the Temple to assure James that he did not forsake the Jewish covenant. But as already detailed, Paul had been removed from the movement in 44 CE, had been party to James' stoning in 62 CE, and vehemently opposed the Everlasting covenant with the Jews. (See Galatians.) If this had occurred in 58 CE, James would have had nothing to do with Paul. Second, according to Paul's own letters, the Temple no longer had any spiritual meaning. If Paul really did return to the Temple, then at best, he was being extremely hypocritical. Placing Paul at the Temple was absurd, for the Jewish Christians believed him to be a liar and the enemy of the law. The only safe place for Paul in Jerusalem would have been the Upper Palace of King Agrippa.

As with the other stories, the writer of Acts was careful to place Paul in an earlier timeframe. The 58 CE arrest was four years before the stoning of James and eight years before the start of the Jewish war. To further cement its fictitious timeline, Acts had people confusing Paul with the Egyptian, a wonder-worker who led a failed revolt at the Mount of Olives around 58 CE. (*Ant.* 20.169-172 and Acts 21:38) The Acts' timeline cannot be correct as Saul escaped the Jews around 66 CE, many years after the death of James and the time of the Egyptian.

The last mention of Saul by Josephus occurred in 66-67 CE. Saul was sent as an emissary to Caesar to shift blame from himself and his cronies to the Roman procurator, Florus.

> However, Cestius sent Saul and his friends, **at their own desire**, to Achia. to Nero, to inform him of the great distress they were in; and to lay the blame of their kindling the war upon Florus, as hoping to alleviate his own danger, by provoking his indignation against Florus. (*War* 2.558) (Emphasis mine)

In this final passage about Saul, the following should be noted. Saul requested to see Nero in order to shift the blame from Cestius and himself to Florus. This voluntary request was similar to Paul's appeal to Caesar in Acts 26:32. In both stories, Saul (Paul) wanted to lay his case before Caesar. In Acts, Paul was blamed for causing a disruption in Jerusalem because of his misunderstood antinomian gospel. According to the Roman procurator, Festus, and Agrippa II, Paul was an innocent man. In Josephus, Saul also claimed his innocence to Nero concerning the kindling of the Jewish war. The location of the meeting should also be of great interest. According to the *War,* Saul traveled to Greece to meet Nero, while Acts sent Paul to Rome. Obviously, Paul never traveled to Rome and was never imprisoned there.

Who reigned as Caesar in 66-67 CE? The ruler of the world was none other than the madman, Nero. Saul (Paul) had appealed to Nero in both scenarios, in 66-67 CE in Achia and in 60-62 CE in Rome, per the *War* and Acts respectively. In 64 CE, a great fire consumed the city of Rome. Many claimed that Nero had started the fire, so that he could rebuild the city with his own architectural plans. Nero, however, knew that the politics of this was dangerous, so he made the Jewish Christians scapegoats, saying that they had started the fire. No one will ever know for sure who started the fire, but we do know that the punishment of the Jewish Christians included the following:

Besides being put to death they were made to serve as objects of amusement; they were clad in the hides of beasts and torn to death by dogs; others were crucified, others set on fire to serve to illuminate the night when daylight failed. (Tacitus, *Annals*, xv. 44)

Nero tortured these Jewish Christians to such an extent that the population felt sympathy for them, even though they were deemed "a class hated for their abominations." This was Nero, the Caesar whom Saul requested to meet. This meeting was not to chastise Nero for the slaughter, but rather to shift blame from himself to another. Saul could bargain with the devil. After all, he had always sided with the powerful. The letter to the Romans stated:

Everyone must submit himself to the governing authorities, for there is no authority except that which God has established. The authorities that exist have been established by God. Consequently, he who rebels against the authority is rebelling against what God has instituted, and those that do so will bring judgment on themselves. ...This is also why you pay taxes, for the authorities are God's servants, who give their full time to governing. (Romans 13:1-7)

The apostle Paul wrote that all government was established by God and the authorities were God's servants. If this were written around 40 CE or shortly thereafter, then this good-citizen philosophy would have coincided with the regime of Caligula, an equal to Nero in sadistic behavior. As it turned out, Paul's regard for justice and equality was nonexistent, in that he regarded both Caligula and Nero as God's servants. What a sick and perverted mentality!

As noted earlier, Acts sent Paul to Rome in 60-62 CE to remove him from the scene of the crime, or the stoning of James the Just. This trip to Rome was also necessary to help concoct an early death for the apostle, a few years before Josephus' history of Saul. Not even the most ardent supporter of Paul (then and now) could have approved of his meeting with Nero in 66-67 CE, after the great fire of Rome. So a nice ending was written for Paul. Along with Peter, Paul conveniently suffered martyrdom in Rome around 64 CE. So both great Church leaders supposedly died in Rome. Although Cephas (Peter) may very well have been killed in Rome (who knows), Paul definitely was not. Saul (Paul) met with the monster, Nero, in Achia, not Rome, in 66-67 CE.

From the above four accounts concerning Saul in Josephus, we get a much different picture of the great apostle to the Gentiles. This Saul sided with the authorities, hell-bent on destroying the Fourth Philosophy (Jewish Christianity). The book of Acts was simply a complete misrepresentation of the facts concerning Paul's life. The writer of Acts put Paul's later life in the 58-62 CE timeframe in order to distance him from the history of Josephus' Saul. Yet, the real Saul (Paul) worked with the ruling authorities at the time of James' murder (62 CE). He also rubbed elbows with Agrippa and Nero, always working against the Jewish Christians, those fanatics who removed him from their numbers at Antioch, in 44 CE.

PAUL AND ACTS

It is traditionally assumed that the writings of Paul and the Acts of the Apostles go hand-in-hand. In fact, the Acts of the Apostles was primarily the acts of Paul, with only slight mention of the other apostles. And even then, these other apostles learned to accept Paul's new gospel. For example, Peter learned to accept Gentiles in Acts chapter 10, even though the earthly Jesus never taught him these things. As noted above, invented characters such as Stephen, Philip, and Ananias mouthed the philosophy of Paul even though they supposedly predated him. The fallibility of Acts is obvious, but a comparison of Paul's writings to that of Acts may flesh out some truth.

Four main areas of divergence exist between the letters of Paul and Acts: at the conversion of Saul, at the Council of Jerusalem, the argument between Paul and Cephas at Antioch and concerning the famine relief to Jerusalem.

1. The Conversion of Saul

A. Acts 8:1-3; 9:1-2 and Gal. 1:13 - Persecution of the Church

Acts and Galatians both recount Paul's initial persecution of the Jewish Christian movement. Acts stated that:

Saul began to destroy the church. Going from house to house, he dragged off men and women and put them in prison. ...He went to the high priest and asked him for letters to the synagogues in Damascus, so that if he found any there who belonged to the Way, whether men or women, he might take them as prisoners to Jerusalem. (Acts 8:3; 9:1-2)

Paul's hatred for the Way, or the Way of Righteousness, was not hidden. In fact, Acts made Paul into a super-policeman. Note also that Paul worked for the high priest, who was appointed by the Herodians. The author of Acts may have unintentionally connected Paul to the ruling authorities. Considering what we have already seen, Paul was a kinsman to Agrippa. Therefore, any passage declaring Paul to be a Pharisee should be questioned.

Now Paul's version differs only slightly, but each discrepancy will loom large in our study.

For you have heard of my previous way of life in Judaism, how intensely I persecuted the church of God and tried to destroy it. I was advancing in Judaism beyond many Jews of my own age and was extremely zealous for the traditions of my fathers. (Gal. 1:13-14)

Paul and Acts had one main point of agreement: Paul did violently persecute the Church. However, Paul gave no details concerning this persecution. As discussed earlier, the account in Acts mirrored a later persecution by Saul after the stoning of James in 62 CE. (*Ant.* 20.214) A passage from the *Recognitions* also corresponds to the Acts' version, this perhaps happening in the mid 40's. So is it possible that Saul/Paul persecuted the Church three times: right before his conversion, shortly after Paul's removal from the movement at Antioch (44 CE) and once again, near the twilight of his career, in 62 CE? As I have said before, there existed a strong tradition associated with a betrayal. The New Testament turned a Jewish apostle, Judas Iscariot, into the traitor, but I believe the label originally belonged to Paul.

The main difference in the above stories concerns Saul's motivation. In Acts, the high priest was behind the stoning of Stephen, and Saul consorted with this high priest to obtain letters to arrest members of the Way. As we have seen, Stephen's stoning did not occur before Saul's conversion. In Galatians, Paul blamed the whole persecution on his zealotry for the traditions of his fathers. This, too, may not have been the entire truth. Saul may have been zealous, but not with the same zealotry exhibited by the Fourth Philosophy (Way of Righteousness or Jewish Christianity). The reason for this sleight-of-hand is obvious: Paul wanted his Gentile audience to consider him an equal or superior to the Jewish Apostles. Thus, even though Paul now rejected the law, he once followed it closer than any of the other apostles. Put another way, Paul had been zealous for the law, like Cephas and James, but that was before his enlightenment from the Risen Christ. This makes Paul look very big in comparison to James and the other apostles. Remember, the letter to the Galatians was written to prop up Paul's image among this particular Gentile community. They had heard of Cephas' argument with Paul and the resulting expulsion from the movement. Paul had to give them his side of the story, even if biased. They would have known no better.

B. Acts 9:1-30 and Gal. 1:15-17 - Damascus

The story of Saul's conversion on his way to Damascus is familiar to most Bible students. The Lord appeared to him in a vision, and from that point on, Saul followed Jesus. He was led by the hand into the city of Damascus, as the confrontation with the Risen Jesus had temporarily blinded him. There he met Ananias and other disciples of the Way, and the Holy Spirit came upon him. At that moment, Saul transformed into Paul, champion of the Christian movement.

However, Paul's account of his own conversion differs considerably.

But when God, who set me apart from birth and called me by his grace, was pleased to reveal his Son in me so that I might preach him among the Gentiles, I did not consult any man, nor did I go up to Jerusalem to see those who were apostles before I was, but I went immediately into Arabia and later returned to Damascus. (Gal. 1:15-17)

According to Paul, he did not consult any man, for his vision of Jesus had made him the apostle to the Gentiles. There was no need to get approval from Cephas or James or any other man, for Paul had the approval of the Risen Christ, a far higher authority than any man. No doubt, Paul twisted the truth in order to impress his Gentile audience. Remember, Paul was giving his side of the Antioch confrontation, with himself as God's chosen instrument. This being understood, the difference between Paul's account and the Acts' version is huge. While the Acts' account had Saul being taught by others, Paul said he was taught by the Risen Jesus. This means that Paul's gospel was original to him alone and had nothing to do with the earlier hellenized Christian Jews such as Stephen, Philip and Ananias. Christianity, as we know it today, did not start with Jesus, or with the crucifixion of Jesus but rather with the conversion of Saul.

Saul's sojourn into Arabia was omitted by Acts, but there may be some truth here. Saul may have been sorting out his vision of Jesus into a coherent gospel. This wilderness commune with God also raised Paul to the level of the prophets of old. After this time in the desert (a week, a month or a year?), Saul headed to Damascus with his new gospel. Paul never mentioned the helping hands of Ananias or Judas. These men were either not central to his message or were never part of his conversion. To Paul, his conversion centered upon him and the Risen Christ.

Should we believe Paul's account or the story in Acts? My guess is that neither account was entirely true or entirely false. Paul was placing his own present views (44 CE) upon a young convert (22-25 CE). He did this to show that his message was superior to that of James and Cephas. On the other hand,

Acts made Paul into a follower of the new faith, not the inventor. The entire hellenized Jewish Christian movement of Jerusalem was meant to predate Paul's conversion, so that a continuity of belief could be proved. This was the fundamental modus operandi of Acts: moving the Jewish Christians from the law to the gospel of Paul. Note that Peter moved towards Paul's position in Acts chapter 10.

C. Acts 9:19-26 and 2 Cor. 11:32-33 - Escape from Damascus

The story of Paul's escape from Damascus through a window in the wall demonstrates Acts' working method of changing a fact here or there to come up with something completely new.

After many days had gone by, the Jews conspired to kill him [Paul], but Saul learned of their plan. Day and night they kept close watch on the city gates in order to kill him. But his followers took him by night and lowered him in a basket through an opening in the wall. When he came to Jerusalem, he tried to join the disciples, but they were all afraid of him, not believing that he really was a disciple. (Acts 9:23-26)

It is interesting to note that this supposedly occurred a few days after Saul's conversion. By Paul's own admission in Galatians 1:17-18, he "went immediately into Arabia and later returned to Damascus". Then after three years, Paul made his first post conversion trip to Jerusalem. In the above passage, Paul went immediately to Damascus and then left for Jerusalem after escaping the clutches of the evil Jews. Certainly, the chronology in Acts cannot be reconciled to Paul's own account. But why should Acts change Paul's own account? The answer is quite clear: Acts tried to vilify the Jews in the Paul saga, just as the Gospels tried to pin the crucifixion of Jesus upon the Jews, even though crucifixion was the Roman punishment for sedition.

To further refute the Acts' version of events, Paul also wrote about the escape from Damascus.

In Damascus the governor under Aretas had the city of the Damascenes guarded in order to arrest me. But I was lowered in a basket from a window in the wall and slipped through his hands. (2 Cor. 11:32-33)

The antagonist in Paul's story was King Aretas, not the Jews. Paul's purpose for relaying the story was to set forth the many trials and tribulations that he had endured for the sake of his gospel. Paul felt it necessary to brag about his accomplishments because he was contending with Cephas and

James for control of his own churches. By the time Paul wrote 2 Corinthians, he hated the Jerusalem Pillars with a passion, comparing these super-apostles with Satan himself (2 Cor. 11:1-15). So, it is quite revealing that Paul blamed Aretas and not the Jews for his predicament in Damascus. If anyone had reason to hate the Jews, it would have been Paul. But Paul placed the blame squarely upon King Aretas.

Now King Aretas' relations with the Herodians were very poor. Josephus wrote how the people believed that the destruction of Herod Antipas' army in his fight with Aretas had been a sign from God. This was because Herod Antipas had John the Baptist killed. (*Ant.* 18.116-119) Thus, at the time of Paul's escape, the wounds inflicted upon the Baptist and on Aretas would have been fresh. The fact that Aretas was trying to catch a well-known Herodian (Saul) should not surprise us. So, in this instance, Paul's account rings true while the Acts' version appears to be a rewrite to shift blame from Aretas to the Jews.

The chronology of this escape should also be examined. In Acts, Saul was converted around 31-35 CE, and he supposedly escaped from Damascus a few days after his conversion. This is interesting considering John the Baptist was not put to death before 35-36 CE. This question should be raised: was the escape from Damascus at the beginning or at the end of Paul's career? Paul himself stated that he went to Damascus after his conversion, but did he go there later in his career as well?

King Aretas' war with Herod Antipas occurred after Herod divorced the daughter of Aretas in favor of Herodias, his brother Philip's wife. (*Ant.*18.109-115) (Matt. 14:1-12) According to Matthew, John the Baptist was imprisoned because he criticized Herod Antipas for taking his brother's wife. This story was also told in the Slavonic Josephus (After *War* 2.168). This criticism goaded Herod into arresting John, a man with a huge following. Herod eventually put John to death as he feared that the Baptist's followers would rebel. (*Ant.* 18.116-119) This occurred around 35-36 CE.

Shortly after the Baptist's death, King Aretas defeated the army of Herod Antipas, and the people viewed the defeat as punishment for his murder of John. (*Ant.* 18.119). Thus, the dating for Aretas' war with Antipas can be placed at 36-37 CE. It is also fact that this Aretas ruled until 40 CE. Therefore, the altercation with Paul had to be between 37-40 CE. As we have already shown, Saul (Paul) was a member of the Herodian family (*Ant.* 20.214). Further evidence of this relationship will be detailed later in this chapter.

If Paul's escape from Damascus occurred between 37-40 CE, then it could not have been at the beginning of Paul's career within the Jewish Christian movement. Most scholars place Paul's conversion between 31-35

CE, because any later date plays havoc with the traditional timeline. If Paul's conversion occurred as late as 38 CE, then the Council of Jerusalem could not have convened until 55 CE (17 years after Paul's conversion, per Gal. 1:18-2:1). This would have been impossible as Acts 18:2 described the expulsion of Jews from Rome during the reign of Claudius. Since Claudius reigned from 41-54 CE, the chronology of Acts would be completely destroyed.

This is what probably happened. After the Council of Jerusalem, around 38 CE (Paul's later career), Paul went to Damascus. The governor under King Aretas was informed that a Herodian was staying within the city's walls. His orders to capture Paul prompted Paul's escape as explained in 2 Cor. 11:32-33. This was one detail which stood out in Paul's mind, due to its recent occurrence. His other exploits in 2 Cor. 11 were general in nature, with no times or places mentioned. This escape took place **after** the Council of Jerusalem but before Paul's break from the movement in 44 CE.

2. The Council of Jerusalem

A. Acts 15:1-5 and Gal. 2:1-5 - The Trip to Jerusalem

Some men came down from Judea to Antioch and were teaching the brothers: "Unless you are circumcised, according to the customs taught by Moses, you cannot be saved." This brought Paul and Barnabas into sharp dispute and debate with them. So Paul and Barnabas were appointed, along with some other believers, to go up to Jerusalem to see the apostles and elders about this question. The church sent them on their way, and as they traveled through Phoenicia and Samaria, they told how the Gentiles had been converted. This news made all the brothers glad. When they came to Jerusalem, they were welcomed by the church and the apostles and elders, to whom they reported everything God had done through them. Then some of the believers who belonged to the party of the Pharisees stood up and said, "The Gentiles must be circumcised and required to obey the law of Moses." (Acts 15:1-5)

Fourteen years later I went up again to Jerusalem, this time with Barnabas. I took Titus along also. **I went in response to a revelation** and set before them the gospel that I preach among the Gentiles. But I did this privately to those who seemed to be leaders, for fear that I was running or had run my race in vain. Yet not even Titus, who was with me, was compelled to be circumcised, even though he was a Greek. This matter arose because some false brothers had infiltrated our ranks to spy on the freedom we have in Christ Jesus and to make us slaves. We did not give into them for a moment, so that the truth of the gospel might remain with you. (Gal. 2:1-5) (Emphasis mine)

Five fundamental differences can be noted concerning these two accounts. First and foremost, was the Council before or after the conflict at Antioch? In Acts, the disagreement at Antioch between those sent from Judea and Paul **preceded** the Council of Jerusalem. Acts simply made the conflict between James and Paul disappear, as the Council decided the argument in Paul's favor. In Galatians, the conflict at Antioch occurred **after** the Council. This raises the question: why did James renege on his pledge to Paul made at the Council? This will be answered as the passages are further explored.

Second, Paul claimed that he met those "who seemed to be leaders" in **private**. In Acts, Paul was welcomed by the church with great acclaim. In the open, Paul reported about his activities among the Gentiles and all, except a party of the Pharisees, praised God for his successes. This question of private versus public is a very important issue. If the meeting was in private as Paul stated, then Paul could have easily misrepresented his views. In 1 Cor. 9:19-23, Paul described his techniques in dealing with different groups. He stated: "To the Jews I became as a Jew, to win the Jews. To those under the law I became like one under the law (though I myself am not under the law), so as to win those under the law." This is a very cynical way to deal with other people. Paul pretended to be under the law, even though he claimed he was not under the law. So what did Paul actually say to the leaders which garnered support for his ministry? Did he tell them the entire truth or did he tell them what he knew they wanted to hear?

Third, to his audience in Galatia, Paul wanted to stress his importance versus the Pillar apostles. When speaking of James and Cephas, Paul referred to them as those "who seemed to be leaders." This was Paul's way of comparing his credentials to those lowly Jerusalem apostles. Had these Jerusalem leaders ever conversed with the Risen Christ as he had done? Of course not! Remember, Paul was fighting for control of his churches in Galatia. News of the incident at Antioch had surely reached their ears, and they were certainly questioning Paul's legitimacy within the movement. Paul was simply telling them that he had the truth, not the Jerusalem apostles.

Fourth, how did Acts deal with those opposing Paul, those members of the circumcision party? In Galatians 1:12, Paul identified the circumcision group as those sent by James. In Acts, the circumcision was identified as members of a group of Pharisees. Thus, Acts decoupled the circumcision group from James. This was done so that James could later approve of Paul's message. In reality, James had become a bitter opponent of Paul. The Gospels and Acts were consistent in their denigration of the Pharisees. This treatment distanced the early Church from the Pharisees, even though Judas and Sadduc (Jesus and John) were Pharisees.

The fifth point concerns the reason why the Council was ordered. In Acts, the church at Antioch sent Paul and Barnabas to Jerusalem to answer the question of Gentile participation in the movement. (Again, Acts placed the conflict in Antioch before the Council of Jerusalem.) In Gal. 2:1-2, Paul stated that he went to Jerusalem in "response to a revelation." So, which scenario is to be believed? Certainly, Paul's account is more believable, since his story at least placed the Council before his conflict with Cephas at Antioch. And it should be noted that Paul stated that his trip to Jerusalem was due to a revelation, a word from God. There was no ruling body from Antioch which had the authority to order him about. Only the Risen Christ had authority over Paul.

B. Peter and Cornelius

The apostles and elders met to consider this question [Must the Gentiles be circumcised and ordered to follow the law of Moses?]. After much discussion, Peter got up and addressed them: "Brothers, you know that some time ago God made a choice among you that the Gentiles might hear from my lips the message of the gospel and believe. God, who knows the heart, showed that he accepted them by giving the Holy Spirit to them, just as he did to us. He made no distinction between us and them, for he purified their hearts by faith. Now then, why do you try to test God by putting on the necks of the disciples a yoke that neither we nor our fathers have been able to bear? No! We believe it is through the grace of our Lord Jesus that we are saved, just as they are." (Acts 15:6-11)

The purpose of Acts becomes clear in the above passage. Peter recalled his encounter with the Gentile, Cornelius. In Acts 10, Peter was given insights from a dream (or from Jesus) to accept unclean food as clean. He later interpreted this as God's desire for him to accept the unclean Gentiles as worthy of salvation. In short, this Peter/Cornelius event confirmed the Pauline mission to the Gentiles. How convenient! The Jerusalem Pillars were moving towards Paul's gospel, abandoning the teachings of the earthly Jesus.

However, a close examination of the Cornelius meeting shows that this Gentile conversion was simply a rewrite of an event recorded by Josephus.

Accordingly, he [Agrippa I] loved to live continually at Jerusalem, and was exactly careful in the observance of the laws of his country. He therefore kept himself entirely pure: nor did any day pass over his head without its appointed sacrifice. However, there was a certain man of the Jewish nation at Jerusalem, who appeared to be very accurate in the knowledge of the law. His **name**

was Simon. This man got together an assembly, while the king was absent at Caesarea, and had the insolence to accuse him as not living holily, and that he might justly **be excluded out of the temple, since it belonged only to native Jews.** But the general of Agrippa's army informed him, that Simon had made such a speech to the people. So the **king sent for him**; and, as he was then sitting in the theater, he bade him sit down by him, and said to him with a low and gentile voice, "What is done in this place that is contrary to the law?" But he had nothing to say for himself, but begged his pardon. So the king was more easily reconciled to him than one could have imagined, as esteeming mildness a better quality in a king than anger; and knowing that moderation is more becoming in great men than passion. So he made Simon a small present, and dismissed him. (*Ant.* 19.331-334) (Emphasis mine)

In the above passage, Simon preached that King Agrippa should be excluded from the Temple since he was not a native Jew. This was certainly a policy of exclusion. When Agrippa was informed of this, he ordered that Simon be brought to him in Caesarea. Josephus made it appear that Agrippa was very gentile with Simon, but more likely, Agrippa interrogated Simon. Like Jesus before Pilate, Simon remained silent as a way to protect his followers.

The Peter and Cornelius episode recorded in Acts 10, repeated in Acts 11 and finally used in Acts 15 (Council of Jerusalem) has several points in common with the Agrippa passage. First, the names of the preachers were the same, Simon Peter and Simon. In fact, Peter was called Simon by the Holy Spirit (Acts 10:19). Both Peter and Simon believed that Gentiles were not to be part of the covenant. Simon wanted to exclude Agrippa while Peter just assumed that the Gentiles were unclean. In the Acts' story, Peter had a vision which turned his whole outlook around. This vision actually connected Peter with Paul. After all, Paul claimed in Gal. 1:12: "I did not receive it [gospel] from any man, nor was I taught it; rather, I received it by revelation from Jesus Christ." In short, Peter had a Pauline revelation. Could this have really happened? Of course not!

When Agrippa heard that Simon preached against his use of the Temple, he immediately had Simon brought to Caesarea. According to Josephus, Agrippa was "careful in the observance of the laws of his country." In Acts, Cornelius was told in a dream to have Peter brought to Caesarea. Like Agrippa, Cornelius was "a righteous and God fearing man, respected by all the Jewish people." (Acts 10:22) In short, Acts substituted Cornelius for Agrippa, one righteous Gentile for one righteous half-Jew. It is interesting that the writer of Acts did not even attempt to disguise this episode, as both stories had a Simon being brought to Caesarea.

The purpose of this rewrite was no different than the mythical hellinized

Jerusalem group described in Acts 6-8. In both cases, the Jews were being brought towards the Pauline position. In fact, even though Paul was not a major physical player in the first half of Acts, his gospel was being touted throughout. In the case of Simon Peter and Cornelius, an historical exclusionary event (the barring of Agrippa from the Temple) was turned into an inclusionary event (the acceptance of Gentiles into the movement.) Nothing could have been farther from the truth.

C. The Outcome of the Council

In Acts 15:12-18, Paul told the Jews the wonderful signs and miracles that had been performed among the Gentiles. This was added to the powerful message already provided by Peter. After quoting the prophets, James spoke:

"It is my judgment, therefore, that we should not make it difficult for the Gentiles who are turning to God. Instead we should write to them, telling them to abstain from food polluted by idols, from sexual immorality, from the meat of strangled animals and from blood. For Moses has been preached in every city from the earliest times and is read in the synagogues on every Sabbath." (Acts 15:19-21)

After this, Judas and Silas were chosen to accompany Paul and Barnabas to deliver a letter to the church in Antioch. The letter contained the above message from James. Compare this supposed history to the letter of Galatians.

As for those who seemed to be important - whatever they were makes no difference to me; God does not judge by external appearances - those men added nothing to my message. On the contrary, they saw that I had been given the task of preaching the gospel to the Gentiles, just as Peter had been given the task of preaching the gospel to the Jews. For God, who was at work in the ministry of Peter as an apostle to the Jews, was also at work in my ministry as an apostle to the Gentiles. James, Peter and John, those reputed to be pillars, gave me and Barnabas the right hand of fellowship when they recognized the grace given to me. They agreed that we should go to the Gentiles, and they to the Jews. All they asked was that we should remember the poor, the very thing I was eager to do. (Gal. 2:6-10)

Paul's account has several important threads which help decipher this whole situation. First, Paul made every effort to minimize the importance of Cephas and James. When mentioning these Jewish leaders, Paul stated that they "seemed to be important," but they added absolutely nothing to his message, his gospel to the Gentiles. This was central in Paul's line of defense. He had to be superior to these Jewish leaders, at least in the eyes of his Gentile audience.

Second, Paul was drawing a comparison between himself and Cephas, and also between his gospel and the other gospel. Paul stated that these Jewish leaders recognized the grace given him by God and therefore had left the Gentile ministry to him alone. This exclusiveness was omitted in the Acts' version.

Third, Paul stated that the task of preaching the Jewish message was given to Cephas (Peter). As mentioned earlier, it is possible that this Council of Jerusalem had more on its agenda than Paul's Gentile mission. After the death of John the Baptist in 36 CE, James became the leader of the movement. He had the problem of uniting the various elements which had grown up around several charismatic leaders. The John crowd had to be brought under his control. This council may have been a meeting which outlined James' new approach to spreading the message of "Jesus". (This can be dated at between 36-39 CE). Note that Cephas (Peter) was given the task of preaching the message to the Jews. From what we know of Cephas from Galatians and Corinthians, he was traveling about the Roman Empire preaching the revolutionary message of Jesus, or of the Fourth Philosophy. He was not overly concerned with the Gentile message. In fact, the so-called commission of Paul as the apostle to the Gentiles, may have been of very low importance. James would have been primarily concerned with the spread of the message throughout the Jewish world. However, to Paul, his message to the Gentiles was the focus of the meeting.

Fourth, according to Paul, he was to collect monies for the poor in Jerusalem. This is exactly what Paul was doing. However, the argument between Cephas and Paul may have put a damper on his collections. That is why it was so important for Paul to tell the Galatians that his money collecting effort was part of an agreement between James and himself. He did not want to be accused of taking the money for his own purposes. Paul's own background of corruption may have been part of the attack on him. (This will be explained further in the next section, Paul and Josephus.)

3. The Argument at Antioch between Paul and Cephas

The argument between Paul and Cephas was a turning point in the history of the movement. According to Paul, this occurred **after** the Council of Jerusalem and resulted in a final split between his gospel and the inferior gospel of James and Cephas. However, this split was entirely whitewashed by the book of Acts. In Acts, the question of fellowship with Gentiles occurred **before** the Council.

Some men came down from Judea to Antioch and were teaching the brothers: "Unless you are circumcised, according to the custom taught be Moses, you cannot be saved." This brought Paul and Barnabas into sharp dispute and debate with them. So Paul and Barnabas were appointed along with some other believers, to go up to Jerusalem to see the apostles and elders about this question. ...We have heard that some went out from us **without our authorization** and disturbed you, troubling your minds by what they said. ... Some time later Paul said to Barnabas, Let us go back and visit the brothers in all the towns where we preached the word of the Lord and see how they are doing." Barnabas wanted to take John, also called Mark, with them, but Paul did not think it wise to take him, because he had deserted them in Pamphylia and had not continued with them in their work. **They had such a sharp disagreement that they parted company.** (Acts 15:1-2; 36-39) (Emphasis mine)

I am astonished that you are so quickly deserting the one who called you by the grace of Christ and are turning to a different gospel - which is really no gospel at all. Evidently some people are throwing you into confusion and are trying to pervert the gospel of Christ. But even if we or an **angel from heaven should preach a gospel other than the one we preached to you, let him be eternally condemned!** (Gal. 1:6-8) (Emphasis mine)

When Peter came to Antioch, I opposed him to his face, because he was in the wrong. Before certain men **came from James**, he used to eat with the Gentiles. But when they arrived, he began to draw back and separate himself from the Gentiles because he was afraid of those who belonged to the circumcision group. The other Jews joined him in his hypocrisy, so that by their hypocrisy **even Barnabas was led astray**. (Gal. 2:11-13) (Emphasis mine)

It should be noted that the letter to the Galatians was a plea from Paul for his Gentile disciples to abandon a new and inferior gospel. Paul clearly stated that if anyone preached a gospel different from his own gospel, that this person would be eternally condemned, even if that person were an angel from heaven or perhaps an apostle from Jerusalem. This statement puts the rest of Galatians into perspective. Paul was trying to win back his disciples as they had been alienated by news from Antioch.

As mentioned earlier, Acts simply placed the confrontation before the Council of Jerusalem. Acts never mentioned an argument between Peter

(Cephas) and Paul. That would have put the Pillar Apostles of Jerusalem against Paul. Instead, Acts placed the blame on those who had not been authorized by James. So Acts not only misrepresented the timing of the argument but also changed the combatants.

Paul's account, though biased, is much closer to the truth. He portrayed the Jews as hypocrites and himself as the hero of the Gentile Gospel. Paul clearly placed the Antioch argument as post Council. He stated that only after receiving news from James did Peter begin withdrawing from fellowship. What could have been in James' letter to produce such a reaction from Peter?

In 1 Corinthians 9:19-23, Paul admitted that his philosophy towards others was a bit dishonest. To Paul, this dishonesty was simply a way to win souls for Christ. Would we teach our children to act one way with one group and another way with a different group? A good parent would try to instill honesty and consistency with all people. But that was not Paul's way. He acted differently with the Jews than with the Gentiles. With the Jews, he pretended to be under the law, to follow the law with fervor, even though he stated that "I myself am not under the law." (1 Cor. 9:20)

It is very possible that Paul fooled James and Cephas at the Council of Jerusalem. Paul probably convinced the Pillars that he taught the Gentiles the way of the law, which included circumcision. This did not mean that all Gentiles had to be circumcised. Only those who wanted to become full participants with the Jewish nation had to submit to the whole law. All other Gentiles could have remained God-fearing or admirers of the Jews, just as Cornelius had been portrayed. (Acts 10:2) This would have been acceptable to the Jewish leaders. However, as one read Galatians, it becomes very clear that Paul never expected his Gentile followers to become full Jews. Instead, he taught them the gospel of faith, not the way of the law. "Now that faith has come, we are no longer under the supervision of the law." (Gal. 3:25)

Paul's real message eventually became known to James, and he sent out emissaries to combat Paul's gospel. These were the men who came from James. (Gal. 2:12) They informed Cephas (Peter) of Paul's actual gospel. This is what caused Cephas to withdraw from Paul's converts and from Paul himself. The jig was up. Paul was removed from the movement. The argument at Antioch was the official split between the Jerusalem apostles (James, Cephas and John) and Paul, the self proclaimed apostle to the Gentiles.

One other point should be noted. According to Paul, Barnabas was swayed by Cephas' argument and turned his back upon Paul's gospel. "The other Jews joined him [Cephas] in his hypocrisy, so that by their hypocrisy even Barnabas was led astray." (Gal. 2:13) This conflict was the reason why Barnabas and Paul parted company. However, the version of their parting in

Acts is quite different. According to Acts, they parted company because of an argument over John Mark. After this event, Barnabas was never mentioned again. Of course, the Acts' version was not history but an alternate storyline to cover-up the real reason behind the split.

4. The Famine

In Acts 11:27-30, the church at Antioch sent Paul to Jerusalem with famine relief.

During this time some prophets came down from Jerusalem to Antioch. One of them, named Agabus, stood up and through the Spirit predicted that a severe famine would spread over the entire Roman world. (This happened during the reign of Claudius.) The disciples, each according to his ability, decided to provide help for the brothers living in Judea. This they did, sending their gifts to the elders by Barnabas and Saul.

Acts has a window of opportunity here of 13 years for the famine. The reign of Claudius was from 41-54 CE. Josephus does narrow the gap by his mention of the famine in *Ant.* 20.101. "Under these procurators [Fadus and Tiberius Alexander] that great famine happened in Judea, in which queen Helena bought corn in Egypt at a great expense, and distributed it to those that were in want..." Fadus and Tiberius Alexander were procurators from 44-48 CE. This narrows the dating of the famine to the mid to later 40's. As mentioned before, Paul was already out of the movement by this time. If that were the case, then why did Acts have Paul go to Jerusalem for the famine relief effort?

Surely, helping those in need would be a feather in one's cap. Acts made Paul out to be a rescuer of the poor. But did Paul really do this? In Galatians, Paul only mentioned two visits to Jerusalem: one 3 years after his conversion and the other 14 years later at the Council of Jerusalem. The reason why Paul did not mention the famine visit was because it had not yet occurred. Even if Paul truly took part in the famine relief in Jerusalem, the timing of this visit has repercussions for the traditional timeline. If Galatians were written as traditionally supposed, then why did Paul not mention the visit? This would have been excellent propaganda. However, if Paul was ridden out of the movement at 44 CE as I have proposed, then he could not have known about a later visit: it had not yet occurred!

PAUL AND JOSEPHUS

There are two points of intersection between the writings of Paul and the *Antiquities*: one before Paul's conversion and the other at the end of his career with the Fourth Philosophy. The short description of Paul's beginnings will be compared to an unnamed Jew from Josephus' writings.

For you have heard of my previous way of life in Judaism, how intensely I persecuted the church of God and tried to destroy it. I was advancing in Judaism beyond many Jews of my own age and was extremely zealous for the traditions of my fathers. ...I was personally unknown to the churches of Judea that are in Christ. They only heard the report: "The man who formerly persecuted us is now preaching the faith he once tried to destroy." And they praised God because of me. (Gal. 1:13-14; 22-24)

Before we examine Paul's own account of his pre-conversion extremes, we must rid our minds of the picture of Paul as painted by Acts. As already shown, the book of Acts had no authentic information concerning the first persecution by Paul. In fact, Acts cobbled together two different accounts: the initial appearance of Saul was taken from *Ant.* 20.214, where Saul persecuted those weaker than himself after the stoning of James, and the second account was recorded in the *Recognitions* 1.70,71, where the "Enemy" attacked James. When combined, these two attacks on James served as a wonderful picture of evil. So, in consideration of this information, we must jettison our prior ideas about Saul's first persecution of the Church.

Since we cannot count on the book of Acts for this first persecution, we must turn to Paul's own letters. The passage from Galatians has been included above. Before considering Paul's account, we must realize that Paul wrote to a Gentile audience, who had heard of the conflict between Paul and Cephas. Even though Gentile, surely they had some conception of Cephas' importance within the movement. So when we read Paul, we must understand that Paul was in a competition with both Cephas and James for the Gentile's affections. Thus, he exaggerated his own importance as he downplayed the importance of the Pillar apostles. For example, Paul referred to the Pillars (James, Cephas and John) as those who **seemed** to be important.

With Paul's motives in mind, three points in his account should be considered. First, Paul emphasized his zealousness for the law, beyond that of his peers. This comparison is extremely revealing. In essence, Paul was comparing his pre-conversion self to that of James and Cephas. This could be rephrased as such: "Before I became one with Christ, I followed the law as zealously as Cephas and James." It should be noted that Paul's audience would not have known the truth of the matter. Their ignorance played to Paul's advantage.

Second, Paul claimed that he was personally unknown to the churches in Judea. This suggests that Paul was not in the area for an extended period of time during the persecution. What exactly did Paul do which so injured the Church? Paul does not say. He only said that the churches heard the report that "the man who formerly persecuted us is now preaching the faith he once tried to destroy." Although we cannot know what Paul actually did to the faith, we do know that the faith forgave him for his actions. If Saul's persecution occurred after the death of Jesus (Judas the Galilean), then his conversion took place during the leadership of John the Baptist (the Sadduc). The forgiveness of Saul makes perfect sense during this forgiveness phase of the Fourth Philosophy.

Third, Paul claimed that the people "praised God because of me." (Gal. 1:24) If Paul were just an ordinary Jew or even a Pharisee, his turnaround would not have been so miraculous. However, as suggested above, Saul was a Herodian. If this were the case, then the conversion of Saul was, in effect, like the conversion of an important figure within the opposition party. How strange that a Herodian would deny his own family's right to govern and throw his lot in with the "troublemakers!"

The passage from Josephus which may detail the early years of Saul can be dated to approximately 19 CE. This would be consistent with my Judas the Galilean timeline. The unnamed Jew comes after the spurious Jesus passage in *Antiquities* and can be tied to passages from Tacitus and Suetonius which tell of the Jews' banishment from Rome in 19 CE.

There was a man who was a Jew, but had been driven away from his own country by an accusation laid against him for transgressing their laws, and by the fear he was under of punishment for the same; but in all respects a wicked man: - he then living at Rome, professed to instruct men in the wisdom of the laws of Moses. He procured also three other men, entirely of the same character with himself, to be his partners. These men persuaded Fulvia, a woman of great dignity, and one that had embraced the Jewish religion, to send purple and gold to the temple at Jerusalem; and, when they had gotten them, they employed them for their own uses, and spent the money themselves. ...Thus were these Jews banished out of the city by the wickedness of four men. (*Ant.* 18.81-85)

The above passage has never been positively attributed to Saul, mainly because the traditional timeline has Saul persecuting the church in the early to mid 30's. However, if the traditional timeline is off by a generation, then the similarities between the unnamed Jew and Saul become apparent.

It is interesting that Josephus did not name the Jew in the above account. He generally was quite adept at identifying individuals. Why tell a story of the Jewish banishment from Rome if you do not even have the names of those responsible for the crime? Is it possible that the name was deleted in the pious editing of Josephus? After all, this is only twenty or so verses after the altered Jesus passage. (*Ant.* 18.63-64 vs. *Ant.* 18.81-85) Without the name Saul, we are only left with similar behavior patterns and cannot place this event upon Saul's shoulders with total certainty.

This Jew was driven from Judea because he had transgressed their laws. His flight from Judea was necessitated by the fear of punishment. This type of individual would never be able to openly mingle with the fanatical Jews again. After Paul's conversion, he traveled to Jerusalem twice by his own account (Gal. 1:18 and 2:1-2), but each time he only conversed privately with the leaders. Obviously, Paul knew of the dangers lurking in Jerusalem. It is probable that there was an ongoing debate within the Fourth Philosophy about Paul's career within the movement. Although the Sadduc (John the Baptist) preached repentance and forgiveness, the more pragmatic parts of the movement would have been very wary of this Herodian within their midst. This may explain why Barnabas traveled with Paul. Perhaps, Barnabas was the eyes and ears for the Jerusalem community concerning Paul's activities.

After being driven from Judea, the unnamed Jew settled in Rome to make a living. Even though he had been forced to leave Judea for transgressing the Law, he professed to "instruct men in the wisdom of the law of Moses." This seems quite unusual. If a man knows the Law in Rome, he should know the same Law in Jerusalem. However, this pattern fits perfectly with Paul. Paul was always criticized by the circumcision (those from James, the brother of Jesus), but he claimed to have a superior knowledge of the Law to his own followers. These followers were generally Jewish converts, and later, simply Gentiles. These converts would know no better. They generally took Paul at his word, even though the circumcision called him a liar. In the Josephus passage, the unnamed Jew had convinced Fulvia, a rich Jewish convert, of his qualifications.

With the help of three other men, the unnamed Jew convinced Fulvia to contribute a vast sum to the Temple in Jerusalem. First, the unnamed Jew worked his scam with the help of others. In the four passages about Saul in Josephus (see Acts and Josephus), this Saul was always accompanied by others, namely Costobar, Antipas and hired hands. Note that Josephus called the followers of Saul "wicked wretches" (*Ant.* 20.214) just as he called the unnamed Jew a "wicked man" and his friends "of the same character as himself."

The scam concerned the contribution of purple and gold to the Temple in Jerusalem. This wealth never left the unnamed Jew's possession. Compare these actions to those of Paul.

Now about the collection for God's people: do what I told the Galatian churches to do. On the first day of the week, each one of you should set aside a sum of money in keeping with his income, saving it up, so that when I come no collections will have to be made. Then, when I arrive, I will give letters of introduction to the men you approve and **send them with your gift to Jerusalem. If it seems advisable for me to go also, they will accompany me.** (1 Cor. 16:1-4) (Emphasis mine)

Like the unnamed Jew, Paul collected money from his converts to be sent to Jerusalem. Paul also made sure that he would accompany the funds to the city. He was quite sure that no one would object to his plan.

The above instructions were for the Galatians and Corinthians. However, it seems as though Paul's credibility was being challenged by the Jews. It is possible that Paul's history of deceit had made him a target of the unrelenting James and his Jewish Christian disciples. Galatians and 1 and 2 Corinthians are merely documents which defend Paul's honesty and hard work. With the faith of a televangelist, Paul stated:

Remember this: whoever sows sparingly will also reap sparingly, and whoever sows generously will also reap generously. Each man should give what he has decided in his heart to give, not reluctantly or under compulsion, for God loves a cheerful giver. …This service that you perform is not only supplying the needs of God's people [Jews in Jerusalem] but is also overflowing in many expressions of thanks to God. (2 Cor. 9:6-12)

After calling the Jewish apostles "deceitful workmen, masquerading as apostles of Christ" (2 Cor. 11:13), Paul repeated his claims of personal sacrifice and suffering (2 Cor. 11:16-33). He then topped off his sales pitch with the boastful claim that he had been called up to heaven (2 Cor. 12:1-10). This all leads up to this passage: "Now I am ready to visit you for the third time, and I will not be a burden to you, because **what I want is not your possessions but you.**" (2 Cor. 12:14) However, I am quite sure that Paul accepted the possessions with open arms. These possessions never made it to the Jewish Christians in Jerusalem.

So what happened to the money that Paul collected from those dear souls in Corinth and Galatia. Surely, James' Jewish Christians did not receive any assistance from Paul. Most likely, Paul used the money to further his own agenda and those goals of his Herodian friends and family. In the 60's, Saul had the resources to hire men to attack the Church. It is possible that he used the money collected in the 40's to stir up trouble for James and Cephas. In the 40's, the Fourth Philosophy came under attack: Theudas was beheaded and the sons of Judas the Galilean were crucified. Could Paul have had a hand in this persecution? And if he did, then the genesis of the betrayer myth can be identified. (This will be explained in detail later.)

This question should be asked: Why should a wealthy Herodian steal from others? It is possible that Saul's finances were no better than that of Agrippa I, the Herodian King of Israel from 37-44 CE. In Robert Graves' historical novel, *Claudius the God*, Agrippa's history was traced, and he often asked for bailouts from this source or that. There is no reason to believe that Saul would have had greater resources than Agrippa. So it is quite possible that a Herodian would trick his way to wealth.

There is one more possible tie between Paul and the unnamed Jew, and that is the city of Rome. The unnamed Jew's con game caused quite an uproar in Rome, to the extent that all Jews were punished. Surely, this unnamed Jew could never show his face in Rome again. Is it just coincidence that Paul never traveled to Rome as attested by himself (Rom. 1:8-15)? In his letter to the Romans, Paul claimed he wanted to visit Rome but other factors always prevented the trip. Also, the book of Acts only had Paul going to Rome to visit Nero in 62 CE (Acts 28:11-31). This meeting in Acts is pure fiction as Saul's meeting with Nero actually occurred at Achia in 66-67 CE. As such, there was no trip to Rome! With Paul's unmatched ego, it seems incredible that he would never visit the greatest city of his day, the seat of ancient power. One would think that Rome would have been his base of operations. The unnamed Jew incident may explain why only letters went to Rome. Paul knew that he could never show his face in that great city again. How ironic that the seat of Imperial power (Rome) and the center of religious devotion (Jerusalem) were both off limits to the apostle to the Gentiles.

The beginning of Paul's career can be tentatively tied to the unnamed Jew. The end of Paul's career can be positively tied to the King Izates conversion of 44 CE, recorded by Josephus.

Now, during the time Izates abode at Charax-Spasini, a certain Jewish merchant, whose name was **Ananias, got among the women that belonged to the king**, and taught them to worship God according to the Jewish religion. ...and as he [Izates] supposed that he could not be thoroughly a Jew unless he were circumcised, he was ready to have it done. ...and he [Ananias] said, that he [Izates] **might worship God without being circumcised,** even though he did resolve to follow the Jewish law entirely; which worship of God was of a **superior nature to circumcision.** He added that God would forgive him, though he did not perform the operation, while it was omitted out of necessity, and for fear of his subjects. So the king at that time complied with these persuasions of Ananias. (*Ant.* 20.34-42) (Emphasis mine)

The first half of the Izates conversion contains some interesting points which have been highlighted above. The Jewish merchant, Ananias, taught his version of Judaism to the king's harem. This would suggest that he was either a eunuch or knew a eunuch who granted him access to the women. Both the name, Ananias, and the profession, eunuch, were used by Acts to weave its yarn about the early Church. An Ananias supposedly learned from a vision that he was to lay hands upon Saul, and to tell Saul of the mission to the Gentiles. (Acts 9:10-19) This, of course, is totally different from Paul's own account, where no man had instructed him. (Gal. 1:11-12; 1:16-17) The inaccuracy of Acts can also be determined by the vision given to Ananias. Visions were often used by the author of Acts to further the storyline with the sanctions of God. This methodology was employed in Acts chapter 10, where both Peter and Cornelius were given visions. As already mentioned before, Acts 10 was simply a rewrite of the Simon/Agrippa meeting from *Ant.* 19.332-334. The eunuch was used in the story of Philip and the eunuch (Acts 8:26-39). Like the supernatural account of Saul and Ananias, Philip was told by an angel of the Lord to go south from Jerusalem to Gaza, where he met up with the eunuch. There Philip preached the Pauline message of inclusion into the movement, where baptism replaced circumcision.

In the above passage by Josephus, Ananias preached that circumcision was **not** necessary for Gentiles who wanted to follow the Jewish law. This new "Jewish" worship of God was superior to circumcision. It is not as though Ananias overtly preached against circumcision, but he realized that circumcision might compromise Izates' position with his subjects. This was extremely pragmatic, but it would not appear so to the more zealous Jews, who considered circumcision as the sign of the everlasting covenant between God and man. To the zealous Jews, one must have been circumcised to follow the entire law.

What exactly did Paul preach concerning circumcision? In Romans 3:21 Paul wrote: "But now a righteousness from God, apart from law, has been made known, to which the Law and Prophets testify. This righteousness from God comes through faith in Jesus Christ to all who believe." And again, in Gal. 3:11, he wrote: "Clearly no one is justified before God by the law, because 'The righteous will live by faith.'" Paul's emphasis on faith was so strong that he also wrote: "I, Paul, tell you that if you let yourselves be circumcised, Christ will be of no value to you at all." (Gal. 5:2) His hatred for James and his circumcision group is graphically described in Gal. 5:12: "As for those agitators, I wish they would go the whole way and emasculate themselves!" Ouch! Paul certainly preached a "worship of God superior to circumcision." In this, Paul was perfectly in synch with Ananias. That is why I date the Antioch confrontation between Paul and Cephas at 44 CE, consistent with the King Izates conversion.

The Izates conversion has a second part. Like the argument between Paul and Cephas at Antioch, Ananias was pitted against Eleazar, who was sent from Galilee.

...a certain other **Jew that came out of Galilee,** whose name was Eleazar, and who was esteemed very skillful in the learning of his country, persuaded him [Izates] to do the thing [circumcision]; for as he entered into his palace to salute him, and **found him reading the law of Moses,** he said to him, "Thou dost not consider, O king! that thou unjustly break the principal of those laws, and art injurious to God himself, [by omitting to be circumcised]; for thou ought not only to read them, but chiefly to practice what they enjoin thee. **How long wilt thou continue uncircumcised? But, if thou hast not yet read the law about circumcision, and does not know how great impiety thou art guilty of by neglecting it, read it now.**" When the king had heard what he said, he delayed the thing no longer, but retired to another room, and sent for a surgeon, and did what he was commanded to do [be circumcised]. (*Ant.* 20.43-46) (Emphasis mine)

Is it just a coincidence that Eleazar came from Galilee to fight the message of Ananias? In Galatians 2:12, "certain men came from James", who were either situated in Jerusalem or in Galilee. It is most probable that James sent emissaries out to combat the Pauline message wherever it had some roots. Thus, Ananias and Paul probably had some shared background in that they preached the same message. The question that must be answered is this: Did Paul head up the entire operation or was there some other force at work? This will be answered within the next few chapters.

This passage about Eleazar and Izates has also been incorporated into the book of Acts. In Acts 8:30-39, Philip heard the eunuch reading the book of Isaiah, just as Eleazar found Izates reading the law of Moses. Philip explained the Scriptures to the eunuch, and the eunuch insisted upon being baptized. Eleazar pointed out to Izates that circumcision was part of the law, and Izates then called for the surgeon to perform the operation. Acts simply substituted baptism for circumcision.

This point should not be missed. In both cases where the two different philosophies clashed, the zealous Jews came out on top. Paul stated that at Antioch: "The other Jews joined him [Cephas] in his hypocrisy, so that by their hypocrisy even Barnabas was led astray." (Gal. 2:13) Izates also sided with the circumcision party in the above passage. Even though Paul tried to paint Cephas as a hypocrite, the damage had already been done. As of 44 CE, Paul no longer shared any ideals with the Jewish Christian movement, and his ministry among the Gentiles was also called into question by James and Cephas.

CONCLUSION

If anything can be gained from the above discussion, it is a healthy skepticism of the traditional timeline as championed by the book of Acts. Acts simply rewrote many of the events in the early history of the Fourth Philosophy and twisted the outcomes using visions and dreams to involve God in the unholy misdirection. This being said, Acts can be very valuable in that it points to issues and events which were of great importance to the early church. For example, the concocted Peter/Cornelius episode (Acts 10) shows us the actual importance of the Simon/Agrippa meeting. The mythical stoning of Stephen covers the legendary stoning of James the Just. And the story of Philip and the eunuch leads us to consider the real impact of the King Izates conversion.

Paul does not fare so well in this investigation. In the traditional timeline, Paul was made into the super-apostle to the Gentiles. In this study of Acts and Josephus, we find that Saul/Paul was not the major player in the whole movement, and that he was even removed from fellowship in 44 CE. His later years were consumed with trying to destroy the movement he once defended. In 67 CE, he went to Achia to meet with Nero. This despicable action sums up the career of Paul.

CHAPTER 8

THE GOSPEL OF PAUL

The subject of Paul the Apostle is a complex one, yet even the study of Judas the Galilean and the Fourth Philosophy is impacted by his life and beliefs; for Paul was opposed to the basic tenets held by Judas and his loyal followers. This Fourth Philosophy held fast to the teachings of Moses, which included all of the law, especially circumcision. Circumcision was the sign between God and man concerning the Everlasting Covenant, no small insignificant matter. Circumcision was central to the Jewish religion. Without it, the Jews were just like everyone else. Yet Paul opposed circumcising his Gentile converts.

This strong opposition between Paul and the Fourth Philosophy explains why so much confusion exists in the interpretation of the New Testament. In its pages, we see a primitive law abiding Jesus (Judas the Galilean) and an other-worldly Jesus, centered upon the Pauline goal of individual salvation. This New Testament Jesus is no doubt a composite character, combining much of Judas' actual teachings with preconceived notions about those teachings. For example, when Jesus criticized the Pharisees for holding onto the traditions of man over the laws of God (Mark 7:1-23), the New Testament added this Pauline touch: "In saying this, Jesus declared all foods 'clean.'" In reality, Jesus defended the laws of God, which included clean and unclean foods. He was not declaring these purity laws null and void. So you see, nothing can be accepted at face value. We must sort out the real from the counterfeit. We must better understand Paul in order to separate his beliefs from those of Judas/Jesus.

PAUL AND HEROD

The Fourth Philosophy was a reactionary movement patterned upon the Maccabees, with Herod the Great as the chief antagonist. Herod introduced foreign practices among the Jews just as Antiochus Epiphanes did some one hundred and fifty years earlier. That Judas the Galilean simply opposed Herod is an understatement. The disciples of Judas were willing to give their very lives in order to stop the hellenizing tendencies of Herod. This fervor continued from the time of Matthias, through the death of John the Baptist to the murder of James, the brother of Jesus (Judas). Thus, if we can tie Paul to Herod, his credibility is severely compromised. In fact, if Paul were a Herodian, then our picture of Jesus is grossly distorted, because much of the New Testament Jesus comes from the life and teachings of Paul.

First, we will look to Paul's own writings for insights. In Romans 16:11, Paul said, "Greet Herodian the kinsman of me." The Greek word for kinsman is different than the word for brother. It is most likely that this kinsman would be a flesh and blood relative while brother could very well denote a spiritual relationship. This "Herodian" may have been related by blood ties, but this by itself would still leave doubt. So Paul went on and said, "Lucius and Jason and Sosipater the kinsman of me." (Rom. 16:21) This suggests that Paul had ties in Rome to several of his relatives who were Herodians. In all the other epistles, Paul did not specifically mention any other relatives. So the case against Paul based upon his own letters is meager at best, but a possible tie to Herod is clearly present.

The Book of Acts, although historically flawed, may shed more light upon Paul's background. Saul (Paul) was first mentioned in Acts 8:1, where he gave approval to the death of Stephen and to the general persecution of Christians. "But Saul began to destroy the church. Going from house to house, he dragged off men and women and put them in prison." (Acts 8:3) Saul intended to widen his search beyond Jerusalem so "he went to the high priest and asked him for letters to the synagogues in Damascus, so that if he found any there who belonged to the Way, he might take them as prisoners to Jerusalem." (Acts 9:2) Our focus should be upon Saul's influence at such a young age. Even though he was employed as a lowly thug by the High Priest, he did seem to have a certain pull with this particular priest. This does not prove that Saul was of Herodian descent, but the authority given him was extraordinary if he came from Tarsus and was unrelated to those in power. Note that the parallel passage in *Ant* 20.214 directly stated that Saul was of the royal family. This explains Saul's pull with the high priesthood. In general, those who persecuted Jesus and the Church were the Sadducees, High Priests and Herodians. Pharisees had a better feel for the people's pulse, and association with Rome and its policies was not at all popular. If Paul were really a Pharisee as he claimed, he would not have associated with the High Priest in this persecution. This persecution proves that Paul had no ties to the Pharisees.

In Damascus, Paul escaped the governor under King Aretas by being lowered by a basket from a window in the wall. (2 Cor. 11:32-33) This scene was obviously altered in Acts 9:23-25, where Paul was lowered from the wall to escape the Jews. Certainly, the letter of Paul should be trusted more than the sanitizing Acts. And if this is so, the enemy of Paul was King Aretas, the same king who opposed Antipas (Herod the Tetrarch) because Herod had jilted his daughter and had also murdered John the Baptist, a vocal critic of Herod's personal life. (*Ant.* 18.109-119) This hatred of Saul (Paul) may have had more to do with his Herodian background than with his preaching. As I have detailed earlier, I believe this escape from Damascus was near the end of Paul's career with the movement (late 30's). If Paul had been a solid supporter of John the Baptist, then it is doubtful that Aretas would have been so keen on arresting him. But Paul was becoming more and more aligned with his old pals, the Herodians, by this time.

In the church at Antioch, there was one Manaen, a member of the court of Herod the Tetrarch (Antipas). (Acts 13:1) Saul was mentioned right after him and a few others, as leaders of this particular church. Again, Saul was placed right next to a Herodian. Maybe Aretas' mistrust of Saul was well deserved!

Being a member of Herod's family had considerable advantages. For instance, they were given Roman citizenship at birth. Now in Acts 17:3, Paul and Silas were both said to be Roman citizens. If Paul were a Pharisee, a Hebrew of Hebrews and a member of the tribe of Benjamin, it is doubtful that he would also have had Roman citizenship. Paul compared himself to the Jerusalem Apostles: "I was advancing in Judaism beyond many Jews of my own age and was extremely zealous for the traditions of my fathers." (Gal. 1:14) Here Paul used the term "zealous" for the law, placing himself as an equal or superior position vis-a-vis Cephas and James. If this were true, then Roman citizenship cannot be believed. It is much more likely that Paul's Roman citizenship came from his birthright as a member of the royal family.

After being threatened by the Jewish Christians (Fourth Philosophy), Paul was arrested by the Roman guard, thus saving his life. (Acts 21:27-36) It is interesting that Paul's nephew was there to protect Paul after the arrest, supplying information to the Romans. The original story, recorded by Josephus in *War* 2.556-557, had Saul and his brother escaping from Jerusalem to the Roman commander, Cestius. In both scenarios, Saul (Paul) escaped the zealous Jews with the help of family and was rescued by the Romans.

After escaping Jerusalem, Paul was sent to Caesarea (58 CE) to answer charges in front of the Roman Procurator, Felix (52-60 CE). (This, of course, is not actual history as Saul escaped to Cestius. However, certain aspects of this story have some bearing on our question of Herodian affiliation.) From the narrative in Acts 24:22-26, we learn that Felix was married to Drusilla, the daughter of Agrippa I and sister of Agrippa II. Felix often spoke with Paul, listening to Paul's gospel. The reason for this frequent discourse was the hope for a bribe, for Felix believed that Paul possessed a large sum of money. That the friendly conversations actually occurred should not be doubted for Drusilla was a member of the Herodian family. This, in and of itself, may indirectly indict Paul. And could the bribe issue relate to the sum of money sent by Paul's churches to the Church in Jerusalem? (1 Cor. 16:1-4) Per this passage from Corinthians, Paul stated that he might accompany the money to Jerusalem. Obviously, the money never changed hands between Paul and James.

In 60 CE, Felix was replaced by Porcius Festus. Felix never received his bribe for he left Paul in prison as a favor to the Jews. (Again, this is not history. Paul was never imprisoned!) Festus convened a court, and it was decided that Paul should be sent to Rome to stand trial there. (Saul actually met Nero in 67 CE in Achia, not Rome.) A few days later, King Agrippa II and his sister Bernice arrived in Caesarea to talk with Festus. (It should be noted that this Bernice later became the mistress of Titus, the Roman general who destroyed Jerusalem. It was also rumored that Bernice was having an incestuous relationship with her brother, Agrippa II. (*Ant.* 20.145)) Festus informed Agrippa of Paul's case, and Paul was granted an audience. Paul made the most of his opportunity, praising the King with flattery upon flattery (Acts 26:2-3; 26:26-28) This action by Paul was opposite that of Jesus (based upon Simon and Agrippa I - *Ant.* 19.332-334) who was silent before Pilate. And consider Paul's attitude towards these Herodians, that of cordiality. The Fourth Philosophy, especially John the Baptist, would have vomited over this friendship. (The actual meeting with Agrippa II occurred in 66 CE, and Saul was trying to convince Agrippa to send troops to Jerusalem to suppress the insurgents. (*War* 2.418-419))

The ties between Paul and the Herodians appear fairly secure, but Paul's teachings make it a certainty. In Romans 13:1-7, Paul wrote that the believers should pay their taxes to Rome and should also follow Caesar without reservation. From our analysis of Judas the Galilean, we know that his followers would rather die than be slaves to Rome. And it should be noted that Jesus was arrested and crucified because of his teaching against the payment of taxes to Rome. However, since the Herodians were Rome's tax collectors, it is easy to see why Paul sided with the power of Rome. This may also explain the passage attributed to Jesus where he was a friend to tax collectors and sinners. This was Paul and **not** Jesus.

WAS PAUL A PHARISEE?

This statement appeared in Philippians 3:4-6 as a response to those from the circumcision:

If anyone else thinks he has reasons to put confidence in the flesh, I have more: circumcised on the eighth day, of the people of Israel, of the tribe of Benjamin, a Hebrew of Hebrews; **in regard to the law, a Pharisee**; as for zeal, persecuting the church; as for legalistic righteousness, faultless.

Before going forward, we should first consider the source of information. This is what Robert Eisenman states about Paul's letters:

Though there is continuing discussion among scholars about aspects of the Pauline corpus - the New Testament letters attributed to Paul - there is general agreement on the authenticity of the main, particularly those letters...like Galatians, 1 and 2 Corinthians, Romans and Philippians. These give us insights of the most intimate kind into the mind of Paul and historical insights into this period, which no defender of the integrity of the early Church and its doctrines would have had the slightest interest in forging or, for that matter, even preserving. (1)

I agree with Eisenman that no one would have invented the story of Paul, as his letters raise questions concerning the truthfulness of the Gospels and Acts. For example, Paul's Pillar Apostles were James, Cephas and John. Paul's James and John were the brothers of the Lord. (Gal. 1:19; 2:7-10; 2:12; 1 Cor. 9:5) The Gospels present a James, Peter and John as being the core apostles with Jesus. However, the Gospels' James and John were the sons of Zebedee, not the brothers of Jesus. Why would a later writer make such an incredible blunder as changing the sons of Zebedee into the brothers of Jesus? Considering that the Gospels minimized the role of Jesus' family throughout, it is fair to say that the Gospel writers turned the brothers of Jesus into the sons of Zebedee. Thus, this one example illustrates that Paul's information was closer to the truth than the Gospel accounts.

But should these five letters listed by Eisenman be accepted as Paul's own letters? The only letter which I have any reservations about is the letter to the Philippians. The reason behind this apprehension goes back to the last chapter. It has already been determined that Paul was never arrested and sent to Rome to meet Caesar. According to Josephus, Saul traveled to Achia to meet with Nero in 67 CE. Acts sent Paul to Rome to simply get him out of town (Jerusalem) before the murder of James. According to Josephus, Saul approved of the murder of James and persecuted the poor afterwards. (*Ant.* 20.200-214) Now Philippians opens up in chapter 1:12-14 with Paul writing about his imprisonment. This cannot be the Rome imprisonment because that never occurred. Perhaps this was added later or perhaps the whole letter is a forgery. Such a possibility makes Paul's Pharisee claim a bit questionable.

Let us assume that the letter to the Philippians was from the hand of Paul. If authentic, then three possible alternatives exist concerning his claim of being a Pharisee: he may have been a Pharisee, he may have lied about being a Pharisee, or he was exaggerating his own credentials. The second and third scenarios are similar in that in either case, Paul was not a Pharisee. Each scenario will be explored below so that the background of Paul can be fully understood. This background will help decipher his message as given in his letters.

The first scenario can only be supported by this lone passage in Philippians. However, there is a close tie to a passage in Galatians 1:13-14. In that passage, Paul claimed that he was "extremely zealous for the traditions of my fathers." It appears as if Paul associated himself to the most zealous of the Pharisees, or to the Fourth Philosophy. (Josephus claimed that Judas the Galilean and Sadduc were both Pharisees. (*Ant.* 18.4; 23)) The Pharisees followed the written and oral law. The "traditions of my fathers" may relate to this oral law. How interesting that Paul claimed association with the Fourth Philosophy before he actually became part of it. The answer is quite simple: Paul was telling his converts that he once lived like the Pillar Apostles or the circumcision group (mutilators of the flesh). However, that preceded his mystical meeting with the Lord. After meeting the Risen Christ, Paul realized that the law was dead, and only faith in Jesus Christ could win salvation. (Gal. 1:15-17; Phil. 3:7-11)

So is it possible that Paul lived as a Pharisee before his conversion to a Pharisaic movement? By Paul's own admission, he persecuted the Church (Gal. 1:13). If Paul were a Pharisee, then how could he have acted the part of persecutor? According to Acts 9:1-2 and the *Recognitions* 1.70-71, Paul was also employed by the High Priest, a member of the Sadducees. A zealous Pharisee would never stoop to such a low. By Paul's own admission of persecuting the Church, he ruled out the possibility of himself being a Pharisee. The picture of Saul in Acts and the *Recognitions* only reinforces the unlikely picture of Paul as Pharisee.

The unnamed Jew in *Ant.* 18.81-85 was driven from Israel "by an accusation laid against him for transgressing their laws." This may be the true picture of the young Saul. This unnamed Jew later went to Rome where he "professed to instruct men in the wisdom of the laws of Moses." This religious knowledge was used to swindle unsuspecting Jewish converts. Obviously, the unnamed Jew could not have been a zealous Pharisee as he was accused of transgressing the laws of Moses. However, that same man claimed to know the laws of Moses when speaking to the uneducated Jewish converts. This pattern of braggadocio fits perfectly with Paul.

From the above, it appears likely that Paul was not a Pharisee. But what about the writing style of Paul's letters? Many have claimed that the Pharisee in Paul comes out through his letters. This was examined by Hyam Maccoby in his book *The Mythmaker*. Maccoby's background in sacred Jewish writings gives his views on Paul's writings a bit more weight than most scholars. Maccoby focused upon three points: the *qal va-homer* argument of light and heavy, Paul's alleged use of Pharisaic argument and Paul's use or non-use of the Hebrew Scriptures.

The light and heavy argument can be illustrated as follows: "if offending a father (a relatively light thing) is punished by banishment for seven days, offending God (a relatively heavy thing) should all the more receive such a punishment." (2) Note that offending God does not get 14 days or any other term. The argument simply states that if a light offense gets seven days, the heavy offense should also get at least seven days. According to Maccoby, Paul used this form of argument often and usually did not get it right. Maccoby gave four examples of this light and heavy argument from Paul's writings and found only one to be properly stated. (Romans 5:10; 5:17; 11:15 and 11:24) To Maccoby, this imprecision on Paul's part proved that he was **not** a trained Pharisee.

Maccoby's next argument concerns Paul's interpretation of Scriptural passages. Many scholars argue that Paul used *midrash* or biblical exegesis to support his positions. Maccoby used the passage from Gal. 3:13 to show that Paul did not understand the Pharisee exegesis of that verse. The verse is as follows: "Christ redeemed us from the curse of the law by becoming a curse for us, for it is written: 'Cursed is everyone who is hung on a tree.'" Paul claimed that everyone who hung on a tree or crucified was cursed. Thus, Jesus, by being crucified, became a curse for us. But this was not part of the Pharisaic tradition. Maccoby wrote:

The idea that anyone hanged on a gibbet is under a curses was entirely alien to Pharisee thought… Many highly respected members of the Pharisee movement were crucified by the Romans, just like Jesus, and, far from being regarded as under a curse because of the manner of their death, they were regarded as martyrs... The Pharisees never thought that God was either stupid or unjust, and he would have to be both to put a curse on an innocent victim. (3)

Who then was cursed in the above passage? The curse was upon those who would allow the victim to hang upon the gibbet, to desecrate the body, made in the image of God. This was the Pharisaic interpretation, so unlike Paul's version.

Maccoby's third argument centered upon Paul's non-use of the Hebrew Scriptures. Paul exclusively used the Greek translation which sometimes differs from the Hebrew. Maccoby claimed that a trained Pharisee could not play so loosely with the word of God.

In short, Maccoby believed that nothing in Paul's letters proved that he was a Pharisee. On the contrary, his analysis proved that Paul was not a Pharisee. This brings me to the third alternative which is resume padding. Paul was not a Pharisee but his Gentile followers did not know anything about the Pharisees or their teachings. Paul could simply state that he was the most learned man in Israel and his gullible disciples would take the bait. From the above, Paul was certainly not a Pharisee before his conversion to the Fourth Philosophy, a Pharisaic movement. But could Paul have become a Pharisee after being converted?

In Gal. 1:15-18, Paul wrote that he did not visit Jerusalem for three years after his conversion. It is very likely that the Herodian Saul was part of an initiation which took up to three years to complete. In these three years, Saul would have been taught much about the Pharisaic teachings. This is evident from Maccoby's own presentation of the light and heavy argument. According to Maccoby, Paul only properly stated the argument in one of four cases. This may prove that Paul was not a Pharisee, but it may also prove that Paul was somewhat educated in the methods of Pharisaic argument. After all, he did get one right out of four.

Paul did exaggerate his credentials, and he purposely misled his followers. Paul never had the religious prowess of a Cephas or of a James. That is why he told his followers that he was as zealous in the observance of the law as any of those men. This was a downright lie. He then placed this lie before his conversion to the movement. As seen above, Paul may have learned about Pharisaic argument after his conversion but not before. Before his conversion, he was in cahoots with the High Priest and the Sadducees. Thus, Paul painted a pretty picture of himself: a reformed ex-Pharisee who now served the Risen Christ. In actuality, Paul was a Herodian who converted to the Fourth Philosophy and studied with the Pharisees. He later devised his own world view of Judaism where he, Paul, was the representative of the Risen

Christ, and where James and Cephas still held onto the discredited Law and circumcision.

THE GOSPEL OF PAUL

When examining Paul's letters for his true teachings, we must keep in mind that Paul's gospel was different than anything that went before. Paul stated:

I want you to know, brothers, that the gospel I preached is not something that man made up. I did not receive it from any man, nor was I taught it; rather, **I received it by revelation from Jesus Christ.** (Gal. 1:11-12) (Emphasis mine)

This should be shocking to most present day Christians, who assume that Jesus taught the gospel to his disciples (the Twelve) and they then taught it to the world. According to Matthew 28:19-20, Jesus said: "Go and make disciples of all nations, baptizing them in the name of the Father and of the Son and of the Holy Spirit, and teaching them to obey everything I have commanded you." This great commission was given to the Eleven (per the Gospels, Judas had committed suicide). How can it be that Paul's gospel was a direct revelation from Jesus? Why was Paul's gospel different than the one preached by Cephas and James? After all, Cephas and James had contact with the earthly Jesus and the resurrected Jesus. Was Jesus just a poor communicator or were Cephas and James a bit too slow to understand the real message of Jesus?

GRACE, THE LAW, AND CIRCUMCISION

The best way to approach this matter is by outlining Paul's gospel, by using Paul's letters to the Romans, Corinthians and Galatians. A wealth of information comes from these documents, making it unnecessary to entertain the disputed letters attributed to Paul. By far the most important aspect of Paul's gospel was his application of the concept of Grace upon his Gentile converts.

It is important to keep in mind that Paul was a Jew and that his Christ Jesus figure also lived as a Jew. He could not get around those facts. This Jewish history had to be accounted for in his message. The question for Paul boiled down to this: How could he bring his Gentile flock within the Jewish Christian movement? He had to make them Jews as well, not through circumcision but through the concept of Grace. His Gentiles would become the true Israel, through faith in the blood of Christ.

But now a righteousness from God, **apart from Law**, has been made known, to which the law and the Prophets testify. This righteousness from God comes through faith in Jesus Christ to **all** who believe. There is no difference, for **all** have sinned and fall short of the glory of God, and are justified freely by his grace through the redemption that came by Christ Jesus. God presented him as a **sacrifice of atonement, through faith in his blood.** (Romans 3:21-25) (Emphasis mine)

This short statement summed up Paul's Gospel to the Gentiles. The Gentiles could now attain righteousness apart from the Law. This righteousness was available to all, Gentiles and Jews alike, for all need the atoning sacrifice of Christ Jesus. And, the only way to attain this atonement was through faith in Christ's blood. So in one fell swoop, Paul lumped his Gentiles with all Jews. He then separated the two groups by declaring that only those with faith in the blood could be the true followers of God. Since the Jews followed their own covenant with God through the law and circumcision, Paul effectively replaced the Jews with the Gentiles as the chosen people of God. This is why James so fiercely opposed Paul, once this message became known.

As for the Law, Paul stated: "No one will be declared righteous in his sight by observing the law; rather, through the law we become conscious of sin." (Rom. 3:20) It is ironic that the followers of James were known as the "Way of Righteousness" or the "Way". These zealous Jews were fanatical in their attention to the Law. According to Paul, this misplaced emphasis on the law could never earn righteousness for the Jews. They needed to have faith in the blood, not faith in the word of God.

Circumcision is perhaps the central issue concerning the law. This is what Paul told his Gentile readers:

Circumcision has value if you observe the law, but if you break the law, you have become as though you had not been circumcised. **If those who are not circumcised keep the law's requirements, will they not be regarded as though they were circumcised?** The one who is not circumcised physically and yet obeys the law will condemn you who, even though you have the written code and circumcision, are a lawbreaker. A man is not a Jew if he is only one outwardly, nor is circumcision merely outward and physical. No, a man is a Jew if he is one inwardly; and circumcision is circumcision of the heart, by the Spirit, not by the written code. (Rom. 2:25-29) (Emphasis mine)

Paul did not invent anything when he wrote that a Jew had to have a circumcision of the heart. Many Christians today believe that this was a new concept. However, the Jews knew about the circumcision of the heart. In Deut. 10:16, God told the Jews to "Circumcise your hearts, therefore, and not be stiff-necked any longer." The Jews of New Testament times knew full well of the inward and outward circumcision. Paul, on the other hand, rejected the concept of physical circumcision, claiming that only the circumcision of the heart was necessary. But again, the Jews believed in both the circumcision of the body and the circumcision of the heart.

The denigration of the physical circumcision was necessary for Paul's gospel to the Gentiles. Paul claimed that the spiritual circumcision made them as though they were circumcised. Once again, Paul was transforming his physically uncircumcised Gentiles into the true Israel. Through faith in the blood, the Gentiles would be as though they were circumcised.

This circumcision argument can date the letter to the Romans as before 44 CE. In the King Izates episode as related by Josephus, Ananias said this to King Izates concerning circumcision:

[King Izates] might worship God without being circumcised, even though he did resolve to follow the Jewish law entirely; which worship of God was of a superior nature to circumcision. (*Ant.* 20.41)

This is the exact argument that Paul used in the letter to the Romans. Both Paul and Ananias stated that the Gentiles could follow the law entirely without being circumcised, and that this mode of worship was superior to physical circumcision. Neither Paul nor Ananias explained how one could follow the law without obeying the law of circumcision. A rational mind would see a major flaw in logic in this argument. Regardless, it is very important that we understand that this gospel of Paul's was being preached by others. The question is this: Was this new gospel the invention of Paul's or was someone else behind it? Paul wrote in Galatians 1:12 that his gospel to the Gentiles came directly from the Risen Christ Jesus. It is very likely that Paul did invent his gospel to the Gentiles, but there still may have been another factor in its spread. That factor may have been Agrippa I, king of Israel from 37-44 CE. This will be detailed in Chapter 10.

Paul's gospel of Grace, based upon faith, was based upon Paul's interpretation of the life of Abraham. In Romans 4:1-12, Paul wrote that Abraham was justified by faith before his circumcision. Therefore, Abraham was the father of both the circumcised and of those who believe but were not circumcised. Thus, his Gentiles were sons of Abraham through faith in the blood of Christ. This theology was based upon the passage in Genesis 15:6, where the Scriptures state: "Abram believed the Lord, and he credited it to him as righteousness." To Paul, this belief brought righteousness.

If Paul had analyzed the Genesis passage in context, he would have had trouble preaching his new gospel. Concerning circumcision, Genesis was very clear.

As for you, you must keep my covenant. ...Every male among you shall be circumcised. You are to undergo circumcision, and it will be the sign of the covenant between me and you. ...Any uncircumcised male, who has not been circumcised in the flesh, will be cast off from his people; he has broken my covenant. (Gen. 17:3-14)

Paul never commented upon how his new gospel would impact the Jews. He either did not care about their sensibilities or assumed that some would eventually see the light. I believe that Paul was centered strictly upon his Gentile converts and was content upon them becoming the new Israel. The end of old Israel, the everlasting covenant between God and the Jews, was just a by-product of his new and improved covenant between God and the Gentiles.

Paul's emphasized faith using the example of Abraham. He quoted the passage in Genesis where God told Abraham that he would be the father of many nations. In Paul's reasoning, that included all Gentiles. And his promise was made to Abraham before Abraham's circumcision. Therefore, in Paul's interpretation, faith, not circumcision, was necessary. If Paul had read a little farther, he would have encountered the passage where God told Abraham: "It is through Isaac that your offspring will be reckoned." (Gen. 21:12) This promise to Abraham was after circumcision and related to the father of the Jewish nation, Isaac. If Paul had been honest in his interpretation of Genesis, he could not have switched the everlasting covenant from the Jews (offspring of Isaac) to the Gentiles (offspring of Ishmael). Incredibly, Paul did use the passage from Gen. 21:12, but his interpretation of the offspring of Isaac was not the Jews, but rather, the children of the promise. (Rom. 9:7-9) These children of the promise were his Gentile followers. Paul magically changed a passage, which, without a doubt, referred to the Jews, into a proof text for his Gospel to the Gentiles. How bizarre is that reasoning?

THE ROLE OF GOVERNMENT

Paul's gospel was radically different than the one taught by James and Cephas, the original disciples of Jesus (Judas the Galilean). Paul had changed the chosen people from the Jews to the Gentiles. He also preached a very different message concerning the Church's relationship to the authorities. The mantra of Judas the Galilean was that "God [was] to be their only Ruler and Lord." (*Ant.* 18.23) In the Gospel of Matthew, Jesus said: "No one can serve two masters. You cannot serve both God and Money [Rome]." Paul had turned this exclusive service to God on its head. According to Paul, you could serve God in the spiritual sphere of life and Rome in the physical sphere. The Jews could not separate the two; to them, service to God was in the everyday practice of life.

The following passage illustrates Paul's attitude towards the rulers of his age, which included such monsters as Caligula (37-41 CE) and Nero (54-68 CE).

Everyone must submit himself to the governing authorities, for there is no authority except that which God has established. **The authorities that exist have been established by God.** Consequently, he who rebels against the authority is rebelling against what God has instituted, and those who do so will bring judgment on themselves. **For rulers hold no terror for those who do right, but for those who do wrong.** Do you want to be free from fear of the one in authority? Then do what is right and he will commend you. For he is God's servant to do you good. But if you do wrong, be afraid, for he does not bear the sword for nothing. **He is God's servant, an angel of wrath to bring punishment on the wrongdoer.** Therefore, it is necessary to submit to the authorities, not only because of possible punishment but also because of conscience. This is also why you pay taxes, for the authorities are God's servants, who give their full time to governing. Give everyone what you owe him: **if you owe taxes, pay taxes;** if revenue, then revenue; if respect, then respect; **if honor, then honor**. (Romans 13:1-7) (Emphasis mine)

Depending on when this was written, the concept that the authorities were established by God has been largely overlooked by scholars. If this was written in the late 50's, as proposed by traditional scholars, then Paul was writing that God had established the reign of Nero. If this were written in the early 40's, then Paul was referring to either Caligula or Claudius. We know that Paul was removed from the movement in 44 CE, so the above passage had to predate this time marker. In Chapter 1, another time marker was the expulsion of Jews from Rome under Claudius. This was determined to be at the beginning of Claudius' reign. This would also have been the time when Agrippa I, the King of Israel, had great influence over Claudius. Because Agrippa was at odds with the Messianic Jewish Christians, he might very well have convinced Claudius to expel these rabble-rousers from Rome. It is interesting that in the above passage, Paul tried to convince his followers to behave themselves. He asked them to submit to the authorities and if they did not, then they would suffer the consequences. If you were a follower of Paul, how would you interpret this line: "But if you do wrong, **be afraid**, for he does not bear the **sword** for nothing."? Certainly, Paul wanted to separate his own Gentile followers from the Jewish Christians in Rome. This may date Romans to between 41-43 CE.

The Fourth Philosophy was founded on the belief that only God was their Lord and Ruler. These patriots agreed with the Pharisaic teachings but had "an inviolable attachment to liberty." (*Ant.* 18.23) This dream of liberty from Rome was supported by the language of the book of Revelation, where Jesus would return to defeat the beast, to defeat Rome. (Rev. 17:1-9; 19:11-21) This light versus darkness scenario, which guided the Jewish followers of Judas the Galilean (Jesus), was totally ignored by Paul. According to Paul, these evil agents were established by God. His argument was simple but effective. If he could convince his listeners that the governments were ordained by God, then disobeying the earthly rules would be tantamount to fighting against God.

These earthly rulers were also called angels of wrath to bring punishment to the wrongdoers. It is very telling that Paul compared the Pillar Apostles to disciples of Satan, who himself "masquerades as an angel of light." (2 Cor. 11:13-15) Paul condemned the very disciples of Jesus yet supported the so-called authorities of God. This was an incredible departure from the message of Jesus and James. Paul separated religion from the state. He believed you could worship Christ Jesus and still be a good Roman citizen. On the other hand, Cephas and James commanded a following which demanded autonomy from Rome. In fact, their Messiah would soon return to destroy Rome. These two visions of working in the Roman Empire were polar opposites. (It is amazing that more scholars do not investigate these differences.)

Paul openly supported the earthly rulers. Two very concrete issue differences existed between the religion of Jesus and James and that of Paul. First, there was the taxation issue. Paul plainly stated that if you owed taxes to the government then you should pay those taxes, regardless of your opinion of the particular government. Remember, Paul taught that the governments were an extension of God himself. On the other hand, Judas the Galilean led a tax revolt against Rome in 6 CE, declaring "that this taxation [to the Romans] was no better than an introduction to slavery, and exhorted the nation to assert their liberty." (*Ant.* 18.4) It should also be noted that the Gospel Jesus was crucified because he claimed to be the Messiah, and he opposed Roman taxation. (Luke 23:2) The Romans surely believed these charges against Jesus were true because they crucified him. There is no way around that fact! Knowing that Jesus actually opposed Roman taxation gives an alternative interpretation of Matt. 22:17-21.

"Tell us then, what is your opinion? Is it right to pay taxes to Caesar or not?"

But Jesus, knowing their evil intent, said, "You hypocrites, why are you trying to trap me? Show me the coin used for paying the tax." They brought him a denarius, and he asked them, "Whose portrait is this? And whose inscription?"

"Caesar's," they replied.

Then he said to them, "Give to Caesar what is Caesar's, and to God what is God's."

The traditional interpretation is based upon the Pauline gospel, where one should obey the government and pay one's taxes. This pro-Roman philosophy has been placed upon the Jewish Messiah, Jesus. From a common sense standpoint, this interpretation is ludicrous. Would a popular Messiah figure endorse an occupier's taxation? If he actually did follow Paul's gospel, then how could he have had any popular support among the poor? Human nature has not changed over the ages. People today generally despise taxation. How much more would we despise the taxation of a foreign power? Jesus could not have preached the Pauline stance on Roman taxation!

The alternate interpretation states that the above argument by Jesus was a Zealot slogan. First, note that Jesus did not carry any of this Roman coinage. This would have been common Zealot practice. Second, the phrase "Give to God what is God's" should be put into context. Picture Jesus uttering this phrase while sweeping his arms wide. What was God's? According to Genesis, God had given the land of Israel to Abraham and his descendants. What Jesus actually meant by the passage was this: You Romans, take your money and leave our land. He was calling for the Romans to give back God's land to the Jews. This was pure Zealot ideology. The Slavonic Josephus adds to this interpretation: "[The Jewish people] bade him enter the city, kill the Roman troops and Pilate and reign over these." (After *War* 2.174) Surely, this Jesus was not a pro-Roman Messiah figure.

Paul's philosophy concerning government had one more troubling aspect. In the above passage, Paul stated that everyone should submit to the ruling authorities and that the Christian should respect and honor these same God appointed officials. In 1 Corinthians chapter 8, Paul spoke to the topic of food sacrificed to idols. Paul wrote to his Gentile audience that they were strong in their faith and that these idols had no effect upon them. He did tell these followers to be sensitive to those who did have a problem with food sacrificed to idols. These weaker brothers were, no doubt, the Jews. The Jewish Christians would not partake in food offered in sacrifice to Gods and certainly would not participate in Emperor worship. Paul understood this, and he at least told his followers to respect the Jews' weaknesses.

Would Paul's Gentile followers have actually participated in Emperor worship? We know that the proposed placement of Caligula's statue in the Temple would have caused a war between the Romans and Jews. Only the assassination of Caligula stopped the insane installation. The followers of Judas the Galilean would have gladly died before worshipping a false God. However, Paul's split of the spiritual from the worldly did give his followers the freedom to participate more fully in Roman culture. As long as his disciples had faith in Christ Jesus, they could function in Roman affairs. This split between spiritual and worldly affairs was a sure winner. Most Christians today have the same outlook as preached by Paul. They worship Jesus, and at the same time, they participate in a consumer driven world of excesses. The followers of James would have never divorced their actions from their beliefs. That was a major difference between Paul's and James' Gospels.

MARRIAGE

Was Jesus married? Certainly, the Gospels depicted Jesus as a leader of a small band of male apostles with only sporadic mention of any females. Nowhere in these documents is there overt mention of him being married. However, several passages suggest otherwise. In Matt. 8:14, Jesus healed Peter's mother-in-law. Even though the Gospels did not directly state that Peter or any of the other Apostles were married, this passage tells us contrary. Peter was married, and his wife probably traveled with him. If Jesus headed a band of married apostles, then could he have been married as well?

In the *War* and *Antiquities*, Josephus wrote that the Pharisees and one sect of the Essenes married. In fact, the Fourth Philosophy of Judas the Galilean followed the tenets of the Pharisees (*Ant.* 18.23). We know that the later Sicarii married and had children as those at Masada were comprised of whole families. Of the last mention of the Sicarii, Josephus wrote this about their children, who showed great courage under persecution:

But what was most of all astonishing to the beholders, was the courage of the children; for not one of these children was so far overcome by these torments as to name Caesar for their lord. (*War* 7.419)

Considering that the Pharisees, Fourth Philosophy and one sect of the Essenes married, it is hard to believe that Jesus did not marry as well. His disciples had wives, per Matt. 8:13 and 1 Cor. 9:5, where Paul asked: Don't we have the right to take a believing wife along with us, as do the other apostles and the Lord's brothers and Cephas?" Everyone must have been married except Jesus! This is so improbable that only the most devout practitioners of the traditional view could possibly accept it. In fact, Jesus did marry. If Jesus were Judas the Galilean, as I claim, then he would have had many sons and daughters. According to Josephus, Judas had at least three sons, named James, Simon and Menahem. He very well could have had more but those are the only ones central to Josephus' narrative.

In Matt. 13:55, the mother and brothers of Jesus are enumerated. "Isn't this the carpenter's son? Isn't his mother's name Mary, and aren't his brothers James, Joseph, Simon and Judas?" We are to believe that the great prophet and Messiah, Jesus, was being followed by his mother and brothers, who themselves did not believe in him. My alternate solution is as follows: Mary was the wife of Jesus and his sons were James, Joseph, Simon and Judas. It certainly would be appropriate for the wife and children of the Messiah to be traveling with him.

The wedding at Cana (John 2:1-11) has been transformed from a wedding to a miracle. Taking away the miracle, Jesus and Mary ordered servants concerning the wine situation. In all likelihood, Jesus and Mary were the bridegroom and bride. This has been taken to unrecognizable directions by some, claiming that the heirs of this couple traveled to France. This is interesting stuff but beyond this inquiry. I think it is fair to say that Jesus was a married man with several children.

By Paul's own words, all of the other apostles were married. So why was Paul single? He gave a hint of his own situation in 1 Cor. 7.

It is good for a man not to marry. …I wish that all men were as I am. …But since there is so much immorality, each man should have his own wife, and each woman her own husband. …I would like you to be free from concern. An unmarried man is concerned about the Lord's affairs - how he can please the Lord. But a married man is concerned about the affairs of this world - how he can please his wife - and his interests are divided. (1 Cor. 7:1-2, 7, 32-33)

Paul was single because he only had concern for the Lord's business. He later brought this up when comparing himself to the Jewish apostles, Cephas and the Lord's brothers (1 Cor. 9:5-6). His stand on marriage was, therefore, another way to compare himself positively against his rivals for the faith. The above passage was also instrumental in creating an unmarried Jesus. The argument would go as such: If Paul were celibate, surely Jesus was as well. How untidy it would seem for the Savior of the world to be henpecked and taken away from the Lord's work!

This same passage was the underpinning of the Catholic Church's ban on marriage for the priesthood. This is particularly odd considering the Catholics consider Peter their first Pope. We have already noted from Matthew and I Corinthians that this Cephas (Peter) was married. The real reason behind the ban on marriage for the priesthood was purely economic. The Church did not want any church property being inherited by the sons and daughters of the priesthood. So much for being unconcerned about the world's affairs!

THE LORD'S SUPPER

Did Paul invent the Lord's Supper? Surely, the Jewish apostles shared bread together, but did they really celebrate the Lord's Supper as claimed by Paul? Let us look at the passage concerning the Lord's Supper from 1 Corinthians.

For **I received from the Lord** what I also passed on to you: the Lord Jesus, on the night he was **betrayed [handed over]**, took bread, and when he had given thanks, he broke it and said, "This is my body, which is for you; do this in remembrance of me." In the same way, after supper he took the cup, saying, "This cup is the **new covenant in my blood;** do this, whenever you drink it, in remembrance of me." For whenever you eat this bread and drink this cup, you **proclaim the Lord's death until he comes.** (1 Cor. 11:23-26) (Emphasis mine)

It must be remembered that this was the earliest attestation to the Lord's Supper. The Gospel accounts were at least a generation later. So it is extremely interesting that Paul received this Lord's Supper directly from the Lord Jesus. Since Paul never met Jesus in the flesh, any message received from the Lord had to come through revelation. This is exactly what Paul wrote in Gal. 1:12 about his own gospel: "I did not receive it from any man, nor was I taught it; rather, I received it by revelation from Jesus Christ." Certainly, this Lord's Supper did not come from any other man as well. It, too, was a revelation from Jesus Christ. Consider what this means. Paul invented the Lord's Supper and the Gospel writer's simply incorporated this ritual into their rewrite of history.

This invention scenario is not far-fetched. What law abiding Jew would have spoken about a cup of wine being the "new covenant in my blood." First, that Jew had to assume that the old covenant was not everlasting. This, in and of itself, made the statement unacceptable to the Jews. Second, God did not approve of human sacrifice. In Leviticus 20:1-5, the Lord told Moses that anyone sacrificing his children to Molech must be put to death. As the Pharisees would have argued: if it were a sin for the people to sacrifice their children, how much greater a sin for God to sacrifice one of his children. Third, Paul claimed that righteousness was given by God through faith in the blood of Jesus. (Rom. 3:22) This was not part of any Jewish group's belief system, especially the Fourth Philosophy. They believed that righteousness was given by God based upon a person's actions and intentions. Therefore, the law abiding followers of Jesus (Judas the Galilean) would never have practiced this pagan exercise, coined the Lord's Supper.

The universally translated phrase "on the night he was betrayed," has been incorporated into the Gospel lore. The Greek word translated as betrayed actually means "handed over" or "delivered over." This is incredibly important for our current study. According to my theory, Judas the Galilean was the historical Jesus of Nazareth. In this theory, Judas Iscariot never even existed. Note that Paul did not mention a betrayer, only that Jesus had been handed over. Did not the High Priests hand Jesus over to Pilate? Could this passage by Paul have nothing whatsoever to do with Judas Iscariot? Later in this same letter, Paul stated that the resurrected Jesus appeared to Cephas and then to the **Twelve**. (1 Cor. 15:5) In the Great Commission, recorded in Matt. 28:16, the **Eleven** disciples were instructed by Jesus. (See also Mark 16:14 and Luke 24:33. John 20:24 had Jesus appearing to Ten, as Thomas was not with the others.) Now either the Gospels were wrong about the Eleven or Paul about the Twelve. The earlier passage by Paul, no doubt, related the real story. Jesus appeared to the Twelve, proving that a betrayal did not occur.

Finally, Paul stated that his disciples would continue to celebrate the Lord's Supper until Jesus returned. In this, Paul was no different that the Jerusalem apostles. They too believed that Jesus would return, not as the Prince of Peace but as an avenging destroyer of Rome (See Revelation!) So while Paul also taught that the end was near, his vision of the return of Christ was much different than that of the Twelve.

RESURRECTION

The Jewish apostles, led by John the Baptist and James the Just, convinced themselves and others that they had witnessed the resurrected Jesus (Judas the Galilean). This was necessary to keep the movement relevant, as Judas had just been crucified by the enemy, Rome. Since Judas was considered the Messiah (King), it would have been very difficult peddling a dead King to the masses. This is why the resurrection took place. Death could not defeat this Messiah. In fact, according to Revelation, this Messiah was to return in glory to destroy the Roman occupiers.

Paul inherited this resurrection story from the Jewish apostles, but he did his best to place his own unique interpretation to it. Here was Paul's take on the resurrection of Jesus.

For what I received I passed on to you as of first importance: that Christ died for our sins according to the Scriptures, that he was buried, that he was raised on the third day according to the Scriptures, and that he appeared to Peter [Cephas], and then to the Twelve. After that, he appeared to more than five hundred of the brothers at the same time, most of whom are still living, though some have fallen asleep. Then he appeared to James, then to all the apostles, and last of all he appeared to me, as to one abnormally born. (1 Cor. 15:3-8)

In this passage, Paul did not tell who passed on this information to him. This, no doubt, was a well known doctrine within the Jewish Christian movement which Paul incorporated into his own gospel. Note that Paul stated that Christ's death was for the forgiveness of sins, consistent with his message that salvation came through faith in the blood of Jesus. According to Josephus' account of John the Baptist's teachings, forgiveness of the soul came from righteousness. (*Ant.* 18.117) Thus, Paul's interpretation was his alone.

The rest of the passage may have come from Paul, or may include one or more interpolations. The use of the Twelve may be a later addition as Paul generally did not put a definite number on the apostles. However, the genius of Judas the Galilean (Jesus) may have been behind the Twelve apostle scheme. They were his representatives of the Twelve tribes. So this mention of the Twelve may be authentic. (If authentic, it does nullify the Judas Iscariot story!) Another part that may be an interpolation is the five hundred brothers. This would directly contradict Acts 1:15, where the number of believers after the resurrection numbered only one hundred and twenty. This may have been added by Paul or by a later pen to lessen the importance of James. Surely, James' importance was limited as Jesus did not appear to him before over five hundred others.

Paul mentioned himself last in the list, but he did distinguish himself from all others. They had all seen the resurrected Jesus as a man on earth, while he, Paul, had seen the Risen Christ in heaven. In the second letter to the Corinthians, Paul wrote about his meetings with the Lord.

I must go on boasting. Although there is nothing to be gained, I will go on to visions and revelations from the Lord. I know a man in Christ who fourteen years ago was caught up to the third heaven. Whether it was in the body or out of the body I do not know - God knows. And I know that this man ... was caught up to Paradise. He heard inexpressible things, things that man is not permitted to tell. ...To keep me from becoming conceited because of these surpassingly great revelations, there was given me a thorn in my flesh, a messenger of Satan, to torment me. (2 Cor. 12:1-7)

If this were written today by a religious leader, the Psych wards would be awaiting a new inmate. This is incredibly troubling! Paul was brought up to heaven to hear things "that man is not permitted to tell." These great revelations from the Lord were the backbone of Paul's gospel. Consider the meaning of the revelations: Cephas and James had been with Jesus throughout his earthly ministry and had even witnessed his resurrection, yet Jesus had left them totally in the dark. Only Paul could understand the heavenly message of Jesus.

This one on one with the Risen Christ is hard to swallow, but then Paul finished off the thought by attributing his thorn in the flesh to the revelations. So, in Paul's mind, his thorn in the flesh was a result of the great revelations. What was the thorn in his flesh? Many have guessed that the thorn was a physical ailment. This is possible if Paul went into catatonic trances when visiting the Lord. Paul could also have been schizophrenic. The thorn may not have been a physical ailment but rather a force which would not quit bothering Paul. In context, Paul wrote about the "super-apostles" just a few verses before boasting about his hard work and about his admission of revelations from the Risen Christ (2 Cor. 11:1-15). This boasting was simply a way to place him above the "super-apostles." And it is interesting that Paul associated these "super-apostles" (Cephas and James) to the servants of Satan (2 Cor. 11:13-15). If James and Cephas were messengers of Satan then could they have been the thorn in the flesh or the "messenger of Satan?" (2 Cor. 12:7) In addition, after making his fantastic claims, Paul chided the Corinthians: "I ought to have been commended by you, for I am not in the least inferior to the "super-apostles." (2 Cor. 12:11) In short, all the boasting about hard work and the wonders of heaven was to simply make himself look more favorable to his congregation. Certainly, at this point in time, the Jewish Apostles were making a huge impact on Paul's disciples. This dates 2 Corinthians to 44 CE, the same as for the letter to the Galatians.

To the followers of Judas the Galilean, the resurrection of "Jesus" was a continuation of their struggle against Rome. Through this resurrection, there was no magical formula for the forgiveness of sins. These Jewish fanatics looked to the law of Moses and to the everlasting covenant between themselves and God. Their covenant with God did not need an amendment; it did not need a death or a resurrection. On the other hand, Paul's Gentiles were not part of Israel. To them, resurrection had much to do with their **personal** salvation. Paul wrote: "For if the dead are not raised, then Christ has not been raised either. And if Christ has not been raised, your faith is futile; you are still in your sins." (1 Cor. 15:16-17) Paul's emphasis on the death, burial, and resurrection of Christ was no different that the rebirth of the mystery religions.

One last passage about the death and resurrection should further illustrate the difference between Paul and the original followers of Jesus.

And he [Jesus] died for all, that those who live should no longer live for themselves but for him who died for them and was raised again. …Therefore, if anyone is in Christ, he is a new creation; the old has gone, the new has come! All this is from God, who reconciled us to himself through Christ and gave us the ministry of reconciliation: that God was reconciling the world to himself in Christ, not counting men's sins against them. …God made him who had no sin to be [a sin offering] for us, so that in him we might become the righteousness of God. (2 Cor. 5:15-21)

Once again, Paul was telling his disciples that he, Paul, had been given the ministry of reconciliation. This reconciliation to God came through the death and resurrection of Christ. Anyone in Christ would then become the righteousness of God. This union with the dead and resurrected Christ was simply a new packaging of the old mystery religions. According to John the Baptist, righteousness (obeying God) was the means of forgiveness. (*Ant.* 18.116-119) To Paul, identifying with the death and resurrection of Christ was the means of righteousness. Is there any doubt that the Fourth Philosophy removed Paul from their fellowship once they understood his true teachings?

TEACHING CERTIFICATION

In the letter to the Galatians, Paul wrote of his clash with Cephas and James. The second letter to the Corinthians also has some of the same antagonism between Paul and those who came from James. In fact, the spread of an anti-Paul message was becoming a nightmare for Paul. In *Ant.* 20.34-48, Josephus wrote of the King Izates conversion where the pro-Paul position was overtaken by the pro-James position. Thus, King Izates underwent full conversion to Judaism, which included circumcision. The same argument was also recorded in Galatians, and it appears as if the argument also raged in Corinth. This all can be dated at 44 CE, the time when Paul's gospel was officially condemned by the Pillar apostles, led by James.

Paul broached the subject of teacher certification in the following passage:

Are we beginning to commend ourselves again? Or do we need, like some people, letters of reconciliation to you or from you? You yourselves are our letter, written on our hearts, known and read by everybody. You show that you are a letter of Christ, the result of our ministry, written not with ink but with the Spirit of the living God, not on tablets of stone but on tablets of human hearts. (2 Cor. 3:1-3)

Many have viewed this passage as noble. Paul was telling his disciples that they were proof that his ministry was approved by God. In short, Paul was complimenting himself by complimenting his disciples. But what this really shows is that Paul's message was not approved by those in authority. By this time, approximately 44 CE, James was sending out messengers to dispute the gospel of Paul. This occurred in Antioch (Galatians 2:11-13) and also at the conversion of King Izates (*Ant.* 20.34-48). All three of these interventions by James were related, and they all attacked the fundamental teachings of Paul. That is why Paul lashed out at the Pillar apostles in 2 Corinthians and in the letter to the Galatians. Without authority to teach, Paul was left with nothing. If he could not teach, then he could not collect contributions and could not enlarge his donor base.

CONCLUSION

The gospel of Paul was simply a new interpretation of the Old Testament Scriptures. Stories about Abraham and Isaac were twisted in a way to show that the Gentile followers of faith were the true Israel, and that the Jews were not really Jews at all. In addition, his new faith was a reworking of the mystery religions, where the disciples became one with a dead and resurrected God, through the blood of that God. Paul's faith in the blood of Christ replaced the Jewish adherence to the Law.

The very fact that Paul reworked the Jewish Law proves that an earlier gospel of "Jesus" was well known around the Roman world. Certainly, a human "Jesus" once walked the earth and did teach the Jews. Paul could not change that fact. What he did change was the definition of Jew. Through his convoluted reasoning, passages which confirmed the special place of the Jews were shown to be describing his Gentile followers. That is one reason why Paul's preaching was so powerful. We all want to feel special. While the real gospel of Jesus (Judas the Galilean) appealed only to Jews, Paul's gospel was available to all, generally accompanied by a small contribution. (See 2 Cor. 8:1-15).

CHAPTER 9

JAMES AND PAUL

We have already examined Paul's gospel in some detail. Now, we will compare the letter attributed to James to the four legitimate letters by Paul (Romans, 1&2 Corinthians and Galatians). The letter of James may not have been written by James the Just, but it certainly represents his religion and views on the Law. As I have claimed, Paul tried to kill James in the 40's and he persecuted the poor priests soon after the stoning of James. It is safe to say that James and Paul had a very rocky relationship. If Paul converted in the early 20's, then it was during the leadership of John the Baptist, who preached repentance and forgiveness. While James may have reluctantly accepted Paul within the movement, surely a bond of trust never formed. After John the Baptist was executed (36 CE), James became leader by default with Cephas as his number two man. James' guidance of the movement may have been more confrontational than John's leadership. Under James' influence, Agrippa I was excluded from the Temple. At this approximate time (43-44 CE), James sent out his messengers to hound Paul. This action was taken because James had information that Paul preached against the Law. In this, James was correct.

To solidify my position that James and Paul had become enemies, I will examine the letter of James in regards to the teachings of Paul. Were James and Paul preaching the same gospel or were Jewish Christianity and Gentile Christianity two distinct religions?

RICH AND POOR

The letter of James had one consistent theme relating to the Scripture: "Love your neighbor as thyself." The only way to love your neighbor was to consider your neighbor's needs: if he needed food, you should feed him.

However, according to James, the rich exploited the poor and would be judged for their wickedness. This shabby treatment of the poor by the rich was soundly condemned, promising that God would be the final judge of these wrongdoers. A few passages from James concerning the rich and poor are as follows:

The brother in humble circumstances ought to take pride in his high position. But the one who is rich should take pride in his low position, because he will pass away like a wild flower. For the sun rises with scorching heat and withers the plant; its blossom falls and its beauty is destroyed. In the same way, the rich man will fade away even while he goes about his business. (James 1:9-11)

If you show special attention to the man wearing fine clothes and say, "Here's a good seat for you," but say to the poor man, "You stand there" or "Sit on the floor by my feet," have you not discriminated among yourselves and become judges with evil thoughts? Listen, my dear brothers: Has not God chosen those who are poor in the eyes of the world to be rich in faith and to inherit the kingdom he promised those who love him? But you have insulted the poor. Is it not the rich who are exploiting you? Are they not the ones who are dragging you into court? Are they not the ones who are slandering the name of him to whom you belong? (James 2:3-7)

Now listen, you rich people, weep and wail because of the misery that is coming upon you. Your wealth has rotted, and moths have eaten your clothes. Your gold and silver are corroded. Their corrosion will testify against you and eat your flesh like fire. You have hoarded wealth in the last days. Look! The wages you failed to pay the workmen who mowed your fields are crying out against you. The cries of the harvesters have reached the ears of the Lord Almighty. You have lived on earth in luxury and self-indulgence. You have fattened yourselves in the day of slaughter. (James 5:1-5)

There should be no doubt that James disapproved of hoarding wealth. It is interesting that James claimed that this wealth came from those who actually did the work, namely the poor. His analysis of the situation was no different than the analysis of Marx, who claimed that profit was wealth created by the workers. From the above passages, it appears as if James wanted nothing to do with the rich. This money that they hoarded was nothing more than an idol.

This attitude of James was no different than that of Jesus. Jesus said: "Blessed are you who are poor, for yours is the kingdom of God. ...But woe to

163

you who are rich, for you have already received your comfort." (Luke 6:20-24) But perhaps the most telling parable from Jesus about the rich was "The Rich Ruler". (Luke 18:18-25) In this parable, the rich man insisted that he had kept all of the commandments since his childhood. Even so, Jesus told him he still lacked one thing essential for salvation. Jesus said: "Sell everything and give to the poor, and you will have treasure in heaven. Then come, follow me." The rich man went away sad because he could not part with his great wealth. In essence, Jesus believed that if you had wealth while others starved, then you were not following the commands of God, especially the most important law to "love your neighbor as thyself."

This insistence on equality was central to Judas the Galilean's Fourth Philosophy. During the war with Rome, the Sicarii burned down the Record Office so that the poor would be freed from their debts to the rich. (*War* 2.426-427) As noted in Chapter 5, James led the Sicarii movement, and this act was consistent with James' teachings on the rich and the poor.

Continuity existed between the teachings of Judas the Galilean (Jesus) and James concerning the rich and poor. But how did Paul treat the rich in his dealings throughout the Roman Empire? In Josephus' account of the unnamed Jew who swindled the Jewish convert in Rome, the unnamed Jew (Saul) certainly courted the wealthy. (*Ant.* 18.81-84) In his dealings with his churches, Paul encouraged his wealthier patrons to give to those in need. (2 Cor. 8:1-15) Although this appears to be similar in nature to the plea of Jesus for the wealthy to give all they owned to the poor, Paul asked that those with plenty would voluntarily share with those in need. So, in Paul's churches, wealth was not discouraged. In fact, if one were wealthy, then one could help out more people. Unfortunately, we do not know if the contributions of the rich ever made it to those in need. There is a good chance that Paul simply took the money for himself. (This type of extortion takes place today under the name of God.)

In the words of Jesus, one had to give all possessions to the poor before becoming a follower. To Paul, one only had to have faith in the blood of Christ to become a follower. Therefore, the rich and poor were alike. Both could believe in the blood of Christ.

In James 2:3-7, the point was made that the rich were pulling the poor into court in order to take away the little that the poor owned. In 1 Cor. 6:1-11, Paul scolded his disciples from taking each other to court. Paul was not proud of this behavior, but it illustrates that his gospel's qualifications for entry into the movement were not very strict. In fact, people of all walks entered into his new covenant with God. Paul assumed that the Holy Spirit would cleanse them and lead them in holy living. This did not work then and it does not work today. Wicked people often remain wicked people. Such people would have needed to repent (change) before following Jesus and John the Baptist.

FAITH AND DEEDS

As noted in the preceding chapter, Paul used the example of Abraham to illustrate the ideal of faith. In Genesis 15:6: "Abram believed the Lord, and he credited it to him as righteousness." This passage underpinned Paul's gospel. According to Paul, anyone who believed or had faith in the blood of Christ would be considered righteous and forgiven before God.

James also used Genesis 15:6 in his letter. According to James' interpretation, it was not just faith but faith accompanied by works which set Abraham apart.

You foolish man, do you want evidence that faith without deeds is useless? Was not our ancestor Abraham considered righteous for what he did when he offered his son Isaac on the altar? You see that his faith and his actions were working together, and his faith was made complete by what he did. And the scripture was fulfilled that says, "Abraham believed God, and it was credited to him as righteousness," and he was called God's friend. You see that a person is justified by what he does and not by faith alone. (James 2:20-24)

Let us apply some logic to the example of Abraham. If Abraham had refused to offer Isaac on the altar, would Abraham have been considered righteous by God? Abraham could have said, "I believe in you God, but I will not do what you ask. Try me again next week!" No, Abraham went against his own better judgment and began offering his son in sacrifice. That was faith. An utterance from our lips does not prove faith, yet our actions show our worship. If we cheat and steal, our actions show that we worship money, even though we may go to church twice a week and proclaim Jesus.

James wrote: "Faith by itself, if it is not accompanied by action, is dead," (James 2:17) and "Show me your faith without deeds, and I will show you my faith by what I do. You believe that there is one God. Good! Even the demons believe that - and shudder." In short, faith is not really faith without good works. In essence, James was telling Paul and his disciples that their faith was absolutely worthless unless accompanied by action. And the first action would be circumcision, the seal in the everlasting covenant between God and man.

In Galatians, certain men came from James who taught that following the law of God was necessary for salvation. (Gal. 2:12; 3:1-4) This also was the case in the King Izates conversion as related by Josephus (*Ant.* 20.34-48).

Paul, afraid to lose his following, asked them, "Did you receive the Spirit by observing the law, or by believing what you heard?" Here, Paul directly opposed James' theology of faith made relevant by actions.

Remember, James stated that even the demons believe. He, therefore, did not hold to the simple faith or belief as espoused by Paul. Paul wrote in Romans 10:9: "That if you confess with your mouth, 'Jesus is Lord,' and believe in your heart that God raised him from the dead, you will be saved. For it is with your heart that you believe and are justified, and it is with your mouth that you confess and are saved." Paul substituted believing in the resurrection for obeying the law. James certainly believed in the resurrection, yet he also knew that God required man to obey His laws. According to James, you could not substitute belief for following the law. To James, belief was made alive by following the law.

Paul wrote about the difference between his Gentiles and the Jews, the difference between faith and works:

What then shall we say? That the Gentiles, who did not pursue righteousness, have obtained it, a righteousness that is by faith; but Israel, who pursued a law of righteousness, has not attained it. Why not? Because they pursued it not by faith but as if it were by works. (Romans 9:30-32)

This Pauline theology has been accepted over the past 1900 years by the Gentile Church, but it was never accepted by the Jewish Christians as represented by James and Cephas. Certainly, Paul did not preach his new gospel in the early years of his ministry. This evolution in thought, prodded by revelations from the Risen Christ, made Paul view the Gentiles differently. He planned to reach them through a unique message, a mixture of the Jesus story with the prevalent mystery religions of the day. In that way, his Gentile followers really did not need to change dramatically. If Paul had followed the ways of Jesus, James and Cephas, then he would have had to preach the law and circumcision to his followers. This would have slowed the growth among the Gentiles. In his desire to reach and convert as many Gentiles as possible, Paul abandoned the original message of Jesus and created his own hybrid religion. In the end, due to the Jewish war with Rome, Paul's version won out.

TAMING THE TONGUE

This is an interesting topic if we consider the Apostle Paul. Could James have had Paul in mind when he wrote about the tongue?

...the tongue is a small part of the body, but it makes great boasts. Consider what a great forest is set on fire by a small spark. The tongue also is a fire, a world of evil among the parts of the body. ...Out of the same mouth come praise and cursing. My brothers, this should not be. (James 3:5-6, 10)

First, James emphasized that the tongue makes great boasts. This could be true of just about everyone, but no one fits the bill more than Paul. The following came from Paul's letters to his congregations. Note that the bragging is mostly from 2 Corinthians and Galatians. These two letters were written after Paul involuntarily left the movement. That is why Paul spent so much time boasting about his qualifications. He wanted his disciples to compare his real (or invented) activities with those of mere mortal men.

Are we beginning to commend ourselves again? Or do we need, like some people, letters of recommendation to you or from you. (2 Cor. 3:1)

Rather, as servants of God we commend ourselves in every way: in great endurance; in troubles, hardships and distresses; in beatings, imprisonments and riots; in hard work, sleepless nights and hunger; in purity, understanding, patience and kindness; ...genuine, yet regarded as imposters. (2 Cor. 6:4-10)

I must go on boasting. Although there is nothing to be gained, I will go on to visions and revelations from the Lord. ...To keep me from becoming conceited because of these surpassingly great revelations, there was given me a thorn in my flesh, a messenger of Satan, to torment me. (2 Cor. 12:1-10)

I was advancing in Judaism beyond many Jews of my own age and was extremely zealous for the traditions of my fathers. But when God, who set me apart from birth and called me by his grace, was pleased to reveal his Son in me so that I might preach him among the Gentiles... (Gal. 1:14-16)

The boasting is quite amazing. Paul defended his own ministry in several ways. In the first passage (2 Cor. 3:1), Paul explained why he did not have letters of recommendation from the Pillars. He simply stated that they were unnecessary, and that his letters were his followers, who were filled with the Holy Spirit. This bait and switch worked well as most people enjoy being flattered.

In the second passage, Paul recounted (or invented) his great number of sacrifices for the faith. He endured all sorts of trials and tribulations as a servant of God. Surely this hard work counted for something. When reading this, one is almost in awe. Could any man have worked as hard as Paul? But then we must see why Paul recounted these hardships. He stated: "[We are] genuine, yet regarded as imposters." Who regarded Paul and his fellow teachers as imposters? This had to be those nasty followers of James.

Perhaps the greatest boast was Paul's claim of revelations from God. Paul was the ultimate name dropper. This boast was not traceable by anyone, as the Lord only spoke to Paul. How convenient for Paul! Paul himself stated that any man would become conceited by these great revelations. Only the thorn in his flesh kept Paul grounded in this world. Those listening to this claim would either be greatly impressed or incredibly concerned. Today, such an individual as Paul would become a cult hero, just as he was two thousand years ago. Did James approve of Paul's claims? James was the brother of Judas (Jesus), and he knew that Paul's claims concerning the Risen Christ were not true. How could Jesus have preached one message all his years on earth and a different message to Paul after the resurrection? We should ask the same question today.

The last passage goes even further than the claim of revelations from the Risen Christ. Paul wrote that God had set him apart from birth, revealing his Son in him. Paul was, therefore, part of God's cosmic plan for salvation. Even before the crucifixion of Jesus, God had set Paul's future from birth. And Paul was to embody Jesus to the Gentiles. This is incredible boasting. I have no doubt that James had Paul in mind when he wrote about the evils of boasting. I am not sure that James knew the extent of Paul's boasting. After all, 2 Corinthians and Galatians were written after Paul's removal from the movement. Paul was free from hiding any of his wild revelations from the Pillars. They no longer ruled him.

WISDOM

James wrote about wisdom, but once again, James' interpretation was much different than the one given by Paul. James tied wisdom to actions.

Who is wise and understanding among you? Let him show it by his good life, by deeds done in the humility that comes from wisdom. But if you harbor bitter envy and selfish ambition in your hearts, do not boast about it or deny the truth. Such "wisdom" does not come down from heaven but is earthly, unspiritual, of the devil. (James 3:13-15)

To James, life and religion were intricately intertwined. You could not separate the two. Therefore, wisdom was shown through living a good life with deeds illustrating the person's humility. On the other hand, wisdom was much different for Paul. To Paul, the wisdom of God was simply the crucifixion of Christ Jesus. This spin on wisdom removes all human activity.

For the message of the cross is foolishness to those who are perishing, but to us who are being saved it is the power [and wisdom] of God. …When I came to you, brothers, I did not come with eloquence or superior wisdom as I proclaimed to you the testimony about God. For I resolved to know nothing while I was with you except Jesus Christ and him crucified. …we speak of God's secret wisdom, a wisdom that has been hidden and that God destined for our glory before time began … but God has revealed it to us by his Spirit. (1 Cor. 1:18; 2:1-10)

Apart from Christ Jesus crucified, nothing existed but worldly wisdom. To Paul, one could not know the wisdom of God except through the Spirit of God, made possible by the resurrection of Christ Jesus. To Paul, wisdom came from God through the actions of another (Christ Jesus), but to James, wisdom came through good deeds and humility. These views were diametrically opposed. James would never have considered the crucifixion of his brother, Jesus, as necessary to show mercy and kindness to others. The death of Jesus was not a prerequisite to the wisdom described by James. But to Paul, this death of Christ Jesus was a wisdom hidden from the world since the creation.

James believed that God was totally revealed through the Everlasting Covenant between God and Abraham. With this Everlasting Covenant, man had a responsibility to his fellow man, to love thy neighbor as thyself. This was the wisdom as expressed by James. Paul claimed that the Everlasting Covenant was being pushed aside for something that God had hidden from the Jews: Christ Jesus crucified. This wisdom could only be accessed through faith in the blood of Christ. James held on to the Jewish concept of wisdom while Paul wandered into his own pagan-influenced version of wisdom.

THE LAW

From the letters of Paul as well as selected passages from Acts, it can be confidently argued that James zealously supported the law. In his letter to the Galatians, the circumcision group had come from James. In the remainder of that letter, Paul denounced the law as compared to his new religion of faith. (Gal. 3-5:12) In fact, Paul called upon the Jews who represented James to "go the whole way and emasculate themselves." (Gal. 5:12) This hatred for James and his steadfast observance of the law helps define James. He was zealous for the law. This fact slipped out in Acts 21:20, where James and the elders were describing the Jerusalem followers: "You see, brother, how many thousands of Jews have believed, and all of them are zealous for the law."

If the Jews who believed were zealous for the law, then it follows that James and the apostles were preaching the law of Moses. Many scholars have assumed that the leadership (James and Cephas) were really moving towards Paul's position (See Acts 11-15), and were just humoring their own dim-witted disciples. There could be nothing farther from the truth. James was just as much obsessed with the law as his believing disciples. Therefore, when we read the letter of James, we must be mindful of this steadfast observance of the law.

James wrote this concerning the law:

Anyone who speaks against his brother or judges him speaks against the Law and judges it. When you judge the Law, you are not keeping it, but sitting in judgment on it. There is only one Lawgiver and Judge, the one who is able to save and destroy. But you - who are you to judge your neighbor? (James 4:11-12)

Again, James tied his interpretation of the Law to his relationships with others, with his neighbor. In essence, James taught his disciple to treat others with respect and let God be the Judge. But with this judgment by God there was also mercy, for James wrote that the Lawgiver and Judge was able to save and destroy. This Judge did not need the human sacrifice of Jesus to be able to save. God had always had the power to save. After all, is it not God who is all powerful?

Paul did not share this interpretation of the Law. Paul sincerely believed that the Law was dead. Here are a few passages which help frame Paul's view of the Law.

I found that the very commandment that was intended to bring life actually brought death. (Rom. 7:10)

For what the law was powerless to do in that it was weakened by the sinful nature, God did by sending his own Son in the likeness of sinful man to be a sin offering. And so he condemned sin in sinful man, in order that the righteous requirements of the law might be fully met in us, who do not live according to the sinful nature but according to the Spirit. (Rom. 8:3-4)

In the first passage, Paul stated that the commandments of God actually brought death and not life. This revelation from Paul would have sent the Jews howling in disgust. Paul believed that it was impossible to follow the law and therefore the law only brought death and despair. But did God ever intend for the Jews to be perfect? If God created man, He would have known that man was not perfect. What God desired was for the Jews to constantly work towards following the law. A passage in Deuteronomy clarifies the Old Testament's position concerning the law.

The Lord your God will circumcise your hearts and the hearts of your descendants, so that you may love him with all your heart and with all your soul, and will live. ...Now what I am commanding you today is **not too difficult for you or beyond your reach**. It is not in heaven, so that you have to ask, "Who will ascend into heaven to get it and proclaim it to us so we may obey it?" ...No, the word is very near you; it is in your mouth and in your heart so you may obey it. (Deut. 30:6-14) (Emphasis mine)

According to this passage, the law was to be followed by the present and all future generations. And, unlike Paul's position, the law was not too difficult to follow. This is important because Paul's theology rests on the inability of man to follow the law perfectly. Man was never intended to be perfect, so to assume that God gave man a law that would condemn him by his imperfection, makes God out to be sadistic and illogical. Is it any wonder why James rejected Paul's take on the law?

In the Rom. 8:3 passage, Paul's answer for the imperfection of man was a sin offering in the form of Christ Jesus. Through this sacrifice, God was making it possible for man to fulfill the righteous requirements of the law. But Paul never really explained how this sacrifice should nullify an Everlasting Covenant. First, a human sacrifice was abhorrent to God. That God offered Jesus to be a sin offering smacks of sheer paganism. The Jews would and could not accept this. But Paul was not taking his message to the Jews. This sin offering was for his Gentile audience.

THE LIAR, THE ENEMY, AND THE TRAITOR

Knowing that James thoroughly discredited Paul's gospel, it is not much of a stretch to attribute to Paul the Dead Sea Scroll moniker of "The Liar." Robert Eisenman does just that in his 1997 book, *James the Brother of Jesus*. As noted above, the conflict between the two opposing viewpoints went far beyond reconciliation. Paul wanted to supplant the Jews as God's chosen people. What do you think was the response to this "gospel?" The Jewish Christians (Fourth Philosophy) hounded Paul and his congregations calling Paul a liar and the enemy.

Certainly, the later Church did as much as possible to deflect such criticism from its main apostle, Paul. The Book of Acts made Paul into a hero and diminished the roles of Cephas and James. However, there are telltale passages in Paul's letters which suggest that he was indeed branded as "The Liar." The following passages in question are as follows:

I speak the truth in Christ - I am not lying, my conscience confirms it in the Holy Spirit. (Romans 9:1)

We are treated as imposters, and yet are true. (2 Cor. 6:8)

The God and Father of the Lord Jesus, who is to be praised forever, knows that I am not lying. (2 Cor. 11:31)

I assure you before God that what I am writing you is no lie. (Gal. 1:20)

Obviously, the charge of lying to the Gentiles was put forth more than once. Note that the denial was to the Romans, Corinthians and to those in Galatia. In fact, the charge of lying followed Paul wherever he went. This may be one reason why Paul developed such an overwhelming hatred of the Fourth Philosophy and was active against them from 44 CE to the beginning of the Jewish War (66-67 CE).

Paul's defense against the charge of lying was simple: he simply denied lying and swore by the name of God or by the Holy Spirit. How could you not believe Paul if he said that the Holy Spirit confirmed his message? After all, did not Paul have direct revelations from God? This method of hiding behind God worked well for Paul. In fact, many preachers and politicians use the same ploy today. But Paul's argument was made stronger by his supposed ties to the Risen Christ. Like any cult, the Gentile followers of Paul would have believed almost anything. He must have been very smooth as well. Barnabas was his fellow teacher until Cephas and James removed Paul from fellowship. Barnabas sided with Cephas because the truth of the Jewish law was stronger than Paul's dreams.

"The Liar" label certainly fit Paul, but what about "The Enemy?" A liar could describe someone still active in the movement, but an enemy has already been removed and is now in the process of opposing the movement. This was the case with Paul. While still in the movement, Paul was beset with charges of lying to his followers. This came to a head in the Antioch argument with Cephas, and Paul was removed from fellowship. At this point, Paul became the enemy.

This enemy terminology is present in the letter of James and in Paul's second letter to the Corinthians.

You adulterous people, don't you know that **friendship with the world is hatred towards God**? Anyone who chooses to be a friend of the world becomes an **enemy of God**. (James 4:4)

I beg you that when I come I may not have to be as bold as I expect to be toward some people who think that **we live by the standards of this world**. ...For if someone comes to you and preaches a Jesus other than the Jesus we preached, or if you received a different spirit from the one you received, or a different gospel from the one you accepted, you put up with it easily enough. But I do not think I am in the least inferior to those "super-apostles." (2 Cor. 10:2; 11:4-5) (Emphasis mine)

James adamantly insisted that living by the world's standards was equivalent to being an enemy of God. This was consistent with the words of Jesus: "No one can serve two masters. Either he will hate the one and love the other, or he will be devoted to the one and despise the other. You cannot serve both God and Money [Rome]." By the time of the Antioch argument, James was well aware that Paul preached against the law, that he denigrated circumcision and that he taught his disciples to accept eating food sacrificed to idols. To James, anyone who preached against the law was a friend of the world and an enemy of God.

To Paul, his gospel to the Gentiles was God-given. His new gospel broke down the barriers between the God of the Jews and his Gentile disciples. Therefore, "living by the standards of this world" had no true meaning for Paul. In fact, his gospel blurred the line between God and this world. With only the "Spirit" to guide them, his disciples had little chance to live a godly life. In 1 Cor. 5:1, Paul admonished his disciples: "It is actually reported that there is sexual immorality among you, and of a kind that does not occur even among pagans: A man has his father's wife." In response to this immoral action, Paul asked that his church not associate with this type of individual. In a sense, Paul was then setting down his own law as the "Spirit" was unable to guide these poor souls. His "Spirit" theology was often used by his followers to cover their own sins. This same mind-set is used today in Christian churches. If I sin, then God will forgive me because I am saved through the blood of Christ. Maybe Paul did not realize the implications of his new gospel, but when he saw the results, he did try to impose some sort of law. He said this to the Romans: "What then? Shall we sin because we are not under law but under grace? By no means!" Is it any wonder why James considered Paul and his followers to be friends of this world?

Paul became the enemy of the Fourth Philosophy after the Antioch argument with Cephas, around 44 CE. Paul, then, was left with a Gentile following but no mother Church forcing him to play second fiddle to the Pillar Apostles. Initially, Paul still continued to gather contributions for those in Jerusalem. These funds, no doubt, ended up in his own pockets. The title, The Enemy," may have been cast in stone by Paul's dealings with James and Cephas after the fallout at Antioch.

The Recognitions of Clement, a second century document, described Paul as being the Enemy of the Church around the mid 40's. The story may have been a distant memory handed down as an assault upon James at the Temple in Jerusalem. This probably took place when Paul brought his contributions to Jerusalem after the Antioch incident. (This money never went to James but to Paul's own coffers, as Josephus tells us that Saul was very influential in 60's Jerusalem. Influence was gained primarily through wealth and family connections.) In Jerusalem, Paul encountered James.

Much blood is shed; there is a confused flight, in the midst of which that enemy attacked James, and threw him headlong from the top of the steps; and supposing him to be dead, he cared not to inflict further violence upon him. …Then after three days one of the brethren came to us from Gamaliel, … bringing to us secret tidings that the enemy had received a commission from Caiaphas, the chief priest, that he should arrest all who believed in Jesus, and should go to Damascus with his letters, and that there also, employing the help of the unbelievers, he should make havoc among the faithful; and that he was hastening to Damascus chiefly on this account, because he believed that Peter had fled thither. (*Recognitions of Clement* 1.70-71)

When the enemy was first announced in this account, a marginal note in one of the manuscripts stated that the enemy was Paul. (1) This is further supported by the enemy receiving a commission from the high priest to go to Damascus to persecute the Church. This is the same account that the book of Acts attributed to Paul **before his conversion** (Acts 9:1-2). In *The Recognitions*, the Enemy was Paul, but the actions occurred **after his expulsion** from the movement. So, is it possible that Paul attacked and almost killed James shortly after James had pulled the plug on Paul's ministry? From the differences between Paul and James that have been noted above as well as the account from *The Recognitions*, it would be hard to discount such a possibility.

But we must go one step further. Paul was not only "The Liar," and "The Enemy," but "The Traitor" as well. The term traitor has always been assigned to Judas Iscariot, but I propose that Paul, the Apostle to the Gentiles, was the original traitor. (Judas Iscariot will be examined in Part III, Chapter 17.)

First, a traitor is someone who switches allegiances. This was certainly true for Paul. When Paul first converted, he probably spent three years studying with the Fourth Philosophy. In Gal. 1:18, Paul stated that he went up to Jerusalem three years after his conversion. The Essenes had a three year probation for new recruits, and Judas the Galilean copied many of the same practices. This training would have grounded Paul in the Zealot philosophy. In his letters, it is quite apparent that Paul understood the intricacies of the Fourth Philosophy even as he turned the Scriptures on its head. He used the same Genesis passage as James to prove his justification by faith. This took knowledge and guts, to say the least. That Paul stayed within the movement for at least seventeen years is testament that he had once followed the original gospel of Judas (Jesus), John the Baptist, James and Cephas.

Second, Paul denigrated the Jewish religion by twisting the Jewish Scriptures to meet his own desires. He somehow took the Abraham story and made it a promise to the Gentiles. What a feat! This, however, would have angered the leadership of the movement. It is no surprise that the Jews all turned their backs upon Paul at Antioch. And if they had known Paul's entire gospel, they would have probably stoned him as well.

Third, soon after the split at Antioch, James and Simon, the sons of Judas the Galilean were crucified. Could Paul have been behind this decision by the Roman Procurator, Tiberius Alexander? Tiberius Alexander was related to Philo, who knew Agrippa I, a kinsman of Saul. There is a good chance that Paul would have had access to this Alexander. In addition, the *Recognitions of Clement* also had Saul attacking James, almost killing him and chasing Cephas as far as Damascus. It seems as though Saul/Paul wanted to even the score with the Fourth Philosophy.

Fourth, Saul was part of the larger ruling class which had a hand in the stoning of James in 62 CE. This is hidden in Acts as Saul approved of the stoning of Stephen, before his conversion. In reality, Saul approved of the stoning of his longtime nemesis, James the Just.

Fifth, Saul tried to persuade Agrippa II to send forces to Jerusalem to defeat the Zealot and Sicarii forces. There is no doubt that Saul/Paul would have been the object of the most sincere loathing. No one could match Paul's resume concerning the traitor label. He had earned this badge of dishonor with every word he uttered and every action he took. To the Fourth Philosophy, he was the ultimate traitor.

CONCLUSION

The letter of James was sent to a Gentile audience to combat the unlawful teachings of Paul and his disciples. James' representatives reached Corinth, Antioch and to King Izates' kingdom. In each case, Paul's gospel was undercut.

Depending on Paul's strength in these areas, his gospel had a tough row to hoe. In Antioch, Paul stated that all the Jews, including Barnabas, had deserted him. In the case of King Izates, the King accepted the representative of James over Paul's disciple. In Corinth, Paul may have fared better. At least he was still trying, as 2 Corinthians is a testament to his tenacity.

One thing must not be overlooked in this comparison of James and Paul: the two were opposed in everything. This was not just a difference of opinion but one gospel against another. James and Cephas held to the same gospel (good news) that Judas (Jesus) had championed. Paul's gospel shifted the chosen people from the Jews to the Gentiles and was completely alien to anything taught by Jesus. Paul was rightly called the Liar, the Enemy and the Traitor, for his gospel and his later actions were hell-bent on destroying the Church of Judas (Jesus).

CHAPTER 10

AGRIPPA I AND PAUL

Throughout this book, I have been emphasizing the radically different timeline which emerges using the Judas the Galilean hypothesis. Not only does the beginning of the movement shift back a generation, so too does the history of Paul. In the traditional timeline, Paul converted around 35 CE, visited Jerusalem for the second time around 52 CE and finally sailed to Rome between 60-62 CE. Using this traditional timeline, any connection between Paul and Agrippa I would be nearly impossible, since Agrippa I ruled as King of Israel from 37-44 CE.

Under my revised timeline, Paul converted to the movement around 21-25 CE, visited Jerusalem for the second time around 38-42 CE and was summarily removed from the movement in 44 CE. This revised timeline overlaps the kingship of Agrippa I. Therefore, it would be beneficial to look for any connection between the two individuals. In the book of Acts, Paul conversed with Agrippa II, the son of Agrippa I, also known as Agrippa the Great. Is it possible that Paul actually knew the father as well? If he did, then the actual ministry of Paul can be better defined as a ministry opposed to the Fourth Philosophy, opposed to James and Cephas.

Due to this change in timelines, it is very important to examine King Agrippa I. His history will be detailed in this chapter as it relates to Paul. If one would like to read an interesting account of Agrippa, then the book of choice is *Claudius the God*, by Robert Graves. This is the second part of a two-part account of Claudius, the first being *I Claudius*. In the second installment, Graves invested much time detailing the life of Herod Agrippa. I will not go there, because I cannot match Graves' superb writing style. I will, however, interest the reader with many possible connections between this Agrippa and our beloved Paul, the Apostle.

ALL IN THE FAMILY (1)

In the dynasty founded by Herod the Great, there were several important branches. We will focus upon the branches concerning Agrippa I and Saul. In *Ant.* 20.214, Josephus wrote that Saul was a kinsman of the royal family. As this account of Saul came right after the stoning of James, it is quite natural to compare this to the stoning of Stephen and the persecution by Saul. In short, the Acts' version was a rewrite of the original story as presented by Josephus. From this story, we know that Saul was related to Agrippa. This is further confirmed by another story from Josephus, where Saul was picked to petition Agrippa II for an army to crush the rebellion in Jerusalem. (*War* 2.418-419) Once again, Josephus called Saul a kinsman of the King.

So how exactly were Agrippa and Saul related? From the account given by Josephus, the following can be gleaned. Both Agrippa and Saul had their great grandfather, Antipater, in common. Agrippa came from the line of Herod the Great, being his grandson, while Saul's grandmother was Salome, the sister of Herod the Great. This would make them cousins of a sort, but it definitely does not mean that the two branches were close.

But there is more to this family connection. Agrippa's father, Aristobulus, married Saul's Aunt Bernice. This slightly incestuous relationship produced several children, including Agrippa, who became most important in the story of Israel. So, two different familial connections between Agrippa and Saul existed: one through a great grandfather and one through marriage. This enhances the chance of close relations between the family of Agrippa and the family of Saul, but it in no way positively puts the two men together. It is just a starting point.

It should also be noted that Agrippa I married a Cypros, a cousin descended from Herod the Great's brother, Phasaelus. The instances of niece marriage and cousin marriage were quite high for the Herodian stock. This would suggest that the entire family had somewhat close ties, especially if wives and husbands were taken from their own family. Perhaps this was a way to keep all of their assets in the family.

Would Agrippa and Saul have known each other as children? The answer is no. Agrippa was born approximately 10 BCE and was shipped to Rome shortly after Herod the Great had executed his father, Aristobulus, in 6 BCE. Saul, on the other hand, was probably born between 5-1 BCE based upon his own account and that of Josephus. In *Ant.* 18.81-84, an unnamed Jew, most likely Saul, was run out of Judea for transgressing the law and later swindled a Jewish convert in Rome. This was around 19 CE. In Galatians, Paul stated that he was a young man before converting to the Way. Therefore, it is probable that Paul was born between 5-1 BCE. Thus, Saul and Agrippa never met as children, but certainly, their families were close. This is important because this family connection may well have linked the two later in life.

DIFFERING PATHS

Although Saul and Agrippa were relatives, they traveled very different paths. Agrippa I was born around 10 BCE and was shipped to Rome with his mother in 6 BCE, to live at Augustus' court. Agrippa's father, Aristobulus, was executed by his own father, Herod the Great in 6 BCE. This execution was due to Herod's jealousy toward his son and his irrational fear that Aristobulus might grab his throne. This may very well have been the inspiration for the murder of the innocents, as Herod executed both of his sons by his Maccabean queen, Mariamne.

At a very young age, Agrippa became close friends with Tiberius' son. He was schooled with Claudius, a future Caesar. He also befriended Antonia, Claudius' mother, and eventually became close with Gaius (Caligula), Claudius' nephew. So even though Agrippa's life began in the land of Judea, his friends were the power elites of the Roman Empire.

Agrippa spent money freely as a youth. When his mother, Bernice, died, he quickly ran through his inheritance. A constant search for new funds helped shape Agrippa's fortunes. He became very good at asking for help and borrowed money from Antonia and from Alexander, the alabarch (governor of the Jews) of Alexandria. This Alexander was the brother of Philo and the father of Tiberius Alexander, the procurator of Judea when Judas the Galilean's sons, Simon and James, were crucified. Agrippa also used the help of his sister's husband, Herod the Tetrarch (Antipas). His sister, Herodias, and Herod the Tetrarch were responsible for the death of John the Baptist.

Through Tiberius, Agrippa I became a great friend to Gaius (Caligula). Upon the death of Tiberius, Caligula became Emperor and gave Agrippa the tetrarchy of Philip and the tetrarchy of Lysanius. (*Ant.* 18.237) He was later given the tetrarchy of Herod Antipas by suggesting that Antipas was a threat to Caligula. In short, Agrippa had become a very powerful man in a very short period of time.

Agrippa had aligned himself with the powers of Rome, so it should not be surprising that he and the Fourth Philosophy of Judas the Galilean were diametrically opposed. His own brother-in-law had John the Baptist executed, and he had become friends with Alexander the alabarch, the father of Tiberius Alexander, the man who had the sons of Judas the Galilean crucified. No man could have done more to arouse the disgust and anger of the Fourth Philosophy.

While Agrippa I was rubbing elbows with the rich and powerful, Saul was operating under the radar. Nothing is known of Saul's very early life. At about the age of twenty, Saul was driven away from Judea because he transgressed the law. He later went to Rome where he swindled a Jewish convert, claiming that he was knowledgeable in the law and would take her gifts to the Temple in Jerusalem. (It is noteworthy that Paul only visited Jerusalem twice after his conversion and never went to Rome. There was good reason for him to stay away from these two cities.) In Galatians 1:13-17, Paul claimed that he converted to the church of God (the Way of Righteousness or the Fourth Philosophy). After three years, he traveled to Jerusalem to meet with Cephas. This three year stint after the conversion may have been Paul's initiation into the movement. The Essenes used a three year initiate training period (*War* 2.137-138), and it is likely that the Fourth Philosophy also used a similar training schedule. Paul learned the law from the most zealous of Zealots, and this occurred **after** his conversion. Note that in Galatians 1:13-17, Paul stated that he was zealous for the law **before** his conversion. This was extremely unlikely considering he had been run out of town for transgressing the law just a few years before his conversion. In fact, Paul was simply distancing himself from the Pillar Apostles, those Zealots who did not understand God's grace. If Paul had been telling the truth, he would have acknowledged that he was trained by these men to follow the law, and that the original movement was all about the law. This truth would never be admitted by Paul.

From the years 21-37 CE, Paul was a member of the Jewish Christian movement (Fourth Philosophy). It must be stressed that he followed the law and the guidance of John the Baptist and James for most of this time. It was not until his seventeenth year in the movement that he came once again to Jerusalem, in order to put forth his gospel to the Gentiles. This would have occurred between 38-40 CE. Something had happened around the year 37 CE which triggered the revelations of Paul.

While Agrippa I was returning to Jerusalem in 37 CE as a King, appointed by Caligula, his cousin Saul was also headed back to his roots. Was this convergence a coincidence or was Paul drawn back in order to meet this new king? From Paul's own words, he met privately with the leaders (the Pillars). Could he also have met with his own family? This he does not say, but we must not rule out the possibility.

THE MAKING OF A MESSIAH

A Messiah was simply the Anointed One or the king. In this sense, there had been many Messiahs in Israel's past. But the expectations of a Great Messiah from God percolated throughout first-century Judea. According to Numbers 24:17: "A Star will come out of Jacob; a scepter will rise out of Israel." This was the "Star Prophecy", the prophecy which promised that a world leader would arise in Israel. This "Star Prophecy" was the driving force behind the "Star of Bethlehem" stories.

In the Slavonic Josephus, the "Star of Bethlehem" story was placed at around 25 BCE, around the time of Judas the Galilean's birth. In this account, the star was defined.

And he [Herod the Great] was furious and summoned the priests [who were his] advisors and asked if any of them understood [the meaning of] that star. And they answered him: "It is written: 'A star shall shine forth from Jacob and a man shall arise from Judah'." (After *War* 1.400)

Later in the Slavonic Josephus, the writer explained how the "Star Prophecy" could be interpreted differently by various groups. The important point was that the people did take this prophecy seriously.

But they [the Jews] were impelled to [make] war by an ambiguous prediction found in the sacred books, saying that in those times someone from the Judaean land would be reigning over the whole world. For this there are various explanations. For some thought it [meant] Herod, others the crucified miracle-worker, [Jesus], others Vespasian. (After *War* 6.311)

In a successful effort to save his own life, Josephus attributed the "Star Prophecy" to Vespasian. This shrewd move landed Josephus a steady gig with the future Caesar. It is quite obvious that the followers of the miracle worker (Jesus or Judas the Galilean) believed that their leader, dead or alive, was the Messiah. It is interesting that the personage of Herod was included in this list. This probably refers to Herod the Great, who ruled until 4 BCE, but it very well could also refer to Herod Agrippa the Great or Agrippa I, who ruled from 37-44 CE. In either event, there were some who looked at the Herodians for their Messiah.

Agrippa I benefited from his close ties to Caligula, as this Emperor gave Agrippa the Tetrarchies of Philip and Lysanius and later the Tetrarchy of Herod Antipas. This success for Agrippa would not have imputed any comparisons to the Great Messiah. But his effort to persuade Caligula to forego his desire to place a giant statue of himself into the Temple would have garnered great interest. This may have been the platform which illustrated his abilities to Philo. According to Graves, Philo believed that Agrippa was the promised Messiah. (2)

According to Josephus, Agrippa provided Caligula with a supper that surpassed all others in extravagance and expense. This impressed Caligula so much that he offered to grant any wish that Agrippa desired. Caligula assumed that Agrippa would wish for more power, more land to govern, but Agrippa caught Caligula off guard. He asked that Caligula refrain from putting his statue in the Temple. This bothered Caligula, but he agreed to Agrippa's wish because he had made his promise in public. So with a meal, Agrippa might have saved the Temple. Unfortunately, a letter arrived from Judea, from the commander Petronius. Petronius informed Caligula that the Jews would revolt if he placed the statue in the Temple. The thought that any subject would revolt against his government drove Caligula wild. He wrote to Petronius that he should take his own life as an example of disobedience. Thus, Caligula determined to make the statue a reality in the Temple of Jerusalem. (*Ant.* 18.289-309) Agrippa was defeated for the moment, but luck or good planning later saved the day for Agrippa and Israel.

While the Jews in Jerusalem were preparing for war with Rome, due to the impending defilement of the Temple, Agrippa was active in Rome. In 41 CE, the Emperor Caligula was assassinated. This happened soon after Caligula wrote to Petronius. (Luckily for Petronius, he received word of Caligula's death before he received Caligula's letter demanding his own death.) Although Agrippa was never implicated in the plot, he nevertheless was most opportunistic. The assassination put a stop to Caligula's insane desire to despoil the Temple. No one would have benefited more from the death of Caligula than Agrippa.

According to Josephus, Caligula was slain by Cherea and others. (*Ant.*19.114) There was great confusion as to whether Caligula was dead or just wounded. This afforded time for Agrippa and Claudius to leave the theater where they and Caligula had just been. It is very possible that Agrippa was one of those contributing to the confusion. Although Caligula was clearly dead, there was a report "that although **Gaius [Caligula] had been wounded indeed, yet was not he dead, but alive still and under the physician's hands.**" (*Ant.* 19.134) Was this report from Agrippa?

Later in his account, Josephus wrote:

Now this Agrippa, with relation to Gaius, did what became one that had been so much honored by him; for he embraced Gaius's body after he was dead, and laid it upon a bed, and covered it as well as he could, and went out to the guards, and **told them that Gaius was still alive; but he said that they should call for physicians, since he was very ill of his wounds.** But when he had learned that Claudius was carried away violently by the soldiers, he rushed through the crowd to him, and when he found that he was in disorder, and ready to resign up the government to the senate, he encouraged him, and desired him to keep the government. (*Ant.* 19.237-238) (3)

Agrippa was everywhere, in total command. Somehow, he had control of Caligula's dead body and covered it, assuring the guards that Caligula was still alive. This no doubt caused great confusion for those who supported Caligula as well as those who hated the same man. As soon as Agrippa received word about Claudius, he rushed through the crowd to him and coolly advised the despondent Claudius. If Agrippa was not behind the assassination of Caligula, he nevertheless took full advantage of the situation. The assassination not only saved the Temple of Jerusalem and inevitable war with the Jews, but it placed a malleable Claudius on the throne. This long-time friend of Agrippa would prove beneficial to Agrippa's future plans.

As a reward for masterminding his ascension, Claudius made Agrippa's territory equal to that of his grandfather, Herod the Great. Not only did Agrippa return to Jerusalem with more land to control, but he had also helped save the Jewish nation from war with Rome. Without Agrippa's influence and action, the statue of Caligula would have polluted the Temple. And now, Agrippa was the main counsel of the Roman Emperor. Certainly, to a great number of Jews, Agrippa was beginning to look like the promised Messiah.

PAUL'S REVELATIONS

Most people assume that Paul's message had always been centered upon grace and the blood of Christ. However, by his own words, Paul did not seek a conference with James until seventeen years had elapsed since his conversion (Gal. 1:18-2:2). In most of these seventeen years, Paul was a loyal worker, obeying the dictates of the Jewish Pillars. He was just a grunt, not a very influential man in the movement. This all changed with his wild revelations.

These revelations came late within the seventeen year period. If Paul converted in 21-22 CE, then the Council of Jerusalem took place around 38-39 CE. Therefore, the revelations began occurring around 37-38 CE, some short time before the Council. This date corresponds with the award of titles and land to his cousin, Agrippa. Before the revelations, Paul must have been somewhat despondent over his life within the movement. He was surely a competitive man, as his letters show. While his cousin Agrippa rubbed elbows with the Roman Emperor, he was stuck preaching the law to Jewish converts as well as God-Fearing Gentiles. This may have been a noble profession, but it did not compare to the accomplishments of his cousin. The question is this: Did Paul's revelations have anything to do with Agrippa's rise to power?

The Fourth Philosophy of Judas the Galilean stated that "God [was] to be their only Ruler and Lord." (*Ant.* 18.23) There was no distinction between the spiritual and earthly realms. The book of Revelation also follows this early pattern. The enemy was Rome and the Church would be saved by God through the power of the returning Messiah, Jesus. The early movement never envisioned their resurrected Messiah working hand-in-hand with the earthly powers of the day. No, the resurrected Messiah would return to obliterate the power of the earthly powers.

This concept of good versus evil was not convenient for Paul. On the one hand, Paul preached the resurrected Messiah. On the other hand, Paul's own cousin was now king of Israel and this cousin, Agrippa, had great influence over Claudius, the Roman Emperor. How could Paul follow these two different paths?

The answer was a splitting of the spiritual from the earthly. Christ Jesus became a personal savior god, much like the savior gods which existed throughout the Roman Empire. Paul's Christ Jesus could wash away sins. And when you died, this Christ Jesus would accept you into paradise, far from the troubles of this world. Through the Spirit, Christ Jesus would help you in the present world, but Christ Jesus was not going to come back to earth to conduct an earthly government. That was left to others, ordained by God. In the letter to the Romans, Paul wrote:

Everyone must submit himself to the governing authorities, for there is no authority except that which God has established. **The authorities that exist have been established by God.** Consequently, **he who rebels against the authority is rebelling against what God has instituted**, and those who do so will bring judgment on themselves. **For rulers hold no terrors for those who do right, but for those who do wrong.** Do you want to be free from fear of the one in authority? Then do what is right and he will commend you. For he is God's servant to do you good. But if you do wrong, be afraid, for he does not bear the sword for nothing. He is God's servant, an angel of wrath to bring punishment for the wrongdoer. Therefore, it is necessary to submit to the authorities, not only because of possible punishment but also because of conscience. This is also why you pay taxes, for the **authorities are God's servants**, who give their full time to governing. Give everyone what you owe him: **If you owe taxes, pay taxes**; if revenue, then revenue; if respect, then respect; if honor, then honor. (Romans 13:1-7) (Emphasis mine)

There could be no greater repudiation of the Fourth Philosophy then this little tribute to the ruling authorities. By Paul's own words, the authorities were established by God, to be obeyed as one would obey God. Let us ask a few questions of this philosophy. Did God institute the authorities who crucified Jesus? Was Jesus punished by God's servant of wrath for being a wrongdoer? Were the Jew under Hitler punished because they were in the wrong? And the list goes on.

We must remember that this tribute to the ruling elites was written in the early 40's, just after Claudius became Emperor. Consider that Caligula had recently been assassinated in 41 CE. Was Caligula one of God's servants? Was it not Caligula who planned to place a statue of himself into the Temple? Did God sanction this? Even though Claudius was a capable Emperor, the following Emperor was none other than Nero, the man who tortured the early Jewish Christians in 64 CE. Was this Nero established by God?

This avenue of thought by Paul could have never been condoned by the followers of Jesus (Judas the Galilean), James and Cephas. At this point in time, Paul was more interested in attaining the favor of Agrippa than he was of staying true to James. As pointed out in Chapter 1, an expulsion of followers of Christ occurred during the reign of Claudius. This happened during the very early days of Claudius' reign, when he was being advised by King Agrippa. Only Agrippa could have distinguished one group of Jews from another. Certainly, Claudius would not have known which group included the most incendiary Jews. Agrippa simply suggested that Claudius forbid the activities sanctioned by the Fourth Philosophy. It is interesting that Paul urged his own disciples to steer clear of the other Jewish members of the movement. These fanatics were anti-government. Paul wanted his disciples to be good citizens, good followers of Claudius and a perfect template for Agrippa. Paul wanted to show Agrippa that he could help control this other Messiah movement.

In short, Paul's tribute to government was meant primarily for Agrippa, for Paul wanted to work with his cousin. In a sense, Paul would have been the prophet behind the King. In his work with the Pillar Apostles, Paul was insignificant. But with Agrippa, Paul could have enormous power. This shift of power to Agrippa in 37 CE was the reason why Paul began having his visions, his revelations from God. Of course, these revelations had nothing to do with God and were diametrically opposed to the teachings of the real Jesus. But they were a way of shifting his own position from the earthly Jesus to the earthly Agrippa. Christ Jesus was now simply a spiritual force in individual salvation.

TWO MESSIAHS IN JERUSALEM

With the increased power earned by his close association with Claudius, Agrippa was in a position to vie for the love and approval of the Jews. Not since the days of Herod the Great had the Jewish people had such close relations with the greatest power on earth, Rome. This would have pleased the upper class, the wealthy of society, but the Fourth Philosophy would have seen Agrippa as a threat to its own claim. The Fourth Philosophy claimed that Jesus (Judas the Galilean) was the promised Messiah, resurrected from the dead and soon to return in power and glory. But Agrippa's followers could claim that the Messiah was already here on earth, in the body of Herod Agrippa. This power struggle was between two Messiahs, one governing and one still awaiting God's final plan.

Up until 37 CE, Agrippa would have had little concern for the people of Israel. His prospects did not appear bright as he was actually imprisoned by Tiberius. However, the rise of Caligula had also changed Agrippa's fortunes. He now controlled parts of the Holy Land, and that control would be enlarged through Claudius. Agrippa's reputation also was growing, as Agrippa could claim that he had helped stop the statue from being erected in the Temple. (He would never have actually claimed responsibility for the assassination of Caligula, but his efforts were responsible for slowing down Caligula's plans.) On top of this, Agrippa was now a close advisor to the Emperor of Rome, Claudius. In short, Agrippa had built a formidable resume.

How then did Agrippa deal with the Fourth Philosophy? After a few years in Jerusalem, Agrippa became quite aware of his greatest opposition party. In Rome, Agrippa influenced Claudius to expel the Jewish followers of a Chrestus. Suetonius wrote: "The Jews he [Claudius] expelled from Rome, since they were constantly in rebellion, at the instigation of Chrestus." (4) At this approximate time, Claudius also published an edict proclaiming that the Jews should be treated as other Roman citizens as long as they had shown friendship towards Rome, and that the Jews should be able to keep their religious customs. (*Ant.* 19.278-291) This edict was for the majority of Jews, not those Jews who promised war on Rome. Note that Claudius had expelled the followers of Chrestus (Christ) as they were troublemakers. These troublemakers were members of the Fourth Philosophy and were bitterly opposed to both Claudius and his advisor, Agrippa. So the earliest recorded action by Agrippa against the Fourth Philosophy occurred very early in Claudius' reign, around 41-42 CE.

The next recorded conflict between the two Messiah movements came from Josephus and was also included in the book of Acts as a rewrite of history. This occurred around 43 CE.

However, there was a certain man of the Jewish nation at Jerusalem, who appeared to be very accurate in the knowledge of the law. His name was **Simon. This man got together an assembly, while the king was absent at Caesarea,** and had the insolence to accuse him of not living holily, and that he might justly be **excluded out of the temple,** since it belonged only to native Jews. But the **general of Agrippa's army informed him,** that Simon had made such a speech to the people. **So the king sent for him**; and, as he was then sitting in the theater, he bade him sit down by him, and said to him with a low and gentle voice, - "What is there done in this place that is contrary to the law?" But he had nothing to say for himself, but begged his pardon. So the king was more easily reconciled to him than one could have imagined, as esteeming mildness a better quality in a king than anger; and knowing that moderation is more becoming in great men than passion. So he made Simon a small present, and dismissed him. (*Ant.* 19.332-334) (Emphasis mine)

Before analyzing this passage, it may be prudent to show where the book of Acts rewrote this incident. In Acts chapter 10, at the request of an angel, Cornelius (Agrippa) sent his soldier to Joppa to bring back Simon Peter to Caesarea. At this same time, Simon Peter was having his own visions which instructed him to accept the Gentiles into the movement. This inclusionary message was exactly opposite to that of the real Simon, who preached that Agrippa should be excluded from the Temple because he was not a native Jew. The rewriting of the passage from an exclusionary story to an inclusionary one is important. Certainly, the meeting between Simon and Agrippa had been part of the Fourth Philosophy's tradition. It was a clash between the good Messiah (Simon) and the evil Messiah (Agrippa). Only much later was this famous story changed for the purposes of the early Gentile Church.

This passage shows how much Josephus admired Agrippa and how much disdain he had for Simon and the Fourth Philosophy. Even though Josephus was just a young boy when this event occurred, he added touches that made Agrippa very kingly. Although no one but Agrippa and Simon were in the theater, Josephus wrote that Agrippa spoke with "a low and gentle voice." My guess is that this low and gentle voice carried a veiled threat to stop preaching or suffer the consequences.

There was a tension between Agrippa and Simon. Simon did not consider Agrippa a native Jew, and in this he was right. Agrippa had been raised in Augustus' court beside the likes of Caligula. This alone would have persuaded many to exclude him from the Temple. So this divide between Simon and Agrippa was religious in nature and political as well. The Fourth Philosophy did not distinguish between religion and politics. For them, God was their only

Ruler. They could never accept Agrippa. Agrippa knew this and commanded Simon to stop his preaching. Like Jesus before Pilate, Simon remained quiet before Agrippa.

Simon went back to Jerusalem and began preaching against Agrippa again. This can be deduced by the next event described in Acts chapter 12.

It was about this time that King Herod [Agrippa] arrested some who belonged to the church, intending to persecute them. He had James, the brother of John, put to death with the sword. When he saw that this pleased the Jews, he proceeded to seize Peter also. This happened during the Feast of Unleavened Bread. After arresting him, he put him in prison. ...Herod intended to bring him out for public trial after the Passover. (Acts 12:1-4)

According to this passage, Agrippa arrested James and Simon Peter. James was beheaded and Peter was kept in prison for a preordained guilty verdict to occur after the Passover, after the crowds left Jerusalem. Snippets of truth remain in this passage. From Josephus, we know that the sons of Judas the Galilean, James and Simon, were crucified under the procurator, Tiberius Alexander, around 46 CE. (*Ant.* 20.102) These two were the real James and Simon. Most likely, Agrippa had them arrested shortly before his own death, where they languished in prison. They later were crucified as a way to discourage the Fourth Philosophy. Earlier, during the governorship of Fadus (44-46 CE), a Theudas was beheaded. (*Ant.* 20.97-99) The book of Acts combined these two accounts by Josephus. It took the sons of Judas the Galilean, James and Simon, and changed them into James, the son of Zebedee, and Peter. In addition, James, the son of Zebedee, was beheaded just as Theudas was beheaded.

This account is further bolstered by the Slavonic Josephus.

At this time [during the reigns of Fadus and Tiberius Alexander] there appeared many servants of the previously described wonder-worker [Jesus], telling the people about their master, that he was [still] alive although he had died. And [they said], "He will free you from servitude." ...But the grateful governors seeing the subversion of the people, planned with the scribes to take them and destroy them. (After *War* 2.220)

This account from the Slavonic Josephus corresponds to the account of Theudas and the sons of Judas the Galilean, per *Ant.* 20.97-102. It is interesting to note that the Slavonic Josephus stated that these servants were followers of the wonder-worker, or of Jesus. This directly ties the sons of Judas the Galilean to the wonder-worker or Jesus. The persecution by the governors was a way to silence the movement. It more likely just created more martyrs.

So even though Acts chapter 12 was a rewrite of history, facts about Agrippa come forward. Agrippa opposed the movement and had decided to persecute it, acting as any King would. Agrippa was merely protecting his throne, not wanting the Fourth Philosophy to thrive.

While Agrippa was persecuting the Fourth Philosophy (Jewish Christians), he was reaching out to other kings in the region. According to Graves, King Herod Agrippa had close relations with the following kings: the King of Chalcis, the King of Iturea, the King of Adiabene, the King of Osroene, the King of Lesser Armenia, the King of Pontus and Cilicia, the King of Commagene and the prospective King of Parthia. (5) This would have worried the Roman Emperor, Claudius, as Israel had always been the crossroads to Egypt. This confederation of Kings may have eventually threatened Rome.

There is more information concerning one of the Kings mentioned above. He was named Izates, and his account helps tie Agrippa to Paul. Izates' tale played out near the time of Agrippa's death, around 43-44 CE. There were two preachers who attempted to sway Izates to their viewpoint concerning circumcision and the Jewish law. The agent of Agrippa was named Ananias, and he preached a message consistent with that of Paul. He told Izates "that he might worship God without being circumcised, even though he did resolve to follow the Jewish law entirely; which worship of God was of a superior nature to circumcision." (*Ant.* 20.41) Like Paul, Ananias preached a different type of Judaism, one which placed circumcision on a lower level. This type of new Judaism appealed to the Gentile community. But why would such a new Judaism have been taught?

The reason why Ananias taught this new Judaism was due to political considerations. Surely, Izates subjects would be outraged if he converted to a different religion. (*Ant.* 20.42) This shows the genius of Agrippa. He wanted to court the Kings of the surrounding areas, and this included spreading a type of Judaism which would bind the rulers together. Again, this gospel was no different than the one which Paul peddled. The question which must be raised is this: Was Paul also spreading the gospel of Agrippa? His argument with Cephas, as outlined in Galatians, was no different that the argument between Ananais and Eleazar in the King Izates episode.

It should also be emphasized that the other preacher in the Izates' story was named Eleazar, and he was sent from Galilee. His message was consistent with the Fourth Philosophy. He persuaded King Izates to undergo circumcision and become a full Jew. (*Ant.* 20.43-47) As it turned out, Izates' subjects did not revolt against him but accepted his decision on embracing another religion. Now, Eleazar had been sent from Galilee around 44 CE to combat the preaching of Ananias. This same thing happened at Antioch. While Cephas was with Paul at Antioch, "certain men came from James… those who belonged to the circumcision group." (Gal. 2:12) As you can guess, those of the circumcision group insisted that the Gentiles become full Jews by undergoing circumcision.

It seems as though the Fourth Philosophy was fighting back against Agrippa and his agents (Ananias and Paul). Also, at this time, King Agrippa was poisoned and died a painful death. It may prove worthwhile to recount the death of Agrippa as recorded in Acts as well as in *Antiquities*.

Then Herod [Agrippa] went from Judea to Caesarea and stayed there a while. He had been quarreling with the people of Tyre and Sidon; they now joined together and sought an audience with him. Having secured the support of Blastus, a trusted personal servant of the king, they asked for peace, because they depended on the king's country for their food supply. On the appointed day Herod, wearing his royal robes, sat on his throne and delivered a public address to the people. They shouted, "This is the voice of a god, not of a man." Immediately, because Herod did not give praise to God, an angel of the Lord struck him down, and he was eaten by worms and died. (Acts 12:19-23)

Several important points in this account must be highlighted. First, the author of Acts supplied some data which supports the idea that Agrippa was very energetic in producing alliances with other kings. We have already listed a number of kings who were being wooed by Agrippa. In the above account, the people of Tyre and Sidon were suing for peace because Agrippa controlled their food supply. This very well may have happened. The second point concerns the death of Agrippa. According to Acts, Agrippa died because he did not immediately give praise to God after he had been compared to a god. Of course, to our modern minds, this is absolutely ridiculous. People are not struck down today because they do not credit God with this or that accomplishment. The same held true for the past. Maybe Agrippa was struck down, but we should examine the logical alternatives to the supernatural explanation.

Before exploring the alternatives to the supernatural, we must also examine Josephus' take on Agrippa's death. According to Josephus, Agrippa wore a garment made of silver which shone brilliantly in the sunlight. Certain flatterers cried out that he looked like a god. Agrippa did not dispute these flatteries but immediately looked up and saw an owl, an omen of death. Agrippa became ill but lived with "the pain in his belly for five days" before his death. (*Ant.* 19.343-350) When the news of Agrippa's death reached Claudius, the Emperor was sorry. (*Ant.* 19.361)

The cause of death was not retribution from God! Rather, the pain in Agrippa's belly was due to poison. Agrippa was assassinated. Who would have had the motive for killing Agrippa? Two obvious possibilities exist: the Fourth Philosophy and the agents of Claudius.

No group would have had a greater motive for assassinating Agrippa than the followers of Judas the Galilean. Agrippa had advised Claudius to persecute the followers of Christ and Agrippa had imprisoned the sons of Judas the Galilean. But could the movement, which had once been guided by John the Baptist, commit murder? It is possible considering the threat which Agrippa represented. Agrippa was an alternative Messiah, the polar opposite to Judas the Galilean (Jesus). Such a strike against the Herodians and Romans would have been bold, but this may have appeared to be the movement's best alternative. It is also possible that the death of Agrippa was not caused by the Fourth Philosophy but was still viewed as a gift from God. That is the meaning which comes from the account in Acts.

In the Golden Eagle Temple Cleansing (4 BCE), Matthias and Judas did not murder Herod the Great. But they did take advantage of the supposed death and instigated an uprising against the government of Herod. In the same way, James the Just may have believed that God was providing for the movement by eliminating Agrippa. Right after the death of Agrippa, Acts 12:24 stated that "the word of God continued to increase and spread." If the Fourth Philosophy did not commit the murder, they nevertheless benefited from the power vacuum.

The only other obvious suspects would be the agents of Claudius. As noted above, Agrippa was busy aligning himself with other kings in the region. This would have been worrisome to Rome. Before relating the death of Agrippa, Josephus did mention that Marcus, the president of Syria had concerns.

But Marcus had a suspicion what the meaning could be of so great a friendship of these kings one with another, and did not think so close an agreement of so many potentates to be for the interest of the Romans. He therefore sent some of his domestics to every one of them, and enjoined them to go their ways home without further delay. This was very ill taken by Agrippa, who after that became his enemy. (*Ant.* 19.341- 342)

It is hard to believe that Claudius would have ordered the assassination of Agrippa. Their friendship from an early age would have made such an act difficult. However, poisonings were commonplace among the Caesars. Claudius' grandmother, Livia, made a living out of poisoning her real and perceived enemies. Claudius' brother, Germanicus, was also poisoned by Piso while stationed in the East. (*Ant.* 18.54) So the act of poisoning was not unknown to Claudius. Perhaps the deed was accomplished by an underling who wished to protect the Empire, knowing full well that Claudius could never order the death of such a close friend and advisor. The above passage mentions that Marcus viewed Agrippa's behavior as dangerous to the Empire and he could have acted upon these notions.

It is impossible to know with certainty as to who assassinated Agrippa. But the death of Agrippa must have emboldened the Fourth Philosophy. After his death, Theudas went out to the river Jordan and promised to divide the river as Moses had parted the Red Sea. (*Ant.* 20.97-98) This Messianic act was crushed by the procurator, Fadus. The Messianic fervor must have continued as the next procurator, Tiberius Alexander, ordered the crucifixions of Simon and James, the sons of Judas the Galilean. (*Ant.* 20.102) These two were arrested during the last year of Agrippa's life and were now being put to death. This was a way to dampen the fires of revolution, just as Herod Antipas had perceived when he ordered the death of John the Baptist. (*Ant.* 18.116-119)

The death of Agrippa had also caused James the Just to rethink his policy regarding Gentiles. James had never fully understood Paul's gospel towards the Gentiles, and he most likely did not properly monitor the situation. Agrippa's agents were converting Gentiles to a new Judaism, one which thrived without the law and circumcision. James immediately dispatched envoys to correct the situation. In the cases of Paul and Cephas in Antioch and the King Izates conversion, representatives of James (circumcision group) reestablished the importance of the law to Gentile converts. This was the end of Paul's participation in the movement. His double agent cover had been blown. No longer could he preach a supernatural Messiah (Christ Jesus) and an earthly Messiah (Agrippa).

At this point in history, Paul turned against the Fourth Philosophy. His letters to the Galatians and Corinthians pointed to a severed relationship between himself and the Pillars, those super-apostles whom he compared to the servants of Satan. (2 Cor. 11:1-15) Other literature painted Paul as an enemy of the early church in the 40's. The *Recognitions* 1.70-71 accused Paul of trying to kill James and chasing after Peter with the same intent. This was incorporated into Acts but with a twist. In Acts, this persecution was **before** Paul joined the movement. In reality, the persecutions occurred **after** his expulsion from the movement.

THE GENIUS OF AGRIPPA I

When Agrippa I was given titles by Caligula in 37 CE, it is doubtful that he viewed himself as the Messiah. But after gaining more influence with Caligula and possibly being responsible for Caligula's assassination, Agrippa's reputation among the Jews must have soared. This was only the beginning of his rise to power. As a close advisor to Claudius, Agrippa was assigned the same territory that his grandfather, Herod the Great, had once ruled. Agrippa was a player on the world stage. This status would have been viewed as consistent with the promised Messiah.

The dreams of being Messiah were also followed by action. Soon after the dispatching of Caligula and the installing of Claudius as Emperor, Claudius published an edict on behalf of the Jews. This edict was a reward to Agrippa. Not only did Claudius restore Herod the Great's kingdom to Agrippa but he enhanced Agrippa's reputation around the Roman Empire. The edict that was sent throughout the Roman Empire is as follows:

Upon the **petition of king Agrippa and king Herod**, who are persons very dear to me, that I would grant the same rights and privileges should be preserved for the Jews which are in all the Roman empire, which I have granted to those of Alexandria, I very willingly comply therewith; and this grant I make not only for the sake of the petitioners, but as judging those Jews for whom I have been petitioned worthy of such a favor, on account of **their fidelity and friendship to the Romans**. …It will therefore be fit to permit the Jews, who are in all the world under us, to keep their ancient customs without being hindered so to do. (*Ant.* 19.288-290)

Josephus made it clear that the edict was a result of King Agrippa's petition. The Jews throughout the Roman world would be allowed to follow their religious practices without interference. The only thing the Jews had to do in return was to refrain from showing contempt for other religions and to continue their fidelity towards Rome. In short, as long as the Jews behaved themselves, they could expect religious freedom.

Jews throughout the Roman Empire had Agrippa to thank for this welcome edict. This benefited Agrippa in two ways. First, Agrippa's fame must have spread like wildfire through the synagogues. This would have been perfect propaganda for his claim as the promised Messiah. Second, the edict let Jews work more easily within the Empire. This inclusion of the Jews would have hurt the recruiting efforts of the Fourth Philosophy. A happy Jew would not be as likely to join a revolutionary group. This same principle has been in play throughout history. (The U.S. showed little respect for Moslem sensibilities during the early days of the Iraq war. As a consequence, recruitment for the enemies of the U.S. grew.) Agrippa understood that the way to defeat the extremists was to make life better for the Jews.

The second prong of Agrippa's plan was to attack the enemy, that being the Fourth Philosophy. The followers of "Chrestus", who constantly caused disturbances, were driven from Rome. This was a clear sign of things to come. Back in Jerusalem, Simon preached that Agrippa should be barred from the Temple. Agrippa sent for Simon and gave him a chance to stop his preaching. This did not happen, so Agrippa arrested Simon and James, the sons of Judas the Galilean. This was a clear message that the Fourth Philosophy should stop their work against Agrippa. Thus, not only was Agrippa widening his appeal to all Jews throughout the Empire, but he was tightening his grip around the opposition's throat.

Agrippa's plans went beyond just convincing the Jews of his historic importance. As noted above, Agrippa expended much time and resources wooing the neighboring Gentile kings. This attempt at building military and political alliances was part of his Messianic vision. If he could reach beyond the Jews in Israel and throughout the Roman world, then he could build an empire which would dwarf his grandfather's kingdom. Diplomatic envoys to other nations were not invented by Agrippa, but his emphasis on religion may have been quite novel. In the case of King Izates, Ananias tried to convert the King to a new form of Judaism, one without circumcision. If Agrippa was behind this effort, then it shows his sheer genius. He was attempting to unite kingdoms using his own religion. Objectionable aspects of his own religion, such as circumcision, were removed in order to make it easier for the new converts. After all, circumcision would be a hard sell to any adult male. And this method employed by Ananias seemed to work quite well.

The fourth and final part of Agrippa's plan related to the conversion of Gentiles as noted above. In the King Izates episode, Ananias was the agent. However, another man was also hard at work for Agrippa. That man was Paul. He also preached the same message as Ananias. But Paul was much more. He was part of the opposition movement. By convincing Paul to be part of his Messianic dreams, Agrippa was able to monitor and challenge the Fourth Philosophy. In essence, Paul was a mole within the Fourth Philosophy. Any time that he became privy to important information, the King would also eventually be informed. Paul was a mover and a shaker: he constantly monitored his own congregations and used his own disciples to relay information. It would have been quite easy to keep Agrippa informed concerning any new developments within the opposition.

This helps explain the traitor tradition. Certainly, shortly after Paul's removal from the movement, Paul's infamy became known and widely circulated among the Jewish synagogues. Paul was the original traitor, not a Judas Iscariot. (In a later chapter, I will prove that Judas Iscariot never existed!) After the Jewish war, Gentile Christians were saddled with this traitor moniker. They simply shifted it from Paul to Judas Iscariot. (This will be further explored in Part III, Chapter 17.)

So Agrippa had a four part plan to assert his kingship throughout the world. He persuaded Claudius to extend religious rights to Jews throughout the Roman world. He also began persecuting the Fourth Philosophy, by capturing their leaders. By reaching out to the Gentile kings, he began to further his goals beyond his own Jewish boundaries. And finally, he infiltrated the Fourth Philosophy, using Paul as his weapon of choice. This final part of the plan may have been initiated by Paul. Paul's revelations began once Agrippa reaped benefits from his relationship to Caligula. Paul's dreams may have been behind the whole outreach to the Gentile kings. Unfortunately, we will never know who began the ball rolling. But one thing is sure: both Agrippa and Paul were well equipped to dream of a worldly Messiah, and both had the incentives to make that a reality.

CHAPTER 11

CHRIST JESUS

It is my contention that Paul invented Christ Jesus, the theological framework that sparked the story of Jesus of Nazareth. This is wildly different from the traditional view of Christian origins. In the traditional view, Jesus came and preached a revolutionary message which challenged, if not overturned, the Jewish religion. His disciples, the Twelve, were slow to understand his genius and reverted to the practice of the law and circumcision after his death. Even though the Twelve had witnessed the resurrection, they still could not let go of the law of Moses. Luckily, another group located in Jerusalem, led by Stephen and Philip, gravitated towards the original message of Jesus and preached the power of the Holy Spirit. Later, even Peter was brought back to the truth after his meeting with Cornelius. Thus, in the traditional story, the Pauline view of grace had been restored before Paul became central to the Acts' story.

This fanciful story, as told by Acts, consists of many improbabilities. First, the theological succession from Jesus to the Twelve to Paul is totally illogical. Most interpret the New Testament as ascribing the new Christian religion to Jesus. His closest followers were unable to grasp his teachings and it took others, such as Philip, Stephen, Ananias and Paul, to restore the teachings of Jesus. I reject this view as unrealistic. Jesus (Judas the Galilean) preached the law of Moses which emphasized personal relationships and total fealty to God. This Jesus was also obsessed with freedom from the Roman occupation. This same attitude was followed by the Twelve, specifically by Cephas and James the Just. James the Just was the brother of Jesus, yet even in the New Testament, this James fervently obeyed the law of Moses. (Acts 21:20 and Gal. 2:12) So there never was a split between Jesus and his earthly followers. In Galatians 1:11-12, Paul admitted that his gospel did not come from earthly

196

succession but from the Risen Jesus Christ. This Christ Jesus gospel was a revelation from the mind of Paul. It had nothing to do with Jesus or with the Twelve.

Knowing that Paul invented the gospel of Christ Jesus, it is quite easy to identify the false history of Acts. The author of Acts tried to attribute Paul's gospel of grace to an earlier set of individuals. According to Acts 6:1-7, a group of Grecian Jews were ordained by the Twelve to help minister to the disciples. This group included Stephen and Philip. Stephen was the first martyr as recorded by Acts. However, this story of Stephen (supposedly around 35 CE) was simply a rewrite of the stoning of James the Just (62 CE) (*Ant.* 20.200). In both stories, a Saul was bent on destroying the church or the poor. (Acts 8:1 and *Ant.* 20.214) In the case of Philip, his preaching of the Holy Spirit to the Eunuch (Acts 8:26-39) was a rewrite of the story of King Izates (*Ant.* 20.34-48). The only difference was that Philip instructed the Eunuch to be baptized while Eleazar instructed Izates to be circumcised. In addition to Stephen and Philip, the book of Acts also included Ananias and Paul in the early Christ Jesus (Holy Spirit) branch of the movement (Acts 9:1-19). This Ananias was most likely the same Ananias who taught King Izates that he could become a good Jew without being circumcised. And of course, Paul was none other than the Apostle Paul, the hero of Acts. Note that Stephen, Philip, and Ananias all predated Paul's introduction into the movement. Could they have been behind the new gospel of Christ Jesus? Could Paul have learned this gospel from them? No, according to Paul's letter to the Galatians. Paul wrote:

I want you to know, brothers, that the gospel I preached is not something that man made up. I did not receive it from any man, nor was I taught it; rather, I received it by revelation from Jesus Christ. (Gal. 1:11-12)

So it is quite clear that the section of Acts which included Stephen, Philip and Ananias was meant to smooth out the two different gospels: the original gospel taught by Judas the Galilean (Jesus), John the Baptist, Cephas and James and the new gospel which arrived by revelation to Paul. This reconciliation between the two gospels became final when Peter learned to accept the Pauline philosophy in the Cornelius affair (Acts 10). In this confrontation, Peter learned to include even the Gentiles into the movement. However, according to Josephus, a Simon excluded Agrippa I from the Temple because Agrippa was not a native born Jew. (*Ant.* 19.332-334) Acts made an exclusionary tale into a story of inclusion. With that rewrite, Acts moved the religion of the original movement of Judas the Galilean toward the later gospel as preached by Paul.

WAS THE NAME JESUS A TITLE?

The earliest writings which referred to Jesus came from the pen of Paul, somewhere around 40 CE. How did Paul use the term Jesus? Was Jesus a proper name or a title? To find this out, the letter to the Romans was reviewed and all references to Jesus or to Christ were noted. The results are as follows:

Christ Jesus (1)	11
Christ Jesus, our Lord (2)	2
Jesus Christ (3)	8
Jesus Christ, our Lord (4)	9
Jesus (5)	2
Jesus, our Lord (6)	4
Lord (7)	14
Christ (8)	31
Christ and Lord (9)	2
Christ and Spirit (10)	1

Paul used the above titles interchangeably. The terms Christ Jesus and Christ were used primarily when Paul wanted to emphasize the Gentile converts relationship to the man-god. For instance, Paul would write that the followers were "alive to God in Christ Jesus." (Rom. 6:11) The reference to Christ often related to the death and resurrection and its relationship to the believer: "If we died with Christ..." (Rom. 6:8) By far and away, the term Christ was used most often in Romans.

The term Jesus Christ was used primarily to show how God worked in the converts' lives. Thus, "the righteousness from God comes through faith in Jesus Christ." (Rom. 3:22) Anything good from God came through Jesus Christ. Thus, this term was used to make the man-god a mediator between man and God.

Paul also used the term Lord to go with all the above and in Romans chapter 14, Lord was used exclusively. So what does this all mean? I would venture a logical guess that all the above references were titles and not proper names.

The name Christ was the Greek word for Messiah. The Jerusalem Jews certainly knew their leader as the Messiah. To the Jews, this Messiah was the Anointed One or the King. David was an earlier Messiah or King. However, this promised Messiah was believed to have been raised from the dead and would return once again as an earthly King or Messiah. Paul simply took this Messiah language and adapted it to his Messiah figure or his Christ. Paul's

Christ was much more than the Jew's Messiah. Paul's Christ was a mediator between man and God and was also nearer the level of God. In a way, one can read Paul's letters and say that Christ was the Lord and the Lord was God.

Obviously, Christ was a title, just like Messiah. But what about the name Jesus? If Paul believed that the name Jesus was a proper name, he did not display this knowledge in his letters. In Romans 9:5, Paul wrote: "Theirs are the patriarchs, and from them is traced the human ancestry of Christ, who is God over all, forever praised!" Paul noted that Christ, not Jesus, traced his human ancestry from the patriarchs. If Jesus were an actual name and not just a title, then Paul should have used Jesus at this point instead of Christ. But to Paul, Christ, Jesus, Christ Jesus, and Jesus Christ were all titles for his man-god.

So did Paul just create the title Jesus? As we have already noted, Christ was a Greek word for Messiah, a title meaning King. Paul did not create the title Christ and he did not create the title Jesus. The name Jesus could have originally been a proper name or a title. Jesus was a very common name in that era, so it is possible that the very early movement called their Messiah by his given name, that being Jesus. That is surely the orthodox explanation for the name. After all, the Messiah was called Jesus of Nazareth according to Christian tradition.

It does seem strange to me that Paul would have used Jesus as a title if Jesus had really been a proper name. The above passage in Romans 9:5 suggests that Paul did not consider Jesus a proper name. And considering that Paul was writing this only a generation after the death of the Messiah, it is hard to imagine that the memory of the living man had so ebbed into oblivion.

In the early Christian movement (Fourth Philosophy), most of the leaders had titles. John was named the Baptist because he baptized men into the river Jordan (*Ant.* 18. 116-117). I have also linked John the Baptist to the Sadduc, a name meaning Righteous One. (*Ant.* 18.4) Simon was named Cephas or Peter, the title meaning Rock. James, the brother of Jesus, was titled Just or the Just One. And as I will prove later, James and Simon, the sons of Judas the Galilean, were given the nickname of sons of Thunder. Thunder was a fitting nickname for Judas the Galilean. So in each case, the leader was titled with a name which described his best attributes.

The name Jesus or Joshua means Savior or Salvation. The Messiah, Judas the Galilean, surely would have been regarded as a Savior to these disciples. He led them in their tax revolt, and he preached a religion unlike anyone else. According to Josephus, Judas "was a teacher of a peculiar sect of his own, and was not at all like the rest of those their leaders." (*War.* 2.118) In Josephus' history, Judas and his followers were central figures in the fight against Rome.

This Judas the Galilean was a Messiah figure, and he certainly outshone other figures of his time. So if Jesus of Nazareth really existed, this Jesus would have played second fiddle to Judas the Galilean. Of course, my thesis contends that Judas and Jesus were one in the same person. (I find it hard to believe that the Messiah Jesus could have played second fiddle to anyone.) That is why Jesus of Nazareth does not appear in the writings of Josephus. While Josephus wrote extensively about Judas the Galilean's life, he omitted the death of this great rabbi. This is unbelievable considering Josephus mentioned the deaths of Judas' three sons, James, Simon and Menahem and possibly a fourth son, Theudas. On the other hand, Josephus never mentioned one word about the life of Jesus. There is, however, a passage which describes Jesus' death (*Ant.* 18.63-64). How convenient! The death of Jesus of Nazareth has been placed in a section where we would expect to read about the death of Judas the Galilean.

So the title of Jesus was bestowed upon Judas the Galilean either upon his rise as Messiah (4-2 BCE) or upon his proposed resurrection from the dead. In either case, Judas was now a savior. Judas was now Jesus.

CHRIST JESUS AS GENTILE MAN-GOD

The Fourth Philosophy of Judas the Galilean viewed the Messiah as an instrument of God to help drive the Romans from the Holy Land. They never had any inclination to make this Messiah into a God. That being said, the resurrection of Judas (Jesus) made this Messiah special. The book of Revelation makes it clear that the resurrected Messiah was to return with supernatural powers to fight the Romans. So even in this Jewish literature, Jesus was granted extraordinary powers.

But did these Jewish patriots have any idea what Paul was preaching to his Gentile disciples? From the letter to the Galatians, Paul clearly acknowledged that the Jewish leadership (the Pillars) did not accept his gospel but were teaching an inferior gospel. This inferior gospel was the same gospel preached by Judas (Jesus) during his time on earth. The Pillars removed Paul from the movement based upon their limited information concerning his gospel. Paul was removed because he did not teach the law of Moses and the act of circumcision. It would have never occurred to them that Paul was also elevating Christ Jesus to God status.

This elevation of Christ Jesus to God status had two advantages within the Gentile world. First, Paul could separate the heavenly from the earthly. This was necessary if one wanted to fit nicely within the Roman boundaries for religion. Christ Jesus may have been the spiritual Lord but the earthly Lord was Caesar and the Lord of Israel was his cousin Agrippa. In this way, Paul could bring many Gentiles to obey the earthly masters while he did his best to empty their pockets of loose change. The gifts to the poor in Jerusalem never reached James but most likely remained within the Herodian family.

The second advantage to his new gospel was its ability to envelop other religions of the Empire. The death and resurrection of Jesus easily replaced or complemented other mystery religions. Followers of Paul did not have to give up their own religion; they merely adjusted it to include Christ Jesus. At first, Paul probably insisted on including the history of Israel with every Christ Jesus sale. But after the break with the Pillars, Christ Jesus may have had much less to do with the Jewish people. This combining of religions and the inconsistent message concerning the Jews made for a rich environment for varied belief systems. That is why there were a multitude of Christian groups in the Gentile world.

This co-opting of religion is very evident in the history of modern day Peru. We visited there a few years ago and found many interesting developments which only occurred in this region. Paintings of the Last Supper included Jesus and the Twelve eating guinea pigs, the national food of Peru. Another painting had three identical pictures of Jesus, representing a very foreign concept, the Trinity. And the virgin Mary resembled the cone of a mountain, the very image of homage in pre-Christian days. The Church had simply incorporated the Peruvian customs and beliefs into its regional Christianity. This type of absorption occurred throughout the Roman Empire and can be ultimately credited to Paul, the founder of Gentile Christianity.

THE GNOSTICS

Gnostic Christian groups flourished in the second century, probably originating near the time of Paul. These Gnostic groups had three things in common: they separated the body from the spirit; they believed that the Jewish God was behind the evil in the world and finally, they relied upon a special knowledge or gnosis which set them apart from others. Paul's teachings did not wholly endorse any of these notions, but seeds within his words sprouted Gnostic ideas.

The Jerusalem Jews did not separate the soul from the body. They believed that the two were intertwined. As James stated: "Show me your faith without deeds, and I will show you my faith by what I do." (James 2:18) The body was trained to follow the law and the law led you to God. There was no shortcut to God.

Paul, on the other hand, was antinomian. He did not connect the physical obedience to the law as necessary to be a follower of God. Instead, Paul preached that the Spirit of God or the Spirit of Christ would guide his disciples. This dependence on the Spirit to control behavior did not work for Paul as it does not work in the present day. In his letter to the Romans, Paul emphasized that grace would counter any sin. He then answered a question that surely came to everyone's mind: "Shall we go on sinning so that grace may increase? By no means!" (Rom. 6:1-2) Paul's emphasis on grace was interpreted by some as an excuse to behave as badly as possible. After all, God's grace would be greater than any sin that I could possibly consider. This separation of the body from the soul was a real problem for Paul. In his Corinthian congregation, there was sexual immorality which did "not occur even among the pagans." (1 Cor. 5:1) A man had his own father's wife. Paul condemned this and then laid down his own list of laws (1 Cor. 5:9-11). Paul's theology and his practical knowledge of human behavior clashed. People needed some law, with or without the Spirit.

This gospel of grace was misinterpreted by some, according to Paul. Paul wrote:

But if our unrighteousness brings out God's righteousness more clearly, what shall we say? That God is unjust in bringing his wrath upon us? (I am using a human argument.) Certainly not! If that were so, how could God judge the world? Someone might argue, "If my falsehood enhances God's truthfulness and so increases his glory, why am I still condemned as a sinner?" Why not say - as **we are being slanderously reported as saying and that some claim that we say - "Let us do evil that good may result"? Their condemnation is deserved.** (Romans 3:5-8)

The Gnostics believed that the God of the Jews created the world with its evils. To Marcion, the Jewish God was a "worker of evils, delighting in wars, inconsistent in judgment and self-contradictory." (11) He taught that Jesus came from the Father who was far removed from the Jewish God. Did Paul teach these things about the Jewish God? The answer is a definitive no! However, some passages in Paul's writings may have been used by later writers to make their Gnostic cases.

In the above passage, Paul considered the God of the Jews as being linked with goodness and with Christ Jesus. (Rom. 4:21-22) In fact, if you were to read Romans, 1 & 2 Corinthians and Galatians, you would be amazed at how many times Paul referred to the God of Jesus being the Jewish God. So how did the Gnostics use Paul as their source of inspiration in this matter? One passage which has been taken out of context is as follows:

The god of this age has blinded the minds of unbelievers, so that they cannot see the light of the gospel of the glory of Christ. (2 Cor. 4:4)

According to Irenaeus, Marcion taught that Jesus came to destroy the Law and the Prophets which were devised by the maker of this world. (12) To Marcion, the God of the Jews was the exact opposite to Jesus. This was taking the **law versus grace** argument to a new level, not even attempted by Paul. To make Paul's writings consistent with his own teachings, Marcion removed those passages (which were many) that tied the Jewish God directly to Jesus. (13) So even though Paul never even considered that the Jewish God was not the Father of Jesus, later Christian leaders (Marcion) twisted Paul's words to their own devices.

After Paul had been removed from the movement (see Galatians), he was very critical of the Jewish leadership and of their insistence on circumcision and the law. This negativity, no doubt, fed the anti-Jewish feelings in later Gentile leaders. These later leaders could not reconcile the God of the Jews to their Christ Jesus. Therefore, Christ Jesus was divorced from the Jewish God. The Father of Christ Jesus was now identified with a good God, completely opposite to the Jewish God. Paul did not condone this teaching but his own hatred towards the Jewish leadership helped foster an environment where the God of the Jews was a negative force in the world, equivalent to the Jews themselves.

The third main aspect of Gnosticism centered upon a special knowledge. In fact, the name Gnostic comes from the word for knowledge. As Paul wrote to the Corinthians:

We do, however, speak a message of wisdom among the mature, but not the wisdom of this age or of the rulers of this age, who are coming to nothing. No, we speak of **God's secret wisdom**, a wisdom that has been hidden and that God destined for our glory before time began. None of the rulers of this age understood it, for if they had, they would not have crucified the Lord of glory. ...We have not received the spirit of the world but the Spirit who is from God, that we may understand what God has freely given us. ...But **we have the mind of Christ**. (1 Cor. 2:6-16)

Paul preached that his disciples had the very spirit of God, the mind of Christ. This wisdom came through faith in the blood of the Lord Jesus Christ. Through this relationship with Christ, Paul claimed a superior wisdom from that of the world. This world would have included everyone outside of Paul's groups, including the Jews. To put it another way: Paul's relationship to the Christ gave him greater knowledge and wisdom than the actual followers of Jesus (Judas the Galilean). It is easy to imagine how attractive this concept of wisdom and knowledge was to the later disciples. They held something that no one else could possibly possess. They believed the spirit of God resided in them, and this spirit gave them special knowledge. Certainly, this aspect of Gnosticism had its roots in Paul's teachings.

CONCLUSION

From Part I, we have set forth a claim that Judas the Galilean was the promised Messiah. Josephus wrote about Judas in detail but failed to pen one word concerning Jesus' life. In short, Judas was the basis or main framework for the life of Jesus of Nazareth. This Jesus of Nazareth was also dependent upon the theology created by Paul, the Gentile man-god, Christ Jesus. A mingling of the two stories comes together in the Four Gospels. This will be further examined in Part III.

PART III
JESUS OF NAZARETH
(THE MYTHICAL MESSIAH)

These are the twelve he appointed: Simon (to whom he gave the name Peter); James son of Zebedee, and his brother John (to them **he gave the name Boanerges, which means Sons of Thunder**); Andrew, Philip, Bartholomew, Matthew, Thomas, James son of Alphaeus, Thaddaeus, **Simon the Zealot** and **Judas Iscariot [Sicarios],** who betrayed him. (Mark 3:16-19) (Emphasis mine) (Zealot names)

"From the days of John the Baptist until now, the kingdom of heaven has been forcefully advancing and **forceful [violent] men** lay hold of it." (Matt. 11:12) (Emphasis mine)

"You are not yet **fifty years old**," the Jews said to him. (John 8:57) (Emphasis mine)

Then the whole assembly rose and led him off to Pilate. And they began to accuse him saying, "We have found this man subverting our nation. **He opposes payment of taxes to Caesar and claims to be Christ, a king.**" (Luke 23:1-2) (Emphasis mine)

He [Pilate] took water and washed his hands in front of the crowd. "I am innocent of this man's blood," he said. "It is your responsibility."
All the people [the Jews] answered, "Let his blood be on us and on our children!" (Matt. 27:24-25) (Shifting blame from the Romans to the Jews)

Two robbers [revolutionaries] were crucified with him, one on his right and one on his left. (Matt. 27:38)

"My God, my God, why have you forsaken me?" (Matt. 27:46)

Then they said to Paul: "You see, brother, **how many thousands of Jews have believed, and all of them are zealous for the law**. They have been informed that you teach all the Jews who live among the Gentiles to turn away from Moses, telling them not to circumcise their children or live according to our customs." (Acts 21:20-21) (Emphasis mine)

CHAPTER 12

TURNING JUDAS THE GALILEAN AND CHRIST JESUS INTO JESUS OF NAZARETH

In Part I, I have set forth my argument that Judas the Galilean was the powerful first-century rabbi, crucified for his claim of kingship and his refusal to pay taxes to Rome. These two claims were also attributed to Jesus of Nazareth (Luke 23:2). Could there have been parallel movements in Galilee and Judea where two individuals vied for power? Was Jesus the spiritual leader as described in the Gospels? Was Judas the Galilean just a failed Messiah figure, destined for the scrap heap of history? If there is question, then the Gospels have done their job very effectively.

In Part II, the figure of Christ Jesus was explored. This man-god was the brainchild of the Apostle Paul, the result of personal revelations from the Risen Christ. These revelations corresponded to the rise in power of Agrippa I, the cousin of Paul. By separating the earthly (Judas the Galilean or Jesus) from the spiritual (Christ Jesus), Paul essentially could support both his cousin, Agrippa, and the man-god, Christ Jesus. This message was designed for Gentile consumption, which knew little of the Jewish ways but was all too familiar with the mystery religions. Christ Jesus became a savior god.

The split between the Jerusalem Church, led by the Pillars (James, Cephas and John), and Paul, occurred around 44 CE. From this point on, there were two distinct Jesus movements. The original was guided by the Pillars, and they followed the teachings of Judas the Galilean. In all things they worshipped as the Pharisees except they had an "inviolable attachment to liberty." (*Ant.* 18.23) This made the Jewish Christians (Fourth Philosophy) a party of resistance to both Rome and the Herodian leadership. That is why Jesus was crucified! The second movement, created by Paul, was designed to make the believing Gentiles into the Israel of God. He promised that the Gentiles could be reconciled to God through faith in the blood of Christ Jesus. These two very distinct movements split apart once the Jews discovered the actual teachings of Paul.

From 44-70 CE, these two movements grew independently within the Roman Empire. However, the dominant movement was led by the descendants of Judas the Galilean. The term Christian was used by both Suetonius and Tacitus to describe the Jewish Christian movement.

The Jews he [Claudius] expelled from Rome, since they were **constantly in rebellion**, at the instigation of Chrestus. (1)

Nero set up as the culprits and punished with the utmost refinement of cruelty a class hated for their abominations, who are commonly called Christians. Christus, from whom their name is derived, was executed at the hands of the procurator Pontius Pilate in the reign of Tiberius. Checked for the moment, this pernicious superstition again broke out, **not only in Judaea**, the source of the evil, but even in Rome... (2)

The first passage, written by Suetonius, describes the actions of Claudius against the Jews. Note that his actions were not against all Jews but those who followed a "Chrestus". The date of this expulsion coincided with Claudius' ascension to the throne, around 41 CE. Claudius' main advisor at this time was the Jewish King Agrippa. Agrippa persuaded Claudius to issue an edict which protected the religious practices of the Jews. (*Ant.* 19.278-291) Simultaneously, Claudius was protecting the peace loving Jews and attacking a Jewish sect. This Jewish sect (Christianity) was in rebellion against both Rome and King Agrippa. One thing is clear about this reference to "Chrestus": the followers of Chrestus were Jews, not Gentiles. These were the disciples of the Pillar Apostles, led by James and Cephas.

The second passage, written by Tacitus, describes the persecution of the Christians after the Great Fire of Rome, in 64 CE. Note that Tacitus stated that the "superstition again broke out" in Judaea and in Rome. His further description of the torture these Christians endured aligned perfectly with Josephus' description of the Fourth Philosophy. Again, these Christians were Jewish, not Gentiles. In the 16th century, Edward Gibbon conjectured that the Christians referred to by Tacitus were really the followers of Judas the Galilean. This common sense approach has long been ignored by scholars, but based upon what we know of the Jewish and Gentile Christian movements, little doubt remains that those being persecuted were the Jews. Note that Tacitus stated that the superstition broke out again in Judaea. From what we know of Paul's Gentile churches, they would have had no following in Judaea.

Both Suetonius and Tacitus referred to the followers of Christ, and both understood this to mean a sect of Jews, not Gentiles. This is even more revealing considering these historians wrote around 120 CE. By the early second century, the term Christian, in the Roman mind, conjured up a rebel Jewish sect. This was the atmosphere in which the Gospels were composed.

But why would these historians attach Christ to a Jewish sect and not to Paul's Gentile movement? The Jewish War of 66-70 CE firmly placed the Jewish resistance in the consciousness of every Roman citizen. As already noted, the followers of "Chrestus" were making disturbances in Rome around 41 CE and like-minded followers were accused of setting the Great Fire in 64 CE. The Jewish War was the last act of rebellion by the "Christians" (Fourth Philosophy). It is also important that two emperors were involved in this war. Vespasian and Titus both garnered fame and fortune from their victories in Judea. Titus even took Bernice, the sister and incestuous lover of Agrippa II, as his own mistress. Surely, the Romans would have gossiped about such affairs. In short, everything Christian would have been thought of as wholly Jewish.

The Jewish War decimated the Jewish Christian movement. What remained, scattered throughout the Roman Empire, was the Gentile church founded by Paul. Even though the Gentile church no longer had to contend with hostile Jewish teachers, they still had to deal with the memory of the Jewish Christian movement. This was very difficult because the Jewish Christian movement was viewed negatively by the Roman populace. Note that Tacitus stated that these Christians were a "pernicious superstition" "whose guilt merited the most exemplary punishment." (3) The Gentile "Christ Jesus" had little in common with the Jewish Messiah figure, Jesus (Judas the Galilean), but the image of the rebel Jesus was forever burned into the Roman consciousness. Like it or not, "Christ Jesus" could not be totally disassociated from the rebel Jewish leader.

Since the Gentile Christian movement could never disassociate itself from the original Jewish movement, a new plan had to be enacted. The Gospels, starting with Mark, incorporated the Jewish story of a Jesus. Thus, the actual story of Judas the Galilean was used as a framework for this Jesus of Nazareth. As we will note in Chapter 13, all important elements of Judas' life and death were massaged into the new history of Jesus. But that is not all. Judas' disciples, including John the Baptist and the Pillars, were also used in this grand forgery. This disinformation was included in the Gospels and also within the pages of Acts. Yet the greatest change to history concerned the life of Paul, the apostle to the Gentiles. As noted in Part II, Paul was the Liar, the Enemy and the Traitor. This unlovable figure was turned into the hero of Acts. And much of his attitude towards the law and Rome was transferred to the Gospel Jesus.

The first Gentile Gospel of Mark was written around 100 CE. This Gospel depended heavily upon the writings of Josephus (*Antiquities* was written in 93 CE). (4) The purpose of this Gospel was to turn Jesus against his own family. Thus, Jesus of Nazareth was not only celibate like Paul (1 Cor. 7:8; 7:32-33) but also had little to do with his own mother and brothers (Mark 3:20-21; 3:31-35). This was important considering the movement led by Judas the Galilean had familial connections. Judas' own sons played important roles in the early movement: Simon and James were crucified during the governorship of Tiberius Alexander (45-47 CE) and Menahem was killed in 66 CE after marching on Jerusalem and being declared Messiah. Judas' grandson, Eleazar, was the leader of the Sicarii at Masada and gave the order for mass suicide in order to escape the Roman torture (73 CE). And lastly, James the Just, his own brother, was stoned in Jerusalem in 62 CE. This rich history of family politics was well known in Roman circles as Josephus had recorded it all. The Gospel of Mark simply eliminated the sons of Jesus (Judas the Galilean) by making Jesus unmarried. The brothers of Jesus, including James and John, were portrayed as unbelievers. By the time the Gospel of John was written, around 140 CE, the brothers were willing to send Jesus to a certain death (John 7:1-10).

The connection between Judas the Galilean and his own brothers was understood as being modeled after Judas Maccabee and his brothers. A passage in the Slavonic Josephus, which was placed in the text after the Golden Eagle Temple Cleansing, showed the importance of the brotherly connection.

Come, men of Judaea, now is the time for men to behave like men, to show what reverence we have for the Law of Moses. Let us not be shamed, let us not bring disgrace on our Law-giver. Let us take as **the model for [our] exploits** Eleazar first and **the seven Maccabee brothers** and the mother who made men [of them]. For, when **Antiochus had conquered and subjugated our land and was ruling over us**, he was defeated by the seven youths and [their old teacher and an old woman. (After *War* 1.650) (Emphasis mine)

Note that the Slavonic Josephus added passages to Josephus' *Jewish War* concerning the Christian movement. Thus, the above passage, which commented on Judas the Galilean's movement after the Temple Cleansing, was written to supplement Josephus' treatment of the Christian movement. In this passage, Judas and his brothers were encouraged to model themselves after the Maccabee brothers. Just as Judas Maccabee drove Antiochus from

Judea, so too would Judas the Galilean defeat the Romans. Considering the Gospel of Mark was written for a Gentile Roman audience, it only makes sense that Jesus would be opposed by his own brothers. The author of Mark did not want his Jesus mixed up in any way with revolutionary activities, even though Judas the Galilean and his brothers were revolutionaries, opposed to Rome at every turn.

It was also imperative that the Gospels forever hide the relationship between the invented Jesus and the real Judas. This was done by shifting Church history forward by a generation. In the Gospel of Mark, John the Baptist was introduced but his arrival date was not given. The Gospel of Luke corrected this omission. Luke 3:1 stated that John came baptizing in the fifteenth year of the reign of Tiberius Caesar, or around 28-29 CE. This late date for John the Baptist also affected the dating of Jesus' ministry and the career of Paul the Apostle. Most scholars have accepted this dating for John the Baptist without serious question. (Even Mythicists seem to hold onto this date. That is one reason why they deny a historical Jesus. In this timeframe, a Jesus cannot be found!) What a wonderful way to forever distance the counterfeit (Jesus) from the genuine (Judas the Galilean). But there was another account of John the Baptist's arrival. In the Slavonic Josephus, John came baptizing in the Jordan in 6 CE, right before the nationwide tax revolt led by Judas the Galilean. In that passage, John was brought before Archelaus, the son of Herod the Great, who reigned from 4 BCE to 7 CE. (After *War* 2.110) This passage suggests that Luke's version of John the Baptist may have been a rewriting of history that has gone undetected for two thousand years.

The dating had been changed and the Messiah's familial relationships were denied. But perhaps the most devilish act of rewriting concerned the Jewish people. Judas the Galilean had been a Messiah figure to a great many Jews. The Gospel writers made it their mission to change the Jews from God's chosen to the children of the devil. And conversely, the Romans were transformed from occupiers to those who recognized the son of God. This shift of loyalties has long been recognized by scholars, but the ultimate reason for the shift has eluded most, if not all.

Starting with the Gospel of Mark, the various Jewish sects aligned themselves against Jesus. Josephus described the four major sects of first-century Judaea: the Pharisees, the Sadducees, the Essenes and the Fourth Philosophy of Judas the Galilean. The Gospels portrayed the Pharisee, the Sadducees and the Herodians as working together against Jesus. Left out of the Gospel mix were the Essenes and the Fourth Philosophy. According to Josephus (*Ant.* 18.4, 23), the Fourth Philosophy agreed with the Pharisaic teachings but also desired revolution against Rome. So, it can be argued that the only group not overtly against Jesus was the Essenes and this only because they were omitted from the Gospels. How could this Jesus have been the target of all religious parties?

As noted before, the Fourth Philosophy and the Herodians were enemies, each representing a ruling claim. The Herodians were the kings appointed by Rome while the Fourth Philosophy had their own Messiah figure (Judas the Galilean or Jesus). These two groups were at complete odds with one another. The Gospels expect us to believe that these two groups worked together to rid Judaea of Jesus. In addition, the Fourth Philosophy and the Pharisees represented the poor while the Sadducees represented the rich. From the letter of James, it is not hard to see the utter disgust which the Fourth Philosophy had for the rich. To think that these two groups also worked together is ridiculous. The New Testament's claim that Jesus was at odds with all the Jewish sects cannot be seriously entertained.

A few examples of the Gospel's treatment of the various sects follow:

And the **teachers of the law** who came down from Jerusalem said, "He is possessed by Beelzebub! By the prince of demons he is driving out demons." (Mark 3:22)

He then began to teach them that the Son of Man must suffer many things and be **rejected by the elders, chief priests and teachers of the law**, and that he must be killed and after three days rise again. (Mark 8:31)

The **chief priests and the teachers of the law** heard this and began looking for a way to kill him, for they feared him, because the whole crowd was amazed at his teaching. (Mark 11:18)

They arrived again in Jerusalem, and while Jesus was walking in the temple courts, **the chief priests, the teachers of the law and the elders** came to him. "By what authority are you doing these things?" they asked. (Mark 11:27-28) (Emphasis mine)

The Gospel of Mark initially grouped the opposition to Jesus as the chief priests, the teachers of the law and the elders. However, on issues regarding the law, Mark saw fit to place the Pharisees against Jesus. This occurred when certain issues were discussed: clean and unclean hands (Mark 7:1-23); divorce (Mark 10:1-12) and paying taxes to Caesar (Mark 12:13-17). It is interesting that Mark paired the Pharisees with the Herodians as the questioners of Jesus concerning taxation. Judas the Galilean was a Pharisee and led a great tax revolt while the Herodians were the tax collectors of the age. To pair these groups together on this issue is quite astounding.

When Jesus was arrested, he was taken in front of the chief priests, elders of the law and teachers of the law. (Mark 14:53) These same groups, along with the whole Sanhedrin, then handed Jesus over to Pilate. (Mark 15:1) When Pilate tried to free Jesus through the Barabbas affair, the chief priests convinced the crowd to shout "Crucify him." (Mark 15:11-13) This last act helped unite the whole Jewish nation against Jesus. But this was Mark's goal. He had to set the Jews against Jesus.

This same pattern was followed by Matthew, but he added one major element to the Jews hatred of Jesus. When Pilate washed his hands in front of the crowd, he said, "I am innocent of this man's blood. It is your responsibility." The Jews replied, "Let his blood be on us and on our children." (Matt. 27:24-25) In one short scene, Matthew placed the blame on the Jews and on their children for all time.

The Gospel of John denigrated the Jews more than the other Gospels, if that were even possible. John did mention the Pharisees but he tended to use the term Jew as the opponent of Jesus. A few passages will show this clever shift of blame to the whole nation of Jews.

So, because Jesus was doing these things on the Sabbath, **the Jews persecuted him**. Jesus said to them, "My Father is always at his work to this very day, and I, too, am working." For this reason, the **Jews tried all the harder to kill him**; not only was he breaking the Sabbath, but he was even calling God his own Father, making himself equal to God. (John 5:16-18)

After this, Jesus went around in Galilee, purposely staying away from Judea because **the Jews there were waiting to take his life**. (John 7:1) (Emphasis mine)

In reality, the chief priests were teamed up with the Sadducees to stop Jesus (Judas the Galilean). The Pharisees and Essenes had nothing to hate in Jesus. Jesus was insistent on changing the status quo, the very actions dreaded by the wealthy and powerful. Thus, the Gospel version of the Pharisees, the teachers of the law, the elders and the majority of Jews, did not present a true picture of Jesus' relationship with these various groups. Luckily, the Gospel of Luke unwittingly let a few glimpses of reality get through its editing process.

At that time some Pharisees came to Jesus and said to him, "Leave this place and go somewhere else. Herod wants to kill you." (Luke 13:31)

In this passage, the Pharisees were warning Jesus about Herod's plans. One point should not be missed in Luke's Gospel: the Pharisees had continual access to Jesus. If they were really out to kill Jesus, then it seems as though Jesus and his disciples would have kept their distance. Instead, the Pharisees treated Jesus as one of their own, often comparing their own practices to his practices (Luke 5:27-32; 5:33-39; 6:1-5). It would not have been uncommon for Pharisees to disagree with one another. It would have been strange if they had plotted to kill anyone with different ideas.

Jesus was also repeatedly invited to eat with different Pharisee teachers (Luke 7:36-50; 11:37-54; 14:1-6). The Pharisee and teachers of the law often called Jesus "Teacher" (Luke 7:40; 10:25; 11:45). As noted earlier, Judas the Galilean was a Pharisee (*Ant.* 18.23), "a teacher of a peculiar sect of his own, and was not at all like the rest of those their leaders." (*War.* 2.118) So, it was possible to be a Pharisee and disagree over many areas. If one issue scared the Pharisees, it would have been Judas the Galilean's (Jesus') insistence on freedom from Rome. This would have been the only reason to fully oppose Jesus. All the other issues could be debated, but fighting Rome was a matter of life and death, not just for the individual but for Israel as well. Only this fear would have driven **some** Pharisees to bitterly oppose Jesus.

The Gospels effectively turned all sects and all Jews against Jesus. So, even though Jesus was a Messiah (King), his following was rather small. In Acts 1:15, the number of believers numbered about 120. The great crowds which welcomed Jesus upon his entry into Jerusalem (Matt. 21:1-11) were turned against him by the chief priests and eventually called out, "Crucify him!" (Matt. 27:20-25) According to the Gospels, these Jews were not part of Jesus' kingdom. Jesus said to Pilate: "My kingdom is not of this world. If it were, my servants would fight to prevent my arrest by the Jews. But now my kingdom is from another place." (John 18:36) In this statement, Jesus uttered the philosophy of Paul. Jesus would be a Christ to all nations, to all who believed.

In the Gospel story, the Jews functioned as disciples of Satan while the Romans played the good guys. That is one bizarre rewrite of history. Judas the Galilean fought against Roman occupation. The Gospel writers turned this opposition around, so that Jesus was opposed to the Jews. When Jesus was tried before Pilate, at the insistence of the Jews, Pilate tried to free him. He believed in Jesus' innocence, prompting him to wash his hands of the whole affair. Throughout history, people have sympathized with Pilate over his efforts to free Jesus. However, from the first-century historians, Josephus and Philo, the real Pilate was a cruel and unjust man. (5) Did Pilate really try to free Jesus or was this just another rewrite of history? In addition to portraying Pilate favorably, the Gospels also glorified the Roman soldiers.

With a loud cry, Jesus breathed his last. The curtain of the temple was torn in two from top to bottom. And when the centurion, who stood there in front of Jesus, heard his cry and saw how he died, he said, "Surely this man was the Son of God!" (Mark 15:37-39)

CONCLUSION

Judas the Galilean was a rebel leader who claimed to be the promised Messiah. His disciples came from the most radical elements of Jewish society. Judas wanted nothing to do with Rome. His desire was to free the Jewish nation from Rome and allow God to be their only Lord and Ruler. (*Ant.* 18.23) This was to be done through a tax revolt. In 6 CE, Judas and Sadduc declared that "this taxation was no better than an introduction to slavery, and exhorted the nation to assert their liberty." (*Ant.* 18.4) Perhaps the most misunderstood passage in the New Testament concerns Jesus' attitude towards Roman taxation.

"Is it right to pay taxes to Caesar or not? Should we pay or shouldn't we?"

But Jesus knew their hypocrisy. "Why are you trying to trap me?" he asked. "Bring me a denarius and let me look at it." They brought the coin, and he asked them, "Whose portrait is this? And whose inscription?"

"Caesar's," they replied.

Then Jesus said to them, "Give to Caesar what is Caesar's and to God what is God's." (Mark 12:13-17)

The opponents of Jesus were trying to trap him on the question of paying taxes to Rome. If Jesus really believed in the Jews' duty to pay Roman taxes, then why were his opponents trying to trap him using this line of questioning? On the other hand, if Jesus preached against Roman taxation, the answer to this question might be used against him with the Roman administrator, Pilate. And that is exactly what happened. According to Luke 23:2, this was the charge against Jesus: "We have found this man subverting our nation. He opposes payment of taxes to Caesar and claims to be Messiah, a king." Surely, Jesus' audience believed that he opposed Roman taxation.

What did Jesus really mean by saying: "Give to Caesar what is Caesar's and to God what is God's." Let us suppose that Jesus held the denarius in his hands. He motioned to the Jews that this currency belonged to Caesar. But then he swept his arms wide to direct his listeners to the city of Jerusalem and to Israel itself. This was God's land! In short, Jesus was telling his audience that the Romans should take their money and leave God's holy land. This cry of rebellion reverberated in the minds of his followers. This strong tradition helped keep the tax story in the Gospel accounts.

This Messiah figure had been divorced from his roots by Paul. Paul emphasized the crucifixion of Jesus, the sacrifice for all mankind. Paul never wrote about the circumstances surrounding Jesus' crucifixion. Paul's take on the tax issue was completely different from that of Judas the Galilean. Since Paul came from the line of Herod, his sympathies were with the tax collectors. His plea to the Romans was this: "This is why you pay taxes, for the authorities are God's servants, who give their full time to governing. Give everyone what you owe him: if you owe taxes, pay taxes..." (Romans 13:6-7) Paul supported the taxation of Caesar and even claimed that Caesar was God's servant. This support for the taxation would have been appreciated by any government. Paul did not want to make waves with the ruling elites.

This Pauline view of taxation was placed upon Jesus of Nazareth. As noted above, Judas the Galilean wanted to rid the land of the Roman tax machine. But the Gospels aimed at giving the impression that Jesus was unconcerned about the tax issue. The statement "Give to Caesar what is Caesar's and God what is God's" was framed as an endorsement of Roman taxation. In fact, Roman taxation was all right as long as you also gave God his due. Therefore, Jesus of Nazareth meant to please both God and the Romans. Did Jesus really mean this? After all, Jesus did say, "No one can serve two masters. ...You cannot serve both God and Money" (Matt. 6:24)

CHAPTER 13
FORTY SIMILARITIES BETWEEN JUDAS AND JESUS

It can be easily argued that Jesus was the most influential person who lived and taught in first-century Israel. It would seem logical that his life would have been chronicled by contemporary historians. But that part of the Jesus story is puzzling. How could this giant of his time be ignored by the Jewish historian Josephus and the Roman historians Tacitus and Suetonius? This treatment of Jesus is akin to omitting Babe Ruth from baseball greats of the 1920's and 1930's or Hitler from the causes of World War II. Surely no historian would make such a glaring mistake or omission. Unfortunately, the Gospel Jesus did not exist outside the pages of the New Testament.

The only mention of anything related to Jesus by Tacitus concerned the Great Fire of Rome in 64 CE. Nero blamed the Christians for the fire and mercilessly murdered them in retaliation. From this, we can deduce that the followers of Jesus were scattered throughout the cities of the Roman Empire, but nothing further concerning Jesus was revealed. (*Annals* xv. 44) In fact, the great historian Edward Gibbon conjectured that Tacitus had confused the Christians with the followers of Judas the Galilean. It only made sense to him that Nero would have used a group universally hated within the Empire as his scapegoat. (1) Gibbon realized that the traditional Christian story did not mesh with the Neronian persecution. However, Judas the Galilean's movement would have been a perfect fit. My only difference with Gibbon is that I believe that the Christians were actually the followers of Judas the Galilean (Jesus).

Suetonius mentioned the Jews who were followers of a "Chrestus," who caused disturbances in Rome during the reign of Claudius, around 41 CE. (*Twelve Caesars*, Claudius 25) But once again, Jesus was not detailed in any way. It is interesting to note that the Jews Claudius banned from Rome were "constantly in rebellion, at the instigation of a Chrestus." In the traditional view of Christianity, the Christians were law abiding, meek individuals. However, this report by Suetonius gives us the exact opposite reading of this group. This Jewish Christian group was synonymous with Judas the Galilean's Fourth Philosophy. This conjecture is no different than the conjecture made by Gibbon concerning the passage by Tacitus. The reason for the persecution has been obscured for two thousand years. This occurred in 41 CE, not 50 CE as proposed by Acts. This earlier timeframe coincides with Agrippa's influence over Claudius. Since the Fourth Philosophy was a thorn in Agrippa's side, this persecution in Rome was done as a favor by Claudius. Claudius was not persecuting all Jews, just the followers of "Chrestus". In fact, at this very time, Claudius issued an edict giving the Jews throughout the Empire expanded religious rights, and this from the prompting of Agrippa.

While Tacitus and Suetonius gave their interpretations of Roman history, Josephus wrote of the rich history behind the Jewish nation, from its inception to its final agonizing end at Masada (73 CE). Surely, Jesus would have played an important role in his narrative. After all, Jesus was a sensation according to the Gospels. Jesus walked on water, raised people from the dead, healed the blind and crippled, produced matter out of thin air (the feeding of the five thousand), and his teachings confounded all the learned men of his day. Josephus should have had a field day with this rich material. Amazingly, Josephus wrote nothing about Jesus except one questionable passage which seems more like a later creed than his own skeptical writings. Many Christians believe that this lone passage in Josephus' *Antiquities* proves the existence of Jesus. The passage in question, called the Testimonium Flavianum (TF), will be reproduced below.

Now, there was about this time Jesus, a wise man, if it be lawful to call him a man, for he was a doer of wonderful works - a teacher of such men as receive the truth with pleasure. He drew over to him both many of the Jews, and many of the Gentiles. He was [the] Christ; and when Pilate, at the suggestion of the principal men amongst us, had condemned him to the cross, those that loved him at the first did not forsake him, for he appeared to them alive again the third day, as the divine prophets had foretold these and ten thousand other wonderful things concerning him; and the tribe of Christians, so named from him, are not extinct at this day. (*Ant.* 18.63-64)

Did Josephus write this? The answer is no. There are too many arguments against its authenticity. Did a later Christian edit this section of *Antiquities* and add this testimonial? That will be proved below. There are four main points in my argument against this passage.

First, as noted in Chapter 1 concerning Pontius Pilate, a curious pattern emerges right before the TF. Josephus described a three year tenure for the procurator Gratus, yet the text claimed that he served eleven years. Thus, Pilate must have begun his governorship at 26 CE, at least according to the traditional chronology. Yet everything surrounding the two passages about Pilate can be dated at 18-19 CE. Many of these events, such as the death of Germanicus and the expulsion of the Jews from Rome are also corroborated by Tacitus as 19 CE events. Thus, it is very likely that the term of Gratus was changed from three to eleven years by the same people who inserted the TF. (See *Antiquities* 18.26-84)

Second, the TF is so unlike the rest of Josephus' writings. Note that the TF makes Josephus a believing Christian, and also attests to the resurrection. The TF called Jesus a wonder worker. Later, in *Antiquities*, Josephus blasted those who claimed to be miracle workers (*Ant.* 20.98; 20.160; 20.167-168; 20.169-172; 20.188). Thus, from just a cursory analysis, it is obvious that someone other than Josephus wrote the TF. In addition, Josephus did not mention one word regarding the life of Jesus. This is interesting because Josephus wrote extensively about the life and deeds of Judas the Galilean but did not record his death. This is amazing considering Josephus recorded the crucifixions of Judas' sons Simon and James (*Ant.* 20.102), the stoning of another son, Menaham (*War* 2.433-434) and the suicide of his grandson, Eleazar, at Masada. In each case, Josephus referred back to that clever rabbi, Judas the Galilean. And lastly, even the term "wise man" used in the TF was also given to Judas the Galilean (*Ant.* 17.152). Thus, it appears as if the TF was a replacement passage for the crucifixion of Judas the Galilean. The death of Judas would have been the original Josephus.

Third, an amazing gap exists in the *Antiquities*. After *Ant.* 18.84 discusses the expulsion of the Jews in 19 CE, *Ant.* 18.85 goes directly to the reason for Pilate's dismissal from Judea in 37 CE, an awe inspiring eighteen years of missing information. In *Ant.* 18.89, Pilate was credited with ten years as governor. If Pilate came in 18 CE as claimed in the first point, then he actually reigned for eighteen years, not ten. It is no coincidence that the High Priest, Caiaphas, also held his title from 18-37 CE. Thus, it appears as if pious editing has occurred. How unlikely is it that almost eighteen years had little or no information about it? These years were within the lifetime of Josephus' parents. He would have known quite a lot about this time. It should not be missed that this would have been the first generation to guide the Fourth Philosophy after the death of Judas the Galilean (Jesus). How convenient for the Gospel writers! All contradictory information vanished into thin air.

Certainly, Josephus did not delete his own material. The same individuals who tampered with Pilate's reign and who substituted the TF for Judas' death were responsible for erasing the early Church history. (Note: the *War* also has no information from 19 CE to 37 CE. (See *War* 2.175-177 at 19 CE and *War* 2.178 at 37 CE)).

Fourth, One other passage in *Antiquities* proves that the TF is not from the pen of Josephus. In *Ant.* 20.200, James, the brother of Jesus, was stoned. Our current edition of *Antiquities* is differs from the earliest edition. According to Origen, around 230 AD, the following was said about this passage:

This James was of so shining a character among the people, on account of his righteousness, that Flavius Josephus, when in his twentieth book of the *Jewish Antiquities,* he had a mind to set down what was the cause, why the people suffered such miseries, till the very holy house was demolished, he said, that these things befell them by the anger of God, on account of what they had dared to do to James, the brother of Jesus, who was called Christ; and wonderful it is, that while **he did not receive Jesus for Christ**, he did nevertheless bear witness that James was so righteous a man. He says further, that the people thought they had suffered these things for the sake of James. (Whiston, *The Works of Josephus*, pg. 815) (Emphasis mine)

From this we know that Josephus did not regard Jesus as the Christ as claimed in the TF. In addition, this passage was changed from the original because it attributed the destruction of Jerusalem to the slaying of James. The Orthodox Christians could not tolerate this. They believed the destruction was due to the crucifixion of Jesus.

From the above, much of the Church story has been obliterated from the writings of Josephus by later Christians. The reason for this extensive editing job is obvious: later Christians wanted to hide the relationship between Jesus and Judas the Galilean (the same man!). Also, the early history of the movement could be expunged and later replaced with the Acts of the Apostles, which was largely based upon the works of Josephus and twisted into a quite different story.

From the above analysis of the three historians who either mentioned Christians or should have known about Jesus, it should be appreciated that all three knew of Judas the Galilean and his movement of rebellious Jews. Could their Christians have really been the followers of Judas the Galilean, founder of the Fourth Philosophy? The following pages will list forty similarities between Jesus of Nazareth and Judas the Galilean. Some are general in nature and others quite specific. Although any such listing does not prove a 100% foolproof case, the odds overwhelmingly favor my hypothesis that Jesus was simply a title for Judas the Galilean. Of these forty similarities, let's assume a one in two chance of each event happening to Jesus in the time of Pilate and Judas a generation earlier. The mathematical formula for this would be 2 to the 40th power, or put simply: there would be one chance in 1.1 trillion that Jesus and Judas were separate individuals. Although my case is not 100% certain, this would come very close - 99.999...%. And consider this: would the release of prisoners in 4 BCE under the shaky rule of Archelaus (the real Barabbas event) be only one chance in two or would it be one chance in a million? As one can see, the one chance in 1.1 trillion of Jesus and Judas being separate individuals is a gross understatement of the odds favoring my hypothesis.

To further illustrate the odds against Judas and Jesus being separate individuals, just two similarities will be considered. Josephus stated that Judas was the author of the Fourth Philosophy. (The other three philosophies - the Pharisees, the Sadducees and the Essenes - were founded in the second century BCE.) To found a new philosophy was no ordinary undertaking. According to Josephus, this one new philosophy dominated the Jewish scene until the war with Rome had ended. In that particular timeframe, 4 BCE - 73 CE, Josephus never mentioned the word "Christianity." Could Christianity have been like the stealth bomber, hovering about, but never seen? The odds of this would be one in a million, conservatively. A second event concerning Barabbas also has long odds. Josephus wrote in the *War* and *Antiquities* of a Barabbas-style prisoner release in 4 BCE but never again mentioned such an event. Again, could this have also occurred under the government of Pontius Pilate around 30 CE? The odds of this would be a million to one, conservatively. Thus, these two similarities, when put together, would yield the formula 1,000,000 to the 2nd power, or one chance in a trillion. How can such overwhelming odds be ignored?

A LIST OF SIMILARITIES BETWEEN JUDAS AND JESUS

The following list of forty similarities is meant to draw attention to the fact that the life of Jesus, as portrayed in the Gospels, had much in common with Judas the Galilean, as written about by Josephus. To traditional Christians, this list may be very hard to swallow, as it may force a reexamination of their basic belief system. But this list will also madden the Mythicists, who claim that a Messiah figure named Jesus never really existed. While I agree that Jesus of Nazareth was fictional, I do believe that this Jesus was a rewrite of a real individual, Judas the Galilean. And Judas the Galilean was not fictional! If Judas the Galilean lived, then so did his brothers and sons. Combined, they formed the Fourth Philosophy, the forerunner of the religion which Mythicists claim did not exist until after the Jewish war.

To make it easier for readers to locate individual similarities, each will be numbered.

1. Jesus was born in 8-4 BCE (Matthew) and in 6 CE at the Census of Cyrenius (Luke). Judas was mentioned by Josephus in 4 BCE, relating to the Golden Eagle Temple Cleansing (*Ant.* 17.149-167) and in 6 CE, regarding the Census of Cyrenius (*Ant.* 18.1-10) The birth narratives in Matthew and Luke are both inconsistent with the reign of Pilate and the ministry of John the Baptist. For example, if Jesus were born in 4 BCE and died thirty-three years later, then he would have died around 30 CE, during the reign of Pilate but five years **before John the Baptist's death**. (*Ant.* 18.116-119) If Jesus were born in 6 CE and died thirty-three years later, then he would have died in 39 CE, a few years after John the Baptist but two years **after Pilate** left Judea. Both accounts appear historically flawed. These two birth narratives were strategically placed in an era when Judas the Galilean's ministry flourished. This deception moved the adult Jesus thirty years away from Judas the Galilean, thus hiding the Messiah's true identity. This misdirection by the Gospel writers has worked brilliantly. Very few scholars have even considered Jesus outside of the 30 CE timeframe. This is even more disturbing considering Jesus' brother, James, was purported to be ninety-six years old in 62 CE. Even if this slightly exaggerates his age by ten years, James' birth date can be estimated at approximately 35-25 BCE. Jesus was the older brother and could not have been born any later than 25 BCE.

It should be asked: why would Matthew and Luke pick different dates for the Messiah's birth? If one solid date existed, then both Gospel writers should have easily followed that lone date. However, if the writers were trying to present an alternate date, then it might have been possible for each to tie his birth date to a different event. Matthew tied his birth date to the Golden Eagle Temple Cleansing while Luke used the Census of Cyrenius, the two major events in Judas the Galilean's career.

2. This second coincidence relates to Matthew's Star of Bethlehem story which was placed in 4 BCE (See number 1). In the Gospel of Matthew, the magi were drawn to Jerusalem by a star, near the end of Herod the Great's reign, around 4 BCE. These Magi found the baby Jesus but did not return to Herod to report the findings. Herod was incensed and ordered the slaughter of all the baby boys in the vicinity of Bethlehem, two years old and younger.

In the Slavonic Josephus, Persian astrologers went to Herod the Great identifying the star in the sky and explaining its significance. Herod insisted they return to him after finding the infant. However, the astrologers were warned by the stars to avoid Herod on the return trip. In his rage, Herod wanted to kill all the male children throughout his kingdom. His advisors convinced him that the Messiah would come from Bethlehem, hoping to confine the slaughter to only Bethlehem. This Star of Bethlehem passage was inserted in the *War* during the early years of Herod, between 27-22 BCE. (2)

This Slavonic Josephus passage originated from the same source which supplied the Gospel version. The Slavonic text has some interesting details which are missing from Matthew. Matthew wrote that the chief priests and teachers of the law informed Herod that the infant would be born in Bethlehem. He then sent the Magi to Bethlehem and ordered them to return when they had located the infant. (Matt. 2:3-8) This version does not give Herod much credit, for if he really knew that a king would be born in Bethlehem, he would have had every child slaughtered in Bethlehem before the Magi could even reach the place. On the other hand, the Slavonic version had Herod learning about the location after waiting for the Persian astrologers to return. This blunder on Herod's part wasted precious time, allowing the infant's parents to escape. Herod's advisors also told Herod the meaning of the Star. This star was the promised Star Prophecy, which told of a leader coming from Judah. (Numbers 24:17) The same sentiment was included in Matthew 2:6, but this quote from Micah 5:2 promised that a ruler would come from Bethlehem. All in all, the two versions have much in common and vary very little, the difference being the time: 25 BCE versus 4 BCE.

If Jesus were born in 25 BCE, then he would have been 30 years old at the time of the census (6 CE). This was the exact time when John baptized in the Jordan and proclaimed the coming of the Messiah. (3) This date was also marked by the nationwide tax revolt led by Judas the Galilean, the historical Jesus. (*Ant.* 18.4)

3. The genealogy of Jesus can also be compared to information known about Judas the Galilean. In Matthew 1:15 and Luke 3:24, a Mattan and Matthat are listed as great grandfathers. Since the Gospels added a few generations to distance Jesus from Judas, these great grandfathers may have been Jesus' father. Judas's father may have been Matthias, a name closely resembling Mattan and Matthat.

On Mary's side, a similarity exists concerning the town of Sepphoris. In Christian tradition, Mary's family came from Sepphoris. Judas was also linked to Sepphoris by Josephus. It was written that Judas was the son of Sepphoris, or rather from Sepphoris, and he also raided the armory at Sepphoris. Certainly, Judas was well acquainted with this town.

4. Herod the Great planned to execute Judas after the Golden Eagle Temple

Cleansing. Luckily for Judas, Herod ordered to have his prisoners put to death after his own death, in order to create great sorrow in Israel. After Herod's death, his advisors reneged on the insane plan. (*Ant.* 17.149-167) According to the Gospels, Herod the Great tried to kill the baby Jesus. (Matt. 2) Herod's goal of eliminating Jesus ended with his own death. In both stories, an elderly paranoid Herod tried to destroy elements he perceived as being a threat to his rule. Of course, the infant narrative was not actual history but rather a replay of Moses' infancy.

5. Joseph returned to Israel after the death of Herod the Great but was afraid to settle in Judea because of Archelaus. Having been warned in a dream, Joseph moved his family to Nazareth, in Galilee. (Matt. 2:19-23) The New Testament often moved characters by using dreams, miracles or visions. For example, Philip was whisked away after baptizing the eunuch in Acts 8:39-40. Peter's visit to Cornelius' house in Caesarea was preceded by a vision in Acts chapter 10. And the Magi did not return to King Herod because they were warned in a dream. (Matt. 2:12) All three of these examples have alternative explanations. Philip and the eunuch as well as Peter and Cornelius were patterned after the account of King Izates given by Josephus. (*Ant.* 20.34-48) And as noted in number 2, the Slavonic Josephus explained the Persian astrologers' decision to avoid Herod differently. Either the Star of Bethlehem convinced them not to return to Herod or they had talked to the locals about the King and decided to go home by another route. The point is this: when trying to reconstruct historical events, it may be wise to discount the passages which depend upon a literary devise such as a dream or vision.

After being released by Archelaus, Judas went to Sepphoris in Galilee, where he led an uprising against the son of Herod. (*War* 2.56) Sepphoris was in the tetrarchy of Herod Antipas, not under the control of Archelaus. Since Archelaus was waging war upon the followers of Judas and Matthias, the move to Galilee was prudent in that it allowed reorganization without fear of being attacked by Archelaus. The events in Josephus and the New Testament both occurred because Herod the Great had died and the country was in unrest.

6. The Gospels do not mention the early life of Jesus, except when he taught at the Temple at the age of twelve. (Luke 2:41-52) Otherwise, no information was given from 6 CE (Census of Cyrenius) to 26 CE (supposed date of Pilate - see chapter 1). This lack of information mirrors Josephus' *War* where nothing was written from 6 CE (Census) to 26 CE (Pilate). (*War* 2.167-169) Josephus barely expanded on this paucity of information in *Antiquities*, where he listed the Roman procurators during this twenty year stretch, but little else. (*Ant.* 18.26-35) It is possible that these missing years from Josephus could have

been the result of pious editing. The actual crucifixion of Judas the Galilean may have been deleted. Note that Josephus detailed the deaths of Judas' three sons, James, Simon, and Menahem and his grandson, Eleazar. With each of these occasions, Josephus referred back to Judas the Galilean. It is hard to believe that Josephus omitted the circumstances behind the death of Judas. So it is very possible that the writings of Josephus were edited to remove some interesting details of Judas' life and his eventual crucifixion.

7. When he was only twelve, Jesus spent three days at the Temple. He was "sitting among the teachers, listening to them and asking them questions. Everyone who heard him was amazed at his understanding and his answers." (Luke 2:41-52) Judas taught young men at the same Temple. Judas was "the most celebrated interpreters of the Jewish laws and ... well beloved by the people, because of [the] education of their youth." (*Ant.* 17.149 - 4 BCE) How many other men also taught at the Temple? Is it possible that Judas' early career as teacher at the Temple was made legend by placing his wisdom and knowledge within the body of a twelve year old? Consider this: if Judas had been born around 25 BCE (see number 2), then he would have been just twenty years old at the time of the Golden Eagle Temple Cleansing (4 BCE). His status as one of the finest teachers of the law, at such a young age, must have been legendary. This child prodigy legacy was woven into the Gospel fabric by Luke in his story of the twelve year old Jesus.

8. The story of John the Baptist may very well be the most important link between Judas the Galilean and Jesus. In the Gospels, John the Baptist introduced Jesus to the world in 28-29 CE, per the dating of Luke. (Luke 3:1-3) In fact, this is the reason why scholars look nowhere else for Jesus. It is just a given that Jesus' ministry began around 30 CE.

According to the Slavonic Josephus, this same John came baptizing in the Jordan in 6 CE, right before the mention of Judas the Galilean and during the reign of Archelaus (4 BCE- 7 CE). (4) In addition, the Psuedoclementine *Recognitions* acknowledged John right before describing the various Jewish sects. (5) Josephus described these same sects right after his introduction of Judas the Galilean. (*Ant.* 18.4-22 and *War* 2.118-166) So the 6 CE timeframe for John the Baptist is attested to by more than one source.

Could this John the Baptist have been baptizing and proclaiming different Messiahs in both 6 CE and 29 CE? The odds of that would be millions to one. The only logical conclusion is that Jesus and Judas the Galilean were the same person. This explains why the Slavonic Josephus' version of events has been ignored over the years. If John actually came in 6 CE, then all of New Testament scholarship is, at best, misguided. That would not only make the scholars look foolish but would also prove Pauline Christianity a sham religion.

9. Both Judas and Jesus had a second-in-command, Sadduc and John the Baptist, respectively. This organizational model was fashioned after the Maccabees. Mattathias led the movement and his son, Judas Maccabee, was his lieutenant. After Mattathias died, Simon took his place and Judas Maccabee was elevated to the leadership role. In the later Fourth Philosophy, Matthias and Judas worked together at the Temple and were responsible for the Golden Eagle Temple Cleansing. After Matthias suffered martyrdom, Judas filled this position with Sadduc. (*Ant.* 18.4)

In the Gospel accounts, Jesus picked Simon Peter as his second-in-command. In reality, Jesus was first paired with John the Baptist (Sadduc). When Jesus was crucified, he was replaced by his brother, James the Just. At this stage, John the Baptist and James shared control of the movement. In 35-36 CE, John was beheaded by Herod Antipas. James appointed Cephas (Peter) to be John's successor. The Gospels successfully minimized the roles of John the Baptist and James. According to these accounts, John died before Jesus, but per Josephus, John died after Jesus. Also, James the Just was barely mentioned by Acts, his leadership role unannounced until Acts chapter 15, at the Council of Jerusalem. By bypassing John the Baptist and James the Just, the Gospels were able to skip a generation, placing Peter (Cephas) as the leading apostle after the death of Jesus.

The dual leadership may have safeguarded the movement. If one of the leaders was captured or killed, then the other could take control. The movement of Judas the Galilean (Jesus) was different from that of Judas Maccabee in that the later movement believed in the resurrection of its leader. Thus, even though John the Baptist and James led the movement after the death of Jesus, many throughout the movement still awaited the return of Jesus in power and glory. So, in essence, John and James were merely caretakers. This may account for the divisions in the 40 CE church in Corinth. Paul wrote that some disciples followed himself, others followed Cephas (James the Just), others followed Apollos (John the Baptist) (see Acts 18:24-25), and others followed Christ (Judas the Galilean or Jesus). (1 Cor. 1:10-12) This split may have been inevitable since Judas the Galilean's movement was held together by a common hatred of Rome. Teachers within the movement could have possibly come from both the Pharisees and the Essenes. Differences, in approach to religion, were inevitable.

10. Jesus and Judas were both called the Galilean. Actually, Jesus was referred to as Jesus of Nazareth, a city located near Sepphoris in Galilee. It should not

be missed that Sepphoris was central to Judas the Galilean's ministry. Placing Nazareth close to Sepphoris may have been more than just coincidence. In *War* 1.648, Judas was said to be the son of Sepphoris. This more likely was his place of birth as opposed to his father. And in *War* 2.56, Judas retreated to Sepphoris after being harassed by Archelaus. There, Judas armed his disciples with weapons from the armory. Judas' history with Sepphoris was no doubt changed to Nazareth to hide these embarrassing revelations. After all, both of the above references to Sepphoris were in the context of armed rebellion against Herod the Great and later, Archelaus.

The name Nazareth is probably a corruption of Nazarite, as no references to Nazareth appear in the Old Testament or in Josephus. (A Nazarite was consecrated to God by a vow and included such notables as John the Baptist and Samson). In fact, John Crossan stated that in addition to Josephus' silence concerning Nazareth, "it is never mentioned by any of the Jewish rabbis whose pronouncements are in the Mishnah or whose discussions are in the Talmud." (6) Jesus' disciples were called Galileans (Mark 14:70) and it may have been a sleight-of-hand which changed Jesus the Galilean to Jesus of Nazareth. In John 7:41, the crowd asked, "How can the Christ come from Galilee?" And the leaders had the same reservations about Jesus. "Look into it, and you will find that a prophet does not come out of Galilee." (John 7:52)

Judas the Galilean was mentioned in several passages by Josephus (*War* 2.118; *War* 2.433 and *Ant.* 20.102). Josephus did state that this Judas hailed from Gamala, across the River Jordan (*Ant.* 18.4), but he was known as the Galilean, as attributed to the above references. Galilee was a hotbed for revolutionaries. Both Jesus and Judas would have had a similar background, influenced by those who had struggled for years against Herod the Great.

11. The disciples of Jesus and Judas were zealous for the law. (Acts 21:20) (*Ant.* 17.149-154) It is true that Paul taught his Gentile followers to disregard the law. However, the Jewish Christians, led by James the Just, clearly denounced that teaching and removed Paul and his followers from fellowship. (See Galatians)

Some forty years after the death of Judas (19 CE), a splinter group of the Fourth Philosophy, known as the Zealots, appeared on the scene. Like their name suggests, these individuals were obsessed with the Law and were comparable to the fanatical followers of James the Just. (Acts 21:20)

12. Judas and Jesus were both called wise men by Josephus. (*Ant.* 17.152 and *Ant.* 18.63) As the Jesus passage was a late third or early fourth century interpolation, the use of the term wise man was taken from the description of Judas and Matthias. It must also be noted that Josephus did not freely

use the term wise man. He did, however, use that term when describing himself. If Josephus called himself a wise man then this indeed was a great compliment.

13. Both teachers assigned a high value to the sharing of wealth or pure communism. (Matt. 6:19-27; Acts 2:42-45; James 5:1-6) (*Ant.* 18.7; *War* 2.427) (Essenes - *War* 2.122) In fact, this was the central message in "Love your Neighbor as Yourself." How could one love his neighbor if he let that neighbor go hungry or unclothed? When Jesus confronted the rich young ruler, he did not say give ten percent to the poor, but rather, give everything to the poor and then come follow me. (Matt. 19:16-24) This was a radical message two thousand years ago. How many middle-class Americans would follow that same philosophy today?

Members of the Fourth Philosophy were known as bandits by Josephus, for they exploited the wealthy, a type of Robin Hood movement. During the war with Rome, the debt records were burned in order to free those enslaved to the wealthy by their debt. (*War* 2.426-427) This was truly class warfare! As for the Zealots, Josephus shared his contempt for their practices concerning wealth and private property: "The dregs, the scum of the whole country, they have **squandered their own property** and practiced their lunacy upon the towns and villages around, and finally have poured in a stealthy stream into the Holy City..." (*War* 4.241) Considering what Jesus said to the rich young ruler, Josephus would have had the same attitude towards Jesus' lunacy!

At the beginning of the Church, disciples were urged to share everything in common. (Acts 2:42) This approach to living was in line with the Kingdom of God as preached by Jesus. Also, the feeding of the five thousand was simply the sharing of one's food with another. It had nothing to do with hocus-pocus. In addition, the letter of James favored the poor over the rich. (James 5:1-6)

14. Both Judas and Jesus were considered fine teachers of the Law. (Matt. 5:17-20; Mark 12:28-34) (*Ant.* 17.149; *War* 1.648) Judas followed the basic teachings of the Pharisees as did Jesus. As for Judas' abilities, Josephus wrote: "[Judas and Matthias were] the most celebrated interpreters of the Jewish laws, and well beloved by the people." (*Ant.* 17.149) The earlier assessment from *War* 1.648 stated that "there were two men of learning in the city [Jerusalem], who were thought the most skillful in the laws of their country, and were on that account held in very great esteem all over the nation."

From the Gospels, we know that Jesus used parables in relating his message, in line with Pharisaic practices. Jesus said that the two greatest commandments were to love God and to love thy neighbor. To love God involved obeying God and the Law handed down by God to Moses. To love thy neighbor included sharing one's possessions, so that no one was left hungry or homeless. In addition, both Judas and Jesus followed Judas Maccabee in his interpretation of the Sabbath: the Sabbath was made for man, not man for the Sabbath. Judas Maccabee permitted his disciples to defend themselves if attacked on the Sabbath. Likewise, Jesus preached that it was proper to do good on the Sabbath. In fact, Jesus was reprimanded by some Pharisees for breaking the Sabbath laws as he fled from Herod. Jesus quoted the Old Testament story of David eating consecrated bread in order to maintain strength in his flight from the authorities. Jesus had good reason to follow David and Judas Maccabee: he was a marked man. Both Jesus and Judas Maccabee would not have flouted the Sabbath law for any old reason.

From the above passages from Josephus, Judas the Galilean was known throughout the nation for his ability in interpreting the law. We get the same feeling for Jesus when reading the Gospels. The Pharisees constantly invited him to dinner in order to discuss issues. We are privy to only the negative aspects of those meetings. In reality, most teachers in Israel considered Jesus an important figure and were constantly amazed at his teachings.

15. Judas the Galilean's movement centered in Jerusalem and in Galilee. Judas began his public career in Jerusalem, teaching young men at the Temple. He convinced his students to take part in the Golden Eagle Temple Cleansing and was arrested by Herod the Great. (*Ant.* 17.149-167) Judas was later released by Archelaus and fled to Sepphoris in Galilee. Until his return to Jerusalem, Judas preached in Galilee where he was crowned Messiah by his followers, and later led a tax revolt against Rome. (*Ant.* 17.271-272 and 18.1-10)

Jesus was also in Jerusalem at the start of his career, according to John. Coincidentally, John placed his Temple Cleansing at the start of Jesus' career, consistent with the story of Judas the Galilean. (John 2:12-17) Jesus then returned to Galilee, where he was proclaimed Messiah. From the Gospel accounts, Jesus spent most of his ministry in Galilee. Jesus finally returned to Jerusalem, where he was captured and crucified.

Even after Judas' death, his movement revolved around Jerusalem and Galilee. In fact, Josephus noted that Eleazar was sent by his leaders in Galilee to teach King Izates true Judaism, which included circumcision. King Izates had previously been taught by Ananias that he could become a full Jew without circumcision. The Jewish Christian model also practiced circumcision. Note that Paul and Cephas also had a similar disagreement in Antioch, caused by men sent from James. James may have been centered in either Jerusalem or in Galilee. However, since this occurred around the time of Agrippa's assassination, James probably located himself in a safer place, no doubt, Galilee.

16. Both Jesus and Judas cleansed the Temple in Jerusalem. (Matt. 21:12-13) (*Ant.* 17.149-167) Actually, Judas probably cleansed the Temple twice. The first cleansing was the Golden Eagle Temple Cleansing where Matthias and Judas were captured by Herod the Great. The Golden Eagle was a sign of fealty to Rome, and the teachers could not condone this alliance, considering that God was their only Lord and Ruler. (*Ant.* 18.23) The second cleansing can be deduced from inference. Judas the Galilean's son, Menahem, followed his father's modus operandi and seized an armory before marching upon Jerusalem. Menehem promptly cleansed the Temple after being hailed as Messiah by his disciples. It is most probable that Judas the Galilean marched on Jerusalem some time after the Census of Cyrenius (6 CE) and cleansed the Temple as a Messianic act. It is interesting to note that the Gospel of John placed the Temple cleansing at the beginning of Jesus' career (John 2:12-25) while the Synoptic Gospels have it at the end of his ministry. What are the odds of the two men cleansing the Temple once, not to say twice? Outside of the cleansing in 4 BCE (Judas) and the cleansing by his son in 66 CE (Menahem), Josephus did not record one other Temple cleansing from 4 BCE to 66 CE. It was certainly not an everyday occurrence.

The 4 BCE Temple cleansing concerned the Golden **Eagle**, a graven image paying homage to Rome. The Slavonic Josephus verified that the Golden Eagle was in honor of Caesar and was even named "the Golden-winged Eagle." (7) Josephus stated that Pilate brought his standards into Jerusalem in 19 CE, right before the crucifixion of Jesus. These standards had the **eagle** upon them, the symbol of Rome. In both the Temple cleansing of 4 BCE and the one in 19 CE, the power of Rome was attacked by Judas (Jesus).

17. Judas opposed the Roman tax, and Jesus was crucified for the charge of opposing the Roman tax. (Luke 23.2) (*Ant.* 18.4) The ministry of Judas (4 BCE - 19 CE) focused upon the tax issue. At the Barabbas-style prisoner release ordered by Archelaus in 4 BCE, the Jewish crowd demanded the release of prisoners, the easing of annual payments and the removal of an onerous sales tax. (*Ant.* 17.204-205) Judas then led a tax revolt at the time of the census (6 CE), but this did not end the extortion by Rome. Tacitus stated that Judea was exhausted by its tax burden (16-18 CE). (*Annals*, ii. 42) This struggle against Roman taxation was well documented by both Tacitus and Josephus.

Jesus did not oppose every tax, but his hatred of Roman taxation is beyond doubt. "Give to Caesar what is Caesar's and to God what is God's" was not a pro-tax message. Jesus was saying this: take your money with Caesar's portrait and leave our country. This statement went well beyond a yes or no answer to the tax question. To "Give God what is God's" harkened the Jews back to the days of Judas Maccabee and his struggle for Jewish independence. This is why Jesus was crucified by the Romans.

Paul, on the other hand, taught his disciples to pay their taxes to Rome without hesitation. (Rom. 13:1-7) This accommodation to Roman taxation was totally opposite the view of Judas (Jesus). Many people read Paul's view into the interpretation of Jesus' statement: "Give to Caesar what is Caesar's and to God what is God's." But we must remember that Jesus was crucified and that death was not a result of upholding Roman taxation.

18. According to Josephus, Judas founded the Fourth Philosophy during his fight with Herod the Great's dynasty and Rome. (*Ant.* 18.1-10) Jesus was credited with the founding of Christianity, a new religion. This religion of Jesus was never mentioned by Josephus, an amazing omission. It is my contention that Josephus was very concerned with the followers of Jesus, but this Christian movement was termed the Fourth Philosophy.

The Fourth Philosophy joined the earlier philosophies of the Pharisees, Sadducees, and Essenes. This Fourth Philosophy was similar to that of the Pharisees except that followers of Judas were extremely nationalistic. Also, Judas' disciples shared some practices with the Essenes. Thus, the nationalistic movement had drawing power away from the other philosophies. This may explain why John the Essene was a leader in the war against Rome. Essenes were known as pacifists, so the mention of a warlike Essene has confounded scholars. This John the Essene was no doubt influenced by the Fourth Philosophy.

In reading the New Testament, one must admit that Jesus was quite often friendly with the Pharisees. He did blast those who loved themselves more than their fellow Jews, but his overall feeling for the Pharisees was positive. "You are not far from the kingdom of heaven," Jesus said to one Pharisee. (Mark 12:34) In addition, Jesus preached using parables, a mode of teaching practiced by the Pharisees. Thus, like Judas, Jesus was very close to the Pharisees in belief and action.

19. Josephus detailed the life but not the death of Judas while mentioning the death of Jesus but not one word about his life. Josephus invested much effort in recounting Judas' life, even touching upon the lives of his sons, James, Simon, and Menahem and his grandson, Eleazar. (*Ant.* 20.102; *War* 2.433-434; *War* 7.253) Each time the descendants were recognized, Josephus recounted their pedigree. This did not occur in just one isolated time period. Simon and James were crucified in 46-48 CE, Menahem stoned in 66 CE and

Eleazar led the Sicarii at Masada in 73 CE. This theme of Judas the Galilean ran throughout Josephus' narrative.

It is probable that the death of Judas was removed by a later Gentile Christian who believed the death of Judas by crucifixion might attract too much unwanted attention. Most scholars believe that the passage in Josephus, which details the death of Jesus, is a late third to early fourth century forgery. The question is this: was the spurious Jesus passage (TF of *Ant.* 18.63-64) a replacement for Judas' death by crucifixion? The death of Judas by crucifixion should not be doubted. Judas fought against Rome and such actions were punishable by crucifixion. In addition, Judas' two sons, James and Simon, were crucified a generation later (46-48 CE).

20. Zealots and Sicarii arose from Judas' Fourth Philosophy. Two of Jesus' apostles were named Simon the Zealot and Judas Iscariot (a garbling of Sicarios). Since the Zealots and Sicarii were not introduced until the late 50's and early 60's by Josephus, titles of that sort would not have been used in Jesus' time (4 BCE - 19 CE). These names were placed on the Apostles by Gentile Christians, nearly one hundred years later. In addition, the nickname "Sons of Thunder" denotes a power associated with the Fourth Philosophy, not the mild Christianity of the Gospels.

21. Disciples of both Judas and Jesus were willing to die for their respective cause. The Neronian persecution reported by Tacitus and the description of the Fourth Philosophy by Josephus indicate a willingness to die happily for God. (In fact, Edward Gibbon conjectured that Tacitus really was describing the Fourth Philosophy, not the traditional Christians.) Jesus said: "Blessed [are] the ones being persecuted because of righteousness, for theirs is the Kingdom of God." (Matt. 5:10) In the same way, Judas and Matthias stressed the rewards of righteousness if they were to be punished by Herod the Great. (*Ant.* 17.149-167) The followers of Judas the Galilean gladly accepted death for the sake of righteousness. (*Ant.* 18.23-24)

Unlike the Fourth Philosophy or Jewish Christianity, Paul's Gentiles were taught to pay taxes to Rome and to follow their rulers (Nero and other madmen.) Paul's philosophy of acting like a Gentile to the Gentiles and like a Jew to the Jews was totally contrary to Judas' and Jesus' teachings. Judas (Jesus) was who he claimed to be. He never acted a part as did Paul.

22. The sons of Judas and the "brothers" of Jesus were named James and Simon. How easy it would have been for an early Gospel writer to change children into brothers and a wife into a mother. This would have been done for several reasons. First, by making sons and a wife into brothers and a mother,

the Gospel writers wiped out a generation, making Jesus a much younger man, that of about thirty. Second, to follow in Paul's footsteps, one had to be celibate. Although marriage and sex had no negative connotations in Jewish society, the later Church found it difficult to accept the fact that God's son had sex which resulted in children (mini-gods). Third, it was easier to disassociate Jesus from brothers and a mother. A good father and husband would have been more understanding with his wife and his own children.

23. The sons of Judas were put to death by crucifixion. Jesus was the only other individual crucified to be mentioned by name. Also two Apostles were to drink the same cup as Jesus, namely crucifixion. (Matt. 20:20-23) (Ant. 20.102) It is my contention that these two Apostles were the sons of Jesus (Judas the Galilean).

This is very significant because crucifixion was a form of punishment doled out by the Roman authorities. One was crucified because of political activity, not for religious beliefs. In fact, the Romans allowed all types of religions as long as they did not oppose Rome and its tax machine. Paul's version of Christianity would have been the model Roman religion! Jesus preached against Roman taxation and was proclaimed King or Messiah. That is why he was crucified. The two sons of Judas the Galilean would have been crucified for the same reason: resistance against Rome.

24. Many members of the movement had nicknames. Sadduc was a priestly title denoting righteousness while John the Baptist "commanded the Jews to exercise virtue, both as to righteousness towards one another, and piety towards God." (*Ant.* 18.117) James, the brother of Jesus, was known as the Just. Judas the Galilean was known as Jesus (Joshua or Savior), Saul was renamed Paul (small), and Simon became Cephas (Peter), which means rock. The above nicknames generally described the character of the individual. These internal nicknames would not have been known or used by those outside the movement. Thus, Josephus wrote of Judas the Galilean, Simon and Saul, never using the names Jesus, Cephas and Paul.

Nicknames were also used in the Maccabean movement. Judas was nicknamed Maccabee or the Hammer. Since the Fourth Philosophy (Jewish Christianity) was based upon the Maccabean movement, the use of nicknames should be expected.

Other nicknames in the Jesus movement included the Sons of Thunder (James and Simon, the sons of Judas the Galilean). Only Judas would have been referred to as Thunder. Simon the Zealot and James the Younger may have also been references to these sons of Judas. Remember, the Gospel writers were intent on hiding the true identities of Jesus' sons. One other nickname was Thomas, which may have referred to Judas, another son of Judas the Galilean. The combination of Judas and Thomas may have yielded Theudas or Thaddeus.

25. Jesus was proclaimed Messiah or King in Galilee, or close by. Before the Transfiguration, Jesus and the Twelve were in Caesarea Philippi (Matt. 16:13) and afterwards traveled to Capernaum. (Matt. 17:24) After Jesus was proclaimed King, he marched to Jerusalem.

Judas was also proclaimed King in Galilee, around Sepphoris. This occurred after he captured Herod's armory and equipped his followers. (*Ant.* 17.271-272; *War* 2.56) He also may have marched upon Jerusalem, deduced by examining the behavior of his son, Menahem, who proclaimed himself King after capturing Herod's armory at Masada. He then marched straight to Jerusalem. (*War* 2.433) Judas the Galilean's entrance to Jerusalem may have been in 19 CE, so his kingship may have actually lasted twenty-two years, from 4 BCE to 19 CE. This is different from Jesus who went directly to Jerusalem. However, the Gospels may have telescoped the career of Jesus into a few short years just as Josephus compressed the seventy-five year movement created by Judas into a few paragraphs. (*Ant.* 18.1-10)

26. In Acts 5:37, Judas the Galilean was killed "and all his followers were scattered." This passage was meant to minimize Judas' influence, giving the impression that Judas' movement ended with his death. However, Josephus clearly stated that Judas' movement grew and expanded over the next fifty to sixty years.

After Jesus was captured, his disciples fled and some denied their association with him (Peter). Even after the crucifixion, the disciples were forlorn and in hiding. It seems as if both movements acted the same way after their leaders were killed.

There is an amazing convergence between Judas and Jesus concerning the disciples' reaction to his arrest. In Matt. 26:56, after Jesus' arrest, "the disciples deserted him and fled." In Mark 14:50, "everyone deserted him and fled." These two Gospels are in complete agreement concerning the disciples' behavior after the arrest. The interesting part concerns the Gospel of Luke. In Luke, the disciples did not flee, but Simon Peter followed at a distance. Why is the account in Luke different from the other Synoptic Gospels? The answer may be in Acts 5:37, that passage which distorted the picture of Judas the Galilean. If the author of Acts were the same writer who penned Luke, then a direct correlation between Judas and Jesus can be established. The Gospel of Luke omitted the language of the deserting disciples. However, this scattering of disciples was recorded by Luke in Acts 5, concerning the disciples of Judas the Galilean. Did Luke forget his mission and erroneously credit the disciples of Judas with the same actions accorded the followers of Jesus in Matthew and Mark?

27. After Jesus' arrest, he was brought first to Annas, the father-in-law of Caiaphas and former High Priest. (John 18:12-24) This Annas was appointed High Priest in 6 CE by Cyrenius and Coponius, in the days of the census. Opposing the census and Annas was none other than Judas the Galilean. It would seem that Annas would have been much more interested in the death of Judas the Galilean than the Gospel Jesus. But why would the ex-High Priest take a leading role in the arrest of Jesus? Under the governorship of Gratus (15-18 CE), four different High Priests were appointed. This musical chair approach to the High Priesthood must have maddened the religious people of the day, including Jesus. This may have been one reason why Jesus picked this time to enter Jerusalem. In all probability, Annas may have been calling the shots even after his stint as High Priest. Josephus wrote that this Annas had five sons who were High Priest. (*Ant.* 20.198) The existence of this dynasty means that Annas was a force in first-century Judea.

The Gospel of John may have inadvertently connected Jesus with Judas' old adversary. The Synoptic Gospels were careful to avoid mentioning Annas, preferring to have the whole affair tried before Caiaphas and the elders. Annas certainly lends credence to my Judas the Galilean hypothesis, in that he functioned in a leadership role during the lifetime of Judas. It is also more likely that Annas would have been physically stronger in 19 CE rather than the later date of 30-33 CE, per the traditional dating. Annas may well have been dead by 30-33 CE.

28. In the trial of Matthias in the Golden Eagle Temple Cleansing, the High Priest was also named Matthias. This latter Matthias had once relinquished his office for a day, a day celebrated by a fast, because of a dream where he had sexual relations with his wife. Pilate washed his hands of responsibility on a single day because of his wife's dream concerning Jesus' innocence. (Matt. 27:19-24) (*Ant.* 17.166) In both cases, a dream sequence was used to remove responsibility for a short period of time. In the case of Pilate, this conveniently shifted the blame for Jesus' crucifixion from the Romans to the Jews, even though crucifixion was a Roman punishment. The Jews supposedly said, "Let his blood be on us and on our children." (Matt. 27:25) Unfortunately, this has been used as an excuse to persecute the Jews throughout history.

The whole scene, where Pilate washed his hands and the Jews greedily usurped his power of life and death, appears extremely unlikely. According to the Gospels, the Jews had welcomed Jesus into Jerusalem as Messiah, just a few days earlier. Now they were willing to have his blood on their heads for all eternity. This cannot be logically explained. The alternative is radical but at least logical: this dream scene was adapted from the Matthias episode and reworked using the new Pauline thinking. The Jews were the enemies, not the Romans.

29. Herod the Great sent Matthias, Judas and the rebels to Jericho for questioning concerning the Golden Eagle Temple Cleansing. There, Herod heard the reasons for the uprising. (*Ant.* 17.160) Pilate sent Jesus to Herod for questioning. (Luke 23:6-7) This interrogation was told only by Luke. Luke had a tendency to take events from Josephus and incorporate them into the fictional story of Jesus and the early Church. There were two Temple Cleansings, the Golden Eagle Temple Cleansing and the one recorded in the Gospels at the end of Jesus' career. Two trials or interrogations also occurred, one before Herod the Great in 4 BCE and the other before Pilate in 19 CE. Luke simply combined these two trials in his Gospel.

30. Under Herod the Great's son, Archelaus (4 BCE), prisoners were released to appease the Jewish mob. One of these prisoners may have been Judas the Galilean. (*War* 2.4 and *Ant.* 17.204-205) This same story was repeated at the trial of Jesus. In that account, Pilate released Barabbas to the mob instead of Jesus. (Matt. 27:15-26) One point must be noted: the Romans did not release political prisoners; they crucified them. On the other hand, the release of prisoners by Archelaus rings true as he was dealing with the remnants of the Matthias and Judas following. This crowd would have wished for the release of Barabbas, the son of the Father. The Father would have been either Matthias or God.

A critic of my theory insists that Archelaus never released the prisoners, only that he promised to release them. This scenario does not make sense for two reasons. First, Archelaus could have quickly appeased the mob by releasing prisoners. It could have been done immediately. He also promised to reduce taxes. Since that could not be accomplished immediately, Archelaus may very well have reneged on that promise. Second, after the prisoner release, Archelaus also granted the mob's request regarding the removal of the High Priest. This, too, could be done immediately. With these two points in mind, it is clear that the releasing of prisoners actually occurred.

31. In the Gospel story, Barabbas led an insurrection in the city, Jerusalem. (Mark 15:7 and Luke 23:19) Shortly before the prisoner release of 4 BCE, Matthias and Judas led the Golden Eagle Temple Cleansing, an insurrection

in the city, where many of the rebels suffered martyrdom, while others, Judas included, were held for later punishment. (*Ant.* 17.149-167; 17.204-206)

Insurrections in the city of Jerusalem were not commonplace in the timeframe noted. From 4 BCE to 50 CE, the only ones recorded were the Golden Eagle Temple Cleansing (4 BCE) and the one supposedly led by Barabbas. This should reinforce the statement that Barabbas was really a nickname for Judas (Jesus). (In some manuscripts, Barabbas was known as Jesus Barabbas.) Both insurrections were aimed at Rome. The Golden Eagle was a symbol of Rome, and Barabbas of Gospel fame was undoubtedly a member of the Fourth Philosophy. Judas and Barabbas were also very popular with the Jewish crowd, who were anti-Roman.

32. The trial of Jesus and the release of Barabbas occurred at the Passover feast. (Mark 14:12) The release of prisoners on 4 BCE also coincided with the Passover. (*Ant.* 17.213) As there were three Jewish pilgrim festivals (Passover, Pentecost and Tabernacles), the odds of this coincidence can be calculated as 3 to the 2nd power, or one in nine. (8)

33. King Herod the Great died a week or so before the Passover feast. At his death, Herod was clothed in purple, with a crown of gold upon his head and a scepter in his right hand. (*Ant.* 17.198) Before his death, Jesus was mocked by the Roman soldiers who put a purple robe on him and wove a crown of thorns to be placed upon his head. A staff was used to beat him. (Mark 15:16-20) The Gospel writers had used so much of this section of *Antiquities* regarding Judas they just applied this to Jesus as well.

34. Jesus was mocked by the Roman soldiers. (Mark 15:16-20) Herod the Great was afraid that the people would mourn his death in "sport and mockery" only. (*Ant.* 17.177) The Gospels and Acts often used information from Josephus or the letters of Paul to flesh out the story of Jesus and his Church. Jesus not only wore the same garb as Herod, but he was treated as poorly by his adversaries.

35. Many religious scholars have questioned the silence of Jesus before Pilate. When charged with a crime, Jesus made no reply, to the amazement of Pilate. (Mark 15:3-5) Unlike Paul, who made a speech everywhere in Acts, Jesus remained silent. The only mention of this type of behavior in Josephus concerned Simon, who had been summoned to answer charges by Agrippa I (43 CE). (This Simon-Agrippa episode was the basis for the Simon Peter-Cornelius story of Acts chapter 10.)
Silence was a way to protect the movement. Under interrogation, members

of the movement would not betray their compatriots. The questioning of Jesus may have been more severe than we are led to believe by the Gospel accounts. Pilate and his henchmen would have liked information, and they no doubt tortured Jesus. He, however, did not betray his friends. The Fourth Philosophy, represented by Simon in the Simon-Agrippa episode, also was famous for its steadfast loyalty to God and fellow members. "They do not value dying any kind of death, nor indeed do they heed the deaths of their relations and friends, nor can any such fear make them call any man Lord." (*Ant.* 18.23-25) In short, they would rather die than betray God and their fellow disciples.

36. In the Gospels, the crowd (Pharisees, etc.) preferred Barabbas over King Jesus. (Mark 15:1-15) This was not only an endorsement for Barabbas but also demonstrated an intense hatred for Jesus. Anyone would have been chosen over Jesus.

Josephus described the crowd as followers of Matthias and Judas, who preferred these teachers over King Herod. (*Ant.* 17.204-206) The disciples really loved Judas and Matthias, but their hatred of Herod and all he represented was unparalleled. Their hatred of Herod corresponds to the Gospel story where the Chief Priests and the Jews hated Jesus.

37. In the Golden Eagle Temple Cleansing, Matthias and Judas were captured by Herod the Great. Matthias was put to death by fire, while Judas eventually gained freedom in a Barabbas-style prisoner release. Once released, Judas assumed the leadership role once held by Matthias. The second-in-command role was then given to Sadduc.

In the book of Acts, Matthias replaced Judas Iscariot as one of the Twelve. While the Josephus story had Judas replacing Matthias, the Acts' version had Matthias replacing a Judas. This Matthias was never mentioned in the Gospels and was absent from any subsequent activities as recorded by Acts. Matthias was just a name taken from Judas the Galilean's past and playfully included in the Judas Iscariot story.

In fact, James the Just replaced the crucified Jesus. Since Judas Iscariot was an invented character to further lay blame upon the Jewish people, there could not have been a replacement for him. He never existed! On the other hand, Jesus was crucified. Jesus was the person being replaced. With the death of Jesus, John the Baptist (Sadduc) became the leader of the movement with James the Just as his second-in-command.

38. Jesus was crucified between two bandits. The bandit was Josephus' term for members of the Fourth Philosophy. This term bandit did not refer to

thieves or highwaymen but rather to terrorists (freedom fighters) or those seeking political turmoil. (9) That Jesus was crucified between these two should not surprise. Jesus was their leader.

John Crossan admits that Jesus was an apocalypticist, but that did not mean that Jesus advocated violence. He concludes that if Jesus were a military threat then Pilate would have captured a large number of Jesus' disciples with him and crucified them as well. (10) There are two fundamental errors in Crossan's reasoning. First, the Jesus (Judas the Galilean) movement was not violent as compared to the later Fourth Philosophy as dominated by the Zealots and Sicarii. The early version of the Fourth Philosophy, as preached by Jesus (Judas), would rid Israel of Roman occupation by the power of God, not by armed rebellion or by assassinations. This same philosophy was still in place by the 40's when Theudas called upon God to part the river Jordan. (*Ant.* 20.97) Second, Crossan does not recognize that Jesus was placed between two bandits. Obviously, Pilate had captured some of Jesus' disciples as they hung to his left and to his right. By placing Jesus in the middle and by attaching the charge against him, King of the Jews, Pilate attacked the Fourth Philosophy head on.

The treatment of the bandits in the Gospels is not consistent. John 19:18 simply stated that Jesus was crucified with "two others - one on each side and Jesus in the middle." John had nothing more to say about these two. Mark and Matthew told a different tale. They wrote that "those crucified with him [the bandits] also heaped insults on him." (Mark 15:32) In this, Mark and Matthew placed the bandits along with the High Priest, aligned against Jesus. But no one does the story better than Luke.

One of the **criminals** who hung there hurled insults at him. "Aren't you the Christ? Save yourself and us!"

But the other **criminal** rebuked him. "Don't you fear God," he said, "since you are under the same sentence? We are punished justly, for we are getting what our deeds deserve. But this man has done nothing wrong."

Then he said, "Jesus, remember me when you come into your kingdom."

Jesus answered him, "I tell you the truth, today you will be with me in paradise." (Luke 23:39-43) (Emphasis mine)

Three major discrepancies can be noted from the above passage. First, Luke called the two men criminals and not bandits. This changed the two into common criminals and not part of a religious or political movement, that being the Fourth Philosophy. Second, one of the criminals hurled insults but the other now sided with Jesus, even saying that Jesus had done nothing wrong, thus exonerating Jesus. Third, this second criminal was pardoned by Jesus, a Pauline move. Jesus always preached a lifelong commitment to God. All of a sudden, he now accepted deathbed conversions. Again, this was added to make Jesus accept the Pauline notion of faith; saved by faith, not by works.

39. The movements continued after the deaths of Judas the Galilean and Jesus. It is interesting that Acts downplayed the movement of Judas the Galilean, saying that Judas was killed "and all his followers were scattered." (Acts 5:37) In reality, the Fourth Philosophy of Judas did not end with Judas' death but grew to a great degree according to Josephus. (*Ant.* 18.1-10) So the speech by Gamaliel in Acts was an attempt by Luke to alter history. The author of Acts did not want people to associate the rebellious Jews with the Gentile Christian movement of the second century. It is true, however, that when the story of Acts was written (second century), the followers of Judas the Galilean had been smashed and scattered.

40. The movements of Judas and Jesus expanded throughout the Roman Empire. The Fourth Philosophy of Judas was responsible for the war against Rome. Although centered in Jerusalem and Galilee, Judas' followers were numbered throughout the Empire and suffered greatly during the Jewish war. We know that Paul's Gentile churches were scattered amongst the great cities, but the Jewish Christian movement must have been much greater. While Paul was the lone apostle to the Gentiles, the influence of Cephas and others must have reached a great multitude. In fact, the early Church would have placed most of its resources in the "conversion" of the Jewish community to the Way of Righteousness.

Note also that Suetonius tied the rebellious, trouble-making Jews to Chrestus or Christ. (Suetonius, *The Twelve Caesars*, Claudius 25) This passage definitively connected the Fourth Philosophy to Christ. While this particular disturbance was at Rome, it seems most probable that all large Jewish congregations of the Diaspora would have contained an element sympathetic to the nationalism of Judas the Galilean (Jesus). Near the end of the *Jewish War*, Josephus wrote that some Sicarii had escaped to Alexandria after the destruction of Masada (73 CE). The Sicarii attempted to gain support from the Alexandrian Jews to rebel against the Romans. This attempt would only have been made if there were some sympathy for their movement. However, they were rebuffed by the majority of Jews, caught, tortured and killed by the authorities. (*War* 7.407-419)

CONCLUSION

Many people have concluded that a Jesus never existed because little evidence supports this Messiah figure in the timeframe generally accepted by scholars, around 30-33 CE. Too many problems exist with this late date, and no corroboration comes from the only Jewish historian of the time, Josephus. Could Josephus have missed the greatest story ever told? Considering that Josephus was born in the 30's, it is quite inconceivable that he could have missed out on Jesus.

Josephus did chronicle another Messiah figure, that being Judas the Galilean. This Judas was a great teacher who despised the ruling class and its association with Rome. This rebel led a tax revolt, cleansed the Temple, was pardoned in a Barabbas-style prisoner release, was claimed Messiah and eventually died fighting the injustice of Rome. This death was not recorded by Josephus. This is amazing considering Judas the Galilean was the driving force in the struggle against Rome. Josephus wrote about the deaths of Judas' sons, Simon and James by crucifixion and Menahem by stoning, and a grandson, Eleazar, who committed suicide at Masada. Each time, Josephus emphasized the relationship between these individuals and Judas the Galilean. So why did Josephus omit Judas' death? The answer is obvious: he did not omit the death of Judas. The story of Judas' death was erased by later Christians who inserted the spurious passage about Jesus. (*Ant.* 18.63-64) This passage has long been discounted by most scholars, but these same scholars have not recognized what the passage replaced. It was not just an insertion into the text but rather a replacement passage. Judas the Galilean suffered crucifixion under Pilate, not a mythical Jesus of Nazareth.

The above similarities between Judas and Jesus should convince the reader that a bait and switch game has occurred. The history of Judas the Galilean was transformed into the history of Jesus of Nazareth. Could there have been two separate individuals who experienced such similar events? The odds would be incalculable. So we are left with the only logical conclusion: Jesus of Nazareth was invented to distance the rebel, Judas the Galilean, from the Jewish religion. The catalyst for this ingenious attempt of history building was the apostle Paul, the man known as the Liar, the Enemy and the Traitor. His theology survived through Jesus of Nazareth, not that of Judas the Galilean. The greatest Jewish teacher of first-century Israel has long been forgotten. His glory was usurped by a literary character, Jesus of Nazareth.

CHAPTER 14

ACTS - PROPAGANDA OF THE CHURCH

The story of Acts supposedly chronicled the historical actions of the Apostles after the crucifixion of Jesus. In this account, the Twelve were introduced and quickly minimized as the true hero of the story emerged. Paul became the focus of Acts as Peter and James drifted into oblivion. The question we will answer is this: was this version of history true or simply a jumble of half truths and flat-out falsifications?

In addition to the amazing similarities between Judas the Galilean and Jesus of Nazareth, a great number a parallel passages exist between Acts and other historical documents, namely the writings of Josephus and Paul's own version of events. Each disputed section of Acts will be separately analyzed, so that the reader will be able to catalogue his/her reasons to doubt the Acts' version of history. This is important because the sheer number of contradictions and/or similarities will determine if my Judas the Galilean hypothesis has validity. The following list will number forty-five items. For simplicity, the number and the verse from Acts will be detailed before analysis.

These forty-five areas of concern are not the whole story. Corroboration for most of Paul's actions was not recorded by Josephus and the only confirmation comes from Paul's own letters. For example, Paul stated that he suffered more than all the other apostles. In context, Paul was comparing himself to the Jewish apostles, specifically Cephas and James, and wished to convince the Corinthians that he surpassed those "super apostles" both in faith and in action.

Five times I received from the Jews the forty lashes minus one. Three times I was beaten by rods, once I was stoned, three times I was shipwrecked, I spent a night and a day in the open sea. I have been constantly on the move. I have been in danger from rivers, in danger from bandits, in danger from my own countrymen, in danger from Gentiles; in danger in the city, in danger in the country, in danger at sea; and in danger from false brothers. I have labored and toiled and have often gone without sleep; I have known hunger and thirst and have often gone without food; I have been cold and naked. (2 Cor. 11:24-27)

This extensive listing of dangers and hardships provided the author of Acts with the opportunity to include these "trials" in his narrative. The dangers were specific, but Paul gave them no context. Why and where was he stoned? Most stonings resulted in death, examples being Stephen and James, the brother of Jesus. Why did Paul receive the thirty-nine lashes? According to Mel Gibson's recent movie, the lashes themselves could kill. Could anyone survive this torture five times? Where and when was he shipwrecked? Not only did Paul claim to have survived three separate shipwrecks, he spent a night and a day in the open sea. (Paul's travels are detailed in Acts 13 and 14 and later in Acts 16 through 21.) Did all these events really happen as we read them? Could any one person have survived all these Pauline perils? Even the fictional character, Indiana Jones, would have struggled mightily with these exertions. Did Paul exaggerate his life for some personal agenda? After all, he was in competition with the Jerusalem apostles. Everything they could do, he could do better! And is it possible that Acts created a colorful history for Paul with his self proclaimed dangers as support? This cannot be positively proved. However, after the forty-five areas of historical manipulations are explored, the reader may find Paul's travel history hard to believe as well.

1. Acts 1:12-26 - Judas Iscariot was replaced by Matthias, an unknown disciple.

In Acts chapter 1, Judas Iscariot was replaced by an unknown disciple named Matthias. According to Paul, Jesus was "delivered up," generally translated as betrayed (1 Cor. 11:23); but it could not have been a member of the original Twelve, for he later wrote that the resurrected Jesus appeared first to Peter and then to the Twelve (1 Cor. 15:3-5). The Gospels and Acts had Jesus meeting with the Eleven, not the Twelve (Mark 16:14; Acts 1:3 and Acts 1:12-13). It must be remembered that Paul wrote his account at least fifty years before Acts. In this lengthy span of time, the story of Jesus' capture may have evolved to include a betrayal. (As noted earlier, the only real betrayal concerned the actions of Paul. He is the one who betrayed the movement.) The Gospels and Acts created a fictional character named Judas

Iscariot, who became this betrayer. This Judas represented all that was evil to the Gentile Church: the name Judas stood for Judah or the Jews and Iscariot was simply a garbling of sicarios, those rebels aligned against Rome, who used assassination as their method of resistance. Like Josephus' description of the Fourth Philosophy as bandits, Judas was portrayed as a thief. Judas also committed suicide, just as the Sicarii had done at Masada in 73 CE. (The leader at Masada was named Eleazar, and he was the grandson of Judas the Galilean.)

In short, the death of a Judas Iscariot never occurred. On the other hand, a Judas was now dead. Judas the Galilean, known by his title Jesus, was crucified by the Romans for his opposition to Roman taxation and for his Messianic claim. This Judas had to be replaced. A movement cannot continue without leadership. Therefore, it was imperative to install a new leader.

The purpose of Acts chapter 1 was to diminish the importance of James, the brother of Jesus, just as the Gospels had whitewashed the history of John the Baptist. In reality, James replaced Jesus as part of the leadership pairing. With the death of Jesus, John the Baptist assumed leadership of the movement and James became his second-in-command. (John the Baptist lived until 35-36 CE while Judas the Galilean (Jesus) died in 19-21 CE. Even the traditional crucifixion date for Jesus, at 30-33 CE, predates the death of John!) The fact that James replaced the crucified Jesus (Judas) is verified by Paul's letter to the Galatians, where Paul recounted his meeting with the Pillar apostles in Jerusalem. These Pillars were Cephas and the brothers of Jesus (Judas), James and John. The author of Acts refused to give James any credit, but instead made Matthias one of the Twelve. So Acts filled the bogus Apostle vacancy but failed to replace the leadership position left by the crucifixion of Jesus.

The new Apostle, Matthias, was an unknown, never to be heard from again. Was he a real person or a literary device to confound the reader? The only Matthias in the Judas the Galilean (Jesus) tradition was Judas' co-teacher in the Golden Eagle Temple Cleansing of 4 BCE. This Matthias was burnt alive by Herod the Great, and his leadership role was assumed by Judas the Galilean. Did the book of Acts playfully misuse this story? Judas replaced Matthias in 4 BCE as the leader of the rebel movement. Was the name Matthias used as a not so subtle joke to replace Judas? This was just one more way to twist the actual history into the new Church history.

2. Acts 2:1-4 - The Twelve spoke in tongues on Pentecost, drawing attention to themselves.

It is amazing that the Twelve Apostles were made to speak in tongues as proof of the Holy Spirit. Throughout the Gospels, Jesus downplayed the miracles, hoping that people would follow his teachings, not just an occasional miracle. This is not to say that the Twelve could not or would not perform miracles. These were not people of science. Any healing, whether natural or not, was seen as an act of God. However, speaking in tongues was not part of the Jewish Christian movement. Jesus did not speak in tongues and nowhere does Josephus mention this being practiced among the Jews.

The Gentile churches founded by Paul practiced speaking in tongues and the interpretation of these ramblings. In fact, the church in Corinth was fascinated by the gift of tongues. This caused confusion and an unruly worship. Paul tried to curb the excesses of the "Holy Spirit", even though he claimed that this gift emanated from God.

Follow the way of love and eagerly desire spiritual gifts, especially the gift of prophecy. For anyone who speaks in a tongue does not speak to men but to God. **Indeed, no one understands him; he utters mysteries with his spirit.** But everyone who prophesies speaks to men for their strengthening, encouragement and comfort. He who speaks in a tongue edifies himself, but he who prophesies edifies the church. I would like every one of you to speak in tongues, but I would rather have you prophesy. He who prophesies is greater than one who speaks in tongues, unless he interprets, so that the church may be edified. (1 Cor. 14:1-5) (Emphasis mine)

In Paul's Gentile churches, speaking in tongues was a gift of the Holy Spirit, except his version of tongues differed from that of Acts chapter 2. The Twelve spoke in various languages so that others could understand. Why then did the Holy Spirit refuse to perform this same trick among the Gentiles? Paul stated that the gift of tongues did not speak to men but to God. So, in essence, the babbling was the language of God. This supposed gift of tongues was an attention grabbing device. Do people really have another voice within themselves or do they want others to believe so? Is this not similar to the Pharisees who loved attention? Jesus condemned these men as hypocrites.

The Twelve also grabbed the attention of foreigners in the area. But why would they be going after foreigners when thousands of their own were waiting to hear from them? Maybe this whole chapter was meant to undo the Tower of Babel episode where arrogant men were thrown into confusion by God, who used language as a wedge among them. This undoubtedly was behind their use of tongues. The Gospel would unite the world as language had once separated it. But we should not forget Paul's teachings. His emphasis on tongues made the whole story possible.

3. Acts 2:38 - The Apostles baptized for the forgiveness of sins and for the gift of the Holy Spirit.

As I have already noted, the early Jewish Christian movement was led by John the Baptist **after** the death of Jesus. Not surprisingly, the Twelve Apostles baptized converts after the crucifixion and resurrection. This baptism was in-line with John's teachings on purity and righteousness. Josephus wrote:

[John] commanded the Jews to exercise virtue, both as to **righteousness towards one another, and piety towards God**, and so to come to baptism; for that the washing [with water] would be acceptable to him, if they made use of it, not in order to the putting away [or the remission] of some sins [only], but for the purification of the body; supposing still that the **soul was thoroughly purified beforehand by righteousness**. (*Ant.* 18.117) (Emphasis mine)

This passage illuminates two telling points about John and his baptism. First, John preached a message totally consistent with that of Jesus. Jesus said that the two greatest commandments were to love God and to love your neighbor as yourself. Josephus wrote that John preached a righteousness towards one another (your neighbor) and a piety towards God. Second, John's baptism was for those who had already purified their souls beforehand by righteousness. Thus, this baptism did not remove one's sins, and it did not repair one's relationship with God. That had already been done by the practice of righteousness.

The baptism referred to in Acts 2:38 was not the baptism of John, even though John would have been the leader of the movement at this time. Instead, the author of Acts introduced Pauline ideas into this baptism. By dying with the crucified Christ, through baptism, one could identify with Christ and have one's sins forgiven. This concept was totally at odds with John's baptism. In addition, one received the gift of the Holy Spirit at baptism. This baptism by the Holy Spirit was the centerpiece of Paul's program, not that of Jesus or John the Baptist. Note that John would have considered any Jew purified who had practiced righteousness. Thus, the grace versus works argument is present in this baptism passage.

4. Acts 2:44-45; Acts 4:32-37 and Acts 5:1-11 - The disciples held all things in common.

In the very first days of the Church, Acts repeatedly stressed the financial arrangements being made by the disciples. Right after the baptism of the three thousand, Acts 2:44-45 stated: "All the believers were together and had everything in common. Selling their possessions and goods, they gave to anyone as he had need." This same sentiment was followed up in Acts 4:32, where "no one claimed that any of his possessions was his own, but they shared everything they had." Many disciples sold fields and gave to the needy. (Acts 4:34-37) However, in Acts 5:1-11, a husband and wife, named Ananias and Sapphira, sold a property and gave only part of the proceeds to the apostles. As a punishment for keeping some money behind for themselves, God smote them both dead. This fanciful story ended with this very real threat: "Great fear seized the Church and all who heard about these events." (Acts 5:11)

This communal approach to living was certainly consistent with what we know of Jesus in the Gospels. Jesus said "No one can serve two masters. ... You cannot serve both God and Money." (Matt. 6:24) Did Jesus intend for his disciples to share everything in common? After all, if one kept a hoard of cash for security, could one truly trust in God alone? Perhaps the most interesting statement made by Jesus occurred in Matt. 19:21, where he told the rich young man how to gain entrance to the kingdom of God: "If you want to be perfect, go, sell your possessions and give to the poor, and you will have treasure in heaven. Then come, follow me." By this, Jesus meant that the rich man could not truly follow him until he had removed the one great stumbling block in his life, his wealth. Jesus followed up on this point by saying "Again I tell you, it is easier for a camel to go through the eye of a needle than for a rich man to enter the kingdom of God." (Matt. 19:24)

This communal way of living seemed absurd to many well-to-do first-century Jews and Romans. To us today, this would be considered cultic. How would you feel if a close relative joined a religious group and immediately signed over every piece of property to the commune? It seems so exciting when we read of these first-century Christians sharing everything in common. But how many of us would do this today?

This skepticism was shared by Josephus. When writing about the Fourth Philosophy's (Zealots') communal living, he stated, "The dregs, the scum of the whole country, they have **squandered their own property** and practiced their **lunacy** upon the towns and villages around, and finally have poured in a stealthy stream into the Holy City..." (*War* 4.241) Squandering their own property meant that they shared it with the poor. Josephus did not congratulate them on their altruistic sacrifices but simply categorized them as lunatics. Is that not how we would react?

From the above, the Jewish Church's attitude about communal living was perfectly in-line with what we know of the Fourth Philosophy. However, this pure communism was not practiced by Paul's Gentile communities. Paul did encourage his churches to set aside their money to help others, so that there might be equality, but a forced communal way of living was not present. (2

Cor. 8:13-15) As time marched on, the wealthy began controlling the Church just as in every other aspect of life. Against these abuses, small monastic movements periodically emerged and tried to rekindle the early spirit of the Church, by living communally.

5. Acts 5:36-39 - Theudas and Judas the Galilean were cited as examples of failure.

This particular passage is a grand anachronism. This New Testament account had Gamaliel in 35 CE referring to an event in the future, the death of Theudas (45 CE), and then to the death of Judas the Galilean (6 CE). The fact that Gamaliel spoke about the future is a bit disconcerting but then Acts did that one better. Acts also claimed that Judas the Galilean was killed after Theudas. In reality, the author of Acts was simply recounting the history of Josephus, detailed in *Ant.* 20.97-102. Josephus wrote that the sons of Judas the Galilean were crucified (46-48 CE) after the beheading of Theudas. (The death of Judas the Galilean is curiously missing from Josephus. Most scholars accept the Acts' version of events and date his death at 6 CE. This is absurd, considering the inaccuracies of the passage. It is my contention that Judas was crucified under Pilate, and his death was replaced by the spurious Jesus passage (TF) in *Ant.* 18.63-64.)

The passage in Acts also purposely discredited Judas the Galilean, claiming his movement failed after his death, and that it did not emanate from God. From Josephus, we know that Judas' Fourth Philosophy consumed the Jewish nation for over fifty years after his death, from 19 CE to 73 CE. Why would Acts misrepresent the facts about Judas the Galilean? To destroy the legacy of Judas was paramount in importance, to forever distance Judas from the newly created Jesus of Nazareth. This smear campaign worked wonderfully, to such an extent that modern day scholars dismiss Judas even though Josephus portrayed him as one of the most important figures of first-century Israel.

6. Acts 2 through Acts 5 - No corroborating information of the events was noted by Josephus.

Josephus left no corresponding information for us to compare and contrast to Acts chapter 2 to most of chapter 5. From the year 19 CE to 37 CE, little was told of Pilate's reign, the very time when the early Church began growing within the environs of Jerusalem. A glimpse of John the Baptist's demise was recounted by Josephus, but even this leaves impossible questions for the believer. If John died in 36 CE, as reported by Josephus, then why did the Gospels move his death up to 30 CE, before the death of Jesus? But more importantly, this paucity of information makes it impossible to trace the development of the early Church.

Is it possible that the absence of material relating to the Church had been edited by early Christians, eager to hide unflattering information concerning their movement? After all, the spurious passage about Jesus (TF) was a replacement passage for the original, which detailed the death of Judas the Galilean. Also, Pilate's arrival was changed from 18 CE to 26 CE. This alteration moved Jesus' ministry forward to the middle of Pilate's reign, more in-line with the Gospel arrival of John the Baptist in 28-29 CE. (According to the Slavonic Josephus, John the Baptist came on the scene in 6 CE, right before the introduction of Judas the Galilean.) The fact that Josephus' story has been edited must give us pause. Did information about James and Simon Peter also become a victim to the later established Gentile movement?

When reading Acts, one must realize that the beginning of the Church occurred right after the death of Jesus. My estimate for this beginning is 19-21 CE while the traditional dating is 30-33 CE. The dating of the events in Acts 5:37, where Gamaliel related information about Theudas and the sons of Judas the Galilean, can be firmly placed at between 44-48 CE. So where did the intervening years disappear? Even if the traditional dating of 30-33 CE is used for the crucifixion of Jesus, then fifteen years elapsed until the Gamaliel episode. And if my estimate is correct, then the book of Acts skipped about twenty-five years or an entire generation. This explains why no information was recorded by Josephus. Even if Josephus did write about these early Jewish Christians, all records would have been summarily destroyed so that the New Testament version of events could not be contradicted.

7. Acts 6:1-7 - The Twelve chose the Seven to minister to the Greek speaking Jews.

According to this passage, "the Grecian Jews among them complained against those of the Aramaic speaking community because their widows were being overlooked in the daily distribution of food." The Twelve fixed this problem by appointing seven men to look after the widows. The Seven were named Stephen, Philip, Procorus, Nicanor, Timon, Parmenas and Nicolas. From these Seven, Stephen and Philip were highlighted in Acts' development of the Church.

First, it seems very strange that the Church, led by the Twelve, overlooked the daily distribution of food to the widows. According to James 1:27, "Religion that God our Father accepts as pure and faultless is this: to look after orphans and widows in their distress and to keep oneself from being polluted by the world." Now it seems strange that this very explicit command from James was disregarded by the Twelve. What type of message were they preaching: "Do as I say and not as I do?" The passage introducing the Seven contradicts the very message that the Twelve would have preached. Did not Jesus wash his disciples' feet? Were the Twelve too good to wait on others and to help the poor and widows? No, that will not do. This episode was simply invented to bring Stephen and Philip into the story of Acts.

From Galatians 1:11-12, Paul claimed that he had received his gospel through revelation from the Risen Jesus Christ. He further claimed that this gospel was not given to him from any man. In fact, this gospel had nothing to do with the Pillar Apostles and the Twelve. Acts 6:1-7 was an attempt to transport Paul's message back in time, to the days of the early Church, to the Twelve through the Seven. The Seven were stand-ins for Paul. This will be further explored below.

8. Acts 6:8 - 7:60 - Stephen was stoned to death, becoming the first Church martyr.

According to Acts, Stephen was the first martyr of the post-Jesus Christian era. Stephen was not one of the Twelve, but rather the Seven, those representing the Greek speaking Jews in Jerusalem. It is interesting that Acts bypassed the Aramaic speaking Jews for the Greek speaking Jews in awarding this singular praise. This Stephen was "full of faith and of the Holy Spirit. …A man full of God's grace and power, [who] did great wonders and miraculous signs among the people." (Acts 6:5-8) In fact, this mention of the Holy Spirit is remarkably similar to Paul's preaching concerning the Holy Spirit. That Stephen became the first martyr has much to do with this connection. In this case, Paul influenced Stephen even before Paul became part of the movement. That is utterly amazing!

In *Ant.* 20.200, James, the brother of Jesus, was stoned to death. This death by stoning was identical to Stephen's mode of death. Was Stephen a mythical stand-in for the historical James? According to *Ant.* 20.214, after the stoning of James, Saul gathered together a group of "wretches" and did violence to the people. This Saul was none other than Paul. It is interesting to note that Saul also attacked the people after the stoning of Stephen. (Acts 8:1) Is this pure coincidence or is something sinister happening?

The Acts' version of Stephen simply whitewashed Josephus' history of James' death, without giving James any credit for being a martyr. In fact, the storyline in Acts ended in 60-62 CE, before the death of James (62 CE). It is my contention that Acts actually included the martyrdom of James but ingeniously hid it in the fabricated story of Stephen. The identification of a Saul after the deaths of both Stephen and James is a dead giveaway as to

Acts' methodology: take a few events from Josephus and twist them into an acceptable pro-Pauline story.

9. Acts 8:1-3 - Saul approved the stoning of Stephen and then went on a rampage against the Church.

As mentioned earlier, Saul persecuted the Church after the deaths of Stephen and James. The accounts are as follows

And Saul was there, giving approval to his [Stephen's] death. On that day a great persecution broke out against the church at Jerusalem, and all except the apostles were scattered throughout Judea and Samaria. Godly men buried Stephen and mourned deeply for him. But Saul began to destroy the church. Going from house to house, he dragged off men and women and put them in prison. (Acts 8:1-3)

[After the death of James] Costobar also, and Saul, did themselves get together a multitude of wicked wretches, and this because they were of the royal family; and so they obtained favor among them, because of their kindred to Agrippa but still they used violence with the people, and they were ready to plunder those that were weaker than themselves. And from that point it principally came to pass, that our city was greatly disordered, and that all things grew worse and worse among us. (*Ant.* 20.214)

The similarities between these two passages are startling. Both accounts occurred shortly after the stoning of a religious follower of Jesus, Stephen and James, respectively. It is instructive that the Acts' version claimed that Saul gave approval for Stephen's death. Although not explicitly stated in Josephus, Saul's actions after the stoning of James point in the same direction. Did Saul approve the stoning of James, the brother of Jesus? The answer is a resounding yes! (According to the Pseudoclementine *Recognitions* 1.70-71, Paul also attacked James in the 40's. This would have occurred shortly after Paul's removal from the movement at Antioch (44 CE). Certainly, a history of distrust and hatred existed in their strained relationship.)

In both passages quoted above, chaos ensued after Saul's persecution. In Acts, disciples were scattered throughout Judea and Samaria while Josephus wrote that the city was greatly disordered. It is interesting that Acts explicitly stated that the persons being scattered were the Grecian Jews while the Apostles were not hunted. This makes no sense. Would a persecution ignore the leaders? The Acts' version may have used the scattering to Samaria as a way to segue to the next topic of Philip in Samaria. However, in Josephus' version, the closest allies of James (the apostles) would have fled the City, in order to evade Saul's attacks. Josephus did connect this persecution to the general demise of Jerusalem. Could this warfare between Saul's forces and the Fourth Philosophy have been the reason for these worsening conditions among all Jews in the City?

In Acts, Saul had the power to imprison the disciples. Most scholars believe he had some connection to those in power. Josephus plainly stated that Saul was a Herodian, related to Agrippa. That explains why Saul could persecute and imprison with impunity. This tie to the Herodians was present in Paul's writings and in his gospel. His stand on taxation, for example, was pro-Herodian.

The New Testament's version of events had Saul persecuting Christians, or the Church. Josephus only said that Saul persecuted those weaker than himself, probably referring to Jesus' movement. This police action against the poor demonstrated Paul's aversion to Jesus' gospel concerning the poor. Jesus said, "Blessed are you who are poor, for yours is the kingdom of God." (Luke 6:20) The Herodian family had never ingratiated themselves to the poor. Their only goal was power and wealth, thus their aligning with Rome against the poor.

The glaring difference between the two stoning accounts concerns the dating. In Acts, the persecution occurred shortly after the death of Jesus, around 35 CE. In Josephus, Saul's rampage took place after the stoning of James, in 62 CE. Like the earlier Theudas and Judas the Galilean passage, the author of Acts had no qualms about shifting historical events in order to invent a new Church story. To make Saul attack the early Church as opposed to the later Church was not altogether wrong. Saul did attack the early Church. However, it appears from Josephus that Saul also attacked the later Church. By shifting Saul's later attack to an earlier time, the author of Acts did not have to explain why Saul attacked the poor after the stoning of James. Instead, Acts had Paul on the way to Rome in 62 CE. This novelist (writer of Acts) knew how to hide the evidence.

In Galatians 1:13, Paul stated: "For you have heard of my previous way of life in Judaism, how intensely I persecuted the Church of God and tried to destroy it." Surely, the writer of Acts knew that Saul had opposed the Church before his conversion. But we have no idea how Paul had opposed the Church. That is why the bait-and-switch has worked so well for two thousand years. The passage from Josephus dealing with 62 CE was taken and placed in this earlier timeframe (35 CE) to explain the wickedness of the young Saul.

That Saul persecuted the early Church is not in question. The question is this: did Saul attack the later Church in 62 CE? Yes, he did! According to Josephus, Saul also met with Nero in 66-67 CE, the same madman who had massacred the Jewish Christians after the Great Fire of Rome in 64 CE. Only a hater of the Jewish Christian movement could have done such things.

10. Acts 8:4-25 - The message of Jesus and the Holy Spirit was brought to Samaria by Philip, followed later by Peter and John.

The persecution by Saul scattered the Grecian speaking Jews while the Twelve Apostles remained in Jerusalem. Philip, one of the Seven, went to Samaria and proclaimed the Christ. There he performed many miraculous signs so that the people believed. Upon believing, the people were baptized into the name of the Lord Jesus. (Acts 8:16) Thus, the world-wide evangelism started with one of the Seven, a precursor to Paul.

The baptism of the Holy Spirit is the centerpiece of this story. Even though Philip baptized the people of Samaria into the name of the Lord Jesus, the Holy Spirit did not arrive until Peter and John placed hands upon them. Why did the Holy Spirit stay away until the Apostles showed up? In Acts 2:38, the Holy Spirit was promised to all who believed and were baptized into the name of Jesus Christ. However, in Acts 10:44, the Holy Spirit descended upon Cornelius before he was baptized. So, in three different cases, the Holy Spirit came once at baptism, once at the laying on of hands and once before baptism. The obvious connection is that at least one of the Twelve was involved in this flow of the Holy Spirit. But if that were the case, then the Holy Spirit would have ceased to exist after the death of the last Apostle.

Two things are at work here. First, Acts showed the Pauline gospel was directly linked to the early movement and was carried to the world through the Grecian speaking Seven. Second, after the Seven took their message to the world, or Samaria in this case, the Twelve Apostles of Jesus signed on to the message. This confirmed that the Twelve supported the Pauline gospel. This, of course, is utterly absurd. According to Paul's letter to the Galatians, his gospel came from the Risen Christ, not the Jerusalem Apostles. (Gal. 1:11-12) And later in that same letter, the supporters of James turned their backs upon Paul at Antioch. (Gal. 2:11-13)

11. Acts 8:9-25 - Simon the magician attempted to buy the gift of the Holy Spirit.

According to the Acts' account concerning Simon, known as the Great Power, he believed the gospel of Philip but was overwhelmed by the laying on of hands, where the gift of the Holy Spirit descended on the believers. Since Simon had been an important player before the arrival of Philip, Peter and John, he could not resist an attempt to purchase the power of the Holy Spirit.

His offer of money was rejected by Peter. Peter flatly told Simon that he must repent or perish. It seems as though Simon did repent as he answered Peter, "Pray to the Lord for me so that nothing you have said may happen to me." (vs. 24) Thus, according to Acts, Simon the Great Power succumbed to the power of God and was reconciled to the Twelve.

This account in Acts was composed in the middle of the second century, near the time when the Pseudoclementine *Recognitions* painted Simon Magus as the chief opponent of James and Peter. In fact, the *Recognitions* combined two individuals into this "Enemy" of the Church, the first, Simon Magus and the second, Paul. (See #13 below.) The Clementine tradition painted both Paul and Simon Magus as the "Enemy", but the Acts' tradition had both repenting and being accepted by the Church. Surely, these two "Christian" movements concocted different histories for Paul and Simon Magus. As we have already seen and will continue to see, the Acts' version of Paul's life was a whitewash and not based on reality. There is no reason to believe that the Jerusalem Church also accepted this Simon Magus as well. In this case, the *Recognitions* make more sense than the Acts of the Apostles.

Neither Acts nor the *Recognitions* accurately portrayed the historical Simon the magician. Acts attempted to change the exploits of the Fourth Philosophy into a pro-Pauline agenda, while the *Recognitions* were pro-Jewish and anti-Pauline. Thus, Paul and Simon were held in great disdain by the author of the *Recognitions*. This negative view of Paul (Saul) and Simon was also expressed by Josephus. In *Ant.* 20.141-143, Josephus wrote about a Simon, who pretended to be a magician. This Simon was a friend of the procurator, Felix (52 CE). Shortly after Agrippa II received certain lands from Caesar (Claudius), Agrippa II promised to wed his sister, Drusilla, to Azizus, king of Emesa. Felix was enamored with Drusilla because of her great beauty. He sent his friend, Simon, to persuade Drusilla to forsake her present husband and "was prevailed upon to transgress the laws of her forefathers, and to marry Felix." (*Ant.* 20.143) Thus, Simon the magician was associated with this crime against the Jewish religion.

This seems a trifling matter to us today. But it would have been a huge scandal and proof that the Herodians were not fit to rule over Israel. Remember, John the Baptist was beheaded because he objected to the marriage of Herod Antipas to his brother's wife, Herodias. Certainly, this marriage by Drusilla to Felix would have infuriated the Fourth Philosophy, and would have been part of their propaganda against Rome and their hirelings, the house of Herod. So, Simon the magician would have been part of this evil which held sway in Judea. Considering that the Gospels and Acts tried to rewrite the zealous Jewish Fourth Philosophy into a pro-Gentile movement, it should not be surprising that Acts rehabilitated both Paul and Simon the magician.

12. Acts 8:26-40 - Philip baptized the Ethiopian eunuch.

Anytime a Bible story has a supernatural event at its core, we should be careful in analysis. Like the present day, the laws of nature were in effect in the time of the early Church. People do not disappear in the twinkling of an eye as Philip did after baptizing the eunuch. (Acts 8:39) This godly act was just a literary device to transport Philip to another time and place. (If such a story were told about a current day preacher, we would all scoff. But for some reason, Christians today assume God worked differently in the past.)

The story of Philip and the eunuch is familiar to most Bible students and goes something like this. Philip was instructed by an angel of the Lord to go from Jerusalem, where he encountered a eunuch on the road. This eunuch was reading the Scriptures, which he did not fully understand. Philip seized the opportunity to explain the Scriptures concerning Jesus. When the eunuch saw water, he said, "Look, here is water. Why shouldn't I be baptized?" So Philip baptized the eunuch. Then in a flash, God miraculously whisked Philip away to another adventure.

Could this story have actually happened? Probably not, but a parallel passage in Josephus has all the above elements. This historical account detailed the spiritual enlightenment of King Izates. King Izates was not a Jew by birth but was brought to that religion by a man named Ananias, a Jewish merchant who taught the king's harem to follow God according to the Jewish religion. This Ananias gained access to King Izates and taught the King "that he might worship God without being circumcised, even though he did resolve to follow the Jewish law entirely; which worship of God was of a superior nature to circumcision." (*Ant.* 20.41) Thus, we have a Pauline conversion of the King. Ananias preached Judaism without circumcision. This was comparable to Paul's teachings as related in Galatians.

Not long after, another Jew by the name of Eleazar arrived, being sent by his leaders in Galilee.

[Eleazar] was esteemed very skillful in the learning of his country, persuaded him [Izates] to do the thing [circumcision]; for as he entered into his palace to salute him, and found him reading the law of Moses, he said to him, ..."How long will thou continue uncircumcised? But if thou hast not yet read the law about circumcision, and does not know how great impiety thou art guilty of by neglecting it, read it now." (*Ant.* 20.44-45)

When King Izates was confronted by what Eleazar had said concerning the law and circumcision, he did not hesitate to become circumcised. Thus, Izates became a true Jew, a member of the covenant between man and God.

The following parallels between Acts and Josephus are enumerated.

1. Both stories involved a eunuch or one who infiltrated the king's harem, usually thought of as a eunuch.
2. The Eunuch in Acts and the King were both reading Scripture but did not fully understand it. The Eunuch was reading Isaiah while the King read the law of Moses.
3. Philip instructed the Eunuch about Jesus, and he was immediately baptized. Eleazar instructed King Izates to undergo circumcision. The King immediately ordered his surgeon to perform the operation.
4. Eleazar was sent from Galilee to combat the false teachings of Ananias. In the earlier story of Philip in Samaria, Peter and John were summoned to complement Philip's teachings.

The New Testament story imitated the story of King Izates as a way to place the Pauline gospel back into history, to 33-35 CE. Remember, this supposedly occurred before the conversion of Paul. In actuality, this King Izates conversion was similar to the argument detailed by Paul in Galatians. Per Josephus, the dating of Izates' circumcision was 44 CE. This certainly was the dating of the argument between Cephas and Paul at Antioch (See Galatians).

In Galatians, certain men were sent from Galilee, from James. These messengers convinced Cephas to withdraw fellowship from Paul. In Josephus, Eleazar was also sent from Galilee. In both cases, the zealous Jews carried the day, and Paul and Ananias were discredited. However, after the Jewish war with Rome, very few Jews followed Jesus. In the end, therefore, Paul and his gospel of "grace" won the war.

Acts made sure that Paul's gospel would win. While the King Izates argument between Ananias and Eleazar occurred in 44 CE (the same date as the argument between Cephas and Paul at Antioch), Acts placed Philip with the Eunuch shortly after the crucifixion of Jesus, somewhere around 33-35 CE. This anachronism was no different than the one perpetrated earlier in Acts 5:37, where Gamaliel (33-35 CE) spoke about Theudas (44-46 CE) and the sons of Judas the Galilean (46-48 CE).

13. Acts 9:1-2 - Saul persecuted the Way with the help of the Chief Priest.

Before examining this passage, we should remember how Acts and the *Recognitions* treated Simon Magus. In Acts, Simon asked the Apostles for forgiveness while he acted as the chief foe of Peter and James in the *Recognitions*. This same formula was in evidence concerning Saul, who transformed into Paul, the Apostle to the Gentiles. The two passages concerning Saul's persecution of the Church will be reproduced below.

Meanwhile, Saul was still breathing out murderous threats against the Lord's disciples. **He went to the chief priest and asked him for letters to the synagogues in Damascus**, so that if he found any there who belonged to the Way, whether men or women, he might take them as prisoners to Jerusalem. (Acts 9:1-2)

[After James was attacked by the Enemy and left for dead in Jerusalem, the disciples went down to Jericho.] Then after three days one of the brethren came to us from Gamaliel, whom we mentioned before, bringing to us secret tidings that **the Enemy had received a commission from Caiaphas, the chief priest, that he should arrest all who believed in Jesus, and should go to Damascus with his letters**, and that there also, employing the help of the unbelievers, he should make havoc among the faithful; and that he was hastening to Damascus chiefly on this account, because he believed that Peter had fled thither. (*Recognitions* 1.70-71) (Emphasis mine)

In Acts, Saul attacked the Church before his conversion. In the *Recognitions*, Saul not only tried to kill James but was hell-bent on finding Peter as well. Little doubt exists that these passages described the same Saul. However, the timing of the attacks differs. In Acts, this alliance with the chief priest occurred at the beginning of Saul's life, being placed at around 31-35 CE. But the persecution described by the *Recognitions* included both the attack on James and the desire to kill Peter as well. How does this square with Paul's own account in Galatians 1:17-19?

...nor did I go up to Jerusalem to see those who were apostles before I was, but I went immediately into Arabia and later returned to Damascus. Then after three years, I went up to Jerusalem to get acquainted with Peter [Cephas] and stayed with him fifteen days. I saw none of the other apostles - only James, the Lord's brother.

It is extremely doubtful that Saul would have been allowed to set foot in Jerusalem if he had tried to kill James and Peter. By Paul's own account, he did not get acquainted with Peter and James until three years after his conversion. This evidence points to the following: the attack on James did not occur until after Paul's argument with Cephas at Antioch and his prompt removal from the movement. This would have occurred after 44 CE.

So once again, Acts whitewashed an event from Saul's life and twisted the facts to arrive at a new story. The stoning of Stephen and the introduction of Saul was a rewrite of the stoning of James in 62 CE. This persecution and attack on James was a post movement act which Acts twisted into a pre-conversion event. So, in reality, Saul attacked the Church three times. The first time was recounted by Josephus, where Saul was run out of Judea and later swindled a Jewish convert in Rome. (*Ant.* 18.81-84) The second attack was described by the *Recognitions* and resulted in the near death of James. The third attack came after the stoning of James in 62 CE. Acts cleverly combined all three elements into its story of Saul's pre-conversion persecution.

There are a few other clues in the above passages. In Acts, Saul began persecuting the Way. This would have been a shortened version of the Way of Righteousness. This Way of Righteousness rings true as both John the Baptist and Judas the Galilean stressed righteousness towards God. (*Ant.* 18.23 and 18.117)

The *Recognitions* called Saul the Enemy. Paul even admitted that some claimed that he lived by the standards of this world. (2 Cor. 10:2) After all, James stated that: "Anyone who chooses to be a friend of the world becomes an enemy of God." (James 4:4) Surely, this moniker of Enemy was placed upon Saul, even during his sojourn with the Fourth Philosophy.

The *Recognitions* and Acts were both second century documents. Sometimes names were used in these accounts as window dressing, not for historical accuracy. The *Recognitions* used Gamaliel as Acts had done in Acts chapter 5. Was Gamaliel actually a member of the movement or was his name used for simple propaganda purposes? Who knows for sure? The *Recognitions* also mentioned Caiaphas as the high priest. From Josephus, we know that Caiaphas was the chief high priest from 18-37 CE. He may have also exerted great power after 37 CE. His father-in-law, Annas, interrogated Jesus (Judas the Galilean) in 19 CE even though his chief high priest status ended in 15 CE. It is possible that Caiaphas may have worked with Saul in 44 CE, but it is much more likely that the name Caiaphas was used to add flavor to the account.

14. Acts 9:4-19 - Saul converted on the road to Damascus and was instructed in the new faith by Ananias.

Saul's conversion in Acts chapter 9 was much different than Paul's own account in Galatians.

But when God, who set me apart from birth and called me by his grace, was pleased to reveal his Son in me so that I might preach him among the Gentiles, **I did not consult any man**, nor did I go up to Jerusalem to see those who were apostles before I was, but **I went immediately into Arabia** and later returned to Damascus. (Gal. 1:15-17) (Emphasis mine)

The following can be gleaned from the above passage. First, Paul wanted to impress his listeners. From the context of Galatians, much harm had been done to Paul's ministry by his unsuccessful confrontation with Cephas at Antioch. The Jews had all abandoned him. Now he was doing his best to keep hold of the Gentiles. Paul wrote that the Son was revealed in him so that he could preach to the Gentiles. And from that moment on, his attack on those represented by James (the circumcision) would be ongoing. He even wished that they would emasculate themselves. (Gal. 5:12)

Second, Paul stated that he did not consult with any man. The gospel he taught came directly from the Risen Christ. This differed from Acts, where Saul received the gift of the Holy Spirit with the laying on of hands by Ananias. (This Ananias was surely taken from the King Izates conversion, where Ananias preached a Judaism "of a superior nature to circumcision." (*Ant.* 20.41))

Third, Paul claimed that he went immediately into Arabia and later returned to Damascus. The Acts' version had Paul being led by the hand directly to Damascus. What happened to Arabia? The answer is clear. Acts tried to alter the facts, fabricating a new story concerning Paul. According to Acts, Paul was now a member of an ongoing concern, Christianity, and God called all the shots. It made Paul out to be a humble servant, where Paul's account was self centered and arrogant. Paul stated that his gospel was not received from any man but came through the Risen Christ. Paul insisted that human intervention had not resulted in his gospel. Rather, his gospel was an original, coming straight from God. If that were so, then we must ask this question: What type of gospel did Jesus and his Twelve Apostles preach? Surely, it was different from that of Paul.

15. Acts 9:23-25 - Paul escaped from Damascus, evading the murderous Jews.

While in Damascus, Paul angered the Jews by his teaching about Jesus and escaped their wrath by being lowered in a basket through an opening in the wall. (Acts 9:25) Paul played the hero while the Jews acted as villains.

The parallel version according to Paul was much different.

In Damascus, the governor under King Aretas had the city of the Damascenes guarded in order to arrest me. But I was lowered in a basket from a window in the wall and slipped through his hands. (2 Cor. 11:32-33)

Paul still made himself the hero of the story, but the adversary was not the Jews but King Aretas. King Aretas had a very good reason to capture Paul. He held all Herodians responsible for the death of John the Baptist. (*Ant.* 18.109-119) From his letters and his teachings, Paul was definitely a Herodian. Josephus confirmed this about Saul in the following passages: *Ant.* 20.214; *War* 2.418-419; *War* 2.425-429 and *War* 2.556-557.

Once again, Acts altered Paul's account to place blame for an action upon the Jews. It would not have looked good to reveal the true reason for the escape: Paul's ties with the Herodians who had engineered the death of John the Baptist. This would have occurred in Paul's later "Christian" years, post 37 CE, and not shortly after his conversion in the mid 20's. And this certainly did not happen after the date of Paul's traditional conversion in 31-35 CE. Consider these facts concerning the traditional dating. If this really happened after his conversion in 31-35 CE, then John the Baptist would have still been alive and King Aretas would have had no motive in capturing Paul. Consider also the fact that the Jews did not hate the "Jewish Christians". James, the brother of Jesus, was based out of Galilee and Jerusalem. In fact, he was stoned to death by followers of the high priest in 62 CE. Certainly, if the Jews hated the Jewish Christians so much, they would not have allowed them to live freely in Jerusalem. Also, according to Josephus, the Fourth Philosophy (Jewish Christian movement) was a subset of the Pharisees. (*Ant.* 18.23) Would the Pharisees have persecuted its own members? No! This was just another attempt to transform an actual historical event concerning Paul into an acceptable story for the established Church.

16. Acts 9:26-30 - Saul went to Jerusalem after escaping the Jews at Damascus.

According to Acts, Saul was led by the hand to Damascus where he was baptized into the Holy Spirit. Acts 9:19 stated: "Saul spent several days with the disciples in Damascus." After his escape from Damascus, Saul went to Jerusalem where he tried to join the disciples. They were afraid of Saul because of his past history. Barnabas then came to Saul's defense, telling the disciples of all he had done in Damascus. "So Saul stayed with them and moved about freely in Jerusalem, speaking boldly in the name of the Lord."

This was Paul's own account of his first visit to Jerusalem:

Then after **three years**, I went up to Jerusalem to get acquainted with Peter and stayed with him fifteen days. I saw none of the other apostles - only James, the Lord's brother. (Gal. 1:18-19)

According to Paul, he did not visit Jerusalem for three years, and then his visit was quite short. He spent time with Peter and James but did not associate with any of the other apostles. Certainly, Paul's account shows that the rank and file disciples did not trust him as he spent time only with the leadership. This account is totally at odds with the Acts' version where Saul moved freely amongst the disciples just a few days after his conversion. The reason for the deception is obvious. The author of Acts wanted to break down the barriers between the Jerusalem Apostles (the Twelve) and Paul from day one.

17. Acts 9:29-30 - Saul debated the Grecian Jews, but they tried to kill him.

In Acts chapters 6, 7 and 8, the Grecian speaking Jews were represented by the Seven, which included Stephen and Philip. These two literary characters brought the Pauline message to the nascent Church, a clever way to transfer the later gospel of Paul to the earliest days of the movement. In Acts 8:14-25, Peter and John approved of Philip's message. Thus, we are to believe that the Pauline message originated with the Twelve, while the Seven just happened to be a bit more aggressive in their evangelization. In reality, the Jerusalem Apostles (Cephas and James) bitterly opposed the Pauline message as they came to understand it by 44 CE. In the earliest Church, Paul had not yet developed his message. It took seventeen years until he introduced a small piece of this gospel to James and Cephas at the "Council of Jerusalem." When James fully understood the Pauline gospel, he sent his agents to Antioch with the order to withdraw fellowship from Paul.

Now the above passage claimed that the Grecian Jews opposed Paul while the Jerusalem Aramaic speaking disciples favored him. Could anything be farther from the truth? Paul's disciples were generally Greek speaking Jews and Gentiles. He had enjoyed little success with the Jerusalem movement. But again, the motive for this ingenuous passage is clear: the author of Acts wanted to cement the close relationship between Paul and the Twelve (represented by Cephas and James). This also explains why Paul was sent away to Tarsus. The Twelve just wanted to protect him. Remember, according to Paul, he wasn't even in Jerusalem at this time. So this whole episode was a complete fabrication to smooth over the split between Paul and Cephas at Antioch. (See Galatians)

18. Acts 10 - 11:18 - Peter brought the Gospel to Cornelius, a Roman centurion.

The story of Peter and Cornelius was an event which completely bridged the gap between the Jews and Gentiles, between God's Law and God's grace. Even though the Pauline message had already been introduced through the Seven, without this meeting, the Jews would not have accepted Paul's gospel. In fact, this meeting between Peter and Cornelius preceded the majority of Paul's travels. This meant that God was working through both Peter and Paul in His goal of bringing the Gentiles into the fold.

The Acts' version goes something like this. Cornelius had a vision which prompted him to send two servants and one soldier to Joppa, in order to bring Peter to Caesarea. As they were approaching Joppa, Peter had a vision: "Do not call anything impure that God has made clean." While Peter pondered over this dream, the servants of Cornelius arrived at his house and convinced Peter to go back to Caesarea with them. When Peter arrived in Caesarea, he went directly to Cornelius' house. There he met Cornelius and concluded that God had included both Jews and Gentiles into the Church. Then the Holy Spirit came upon the Gentiles, and they began speaking in tongues, prompting Peter to baptize them in the name of Jesus Christ. Thus, the Kingdom of God was opened to the Gentiles, by God through Peter.

Before comparing this story to a parallel passage in Josephus, we must note two things. First, both Cornelius and Peter had visions which helped bring them together. It would seem as though the subject of Gentile inclusion had never occurred to Peter. In all his years conversing with Jesus, they had never discussed the Gentiles. How unlikely is that? Dreams and visions were more in line with the Pauline movement, where everything was based upon revelations from the Risen Christ, the very reason why Paul was branded as a liar by the Jewish Christians (Fourth Philosophy). To think that Peter would also fall into this category is beyond naive.

Second, the baptism of the Holy Spirit and the speaking in tongues was part of Paul's gospel. Remember, the true teachings of Jesus focused upon actions, living a life which never wavered from the goal of God's kingdom. This included the sharing of all property. Of course, in the story, Cornelius was deemed worthy without any period of testing. This, indeed, was Pauline theology thrust upon Peter. The inclusion of Cornelius by Peter helped Paul win the day at the Council of Jerusalem as described in Acts chapter 15.

The parallel passage by Josephus will be reproduced below.

However, there was a certain man of the Jewish nation at Jerusalem, **who appeared to be very accurate in the knowledge of the law.** His name was

Simon. This man got together an assembly, while the **king was absent at Caesarea**, and had the insolence to accuse him of not living holily, and that he might be **excluded** out of the temple, since it belonged only to native Jews. But the general of Agrippa's army informed him, that Simon had made such a speech to the people. So the **king sent for him**; and, as he was then sitting in the theatre, he bade him sit down by him, and said to him with a low and gentle voice, "What is there done in this place that is contrary to the law?" But he had nothing to say for himself, but begged his pardon. (*Ant.* 19.332-334) (Emphasis mine)

The people believed that Simon was very accurate in the knowledge of the law, although Josephus used the words "**appeared to be**" in describing his knowledge. This is exactly how Josephus described Judas and Matthias at the Golden Eagle Temple Cleansing. Josephus wrote that these two "were **thought** the most skillful in the laws of their country." (*War* 1.648) This sentiment from Josephus certainly ties Simon to the movement of Judas. In both cases, the teachers were fomenting revolution against the Herodian king. In the above passage, this Simon may have been one of the sons of Judas the Galilean.

Simon preached that those not living holy lives should be excluded from the Temple. This included the Herodians (Agrippa I) and certainly all Gentiles. When Agrippa heard of this, he sent his soldiers to Jerusalem and brought Simon back to Caesarea. Simon knew that his life was in danger so he said nothing to Agrippa. This silence was similar to how Jesus responded to Pilate, probably a standard operating procedure: do not surrender information on yourself or your compatriots.

The similarities between Josephus and Acts are as follows. In Acts, the holy man was Simon Peter while Josephus mentioned only the name Simon. (This Simon may have been Simon Peter or more probably, Simon, the son of Judas the Galilean.) This Simon was brought to Caesarea by soldiers in both stories: in Acts, it was for the inclusion of Gentiles, while in Josephus, it was for the exclusion of Herodians and Gentiles. This change from exclusion to inclusion is incredible. In reality, the Jewish Christian movement (Fourth Philosophy) was extremely exclusionary. This fact is reinforced by the letter to the Galatians, where Simon Peter and all the Jews turned their backs upon Paul when fully aware of his true teachings. (Paul had deceived them into believing he was teaching the law of Moses. Paul actually taught against the law and circumcision, the very sign of the Everlasting Covenant.)

Changing Simon into a pro-Pauline figure was pure genius by the author of Acts. This revelation to Peter after the death of Jesus negated everything the apostles had learned while Jesus was still on earth. This then confirmed the gospel of Paul.

I want you to know, brothers, that the gospel I preached is not something that man made up. I did not receive it from any man, nor was I taught it; rather, **I received it by revelation from Jesus Christ**. (Gal. 1:11-12) (Emphasis mine)

Revelations from God were present in the construction of Paul's gospel and in the Acts' story of Peter and Cornelius. If Peter preached from these revelations, then it could be argued that Paul's revelations should also be accepted. In reality, Simon never followed revelations but rather followed the teachings of the earthly Jesus (Judas the Galilean), not the Risen Christ. It should be clear that like the Seven, Peter was used as a vessel to carry Paul's gospel, even though Paul, himself, stated that his gospel was completely new and received from the Risen Christ.

19. Acts 11:19-26 - Disciples of the Seven spread the gospel to the Gentiles.

According to this passage, disciples who had been scattered after the stoning of Stephen went to Antioch and began preaching the gospel to the Greeks (Gentiles). The news that the Greeks believed in great number eventually reached the ears of the Jerusalem Apostles. In response, the Jerusalem Apostles sent Barnabas to monitor the situation. Barnabas saw that the Gentiles believed and thought it wise to travel to Tarsus in order to recruit Paul as a co-worker. When they returned to Antioch, Barnabas and Paul worked with the Church for an entire year.

Considering that Paul fashioned himself as the "Apostle to the Gentiles", one should question whether it was the Seven's disciples or Paul who brought the message to the Gentiles. In fact, Paul himself wrote that he informed the Jerusalem Apostles about the ministry to the Gentiles. This being the case, the passage in Acts was simply more of the same propaganda, which shifted Paul's message to others. Paul wrote:

Fourteen years later I went up again to Jerusalem, this time with Barnabas. I took Titus along also. I went in response to a revelation and set before them the gospel that I preach among the Gentiles. ...They saw that I had been given the task of preaching the gospel to the Gentiles, just as Peter had been given the task of preaching the gospel to the Jews. (Gal. 2:1-10) (Emphasis mine)

According to Paul, he went to Jerusalem three years after his conversion and then fourteen years later, to lay his gospel before the Pillar Apostles. From this, the gospel to the Gentiles had not even been considered until Paul brought it to the Jerusalem Apostles' attention. This was near the end of Paul's career with the movement, not at the beginning as suggested by Acts. If Paul had converted around 21 CE, then his meeting in Jerusalem would have occurred around 38 CE. Paul was removed from fellowship in 44 CE, so his approved ministry to the Gentiles lasted somewhere around six years, until the Jerusalem community understood his real teachings concerning the law of Moses.

In the Acts' version of events, Paul entered into an already existing Gentile Christian community, which had been approved by the Jerusalem Apostles. According to the traditional timeline, Paul converted around 31-35 CE and this existing community at Antioch had been established in the mid to late 30's. How could this have been possible? Paul's own gospel to the Gentiles was not even considered by the Pillars until seventeen years after Paul's conversion. Do the math. It does not appear that the traditional timeline could be anywhere near correct. Pauline congregations did not exist at the beginning of Paul's career in the movement.

In one last note, Acts stated that the disciples were first called Christians at Antioch. (Acts 11:26) Considering all the other erroneous information in Acts, the origin of the "Christian" moniker cannot be placed at Antioch with complete certainty. However, this does show the importance of Antioch in the early Church history. Remember, at Antioch, Paul was removed from fellowship on James' command.

20. Acts 11:27-30 - Paul and Barnabas were sent to Jerusalem with famine-relief funds.

Paul's journey to Jerusalem in Acts 11:27-30 may have occurred, but not according to Paul's own timeline as reported in Galatians. Paul never mentioned a trip to Jerusalem at the time of the famine.

[After converting] I [Paul] went immediately into Arabia and later returned to Damascus. Then after three years, I went up to Jerusalem to get acquainted with Peter and stayed with him fifteen days. ...Fourteen years later I went up again to Jerusalem, this time with Barnabas. (Gal. 1:17 - 2:1)

According to traditional dating, Paul converted around 31-35 CE. The above seventeen years would have made it 48-52 CE. Since the famine occurred in the mid 40's, during the reign of Fadus (44-46 CE) and Tiberius Alexander (46-48 CE) (*Ant.* 20.101), is appears as if Paul omitted a very important trip.

In fact, mentioning a famine-relief mission would have been fantastic public relations, the very art where Paul excelled. Therefore, it is my opinion that the famine relief had not yet occurred, if it happened at all. Paul could not have mentioned an event which had not yet taken place.

If this is true, then the whole timeline for the Church must be adjusted. In Chapter 1, Pontius Pilate came to Judea in 18 CE. If Judas the Galilean (Jesus) suffered crucifixion in 19-21 CE, then the conversion of Paul would have been in the early 20's. If Paul converted in 21-25 CE, then the seventeen years puts the council of Jerusalem at 38-42 CE. This would be consistent with the King Izates episode. The same struggle between Paul and Cephas was also being experienced by Ananias and Eleazar (44 CE). (*Ant.* 20.7-47) After the conversion of Izates, he and his mother sent money to Jerusalem to aid in the famine relief. (*Ant.* 20.50)

If the council of Jerusalem occurred in 38-42 CE, then it **preceded** the famine. Two items must be noted. First, Paul's letters to the Romans, Corinthians and Galatians have been misdated by scholars. Instead of being from the early to mid 50's, they would have been from the early 40's (post-council but pre-famine). In Corinthians and Galatians, Paul defended his record against all others because he was attempting to win back his disciples. This was necessary, not because of their souls, but because a collection was underway.

So, if Paul did go to Jerusalem with a large cache of money, he did so after the collections were complete. This would have been in the mid 40's. According to the Pseudoclementine *Recognitions*, Paul attacked James in Jerusalem in the mid 40's. This dating corresponds to my revised history of Paul. Also note that Paul hated James at this point and would have done just about anything. (In 62 CE, Saul was mentioned right after the stoning of James. Could Paul have been involved in this murder?)

If one disagrees with my earlier timeframe concerning Paul, then it must be explained why Paul did not mention the famine relief in Galatians. It must have slipped his mind, some will say. How convenient!

21. Acts 12:1-19 - Peter and James were imprisoned. Later, James was beheaded while Peter miraculously escaped.

According to Acts, Peter and James, the son of Zebedee, were arrested and placed in prison by King Agrippa I, around 43 CE. (Acts refers to Agrippa I as Herod.) Another Simon and James were mentioned by Josephus in this general timeframe. Under the procurator Tiberius Alexander (46-48 CE), the sons of Judas the Galilean were commanded to be crucified. (*Ant.* 20.102) Could the Peter and James of Acts have been the sanitized version of the crucifixions of

Simon and James, the sons of Judas the Galilean? The dating of events is very close and the names are identical.

In reality, the sons of Judas the Galilean (Jesus) underwent the same tortures as their famous father, crucifixion. (To these two, Jesus said: you will indeed drink from my cup. (Matt. 20:20-23) This cup was none other than crucifixion!) The Acts' version was simply a way to take a famous story and turn it into a diversionary device. The deaths of James and Simon (sons of Judas) helped remove a fictional character from the history of Acts. In the Gospels and Acts, James and John, the sons of Zebedee, were part of the central three apostles, along with Peter. But according to Paul, the three Pillars were Cephas (Peter) and the brothers of Jesus, James and John. (Gal. 2:9 and 1 Cor. 9:5) The Gospels and Acts downplayed the actual brothers of Jesus to destroy any of Jesus' familial relationships. Therefore, the fictional sons of Zebedee replaced Jesus' brothers. Again, this was just done to diminish the Jewish ties between Jesus and his family. Also note that Acts never mentioned James, the brother of Jesus, until after James, the son of Zebedee, was removed from the story. Upon escaping from prison, Peter gave orders to tell James and the brothers about his miraculous rescue by God. (Acts 12:17) So, the execution of one James led to the introduction of another James.

The sons of Judas the Galilean (Jesus) were omitted from the Gospels because Jesus never married and had children in these sanitized accounts. Even though all the apostles had wives (1 Cor. 9:5), we are to believe that their leader, Jesus, was celibate. This single lifestyle was patterned after Paul and not the Jewish model as represented by Abraham, Moses, David, Solomon and Judas Maccabee. However, the sons of Jesus were hidden in the apostle lists. James the Younger was the son of Jesus while James, the son of Zebedee took the place of his brother. Simon the Zealot was undoubtedly also the son of Jesus. These two apostles were James and Simon, the sons of Judas the Galilean, the two who drank the same cup as Jesus, namely crucifixion. Writing these sons out of the Gospels was necessary for several reasons. First, Jesus had to be celibate, for the Gentile Christian God could not be sullied by sex. Second, if Jesus had fully grown children by the 40's, then he would have been much older than thirty during his ministry. Third, any mention of children would tie Jesus to Judas the Galilean and the Fourth Philosophy. Like the rest of Acts, this mangling of the deaths of Simon and James distanced Jesus from his true legacy.

So why was the event even recorded by the author of Acts? The story of James and Simon had already been woven into the rich tapestry of Church history by the time Acts was written. Instead of denying the story, Acts simply changed a few details and added a supernatural ending. The same can also be said about the exchange between the sons of Zebedee and Jesus as reported in

Matt. 20:20-23. Jesus really spoke to his two sons, James and Simon, not the sons of Zebedee. This will be further explored in the next chapter.

The only thing which does not perfectly jibe with my presentation is the dating of events. Remember, Peter and James were arrested by Agrippa I in 43 CE while the sons of Judas the Galilean, Simon and James, were crucified in 46-48 CE. Why were they not crucified earlier? First, if Simon and James were arrested in 43 CE by Agrippa I, they would still have been in prison through the rest of Agrippa's reign as he died from poisoning not long after the arrests. This would have brought the timeline to 44 CE. In both Acts and the Slavonic Josephus, the authorities in the mid 40's were not quite sure how to respond to the Jesus movement. (Acts 5:33-42 and Slavonic Josephus, After *War* 2.220) In all likelihood, James and Simon languished in prison until 46-48 CE, when Tiberius Alexander ordered that they be crucified. Note that Tiberius Alexander did not capture the sons but just ordered their execution.

One last point concerning the passage needs to be mentioned. In the fictitious rewrite of history, Acts had James beheaded, an act not simply invented out of thin air. Right before Josephus told about the sons of Judas being crucified, he wrote about a Theudas, who was beheaded. (*Ant.* 20.97-99) Thus, this story of Theudas was told in Acts 5:36 and in the above passage. This would suggest that Theudas was also an important player in the early Church, possibly another son of Judas (Jesus).

22. Acts 12:19-25 - Agrippa I was struck down by God, while Paul and Barnabas returned from Jerusalem.

In Chapter 10, I presented an argument about Paul's relationship with Agrippa I which is totally unique to my Judas the Galilean timeline. By the time of Paul's removal from the Christian movement (Fourth Philosophy), he had for some time been working with Agrippa I. In Paul's mind, Christ Jesus was the spiritual redeemer while Agrippa I had earned the title of earthly Messiah or King of Israel.

The above passage described the death of Agrippa I in terms of God's retribution for Agrippa's pride. Because Agrippa did not denounce some sycophants who claimed his voice was that of a god, not of a man, an angel of the Lord struck him down and he was consumed by worms. This fanciful story excluded all mention of assassination by poisoning. But according to Josephus, Agrippa's fight for life lasted five days, the pain in his belly having worn him out. (*Ant.* 19.350) This poisoning was inflicted upon Agrippa by either the Fourth Philosophy or by Claudius, the Roman Emperor.

It is extremely interesting that Acts had Paul in Jerusalem at the time of Agrippa's death or in 44 CE. As already noted, this visit to Jerusalem (and surrounding areas?) occurred after Paul's removal from the movement. It was not mentioned by Paul in his own history as recorded in Galatians. In Galatians, Paul visited Jerusalem three years after his conversion and then fourteen years later at the Council of Jerusalem. Thus, this visit to Jerusalem around 44 CE corresponds to my timeline for Paul.

There is a good chance that Paul was in Jerusalem to do Agrippa's bidding. First, Agrippa was actively courting the nearby kings, and Paul's message of grace over circumcision was the perfect religion for Agrippa's efforts. Note that King Izates had been courted by a similar message preached by Ananias. (*Ant.* 20.34-48) Paul's confrontation with James and Cephas at Antioch probably occurred before the King Izates' confrontation as Paul was the most influential of these antinomian "grace" preachers. After his removal from the movement, Paul probably reported directly to Agrippa in Jerusalem. When Agrippa was assassinated, Paul wisely left town.

One other touch was added by the author of Acts. He stated that Paul left Jerusalem with his co-worker, Barnabas. Barnabas did accompany Paul on his second trip to Jerusalem, at the Council of Jerusalem (Gal. 2:1), but Barnabas had turned his back upon Paul at Antioch (Gal. 2:13). Keeping Barnabas alongside Paul helped maintain the Acts' chronology. However, since this event occurred after Antioch, we know that Paul and Barnabas were no longer traveling partners.

23. Acts 13:1-12 - Saul and Barnabas were sent off to Cyprus, where they met Sergius Paulus and the false prophet named Bar-Jesus or Elymas.

In the introduction to this story, some of Paul's co-workers at Antioch were named. The most interesting character was named Manaen, who was brought up with Herod the Tetrarch. Herod the Tetrarch or Antipas was the one responsible for the beheading of John the Baptist. (Matt. 14:1-12) Paul's close relationship with a Herodian should not surprise us as he upheld their rule through his own preaching. (Rom. 13)

Saul and Barnabas were sent to Cyprus by the church at Antioch. Acts clearly stated that the Holy Spirit was behind the visit, guiding them at every turn. While in Cyprus, the two evangelists met with Sergius Paulus and with his attendant, Bar-Jesus or Elymas, the sorcerer. Elymas tried to convince Sergius Paulus to reject the faith preached by Saul and Barnabas.

Two points must be noted about this whole episode. First, in verse 13:9, Saul became known as Paul and would be called Paul throughout the rest of Acts. It should be asked if this name Paul was taken from his host Sergius Paulus. This may have been true considering how Paul always seemed to interact so well with the rich and famous. Second, the whole section concerning

Elymas is reminiscent of Peter's interaction with Simon the magician. (Acts 8:9-25) In both cases, Peter and Paul were opposed by magicians or sorcerers. Another example of the similarities concerned the reaction of the apostles to the magicians.

[Peter said to Simon, the magician]: "Repent of this wickedness and pray to the Lord. Perhaps he will forgive you for having such a thought in your heart. For I see that you are full of bitterness and captive to sin." (Acts 8:22-23)

[Paul said to Elymas, the sorcerer]: "You are a child of the devil and an enemy of everything that is right! You are full of all kinds of deceit and trickery. Will you never stop perverting the right ways of the Lord? Now the hand of the Lord is against you. You are going to be blind, and for a time you will be unable to see the light of the sun." (Acts 13:10-11)

In both cases, Simon and Elymas were said to be full of bitterness, deceit and trickery. And in both cases, Peter and Paul offered the same chance for redemption. Note that Peter told Simon to repent while Paul promised Elymas that he would go blind, just as he had gone blind in Acts 9:8-9. The similarities in the account suggest that the stories came from just one source and then applied to both Peter and Paul. In any event, the stories about the magicians were just a way to cover up some truth. In the earlier story of Simon, it was proposed that a Simon was behind the unlawful marriage of Drusilla to Felix. In the case of Elymas, the blindness connected Elymas to Paul just as Sergius Paulus was connected to Paul in name. The source for these stories may have been used by the author of the *Recognitions*, as Paul was connected to Simon Magus in that literature.

24. Acts 13:13 - John Mark left Barnabas and Paul and returned to Jerusalem.

John Mark was introduced into the narrative in Acts 12:25, when Paul and Barnabas were returning from Jerusalem after the death of Herod Agrippa (44 CE). I have already shown that by 44 CE, Paul had been removed from the movement, making this whole sequence very questionable. It should have been after the Council of Jerusalem, not before it. Be that as it may, at least the shadowy figure of John Mark made a short appearance. Nothing else was mentioned concerning John Mark until his surprise exodus back to Jerusalem in Acts 13:13. Why did John Mark leave so suddenly? According to Acts 15:38, Paul believed that John had deserted them, and he refused to travel with him again. Did John Mark desert Paul? Could anything else explain John Mark's trip back to Jerusalem?

It is my conjecture that John Mark was sent back to Jerusalem by Barnabas in order to inform James of Paul's evolving gospel. First, the dating of this passage approximates 44 CE, near the time of the Antioch confrontation between Cephas and Paul. (See Galatians). Second, we should ask ourselves these questions: how did James know of Paul's evolving gospel and how did he know that Paul and Cephas were at Antioch? Did John Mark inform James of all the particulars? Third, according to Acts 15:36-41, John Mark was present in Antioch, shortly after the confrontation between Cephas and Paul. Could John Mark have been one of the representatives sent by James, as related in Gal. 2:12? This may explain why Barnabas turned his back upon Paul (Gal. 2:13) and why Barnabas chose to travel with John Mark and not Paul (Acts 15:36-41).

25. Acts 13:13-52 - Paul and Barnabas preached the gospel to the Gentiles and Paul gave a lengthy speech explaining the purpose of Jesus.

As mentioned earlier, the chapters in Acts which deal exclusively with Paul's travels and deeds are primarily fiction, based upon his own wild description of his life. (2 Cor. 11:16-33) That does not discount the value of this passage. Paul and Barnabas traveled to Perga, where Paul gave a lengthy speech extolling the virtues of Jesus while condemning the Jews for not recognizing the Messiah. This speech was a continuation of the speech given by Stephen in Acts 6:8 - 7:60. Both speeches were concocted by the author of Acts, since we already know that the stoning of Stephen never occurred, being a rewrite of the stoning of James, the brother of Jesus. As for Paul's history, earlier passages in Acts were rewrites of other information from Josephus and the *Recognitions*. And the lack of historical credibility will be become even clearer when Paul's later exploits in Acts are explored in detail.

It was quite common for writers to invent speeches for the heroes or villains of their stories. For example, Josephus related a long speech given by Eleazar, right before the Sicarii committed suicide at Masada. Josephus may have known the general attitude and beliefs of Eleazar, but he did not know the exact words which convinced his fellow Sicarii to commit suicide. The same can be said about the speech attributed to Paul in Acts 13. A few comparisons between that speech and the one supposedly given by Stephen are below.

"The people of Jerusalem and their rulers did not recognize Jesus, yet in condemning him they fulfilled the words of the prophets that are read every

Sabbath. Though they found no proper ground for a death sentence, they asked Pilate to have him executed." (Paul - Acts 13:27-28)

"You stiff-necked people, with uncircumcised hearts and ears! You are just like your fathers: You always resist the Holy Spirit! Was there ever a prophet your fathers did not persecute? They even killed those who predicted the coming of the Righteous One. And now you have betrayed and murdered him - you who have received the law that was put into effect through angels but have not obeyed it." (Stephen - Acts 7:51-53)

In both cases, the Jews were wholly responsible for Jesus' death. The speech by Stephen did not even mention the Romans while Paul's speech claimed that the Jews asked Pilate to execute Jesus. Both speeches were pure propaganda. Jesus was crucified because of his opposition to the Roman occupation and their tax machine.

"Therefore, my brothers, I want you to know that through Jesus the forgiveness of sins is proclaimed to you." (Paul - Acts 13:38)

While they were stoning him, Stephen prayed, "Lord Jesus, receive my spirit." Then he fell on his knees and cried out, "Lord, do not hold this sin against them." (Stephen - Acts 7:59-60)

In both stories, Jesus had the ability to forgive sins, an attribute which the Jews believed belonged to God and to God alone. Note that the author of Acts placed this theology upon Stephen before Paul had even invented it. Paul claimed that his gospel was from Christ Jesus and not from any man. (Gal. 1:11-12) Again, this pre-dating of Paul's gospel was necessary to reconcile Paul to the Jerusalem Apostles. By understanding the events at Antioch, we know a reconciliation between the Way of Righteousness and Paul's antinomian gospel never occurred.

One other element was introduced in Acts chapter 13. After the Jews rejected Paul's message, he decided to offer it to the Gentiles, and they gladly accepted the message of eternal life. (Acts 13:46-48) This same sentiment was also included in Acts 28:28, where Paul said to the Jews: "Therefore, I want you to know that God's salvation has been sent to the Gentiles, and they will listen." In fact, all of Acts was designed to shift the gospel from the ears of the Jews to the Gentiles. And, it was all the Jews' fault!

26. Acts 14:8-20 - Paul survived being stoned in Lystra.

In 2 Cor. 11:24-25, Paul enumerated his most harrowing moments in preaching his gospel.

Five times I received from the Jews the forty lashes minus one. Three times I was beaten with rods, **once I was stoned**, three times I was shipwrecked, I spent a night and day in the open sea... (Emphasis mine)

According to Acts 14:19-20, Paul was stoned in Lystra.

Then some Jews came from Antioch and Iconium and won the crowd over. They stoned Paul and dragged him outside the city, thinking he was dead. But after the disciples had gathered around him, he got up and went back into the city.

The list of hardships taken from the second letter to the Corinthians can be dated shortly after Paul's disastrous dispute with Cephas at Antioch. Paul hated the Jerusalem Apostles at this point, as is evidenced by his tone in 2 Cor. 11:13, where he stated that the "super-apostles" (Cephas and James) were really servants of Satan. This can be dated around 44 CE. The passage in Acts has a traditional dating of around 50 CE, due to this event's proximity to the Council of Jerusalem, which was seventeen years after Paul's conversion. Note, however, that Acts portrayed this scene as one of the first in Paul's career with the movement. Many more such tales were told from Acts 16-20.

The author of Acts used Paul's own list to sketch out his story. Paul did state that he survived being stoned. This, in and of itself, is amazing. How many individuals survived being stoned? Stephen was stoned to death in Acts 7 while Josephus wrote of James the Just, who was stoned to death in 62 CE. (*Ant.* 20.200) According to Acts, Paul was stoned by the crowd, who were led by the Jews. Thinking Paul was dead, they dragged him outside the city as refuse. Amazingly, after his opponents had left, Paul sprang back to life and returned in triumph to the city. Surely, the Holy Spirit healed Paul's internal bleeding! If this seems a bit too convenient to be true, then consider the alternative. This event, as told by Acts, never occurred. It was just a way to incorporate some of Paul's hardships into the narrative and vilify the Jews at the same time.

27. Acts 15:1-35 - The Council of Jerusalem certified Paul's mission to the Gentiles.

The Council of Jerusalem has been fully analyzed in my earlier book, *Judas the Galilean*. In that book, I compared Acts chapter 15 to Paul's account in Galatians. All discrepancies were disclosed, and it was determined that the Council as described in Acts never occurred, or at least not as reported.

Paul verified that a meeting did take place in Jerusalem.

Fourteen years later I went up again to Jerusalem, this time with Barnabas. I took Titus along also. **I went in response to a revelation** and set before them the gospel that I preach among the Gentiles. But I did this **privately** to those who seemed to be leaders, for fear that I was running or had run my race in vain. Yet not even Titus, who was with me, was compelled to be circumcised, even though he was a Greek. This matter arose because some false brothers had infiltrated our ranks to spy on the freedom we have in Christ Jesus and to make us slaves. We did not give in to them for a moment, so that the truth of the gospel may remain with you. As for those who seemed to be important - whatever they were makes no difference to me; God does not judge by external appearances - those men added nothing to my message. On the contrary, they saw that I had been given the task of preaching the gospel to the Gentiles, just as Peter had been given the task of preaching the gospel to the Jews. …James, Peter and John, those reputed to be the pillars, gave me and Barnabas the right hand of fellowship when they recognized the grace given to me. They agreed that we should go to the Gentiles, and they to the Jews. All they asked was that we should continue to remember the poor, the very thing I was eager to do. (Gal. 2:1-10) (Emphasis mine)

Paul stated that he, Barnabas and Titus met privately with the Pillar Apostles. This statement conflicts with the Acts' version, where everything was brought out into the open. In addition, Paul stated that he went to Jerusalem in response to a personal revelation from the Risen Christ but Acts claimed that Paul was sent by the church in Antioch to ascertain the proper teachings in regards to the circumcision question.

It is interesting to note that the beginning of Acts 15 is timed differently from Galatians.

Some men came down from Judea to Antioch and were teaching the brothers unless you are circumcised, according to the custom taught by Moses, you cannot be saved. This brought Paul and Barnabas into sharp dispute and debate with them. So Paul and Barnabas were appointed along with some other believers, to go up to Jerusalem to see the apostles and elders about this question. (Acts 15:1-2)

According to Acts, this supposed meeting in Antioch happened **before** the Council. In fact, it was the reason for the Council. Note that Paul and

Barnabas successfully disputed the circumcision party at Antioch. This whitewashed history is at complete odds with Paul's version of events. In his account, the confrontation at Antioch occurred **after** the Council. And it should be fully noted that Barnabas was won over by the circumcision party's arguments. Acts' history simply made the Antioch confrontation go away. In reality (according to Galatians), Paul was removed from fellowship, and all the Jews turned their backs upon him, even Barnabas. (Gal. 2:11-13) In addition, Paul's attacks on the Jewish Christians were quite savage in the letter to the Galatians. A very unhealthy hatred was simmering in Paul's heart and mind.

This Council at Jerusalem came before the famine. Note that Paul never mentioned the famine trip of Acts 11:27-30 in his letter to the Galatians. The purpose of Acts was simple: make Paul the hero and bend the Pillar Apostles in his direction. Placing the Council after the Antioch fight made for a harmonious Church, where the Jewish Apostles slowly but surely came to Paul's point of view. By knowing that the Council pre-dated the split, we can be assured that the two sides never really reconciled. And if this is true, then all of modern day Christianity follows the teachings of a man who was ceremoniously removed from fellowship, removed from the historical Jesus (Judas the Galilean).

So why did Paul even mention the Antioch confrontation in his letter to the Galatians? Word must have spread that Paul was rebuked by the Jerusalem leadership for his gospel, which de-emphasized the law and circumcision. Paul had to try to convince his Gentile followers that he was correct, not James and Peter. Therefore, he belittled James and Peter throughout this letter, saying such things as: those who appeared to be the leaders and that they (James and Peter) added nothing to my message. He then called Peter a hypocrite and finished the letter by once again trashing the law of Moses. This one-sided history was necessary as Paul was in the midst of a huge collection. He could collect no money if his Gentile followers believed him to be an outcast from the movement. His plea was simple: my message comes from the Risen Christ, not from one of those so-called leaders. We assume that Paul succeeded in his pleas to the Gentile churches. If he were successful, then he gained a huge sum of money. If not, then his career as an evangelist to the Gentiles was over. I believe he persuaded the Gentiles for a little while, long enough to get his money. But from Josephus, we know that Paul's career ended with him living comfortably with his Herodian friends and rubbing elbows with Nero.

One other point must be made. In Acts, the leaders of the Jewish Church did not insist that the Gentiles had to become full Jews. It was definitely encouraged, but consistent with other Jewish sects, Gentiles could accept the moral precepts without following the whole law. These Gentiles were called "God Fearers". To be or not to be "a Jew" was the great question for the Gentiles. This is the same question that King Izates had to answer: Should I become circumcised or not? King Izates chose to become a full Jew and was circumcised. James offered the same choice to all Gentiles. Moses should be preached to them, and they could decide if they wished to be full converts or just God-Fearing Gentiles. Paul, on the other hand, did not follow this agenda. He threw out the possibility of circumcision, saying it had nothing to do with his gospel. This was definitely beyond the bounds of the historic Jerusalem Council. James and Cephas would have wanted every Gentile to convert. That they were willing to accept God-Fearing Gentiles in their movement was misconstrued (dishonestly) by Paul, and the Antioch confrontation was proof of Paul's perverted interpretation of this meeting. Paul always accepted personal revelations over human contact, even if he had to lie and deceive.

28. Acts 15:36-41 - Paul and Barnabas parted company after a sharp disagreement concerning John Mark.

An obvious contradiction between Paul and Acts concerns the reason why Paul and Barnabas parted company. Now, the possibility exists that Barnabas may have been more than Paul's co-worker; he may have been Paul's monitor. In Acts 14:12, Barnabas was called Zeus by the Lycaonians while Paul was referred to as Hermes, the chief speaker. This suggests that Barnabas was the one in charge. Could Barnabas have been more than just a sidekick? Could he have been appointed by James and Cephas to watch Paul's activities? After all, Paul had persecuted the Church before his conversion. Any prudent leadership would have had second thoughts about Paul's loyalty. According to Acts 11:25, it was Barnabas who started Paul on his missionary journey. And per Acts 15, Barnabas still worked with Paul by the time of the Jerusalem Council. By Paul's own reckoning in Galatians, Barnabas was a co-worker past the time of the Jerusalem Council and remained with Paul until the conflict at Antioch, perhaps as many as twenty years after Paul had joined the movement. Needless to say, Barnabas was a very important part of Paul's ministry.

In Galatians 2:13, Paul wrote that all the Jews had turned their backs upon him, and that included his traveling partner, Barnabas. The reason for the separation was the law. Barnabas followed Cephas (Peter) and James, whose teachings supported the law and circumcision, even for willing Gentiles. This support by Barnabas of the Pillar Apostles suggests that he was more closely aligned with their beliefs than Paul admits in his letters. Could Barnabas have been fooled by Paul for such a lengthy period of time? It seems hard to believe, but stranger things have happened. Paul probably pushed the envelope with

Barnabas without ever fully disclosing his antinomian gospel, and it may have been Barnabas, or his friend John Mark (Acts 13:13), who informed James that Paul was going outside of his allotted bounds. In Barnabas' eyes, Paul opposed the Pillar Apostles, an act which discredited him in the eyes of all Jews. Paul was summarily removed from the movement, but his writings in Galatians and Corinthians made it clear that he (Paul) was in the right and deserved the support of all Gentiles. After all, he was the self-proclaimed apostle to the Gentiles.

Acts 15:36-40 portrayed the breakup between Paul and Barnabas in a quite different manner. In fact, the real reason for the split was not even part of the discussion.

Some time later Paul said to Barnabas, "Let us go back and visit the brothers in all the towns where we preached the word of the Lord and see how they are doing." **Barnabas wanted to take John, also called Mark, with them**, but Paul did not think it wise to take him, because he had deserted them in Pamphylia and had not continued with them in their work. **They had such a sharp disagreement that they parted company.** Barnabas took Mark and sailed for Cyprus, but Paul chose Silas and left, commended by the brothers to the grace of the Lord. (Emphasis mine)

The breakup in Acts was due to a petty difference over traveling partners. This seems so ridiculous that the reader assumes that even great apostles have unlimited pride and make poor judgments. Did Acts simply paper over the real reason for the split? According to Galatians, the split was due to the law and circumcision, which Paul interpreted differently than the Pillar Apostles: James, John and Cephas. These three Pillars were also the central three in the ministry of Jesus (Judas the Galilean). Barnabas had good reason to leave Paul. Who would you follow: the men who had worked with Jesus throughout his lifetime and who had first reported the resurrected Christ, or Paul, a man with no firsthand knowledge of Jesus? The answer was obvious to Barnabas. That is why Barnabas sent John Mark back to Jerusalem to warn James about Paul's teachings. So, in a sense, the split between Paul and Barnabas could have been over John Mark, but in a very different way than given in Acts.

29. Acts 16:1-5 - Timothy underwent circumcision out of fear from the Jews, and Paul followed the decisions made by the Jerusalem Council.

The author of Acts tried to bring the Twelve Apostles over to Paul's point of view in the early chapters of Acts. The Seven were introduced to mouth Paul's philosophy and then Peter had visions which commanded him to accept the Gentiles (Acts 10). Now, in the later chapters, Paul moved back towards the Jerusalem Apostles, as a way to smooth out any perceived differences.

First, Paul had Timothy circumcised to avoid any problems with the Jews, because these Jews knew that Timothy's father was a Greek. This does not quite jibe with Paul's own words concerning Titus, another Greek.

> **Yet not even Titus was compelled to be circumcised, even though he was a Greek.** This matter arose because some **false brothers** had infiltrated our ranks to spy on the freedom we have in Christ Jesus and to make us slaves. **We did not give in to them for a moment**, so that the **truth of the gospel** might remain with you. (Gal. 2:3-5) (Emphasis mine)

At the Council of Jerusalem, Paul claimed that Titus was not compelled to be circumcised. This, we are to believe, was a matter of principle for Paul. He stated that they did not give in to the circumcision group (false brothers) so that the truth of the gospel would not be tainted. Most likely, Paul did not have Titus circumcised. The agreement reached at Jerusalem did not insist upon Gentile circumcision. However, the Gentiles would be offered full membership into the movement, which included circumcision. The Gentiles could either become full Jews or they could remain God Fearers. Thus, there was no reason to have Titus circumcised if Titus did not want to be a full Jew. On the other hand, the agreement included giving the Gentiles the option. Paul did not follow this part of the agreement; he preached against the law and circumcision for Gentiles.

Could Paul have refused to have Titus circumcised in Jerusalem but have Timothy circumcised because of the Jews in the regions of Lystra, Phrygia and Galatia? Considering that Paul wrote about Titus in his letter to the Galatians, it would certainly be hypocritical to bring Timothy to that congregation. It is my guess that Paul did not have Timothy circumcised, and that the reason for the Acts' claim was to bring Paul closer to the Jerusalem Apostles.

Second, this passage claims that Paul "delivered the decisions reached by the apostles and elders in Jerusalem for the people to obey." (Acts 16:4) Paul preached his own gospel and not the decisions of the Jerusalem Apostles. After all, Paul claimed that his gospel came directly by revelation from the Risen Christ and not from any man. (Gal. 1:11-12) Paul was not following the decisions of James. He was not preaching Moses, the law and circumcision. In fact, his gospel was diametrically opposed to the law. This new gospel of grace prompted James to remove Paul from the movement at Antioch, in 44 CE. But again, the purpose of the Acts' passage was simply to bring harmony to the relationship between James and Paul.

30. Acts 16:10 - The "we" passages replaced the third person.

The "we" passages begin in Acts 16:10 and are used throughout the rest of Acts. Most scholars believe that Luke joined Paul's traveling companions here and stayed with the apostle, just as Dr. Watson accompanied Sherlock Holmes. This homey touch gives Acts a greater sense of reality, at least say the scholars.

It should be noted that most of Acts has already been proved false or misleading. Therefore, the "we" passages should also be viewed skeptically. The "we" passages revolve around the dating of Paul and the book of Acts. Traditional dating has chapter 16 occurring after the council of Jerusalem, approximately 49-52 CE. Those preaching this date in regards to Paul also believe Acts was written shortly after the Jewish war, anywhere from 75-90 CE. If Luke were thirty years old in Acts 16, then he would have been 50-65 years old at the writing of Acts. If this dating is accurate, then this section could have been penned by Paul's traveling companion.

I have dated Paul's removal from the Jewish Christian movement at approximately 44 CE. If a Luke traveled with Paul, it would have been before the split. Per my earlier book, *Judas the Galilean*, the writings of Matthew and Luke were estimated at 105-125 CE. (1) This dating is due to Luke's heavy dependence upon the writings of Josephus. (Josephus wrote *Antiquities* in 93 CE). If my dating is correct, then the traveling companion would have been between 90 and 110 years old when Acts was penned. This appears incredibly unlikely as few men survived to this age due to poor nutrition and ineffective medicines. Few men last that long today. In my opinion, the "we" passages are just one more example of Acts twisting the truth. These "eyewitness" accounts filled in the mythical story of Paul, using his own list of dangers quoted earlier in this chapter. But like the rest of Acts, we can be assured that nothing is as it seems.

31. Acts 16:16-40 - Paul and Silas were imprisoned and severely flogged.

Two points must be considered. First, the magistrates ordered that Paul and Silas be stripped and beaten and then thrown into prison. The next day, these magistrates ordered their release. Paul and Silas refused to leave until the magistrates personally escorted them out. This sway over the magistrates was possible because Paul and Silas were Roman citizens. The magistrates were afraid because they had beaten, flogged and imprisoned Roman citizens. The natural question is this: why did Paul and Silas withhold their Roman citizenship from the magistrates at the beginning of this interesting episode? It seems that there would never have been a beating, a flogging or an imprisonment if Paul had revealed his Roman citizenship. In Acts 22:25, Paul used his Roman citizenship to avoid a beating.

As they stretched him out to flog him, Paul said to the centurion standing there, "Is it legal for you to flog a Roman citizen who hasn't even been found guilty?"

So, this flogging in Philippi was unusual, perhaps even invented!

Second, the miraculous earthquake, with its power to open prison doors, was meant to show that God fully supported Paul's ministry. This episode compares to the escape of Peter in Acts 12, where another miracle was recorded by the author of Acts. The only main difference concerned the jailers. In Peter's case, the jailers responsible for the escape were later executed for their incompetence. (Acts 12:19) In this current passage, Paul's jailer converted and even brought Paul and Silas into his own home for a little dinner. Was it possible that God showed even greater concern for Paul over Peter?

32. Acts 18:1-11 - Paul met with Priscilla and Aquilla in Corinth and promised to preach only to the Gentiles.

This section of Acts has two topics of interest. The first concerns the expulsion of all the Jews from Rome. According to the Acts' timeline, this occurred shortly after the Council of Jerusalem. If the Council dated to around 50 CE, then the expulsion had to be around 52 CE, give or take a year or so. This means that Claudius ordered the removal of Jews near the end of his reign.

As noted in Chapter 1, the dating of the three Roman historians may be somewhat different than the Acts' dating. Suetonius simply stated that the followers of a Chrestus were expelled from the city. Thus, not all the Jews were expelled, just the Jewish Christians, and this due to their revolutionary teachings. Tacitus associated the actions of Claudius near the time of Caligula's assassination, near 41 CE. And Dio Cassius wrote that the Jews were not really expelled but just forbidden from holding meetings. I also pointed out that the Jewish Christians (Fourth Philosophy) were the opponents of King Agrippa I. Agrippa had great influence over Claudius in his early reign. From this, I believe that the expulsion of Jews under Claudius included only followers of Christ and this around 41 CE.

Second, Paul's attitude towards the Jews will be compared to that of Pilate.

But when the Jews became abusive, he shook out his clothes in protest and said to them, "Your blood be on your own heads! I am clear of my responsibility. From now on I will go to the Gentiles." (Acts 18:6)

When Pilate saw that he was getting nowhere, but that instead an uproar was starting, he took water and washed his hands in front of the crowd. "I am innocent of this man's blood," he said. "It is your responsibility!" All the people answered, "Let his blood be on us and on our children." (Matt. 27:24-25)

The similarities in the two accounts are striking. First, both Paul and Pilate cleared themselves from any responsibility through the shaking of clothes and the washing of hands. The responsibility was then shifted to the Jews. In both cases, the blood of Christ was on the Jews' heads, and they readily accepted this verdict. So, did this account of Paul shaking his clothes in protest really occur? I doubt it. Instead, the author of Acts simply rewrote a popular myth concerning Jesus and Pilate and transferred it to Paul and the Jews. The Jews refused to believe in Jesus during Jesus' lifetime and also opposed the teachings of Paul. Acts simply wanted to reinforce this idea. The benefactors of this drama were the Gentiles. Paul stated that he would then go to the Gentiles since the Jews would not believe, consistent with the final chapter of Jesus' life, where the Roman soldier exclaimed, "Surely he was the Son of God." (Matt. 27:54). The Roman soldier believed in Jesus while the Jews had crucified him.

33. Acts 18:24 - 19:7 - The meeting between Paul and Apollos became a way for Paul to bring the Holy Spirit to more believers.

Apollos was supposedly from Alexandria, and he had been instructed in the way of the Lord but knew only of John's baptism. Note that Acts admitted that many people had been taught about Jesus but had never heard about Paul's baptism by the Holy Spirit. This ignorance of the Holy Spirit baptism was due to the Jerusalem Church's great influence. In Acts 18:25, Apollos knew only of John's baptism or a baptism of repentance, this very baptism taught by John the Baptist, Cephas and James. None of these leaders of the early movement knew anything of Paul's Holy Spirit baptism.

According to Acts 18:26 and 19:2-6, Apollos and others gladly received the Holy Spirit when Paul placed his hands upon them. This passage has two purposes. First, the superiority of Paul's baptism was emphasized. Second, it helped diffuse a difference in teachings between Apollos and Paul. From the perspective of Acts, once Apollos was instructed in the Holy Spirit baptism, his teachings and that of Paul became identical. However, according to Paul, the church in Corinth certainly differentiated between them.

My brothers, some from Chloe's household have informed me that there are quarrels among you. What I mean is this: One of you says, "I follow Paul", another, "I follow Apollos", another, "I follow Cephas"; still another, "I follow Christ." (1 Cor. 1:11-12)

This letter to the Corinthians was written, near the time of the Council of Jerusalem (38 CE?), to Paul's own congregation, comprised primarily of Gentiles. However, the quarrels within this church had to do with leadership. Who should the people follow? Paul mentioned four individuals with their own little following: Paul, Apollos, Cephas and Christ. Paul represented his own developing gospel. Apollos taught the baptism of John and may have been a follower of the Baptist, who had just been slain a few years earlier. Cephas represented James in Jerusalem and held to a strict interpretation of the law and circumcision. And Christ was the historical Judas the Galilean, who still held sway over a number of disciples. Each camp pushed their own leader, but the movement could not successfully thrive with these divisions.

The Council of Jerusalem was convened by James after the death of John the Baptist. After Judas the Galilean (Jesus) had been crucified in 19-21 CE, John the Baptist led the movement, with his emphasis on repentance and baptism. When John was put to death by Herod Antipas in 35-36 CE, a rift developed within the movement. James, the brother of Jesus, called the Council to consolidate power. This occurred around 38 CE. James attempted to take the reign of power from his dead but resurrected brother, and he tried to bring the Baptist's followers along as well. This was largely successful. However, a number of disciples stayed loyal to John the Baptist. Even by the second century, John still had a sizable following, as noted by the *Recognitions*. "Yea, some even of the disciples of John, who seemed to be great ones, have separated themselves from the people, and proclaimed their own master as the Christ." (2)

In short, this was a period of confusion within the movement. James began to consolidate power and Paul was just beginning to push his own gospel. It should not be surprising that James did not give Paul's ministry much attention. Paul was a small bit player in the whole drama. James' focus concerned the Fourth Philosophy, and this was the most zealous element within the Jewish religion. Paul was an afterthought at this point in history. However, within a few years, Paul and Agrippa I would grab James' attention. Agrippa was assassinated in 44 CE and Paul was summarily removed from the movement at the same time.

It should not be missed that the author of Acts slyly placed a number on those who were taught about the Holy Spirit by Paul. Hearken back to Acts 2:4, where "All of them [the Twelve] were filled with the Holy Spirit and began to speak in tongues as the Spirit enabled them." This is parodied in Acts 19:6-7: "When Paul placed his hands on them, the Holy Spirit came on them, and they spoke in tongues and prophesied. There were about twelve men in all." This mention of the twelve was no coincidence. Acts concocted the Holy Spirit story as relating to the Twelve just as the later story of Paul was invented to show a smooth conversion of Jamesian Christians into Pauline Christians.

34. Acts 19:11; Acts 20:10 - Like Jesus, Paul healed the sick and raised the dead.

The book of Acts' primary goal was to reconcile the ministry of Paul to the Jerusalem Apostles. This was accomplished by moving Peter and James to Paul's position and making Paul a bit more flexible concerning the Pillar Apostles' problems with their fanatical followers. However, in the above passages, Acts concentrated on making Paul into an instrument of God, comparable to Jesus. Compare Acts 19:11 to Matt. 9:20.

God did extraordinary miracles through Paul. Handkerchiefs and aprons that had touched him were taken to the sick, and their illnesses were cured and the evil spirits left them. (Acts 19:11)

Just then a woman who had been subject to bleeding for twelve years came up behind him and touched the edge of his cloak. She said to herself, "If I only touch his cloak, I will be healed." Jesus turned and saw her. "Take heart daughter," he said, "your faith has healed you." And the woman was healed from that moment. (Matt. 9:20-22)

While Jesus healed through the woman's faith, Paul healed through his personal touch. This may have been the beginning of the religious relic trade.

In Acts 20:10, Paul raised a boy from the dead just as Jesus had raised Lazarus from the dead. (John 11:38-44) This passage may reveal more than just another miracle. In dating Acts, we know that Acts relied heavily upon Josephus (*Antiquities* 93 CE) and the Synoptic Gospels (100-120 CE). But now it appears as if Acts also knew of the Lazarus episode recorded in John. Most scholars believe that John was the last Gospel written, dated as late as 140 CE. Thus, it appears as if Acts may have been written around the mid second century.

35. Acts 19:13-16 - Others tried to use the name of Jesus and Paul without success.

This passage has some interest because it totally contradicts a similar event during the lifetime of Jesus. The passages will be reproduced below.

Some Jews who went around driving out evil spirits tried to invoke the name of the Lord Jesus over those who were demon-possessed. They would say, "In the name of Jesus, whom Paul preaches, I command you to come out." Seven sons of Sceva, a Jewish chief priest, were doing this. The evil spirit answered them, "Jesus I know and Paul I know about, but who are you?" Then the man who had the evil spirit jumped on them and overpowered them all. He gave them such a beating that they ran out of the house naked and bleeding. (Acts 19:13-16)

"Teacher," said John, "we saw a man driving out demons in your name and we told him to stop, because he was not one of us."
"Do not stop him," Jesus said. "No one who does a miracle in my name cane in the next moment say anything bad about me, for whoever is not against us is for us. I tell you the truth, anyone who gives you a cup of water in my name because you belong to Christ will certainly not lose his reward." (Mark 9:38-41)

In the lifetime of Jesus (Judas the Galilean), anyone who did not oppose the movement was considered an ally against the power elites. Thus, Jesus did not wish to stop the man from using his name while doing good. This positive propaganda would only help strengthen the movement. On the other hand, during the time when Acts was written, there was a desire to eliminate alternative methods of worshipping Jesus. Thus, this passage made it clear that only those who practiced the religion of Paul would be recognized by God as a deserving disciple. While Jesus attempted to bring different factions together, as noted before concerning himself and John the Baptist, the second-century Church tried to coerce everyone into one Universal religion.

36. Acts 20:22; 21:4 and 21:10-11 - The Spirit spoke to several disciples concerning Paul's trip to Jerusalem.

These three passages had the Holy Spirit communicating with Paul, some disciples and a prophet named Agabus. The Spirit compelled Paul to travel to Jerusalem. This same spirit urged some disciples to try to dissuade

Paul from going to Jerusalem. And Agabus was convinced by the Spirit that Paul would be handed over to the Gentiles. In short, all voiced their own opinions, attributing their views to the Holy Spirit. This same type of "faith" is practiced daily throughout the world today. The Holy Spirit allows people to do questionable things in the name of God.

37. Acts 21:17 - 22:29 - Paul met with James and was then arrested at the Temple.

The book of Acts had Paul travel to Jerusalem one last time, at the end of his long career. This was not recorded in any of Paul's writings because his letters all predated this trip. However, Josephus did record Saul's adventures in Jerusalem. The writings of Josephus and the book of Acts both had Paul in Jerusalem, but they differ in both time and tenor. Even so, the parallels are obvious. According to Acts, Paul traveled to Jerusalem between 58-60 CE, two to four years **before the stoning of James.** Josephus mentioned a Saul in Jerusalem around 62 CE, immediately **after the stoning of James.** (*Ant.* 20.200-214) The shift in time in Acts helped shield Paul from the accusations concerning his involvement in the murder of James. In fact, in Acts 28, Paul was sent to Rome before 62 CE, again **before the death of James.** How could Paul have been guilty of James' murder if he was not even in town? I will trust Josephus' account on Saul over the one presented by Acts. Saul/Paul was definitely in Jerusalem after 62 CE.

One important piece of information was provided by Acts even if this was an invented story. James, the brother of Jesus, was portrayed as a leader in Jerusalem. His followers were described as "zealous for the law." (Acts 21:20) Now, if the followers were zealous for the law, then the leaders were as well. Thus, the story as related by Paul in Galatians rings true: Cephas and James were zealous upholders of the law and circumcision. And it should not be missed that the association of James with those zealous for the law also connects him with Judas the Galilean and the Fourth Philosophy. As noted in Chapter 5, the activity by the Sicarii increased in connection with the stoning of James.

The misleading part of the Acts' narrative concerns Paul's position in the movement in 58-60 CE. As discussed earlier, Paul had been removed from the Jewish Christian movement around 44 CE. By 60 CE, James would have had nothing to do with him. In the *Recognitions 1.70*, Paul actually attacked and almost killed James in the mid 40's, after his removal from the movement at Antioch. Ask yourself this: Would you accept a man who had attacked you and had preached a gospel contrary to Jewish law? It should be obvious that the entire story was invented. But why would the author of

Acts do this? The purpose was to keep Paul within the movement, even as a central figure. Remember, the whole story of Acts was designed to further the gospel of Paul. He had to be the hero, and the Twelve had to eventually move towards his gospel.

In reality, Josephus' version of events had Saul escaping the Jews in 66 CE. The attack on him occurred at the Upper Palace and not at the Temple. (*War* 2.556-557) In addition, Saul was saved by the Romans in both Josephus and in Acts. Thus, Acts is a fabrication, pure and simple. Paul never met with James, he never performed a purification rite at the Temple, and he was not considered part of the Jewish Christian movement by this time. Acts shaped these events from Josephus so that Paul could still be in control of Christian history and the future of Christianity as well.

38. Acts 9:1-19; 22:1-21; 26:1-23 - There were three accounts of Saul's conversion.

Long speeches in ancient literature were normally composed by the author of the history. This can be said with certainty about the conversions of Saul. Since the beginning of this supposed conversion involved the stoning of Stephen, and this stoning was really a rewrite of the stoning of James (62 CE), the odds favor that the conversion was also invented. In the first account, Saul's conversion was told third person. In the second and third accounts, Paul simply repeated this story, first to the Jewish crowd and then to Agrippa II. While the first account occurred after the fictitious Stephen stoning, the second and third accounts were also accompanied by false rewrites of history. Paul gave his second account to the Jews after a rewrite of Saul's escape from Jerusalem. (*War* 2.556-557) (See #37 above) The third account, given to Agrippa II, was a rewrite of Saul's mission before Agrippa II in 66 CE. (*War* 2.418-419) (See #42 below) Considering all three accounts were surrounded by rewrites of Josephus' history, the accounts themselves must have been sheer imagination.

39. Acts 22:22 - 23:11 - Paul, the Roman citizen, pleaded his case in front of the Sanhedrin.

In this improbable event, Paul confidently spoke to the Sanhedrin, stating his innocence. Being a Roman citizen would have not helped Paul's case as he was being tried for perverting the law of Moses. To make matters worse, Paul insulted the High Priest, just as he had insulted the Pillar Apostles in his letters to the Galatians and Corinthians. This contempt for Jewish authority showed that Paul soared above these petty leaders, that he only obeyed the

Risen Christ. In addition, the author of Acts shamelessly had the Sanhedrin act like a bunch of idiots. Their supposed argument over resurrection nearly caused a riot. It would seem as though they had never debated this topic before. Finally, after Paul had been removed from the mob, the Lord stood near Paul and said, "Take courage! As you have testified about me in Jerusalem, so you must also testify in Rome." (Acts 23:11) This was simply a literary device to foreshadow the eventual trip of Paul to Rome. But as we shall see, even this trip to Rome was a rewrite of another trip by Saul, a trip to Achia. (*War* 2.558) (See #43 and #44 below.)

40. Acts 24:1-27 - Paul was next heard by Felix, the Roman Procurator.

Considering the arrest of Paul at the Temple was sheer imagination, the following accounts of him before Felix and Festus could also be fiction. Even if fictitious, valuable information can be gleaned. First, in verse 5, Paul was accused of being a leader of the Nazarene movement. This was a name given to the Fourth Philosophy, along with the Way or the Way of Righteousness. These Nazarenes were zealous Jews. It makes little sense that the Jews would be persecuting Paul as a ringleader, considering that Paul actually taught against the law. The Nazarenes would not have been accused of such a charge. In the very least, this whole episode appears a bit fishy: Paul may have been guilty of teaching against the law but he would not have been identified with the Nazarenes.

The second point concerns Felix's wife, Drusilla, who had been convinced by Simon, the magician, to forsake her husband and agree to marry Felix. This scandalous marriage went against the Jewish laws. (*Ant.* 20.141-143) It is interesting that the author of Acts had no problem letting Paul converse freely with these two. John the Baptist had been arrested and put to death because he objected to the marriage of Herod Antipas to Herodias. Paul never questioned the relationship between Felix and Drusilla. Paul may have had a friendly relationship with Felix because in the *Recognitions*, Paul and Simon Magus were viewed as opposing the Church.

Third, Felix spoke to Paul frequently because he knew Paul had money and expected a bribe. Where did Paul get this money? If Paul actually finished his collections from Galatia, then the money followed him to Jerusalem, right into his own pocket. At this point in time, Paul had already been removed from the movement. Therefore, the collection money would have been used to further his own goals and not to help the poor.

41. Acts 25:1-12 - Paul was left in prison by Felix (52-60 CE), who was succeeded by Festus (60- 62 CE).

Festus was responsible for sending Paul from Caesarea to Rome. To please the Jews, Festus promised to send Paul to Jerusalem, where an ambush awaited. To avoid certain death at the hands of the Jews, Paul appealed to Caesar, the perfect vehicle in which the author of Acts could transfer Paul to Rome. Note the timing of this request was shortly before the stoning of James the Just. Considering Saul was mentioned right after the death of James, the author of Acts deemed it necessary to get Paul out of town before the murderous act. (*Ant.* 20.200-214)

42. Acts 25:13 - 26:32 - Paul argued his case in front of Agrippa II and Bernice.

Paul met with Agrippa II in Acts and Saul met with him in Josephus' *War.* In Acts, the meeting occurred in 60-62 CE, with the topic being Paul's faith in Christ Jesus. Josephus had Saul meeting with Agrippa II in 66 CE as part of the "Peace Party", and the discussion had nothing to do with spiritual matters. Saul wanted Agrippa to send an army to Jerusalem to put down the growing threat of an insurrection by the Jewish Christians (Fourth Philosophy). (*War* 2.418-419) Josephus did relate that Saul was a kinsman of the royal family. Agrippa II may have also known that Saul had an earlier relationship with his father, Agrippa I. (This is detailed in Chapter 10.)

As a side note, Agrippa's sister, Bernice, was present at the supposed discussion in Acts. This Bernice was rumored to be having an incestuous relationship with Agrippa. This follows the earlier passage where Paul met with Felix and his wife, Drusilla, a union which flouted the law. Again, it must be noted that Paul's acceptance of these unions was so different than John the Baptist, a man who truly represented the Way of Righteousness. One last note must be made concerning Paul's favorable relationship with Agrippa and Bernice. This same Bernice became the mistress of Titus, the future Roman Emperor who destroyed Jerusalem and tore down the great Temple of God. Certainly, Paul was with like-minded company. Titus destroyed the Temple as Paul tried to destroy the law of Moses.

43. Acts 26:32 - Paul appealed the Jewish charges against him to Caesar.

In Acts, Paul appealed to Rome so that he could defend himself against the Jews. This supposedly occurred between 60-62 CE. As we have already determined, this whole episode was sheer fiction. But even if it were true, consider what Paul was doing. Paul was putting himself into the hands of Nero, the monster who ruled the Empire. Considering that Jesus was put to death by Roman justice, this seems a strange request for a member of the movement. However, since Paul was part of the royal family, a meeting with Nero does not seem so unusual.

This meeting with Nero was totally whitewashed by Acts. In Josephus, Saul traveled of his own accord in 66-67 CE to meet with Nero in Achia, to defend himself against any blame concerning the Jewish war. (*War* 2.558) It should be noted that this conference with Nero occurred after Nero had murdered his mother, wife and unborn child. In addition, this meeting with Nero occurred two years **after** Nero had slaughtered the Jewish Christians in 64 CE, after the Great Fire. (3) There was good reason to hide the real history of Paul concerning this meeting with Caesar.

So, in the later chapters of Acts, the author accomplished two goals: he got Paul out of Jerusalem before James the Just was murdered and he hid the actual meeting of Paul with Nero. It should not be missed that the early Jewish Christians considered Nero as the anti-Christ, the Beast numbered 666. (4) Their opinion of Paul was not much higher. Paul was the Liar, the Enemy and the Traitor.

44. Acts 27 and 28 - Paul traveled to Rome to meet with Caesar.

Knowing that Paul's appeal to Caesar did not really happen as reported in Acts, the final two chapters must be sheer fiction. The author of Acts described the dangerous trip from Jerusalem to Rome, where Paul's ship was grounded on the island of Malta after surviving two weeks of storms and low spirits. In this fictional account, Paul encouraged the crew and ultimately saved the day. Paul's inspiration for his calm demeanor came in the form of an Angel from God, who said, "Do not be afraid, Paul. You must stand trial before Caesar; and God has given you the lives of all who sail with you." (Acts 27:24)

Where exactly did the author of Acts get this story? He may have embellished a passage found in Paul's letter to the Corinthians. Paul stated that he had been shipwrecked three times and had spent a night and a day in the open sea. (2 Cor. 11:25) This little sojourn to Rome was an excellent chance to work in some of Paul's self-confessed travails. However, another source comes very close to the Acts' account, a story written by Josephus about his own experience traveling to Rome.

…It happened that I took a voyage to Rome. …At that time when Felix was procurator of Judea, there were certain priests of my acquaintance, and very excellent persons they were, whom on a small and trifling occasion he had put into bonds, and **sent to Rome to plead their cause before Caesar.** …Accordingly I came to Rome, though it were through a great number of hazards, by sea; for, as our ship was drowned in the Adriatic Sea, we that were in it, being about six hundred in number, **swam for our lives all the night;** when upon the first appearance of the day, and upon our sight of a ship of Cyrene, I and some others, eighty in all, **by God's providence,** prevented the rest, and were taken up into the other ship. (5)

In this account by Josephus, he traveled to Rome to defend some priests who had been arrested by Felix. On the way, the ship was lost, and Josephus and some others swam throughout the night and were rescued by God's providence. All these elements were captured in the story about Paul. Considering that the author of Acts relied heavily upon Josephus, it should not be dismissed that this event was also from Josephus' life.

In the Acts' account, when the weary travelers had been brought to shore, the natives showed them kindness and lit a bonfire to warm the bones from the wind and cold. Paul placed a bundle of sticks upon the fire, and a viper escaped the flames and attached to Paul's hand. The natives assumed that Paul was an evil man for the poisonous snake would take his life even after surviving a shipwreck. But to their surprise, Paul shook off the snake and suffered no ill effects. The natives, seeing that he was unharmed, praised him as a god. This little story has one major flaw. According to the Christian commentator, William Barclay, there are no poisonous snakes in Malta today, and in Paul's time, the snake that resembled a viper was quite harmless. (6) The natives would have known full well that no poisonous snakes lived on the island, and they would not have worshipped Paul for surviving the bite of a harmless snake. Once again, Acts conned the readers, who knew and know nothing about Malta.

This trip to Rome served several purposes for the aims of Acts. First, Paul had to be transported away from Jerusalem, away from the spot where James would soon be murdered. Second, in this story, the Roman centurion treated Paul compassionately, in the same manner as the Roman centurion in the time of Jesus, who said, "Surely he was the Son of God." (Matt. 27:54) Third, the dangers that had been enumerated by Paul in 2 Cor. 11:24-26 could be used once more. Paul had stated that he had endured three shipwrecks. What was one more! Fourth, through the power of God (an Angelic visit or vision), Paul saved all souls on board the ship. This was much better than the results written about by Josephus, where eighty were saved. With Paul, all men could be saved! It just so happened that those being saved were all Gentiles and not Jews. Fifth, Paul conveniently arrived in Rome before Nero savagely persecuted the Jewish Christians. In Reality, Paul met with Nero after Nero had murdered the Jewish Christians in 64 CE.

When Paul arrived in Rome, he was allowed to see visitors with minimum supervision. The Jews of the area came to see him, assuring him that they had heard nothing bad about him. (This seems hard to believe considering James and Cephas were busy preaching against Paul's gospel.) When Paul sensed that he had an impartial audience, he preached his gospel, arguing long and hard. Some of the Jews believed, but most did not. At the Jews stubbornness of heart, Paul said, "For this people's heart has become calloused; they hardly hear with their ears and they have closed their eyes. …Therefore, I want you to know that God's salvation has been sent to the Gentiles, and they will listen." (Acts 28:26-29) And with that, the early history of the church had ended. In one last utterance, Paul took his gospel away from the Jews and stated that the Gentiles were worthy and would believe. This is the only true part of the story. The Jews would never believe in Paul's gospel because it destroyed the importance of their Everlasting Covenant with God. The author of Acts was simply rephrasing Paul's arguments in Galatians and Corinthians, where the Jews were demonized since they would not follow his gospel.

45. Acts 28:30-31 - Paul preached in Rome for another two years.

The author of Acts knew quite well that the Jewish Christians (Fourth Philosophy) were the scapegoats of Nero, blamed for setting the Great Fire in Rome in 64 CE. If Paul came to Rome in 62 CE and stayed there for two years, then we are left wondering at what may have happened to him in 64 CE. Tradition has it that both he and Peter were martyred in Rome. If this really happened, then Paul would have suffered death at the hands of Nero along with the other Jewish Christians. But this cannot be the case. Saul met with Nero in 66-67 CE at Achia. (*War* 2.558) In short, like everything else, the two years preaching in Rome was a lie which placed Paul among the brave souls who actually underwent the tortures of Nero.

CONCLUSION

This long section on the Church's history is necessary to prove the reliability of the Judas the Galilean timeline. Everything within the later years of the Church fit perfectly within this new timeline, this new beginning. Saul's history with the Church began in the early 20's, not the early 30's as traditionally believed. Paul's affiliation with the movement ended around 44 CE, some twenty years after he first joined. Thus, after 44 CE, Paul (Saul) worked against the movement, often aligning himself with his family (Herodians) and official of Rome, including Nero himself. To the Jewish Christians, Paul was the ultimate evil, preaching his hated gospel in the name of Judaism. If it were not for the Jewish war and the utter destruction of the

Jewish Christian movement (Fourth Philosophy), Paul's reputation would never have recovered.

Acts was simply a way to rehabilitate Paul's reputation. For the first 100 years after his removal from the movement, Paul had been associated with the Liar, the Enemy and the Traitor. The traitor label was placed upon the fictitious Judas Iscariot, turning the traitor label upon Judas the Galilean and his later movement, the Sicarii. The enemy and liar labels were taken up by the Jews, who worked tirelessly to defeat Paul's gospel. This effort began with the Gospels and ended with Acts. At the end of Acts, we are to believe that the message of Paul was the original message of Jesus and that Cephas and James were also in agreement with Paul. Nothing could be farther from the truth!

CHAPTER 15

THE BIRTH OF JESUS

The next five chapters will attempt to examine the life and death of Jesus through the prism of the historical writings of Josephus. This will be our main source for evaluating the four Gospels, which tell the story of Jesus of Nazareth. Other sources used in this attempt will be the four letters of Paul (Romans, 1 & 2 Corinthians and Galatians), the Slavonic Josephus, and the writings of Suetonius and Tacitus. The early Church historians will also be consulted, but their contribution will be minimal because of their great bias and distance in time from the actual events.

To make the study easier, the search will begin with the birth of Jesus, will continue with his Messianic movement and will end with his crucifixion. (The history of his later movement has already been examined in Chapter 14.) But why even bother? Should we not just accept the veracity of the Gospels? One should only refer to the analysis of Acts, per Chapter 14. Acts has been shown to be sheer propaganda, stretching the truth at every opportunity. The same will be proved concerning the Gospel account of Jesus of Nazareth.

THE BIRTH OF JESUS

Believe it or not, the Gospels of Matthew and Luke give three different dates for the birth of Jesus. Matthew placed the blessed event during the final years of Herod the Great, approximately 6-4 BCE. (Herod the Great died in 4 BCE). Most scholars accept this date, as the Herod the Great episode included the "Star of Bethlehem." The second date comes from Luke's Gospel. Luke placed his birth date at the Census of Cyrenius. According to Josephus, this Census occurred in 6-7 CE, some ten to twelve years after the "Star of Bethlehem" scenario. The third dating for Jesus' birth also can be calculated from Luke's account. Luke stated that Jesus began his ministry at the age of thirty, at the time when John baptized at the Jordan. Luke assigned John the Baptist a beginning date of 28-29 CE. Thus, if Jesus were thirty years old in 29 CE, he must have been born around 2 BCE. This third date splits the difference between the other dates given by Matthew and Luke. The best guess scholars can give based upon these three calculations is that Jesus was born somewhere between 6 BCE and 7 CE.

One other birth scenario exists for Jesus, not recorded in the Gospels. The Slavonic Josephus also has a "Star of Bethlehem" story which actually gives more detail than Matthew's version. The Messiah's birth date in this version was around 25 BCE, some twenty years earlier than Matthew's account. In this version, a younger Herod the Great tried to kill the infant Messiah but was foiled by the three Persian astrologers. So, in actuality, we must try to decide which of the four birth dates, if any, matches up with the majority of information we have concerning the birth of Jesus.

THE "STAR OF BETHLEHEM" - Matt. 2:1-18 and Slavonic Josephus, After *War* 1.400.

The Gospel of Matthew contains the "Star of Bethlehem" story. A birth narrative was entirely omitted by Mark while Luke's account did not even mention this star. What meaning did this star have? According to Matthew, the Magi saw the future Messiah's star in the east. The Magi interpreted this star as representing a child who would be king of the Jews. (Matt. 2:2) The Slavonic Josephus did explain this star a little better than Matthew. This source stated that the priests told Herod that the star represented a prophecy from Numbers 24:17: "A star will come out of Jacob; a scepter will rise out of Israel." (After *War* 1.400) So it can be argued that both sources referred to this "Star Prophecy".

Later in the Slavonic Josephus, the following was written about the "Star Prophecy".

But they [the Jews] were impelled to [make] war by an ambiguous prediction found in the sacred books, saying that in those times someone from the Judaean land would be reigning over the whole world. For this there are various explanations. For some thought it [meant] Herod, others the crucified miracle-worker, [Jesus], others Vespasian. (After *War* 6.311)

The Messianic Jews favored the explanation that "Jesus" was the predicted world ruler. Others, including Josephus, attributed this prophecy to the eventual ruler of the Roman world, Vespasian. Certainly, after the Jewish war, those favoring Vespasian could simply point to history. Jesus and his movement had been thoroughly crushed in the war with Rome. This may be why the "Star of Bethlehem" story, as told by Matthew, does not overtly mention the "Star Prophecy". In fact, through the ages, very few have even put the two together. This tendency to stress the miraculous over the historical and political meanings is a trademark of the various Gospels. The truth should not get in the way of a good story.

Herod's desire to kill the infant Messiah was present in both Matthew and the Slavonic Josephus. In Matthew, this mad plan occurred near the end of Herod's life. When Herod learned that he had been tricked by the Magi, he ordered that all boys two years and younger, in the town of Bethlehem, should be killed. This dated the birth of Jesus to approximately 6 BCE, as Herod died in 4 BCE. The Slavonic Josephus gave a little more insight into Herod's soul. His advisors convinced him that he should kill only those infants in Bethlehem. Herod was willing to kill all infants throughout Israel.

Early tradition had the Messiah being born in Bethlehem. In Matthew, Mary and Joseph were living in Bethlehem when Jesus was born. An angel of God visited Joseph in a dream and convinced him to flee to Egypt. There they stayed until the death of Herod. Once again, an angel announced to Joseph in a dream that Herod had died, and it was safe to return to Israel. On their return, they settled in Nazareth. It is interesting that Matthew had to use an angel twice to move Mary, Joseph and Jesus from Bethlehem to Nazareth. This use of an angel and miraculous dreams should be viewed skeptically. The angel was necessary to move Jesus to Nazareth when he had originally been in Bethlehem.

The move to Nazareth became necessary because Joseph had been warned in a dream to avoid Judea and its ruler, Archelaus. This suggests that Mary and Joseph never lived in Galilee before Jesus' birth. It was only after the birth that they put down roots in Nazareth, far from Archelaus. It should not be missed that Judas the Galilean also fled to Sepphoris, in Galilee, after Archelaus had released him in the Barabbas-style prisoner release. Like the story of Joseph and Mary, Judas also feared the rule of Archelaus and thought it safer to go beyond his reaches.

The small village of Nazareth has also raised questions about this time in Jesus' life. Josephus never mentioned a Nazareth in his writings and John Crossan states that "it is never mentioned by any of the Jewish rabbis whose pronouncements are in the Mishnah or whose discussions are in the Talmud." (1) So, it is very possible that a Nazareth did not even exist at the time of Jesus' birth. But why would Matthew steer us in this direction? Could the Messiah figure have been associated with a larger town only a few miles from this Nazareth? This city in question was named Sepphoris. Sepphoris was associated with Judas the Galilean. The change to Nazareth can now be understood. Matthew simply twisted the term Nazirite, or one consecrated to God, into a geographical destination. This move from Sepphoris to Nazareth helped distance Jesus from Judas the Galilean.

Perhaps the most important aspect of the "Star of Bethlehem" story is the dating of Jesus' birth. According to Matthew, this took place on or slightly before 6 BCE. When we factor in Jesus' purported age of thirty at the start of his ministry, he must have met John the Baptist around 25 CE. However, according to Luke, John began baptizing in the Jordan around 28-29 CE. These dates do not jibe. In addition, James, the brother of Jesus was reported to have been ninety-six years old at his death in 62 CE. Therefore, James must have been born around 35 BCE. Even if the age of ninety-six was a slight exaggeration, he must have been a very old man at the time of his death. Therefore, we can estimate his birth at between 35-25 BCE, a full generation before the birth of Jesus, according to Matthew's reckoning. Finally, a passage in John 8:57 had the Jews saying to Jesus, "You are not yet fifty years old ... and you have seen Abraham!" This Gospel tradition assumed Jesus was a much older man, one nearer 50 than 40. Once again, this age does not jibe with the birth date of 6 BCE.

The Slavonic Josephus dates the "Star of Bethlehem" story at approximately 25 BCE. First, this is much nearer the birth date of James, his brother. Second, if Jesus were thirty at the beginning of his ministry, then this can be dated at 6 CE, the exact time when the Slavonic Josephus introduced John the Baptist. It is also the same date as the Census of Cyrenius. Judas the Galilean led his nationwide tax revolt against Rome in 6 CE. The age of the Slavonic Josephus' Messiah would also be much closer to the John tradition, where Jesus was close to fifty years old at the end of his ministry. I have pinpointed the death of Judas the Galilean at between 19-21 CE. If Judas (Jesus) had been born in 25 BCE, he would have been in his mid 40's at the crucifixion. This is much closer to all the facts than the traditional timeline as given by Matthew.

One other aspect of the "Star of Bethlehem" story should not be missed. The slaughter of the innocents around Bethlehem was used as a way to connect the life of Jesus to the life of Moses. Many scholars have doubted the veracity of this part of the story. Certainly, Herod the Great was capable of ordering this slaughter, but it does not appear in either the *War* or in *Antiquities*. Josephus would not have missed such a good story! So, is it possible that this slaughter was a combination of the Moses story and another story related to Herod the Great? The answer is yes. The positioning of the "Star of Bethlehem" story in the Slavonic Josephus can be aligned with a story told in *Antiquities* but not in the *War*. In this account, Herod tracked down the last of the Maccabean line and had them killed. (*Ant.* 15.259-266) These two young men, the sons of Babas, could very well have been the original innocents, incorporated into the story of the Messiah. After all, this Messiah was going to restore the Kingdom of God at the very time when Herod was eliminating the last of the Maccabees. This, in and of itself, would be a miracle.

THE CENSUS OF CYRENIUS
- Luke 2:1-40.

If the author of Luke was indeed the author of Acts, then we have much to doubt in this Gospel. In Chapter 14, the book of Acts was shown to be one giant anachronism. The Gospel of Luke might not be too far behind in its inaccurate accounts. According to Luke, Jesus was born at the Census of Cyrenius, or around 6-7 CE, during the Roman governorship of Coponius (6-9 CE). (*Ant.* 18.1-3) Coponius replaced Archelaus, and the Census was meant to raise a tax upon the Jews and to dispose of Archelaus' money. So, from Luke's narrative, both Herod the Great and his son, Archelaus, were out of the picture before Jesus' birth, in total disagreement with Matthew's account.

The dating for the birth of Jesus at 6-7 CE is also hard to believe. Luke's date is a good twelve years later than Matthew's "Star of Bethlehem" scenario. It has already been detailed that the traditional dating of the "Star of Bethlehem" is much too late to explain the age of James and the passage of John, where Jesus was not yet fifty years old. The Census birth is even farther off. Even by Luke's own set of "facts", Jesus began his ministry at the age of thirty, and John the Baptist baptized at the Jordan at 28-29 CE. So, if Jesus' birth was in 6-7 CE and he began his ministry at the age of thirty, the ministry began in 36-37 CE. But John the Baptist, who was also the same age as Jesus, began his ministry eight years earlier. Furthermore, according to Josephus, John was put to death in 35-36 CE. (*Ant.* 18.116-119) Therefore, the account in Luke cannot be correct. Jesus was not born at the Census of Cyrenius!

Why would Luke put the birth of Jesus at the Census? For starters, Luke was not too concerned about historical accuracy. To miss a date by ten, twenty or fifty years was not as important as the story itself. The Census had two very important functions. First, the movement of Joseph and Mary from Nazareth to Bethlehem was explained by the Census, where everyone of the house of David had to register in the town of David or Bethlehem. This Census got Jesus to Bethlehem, in order to fulfill the prophecy of Micah 5:2, where the Messiah of Israel would be born. The fact that Matthew had Joseph and Mary living in Bethlehem and then later moving to Nazareth while Luke had the order reversed has been generally ignored by scholars. Perhaps by the time of Luke's Gospel, the legend of Jesus and Galilee was so strong that only the Census could get him out of Galilee.

The second point concerns Judas the Galilean. Judas was the hero of the Census tax revolt. Luke was simply replacing Judas' heroics with the birth of the Messiah. For all time, the Census of Cyrenius would be remembered for the birth of the Messiah. It would never be remembered for the exploits of Judas the Galilean.

JUDAS AND JESUS

The two Gospel accounts of the birth of Jesus do not jibe. Instead, they have created a mystery for historians. How can these accounts be harmonized? If these are birth scenarios, then they cannot be harmonized, as the two accounts differ by approximately twelve years. However, the two accounts may actually represent two separate events in the life of one individual, that person being Judas the Galilean. Matthew's account of the "Star of Bethlehem" was placed at the end of Herod the Great's reign, the same time when Judas and Matthias spearheaded the Golden Eagle Temple Cleansing. That could be a coincidence, but is it not unusual that Luke's account of the Census of Cyrenius was also an important part of Judas the Galilean's legacy? Judas led a nationwide tax revolt against Rome as chronicled by Josephus. (*Ant.* 18.1-4) And it should not be missed that Jesus was crucified for his opposition to Roman taxation. (Luke 23:2)

Not only were the major events in Judas' life shadowed by the Gospel Jesus, but other smaller ones were also mimicked. Joseph fled to Galilee to escape Archelaus, just as Judas had done after the Barabbas-style prisoner release of 4 BCE. In addition, Joseph and Mary took up residence in Nazareth, just a few miles from Sepphoris, the center of Judas' Galilean movement.

So when did the birth of Jesus occur? It was not in 6 BCE (Matthew) or in 6 CE (Luke). The Slavonic Josephus' "Star of Bethlehem" story was placed in 25 BCE. This dating makes much more sense as James, the brother of Jesus, was born somewhere between 35-25 BCE. Also, an older Jesus (Judas) fits the bill when it comes to the passage in John where Jesus was not yet fifty years old. Only the birth in 25 BCE can explain away these difficulties.

CHAPTER 16

THE FAMILY OF JESUS

In the last chapter, the dating of Jesus' birth was questioned. This chapter will go forward from that beginning, questioning everything which strays from reality. We will attempt to discover Jesus' true family history, using the four Gospels, the four letters of Paul, Josephus and the Slavonic Josephus.

MARY AND JOSEPH

The father of Jesus was named Joseph, a carpenter from Nazareth. That is all we know of Joseph. The Gospels of Mark and John did not even acknowledge the existence of such a figure. When the family of Jesus was mentioned, it was always the mother and brothers, never the father, mother and brothers. (Mark 3:20 and 3:21; John 2:1, 7:1-10 and 19:25-27) That suggests that Joseph either died before the ministry of Jesus even started, or he was a phantom figure, not belonging to history.

According to Matthew, Joseph was of David's line and lived in Judea, in Bethlehem. He took Mary as his wife, even though she was pregnant, and he was not the father. This occurred because an angel came to Joseph in a dream, telling him that Mary had conceived through the Holy Spirit of God. The dream sequence was Matthew's way to explain the unexplainable.

After Jesus was born in Bethlehem, an angel of the Lord appeared to Joseph again, urging him to take the family to Egypt, away from Herod the Great. While in Egypt, an angel once more appeared to Joseph in a dream and declared the death of Herod. Joseph moved the family back to Israel but was again warned in a dream to stay clear of Judea because of Archelaus. Thus, Joseph ended up in Nazareth, and helped fulfill the words of the prophets: "He will be called a Nazarene."

Matthew obviously used Joseph as a tool to move the family from Bethlehem to Nazareth. Matthew's use of the four dream sequences may have gone a bit overboard, but he needed to move the child to Galilee, the place where Jesus was to grow into his great ministry. Other than being a tool for this move, nothing else was divulged about Joseph. Once again we should ask: did Joseph really exist?

The story according to Luke also concerned a Mary and Joseph, but the facts were wildly different. It was Mary who was visited by an angel, not Joseph. While Matthew had the couple living in Bethlehem, Luke had them residing in Nazareth. Luke did not employ a dream sequence to move the couple to Bethlehem. Instead, he used the Census of Cyrenius (6 CE). According to Luke, everyone had to go to his home town to register for the Census. This would have been a logistical nightmare, very unlike the Roman style of precision in government. Regardless, Luke used the Census just as Matthew had used the dream sequences to move the family. Unfortunately, this Census of Cyrenius was a good twelve years after the events recorded by Matthew. After the birth, Joseph and Mary simply returned to Nazareth, with no side trip to Egypt and no massacre of the innocents.

Luke also had Mary and Joseph visiting Jerusalem for Jesus' circumcision and for the Passover festivals in the ensuing years. (Luke 2:41) At one of these Passovers, Jesus taught at the Temple while his parents were on their way home, unaware that their twelve year old child was alone in Jerusalem. When they discovered Jesus was missing, they went back to Jerusalem to claim their boy. After three days of searching, they found him at the Temple discussing the law with the religious authorities. Mary said to Jesus, "Your father and I have been anxiously searching for you." From this, Luke lets us know that Joseph was still a part of Jesus' life, at least through his twelfth birthday. This episode at the Temple may actually help identify the real father of Jesus.

Both Matthew and Luke supplied genealogies for Jesus. However, these genealogies have little in common except that they finish with Joseph. Matthew stated that the grandfather of Joseph was a Matthan while Luke reported a grandfather with the name of Matthat. In addition, Luke included the name Mattathias twice in his list, along with another Matthan and also a Mattatha. Now Mattathias was the name of Judas Maccabee's father. The movement of Matthias and Judas the Galilean was modeled after Mattathias and Judas Maccabee. The Golden Eagle Temple Cleansing was patterned after Judas Maccabee and his Temple Cleansing, some 170 years earlier. Just as Judas Maccabee was the son of Mattathias, Judas the Galilean may have been the son of Matthias. This brings us back to the grandfather of Joseph, named Matthan or Matthat. Considering that the Gospels of Matthew and Luke were purposely placed in a later timeframe, the removal of Joseph and his father may be justified. Without these two generations, the father of Jesus would have been Matthan or Matthat or in all probabilities, Matthias.

In the Golden Eagle Temple Cleansing (4 BCE), Matthias and Judas were both arrested by Herod the Great. Matthias was burnt to death but Judas escaped through a Barabbas-style prisoner release under the kingship of Archelaus. So in the story of Judas the Galilean, both he and his father, Matthias, preached at the Temple. Judas would have been a young man of 20, being born at the "Star of Bethlehem" in 25 BCE (Slavonic Josephus). This corresponds to the story of the twelve year old Jesus at the Temple. This Temple scene was the last time Jesus' father was mentioned in the Gospels. Where did Joseph go? Did he die? In reality, the father of Jesus (Judas) was put to death for an insurrection. Jesus Barabbas, or the son of the father, was left to mourn for his father. This Barabbas (Jesus/Judas) was captured but later released to the crowd.

One other passage from the Slavonic Josephus may help clarify this somewhat confusing story. The Slavonic Josephus added about ten passages to the *War*, related to the Christian movement. These lengthy passages tell us much of what really happened in the early years of the Christian movement. After the Golden Eagle uprising, the movement was exhorted on by the Maccabee example.

Come, men of Judaea, now is the time for men to behave like men, to show what reverence we have for the Law of Moses. Let not our race be shamed, let us not bring disgrace on our Law-giver. Let us take as the **model for [our] exploits Eleazar first and the seven Maccabee brothers and the mother who made men [of them]**. For, when Antiochus had conquered and subjugated our land and was ruling over us, he was defeated by these seven youths and [their] old teacher and an old woman. But even if we are to be tortured for our zeal for God, a greater wreath has been plaited for us. And if they kill us, our souls as it leaves [this] dark abode will return to [our] forefathers, where Abraham and his offspring [dwell]. (After *War* 1.650) (Emphasis mine)

This Messianic movement was to be modeled upon the exploits of the Maccabee brothers and their mother, who made men of them. Although Mattathias started the movement, Judas Maccabee carried on his father's fight. Note that the Maccabees fought without their father. This was also the case for Judas the Galilean. His father, Matthias, was burnt to death by Herod the Great. The above passage stressed the importance of Judas' mother and his brothers. We know from Paul's letters that Jesus had brothers who were very influential in the movement. (1 Cor. 9:5 and Gal. 2:9) In reality, these brothers of Jesus were the brothers of Judas the Galilean, the ones written about in the Slavonic Josephus.

While great doubt exists concerning the historical background of Joseph, most scholars agree that Mary was the real deal. As already noted, Jesus was transformed in the Gospels and Paul was nearly deified in the book of Acts. It should be no surprise that the stories about Mary would be nearly as hard to believe. Was Mary a virgin who delivered Jesus into the world? I doubt it! Were Mary and John the Baptist's mother really close relatives? That is possible, but the story of the fetus leaping in Elizabeth's womb when Mary visited belongs to fiction, not history. (Luke 1:44) So, we will attempt to move beyond the foolishness and focus instead upon the historical probabilities.

While Joseph and Mary hailed from Nazareth (Luke), tradition has it that Mary's parents came from Sepphoris. Sepphoris was a major city in Galilee while Nazareth may not have even existed. Mary's association with Sepphoris is extremely interesting as Judas the Galilean was also tied to this city. In *War* 1:648, Josephus wrote that Judas was the son of Sepphoris. He could have also meant that Judas was from Sepphoris. In *War* 2:56, Judas gathered together a large force at Sepphoris and broke open the royal armory. This tie to Sepphoris makes sense if Judas' family was also from Sepphoris. It is my contention that Sepphoris was the city of both Mary and her son, Judas the Galilean.

Other than the birth narratives, the Gospels contain just a few passages which include Mary. One of the most famous concerns the "Wedding at Cana." (John 2:1-11) According to John, the mother of Jesus noticed that the wine was gone. She involved her son, Jesus, and he miraculously turned water into wine. This was Jesus' first miracle (John 2:11), and it was followed up by a Temple Cleansing. The other Gospels placed the Temple Cleansing at the end of Jesus' career, but for some reason, John inserted this at the very beginning of Jesus' ministry. The answer to this part of the mystery is clear: Judas the Galilean also cleansed the Temple at the beginning of his career, and probably at the end as well. (*Ant.* 17.149-167)

Why did Jesus' mother get Jesus involved if they were just invited guests? It would have been none of their business. However, if Jesus was the one getting married, then the family's involvement becomes understandable. One other question must be asked: Was this Mary, the mother of Jesus, or was this Mary Magdalene? Either way, whether it was mother or future wife, Jesus had to get involved. It would have been his responsibility to keep his guests well fed and happy. And we should not be so naive as to believe that he actually turned water into wine. This was just a way to make Jesus equal to the Greek God, Dionysus, who also turned water into wine.

So, at the very beginning of Jesus' ministry, John stated that Jesus' mother was behind his ministry. After all, she was the one who forced Jesus to perform his first miracle. If that really happened, then why do the other Gospels pretend that Mary and her sons were not supportive of Jesus' ministry? A passage in Mark 3:20 questions the family's faith in Jesus.

Then Jesus entered a house, and again a crowd gathered, so that he and his disciples were not even able to eat. When his family heard about this, they went to take charge of him, for they said, "**He is out of his mind.**" (Emphasis mine)

Mary and the kids seemed quite worked up about this situation, enough to state that Jesus was out of his mind. You cannot get any less supportive than this. Why, then, was the treatment of Mary so different in Mark than in John? The authors had different agendas. Mark wanted to distance Jesus from his mother, his brothers, his wife and his sons. Any association with the family was secondary to his true mission: to save the souls of mankind. Shortly after this passage, Mark gave Jesus' reply to his family. "Who are my mother and brothers? … Here are my mother and brothers! Whoever does God's will is my brother and sister and mother." (Mark 3:33-35) This was not a strong endorsement for keeping the family close. Of course, this never occurred as "Jesus" had very strong family ties.

The Gospel of John was written at least a generation after the Synoptic Gospels. By this time, Jesus had evolved from a Messiah redeemer to the creator of the Universe. (John 1:1-5) This god was now comparable to the other mythical gods. His mother was now like the other mother gods. That is why Mary had become so supportive of Jesus. A rich loving relationship between Jesus and Mary was depicted in John and in later Christian art and literature. So, did Mary work with Jesus as depicted in John or was she aligned with her other sons, trying to stop the insane preaching of Jesus? Jesus founded a family ministry, and I believe that not only Mary worked with Jesus, but Jesus' brothers also shared in the ministry from the very beginning.

One last passage should be examined to try to understand the importance of Mary. On the cross, Jesus made preparations for his mother.

…he said to his mother, "Dear woman, here is your son," and to the disciple, "Here is your mother." From that time on, this disciple took her into his home. (John 19:26-27)

From tradition, this disciple was John, the son of Zebedee. Consider the consequences of this passage. Jesus was entrusting his mother's care to a non-family member. This would be strange in today's society but unheard of in Jesus' day. This was the ultimate insult to the brothers of Jesus. James, the brother of Jesus, eventually became leader of the movement. Yet we are to believe that James would not have been entrusted with the care of his own mother. So, although Mary was rehabilitated in John's Gospel, Jesus' brothers remained outside his circle of trust.

THE BROTHERS OF JESUS

The first mention of the brothers of the Lord came from Paul's letters. The two passages will be reproduced below.

I saw none of the other apostles - only James the Lord's brother. ...James, Cephas and John, those reputed to be pillars, gave me and Barnabas the right hand of fellowship... (Gal. 1:19; 2:9)

Don't we have the right to take a believing wife along with us, as do the other apostles and the Lord's brothers and Cephas. (1 Cor. 9:5)

In Galatians, we learn that James was the brother of the Lord. In Corinthians, Paul wrote of brothers, in the plural. James was one but who were the others? If Jesus' movement was based upon the Maccabee model, then the brothers would have been very important. After Judas Maccabee was killed, his brother assumed control of the movement. Note that Paul mentioned the pillar apostles, naming them James, Cephas (Peter) and John. In Corinthians, he most likely was naming these pillars again, but this time writing the Lord's brothers and Cephas. This indicates that John was also a brother of the Lord. If so, then the central three were comprised of Cephas and two brothers of Jesus. Is it possible that James and John were the brothers of Jesus and not the sons of Zebedee? (In the Gospels, James and John, the sons of Zebedee, were part of the central three, along with Peter (Cephas.))

When discussing the brothers of the Lord, the passage concerning James' death should not be dismissed. Josephus did confirm that James was the brother of Jesus.

...so he [Ananus] assembled the sanhedrin of judges, and brought before them the brother of Jesus, who was called Christ, whose name was James, and some others, [or, some of his companions]; and when he had formed an accusation against them as breakers of the law, he delivered them to be stoned. (*Ant.* 20.200)

As discussed before, this stoning of James was transformed by Acts into the stoning of Stephen. Note that a Saul persecuted the Church after the stoning of Stephen (Acts 8:1) while Saul "used violence with the people" after the stoning of James. (*Ant.* 20.214) In the rewrite of Church history, Acts hid the brother of "Jesus" and also conveniently removed Paul (Saul) from Jerusalem before the stoning. In fact, James, the brother of Jesus, was revered in Jerusalem while Paul worked with his murderers!

The brothers of Jesus received little attention in Paul's letters, but he did state that they were considered pillars of the Jerusalem community. James' death as reported by Josephus was later commented upon by Christian historians, but this never made it into the book of Acts. A purposeful downplaying of the brothers existed in both the letters of Paul and the rewrite of James' stoning in Acts. But what can be said about the Gospels and the rest of Acts? Did the brothers also get bad press there?

In the Synoptic Gospels, the brothers were grouped with Jesus' mother. In Mark, the family stated that Jesus was "out of his mind." (Mark 3:21) Of course, the brothers were part of this little anti-Jesus movement. Later in the Gospel of Mark, the brothers were named.

"Where did this man [Jesus] get these things?" they asked. "What's this wisdom that has been given him, that he even does miracles! Isn't this the carpenter? Isn't this Mary's son and the brother of James, Joses, Judas and Simon? Aren't his sisters here with us?" And they took offense of him. (Mark 6:2-3)

Jesus' brothers were named James, Joses (Joseph - Matt. 13:55), Judas and Simon. From our study of Paul's letters, we know that one of Jesus' brothers was named James. This agrees to the above list. However, the letters also suggest that another brother (a pillar) was named John. John does not appear in the brother list. Two possibilities exist. First, Paul may not have really associated the pillar John with one of the brothers. And second, this list of brothers may actually be a list of Jesus' sons.

Let us look at the Gospel scenario. Jesus traveled with his apostles throughout the towns of Galilee. His mother and brothers were following him as well, not as disciples but as concerned family members. From tradition, James died an old man of ninety-six in 62 CE. At the time of Jesus' supposed ministry in 30 CE, James would have been sixty-four years old. His mother, Mary, would have been in her eighties. At those ages, would they have been following Jesus? And where were James' wife and children? According to Paul, James was married. (1 Cor. 9:5) It just seems a bit odd that a mother and brothers would be shadowing Jesus.

On the other hand, it would be perfectly normal if Jesus' wife and kids were traveling with him. Note that Paul complained about the other apostles,

Cephas and the Lord's brothers. "Don't we have the right to take a believing wife along with us, as do the other apostles and the Lord's brothers and Cephas?" (1 Cor. 9:5) Note that the Lord's brothers and Cephas had their wives traveling with them. This would have also been the norm for Jesus as well. So, as of this point in our study, the list of brothers may really be a list of sons. This will be further explored in the following section: Wife and Sons.

The Synoptic Gospels showed that the family of Jesus did not support Jesus but were well intentioned. The Gospel of John made the brothers into opponents of Jesus, exposing their envy at his success.

After this, Jesus went around in Galilee, **purposely staying away from Judea because the Jews there were waiting to take his life.** But when the Jewish Feast of Tabernacles was near, **Jesus' brothers** said to him, "You ought to leave here and go to Judea, so that your disciples may see the miracles you do. No one who wants to become a public figure acts in secret. Since you are doing these things, show yourself to the world." **For even his own brothers did not believe in him.** (John 7:1-5) (Emphasis mine)

Jesus' brothers did not seem concerned that a trip to Jerusalem was a likely death sentence. This lack of concern reminds us of the story of Joseph and his brothers, who sold him into slavery because of their jealousy. So, we are left with unbelieving brothers who wish to send Jesus to his death. This negative portrayal of the brothers is quite startling, but it was written to distance Jesus from the Jews in general and from his own brothers in particular.

The final indignity against the brothers concerned the last request of Jesus. Jesus supposedly asked John, the son of Zebedee, to take care of his mother after the crucifixion. Why would he ask such a question? The author simply wanted to make the brothers look bad. Could there be any truth to this request? I will soon prove that the sons of Zebedee, James and John, were simply cardboard characters who took the place of real individuals. This being the case, then Jesus could not have really asked a son of Zebedee to care for his mother. Instead, the original story probably revolved around Jesus asking one or more of his brothers to look after their mother. This is the only solution which makes sense. Thus, the disciple who Jesus loved was one of his brothers, probably James or John.

THE WIFE AND SONS OF JESUS

Most people remember reading or hearing about *The Da Vinci Code* by Dan Brown. In this novel, Jesus supposedly married Mary Magdalene and had children by her. This, of course, was a huge financial success, and was derided as anti-Christian by many followers within the Church. Was there any truth in this novel? Was Jesus married?

There are three passages in the New Testament which shed light upon the marriage question. I will discuss these based upon the approximate dates of their writing. The first reference to marriage came from Paul, in his letter to the Corinthians.

This is my defense to those who sit in judgment on me. Don't we have the right to food or drink? Don't we have the right to take a believing wife along with us, as do the other apostles and the Lord's brothers and Cephas? Or is it only I and Barnabas who must work for a living? (1 Cor. 9:3-6)

Paul was defending his ministry against those who questioned his credentials. Note that Paul stated that all the followers of Jesus had believing wives except Barnabas and himself. This is a very revealing statement. If the Lord's brothers and Cephas had wives, then Jesus probably had a wife as well. At least we know that the movement started by Jesus did not practice celibacy. We also know that Paul was not married. Is it possible that the Gospel writers simply placed Paul's celibacy upon Jesus? As noted earlier, Paul's view of taxation and his view of the dietary laws were also placed upon the Gospel Jesus. (Mark 7:1-19 and Romans 14:1-4; Mark 12:13-17 and Romans 13:1-7) Therefore, Jesus' wife may have been hidden to bring his lifestyle in line with that of Paul.

The second passage concerning marriage is surprisingly found in the Gospels.

When Jesus came into Peter's house, he saw Peter's mother-in-law lying in bed with a fever. He touched her hand and the fever left her, and she got up and began to wait on him. (Matt. 8:14-15) (See also Mark 1:29-31 and Luke 4:38-39)

According to this passage, Peter had a mother-in-law. If he had a mother-in-law, he also had a wife. Somehow, this passage got through the censors. But it is interesting that no other references to wives are mentioned in the Gospels. Where did these women go? Were they that unimportant to the movement? Or were these wives purposely hidden to give the appearance of a much more spiritual group of disciples? Again, we have to go back to the example set by Paul and his opinion of marriage. Paul stated:

I would like you to be free from concern. An unmarried man is concerned about the Lord's affairs - how he can please the Lord. But a married man is concerned about the affairs of this world - how he can please his wife - and his interests are divided. An unmarried woman or virgin is concerned about the Lord's affairs: Her aim is to be devoted to the Lord in both body and spirit. But a married woman is concerned about the affairs of this world - how she can please her husband. I am saying this for your own good, not to restrict you, but that you may live in a right way in undivided devotion to the Lord. (1 Cor. 7:32-35)

To Paul, an unmarried man could fully devote himself to the Lord's business while a married man had to please his wife and children. Of course, Paul was unmarried, and he used this as a way to compare himself to the Jerusalem apostles. Who was fully devoted to the Lord's work, Cephas and the Lord's brothers or himself? This celibacy for the Lord's sake was thrust upon Jesus, as he had to be fully committed to the Lord's work. This whole comment upon spirituality, based upon marriage, was beyond the Jewish experience. All the great leaders in Jewish history had been married, including Abraham, Moses, David and Solomon. So why should we insist on Jesus' celibacy? This whole concept originated with Paul. It had nothing to do with Jesus or with his Jewish followers.

This derogatory passage concerning marriage does indeed confirm that marriage was the norm within the movement and not the exception. The later Church used these words to condone celibacy for the priesthood. Today, we would be abhorred if the Pope had a consenting wife, but did not Cephas (Peter) have a believing wife?

The third marriage passage comes from the Gospel of John. This was the famous marriage at Cana, where Jesus supposedly turned water into wine. In this account, a young Jesus took responsibility for the wine situation at the insistence of his mother. However, this wedding may have been Jesus' wedding with Mary Magdalene. This occurred at the very beginning of Jesus' ministry, before the first Temple Cleansing. According to my Judas the Galilean timeline, Judas (Jesus) was born around 25 BCE, he married Mary Magdalene around 7-5 BCE and then cleansed the Temple in 4 BCE. This fits the facts as presented in the Gospel of John.

Was Mary Magdalene Jesus' wife? No one will ever be able to prove this assertion, but Mary Magdalene is as good a guess as anyone else. After all, in some traditions, Jesus appeared first to Mary Magdalene after the Resurrection, a strong case for them being husband and wife or at least very close friends. There are also accounts in later tradition which suggest that Jesus and Mary were more than just friends. The Gospel of Philip supplied these suggestive passages: (1)

There were three who always walked with the Lord: Mary, his mother and her sister and Magdalene, whom they called his lover. (vs. 32)

Wisdom, whom they call barren, is the mother of the angels, and the consort of Christ is Mary Magdalene. The [Lord loved Mary] more than all the disciples, and he kissed her on the [mouth many times] (vs. 55)

Although this was compiled during the third century, it drew from even earlier sources. (2) So this idea of the union between Jesus and Mary did not originate with Dan Brown. However, to be taken seriously, we must investigate the writings of Josephus to fully understand the place of marriage within the major sects.

According to Josephus, four major Jewish sects or philosophies operated during the first century: the Pharisees, the Sadducees, the Essenes and the Fourth Philosophy of Judas the Galilean. Of these sects, only the Essenes practiced celibacy.

These last [Essenes] are Jews by birth, and seem to have a greater affection for one another than the other sects have. These Essenes reject pleasure as an evil, but esteem continence, and the conquest over our passions, to be virtue. They neglect wedlock, but choose other person's children, while they are pliable, and fit for learning; and esteem them to be of their kindred, and form them according to their own manners. ... Moreover, there is another order of Essenes, who agree with the rest as to their way of living, and customs, and laws, but differ from them in the point of marriage, as thinking that by not marrying they cut off the principal part of the human life, which is the prospect of succession. (*War* 2.119-120; 2:160)

The main order of Essenes did not practice marriage. From the passages already presented from Paul and the Gospels, the Apostles were married. Therefore, Jesus and his disciples were not members of the Essenes' main order. However, according to Josephus, a small sect of Essenes did marry. Could this small sect have been led by Jesus? First, it may be instructive to compare the Essenes described in the *War* and the *Antiquities*. In the *War*, the Essenes married (at least one small subgroup) and were willing to undergo all sorts of torture rather than blaspheme their God. (*War* 2.152-153) These same attributes were given to Judas the Galilean's Fourth Philosophy in *Antiquities*.

But of the fourth sect of Jewish philosophy, Judas the Galilean was the author. These men agree in all other things with the Pharisaic notions; but they have an inviolable attachment to liberty; and say that God is to be their only Ruler and Lord. They also do not value dying any kind of death, nor indeed do they heed the deaths of their relations and friends, nor can any such fear make them call any man Lord. (*Ant.* 18.23)

In the above passage, the Fourth Philosophy married as did the Pharisees. They also underwent all types of tortures at the hands of the Romans. Josephus assigned these attributes to the Essenes in the *War* while saying very little about Judas the Galilean. This change from the Essenes to the Fourth Philosophy may simply have been a correction, since the *War* was written shortly after the Jewish war while Josephus may have had more time to put everything together properly in *Antiquities*. Regardless, one thing is clear: the followers of the Messiah (Judas/Jesus) practiced marriage. And it is not too much of a stretch to state that Jesus may also have been married. After all, marriage was the norm for his particular group.

The leap of faith which states that Jesus was a married man is not that great. And if married, he no doubt had children as well. On this account, the Gospels are silent. Or are they?

The passage universally interpreted about his mother and brothers may really have been about his wife and sons. As noted earlier, if "Jesus" preached during his mid forties, then it is incredibly unlikely that his brothers and aged mother were traveling from town to town keeping tabs on him. Like Cephas and the Lord's brothers (1 Cor. 9:5), Jesus most likely had a believing wife traveling with him. Assuming Jesus was married with children, let's reexamine the following passage.

Coming to his home town, he began teaching the people in their synagogue, and they were amazed. "Where did this man get this wisdom and these miraculous powers?" they asked. "Isn't this the **carpenter's son**? Isn't his mother's name Mary, and aren't his brothers James, Joseph, Simon and Judas." (Matt. 13:54-55) (Emphasis mine)

The parallel passage in Mark 6:3 is slightly different. There the people asked, "Isn't this the carpenter?" This change from Mark to Matthew lends credence to the current interpretation that Jesus was thought of as the son of the carpenter, not a man standing on his own two feet, making it easier to accept that the family traveling with Jesus would be a mother and brothers. However, in Mark's Gospel, there is no mention of the father, and the association with a mother and brothers is not as strong.

To get to the truth, we must try to identify these brothers or sons. According to Paul, the Lord's brothers and Cephas (1 Cor. 9:5) may very well have been the Pillars as described in Galatians. These Pillars were named James, Peter (Cephas) and John. (Gal. 2:9) Thus, two of the brothers were probably named James and John. Only the name James matches the list quoted above. Why was John omitted from the list? Many will dismiss this as evidence that John was not a brother, but the names should be interpreted in a different light before excluding John from being a brother.

Could James, Simon, Judas and Joseph have been the sons of Jesus? This will be explored from the vantage of my Judas the Galilean hypothesis. If Jesus and Judas were really one, then the sons listed above would have been Judas' sons. A number of Judas' sons can be identified from the writings of Josephus. They are noted in the following passages:

Under these procurators [Fadus (44-46CE) and Alexander (46-48 CE)] that great famine happened in Judea, in which queen Helena bought corn in Egypt at a great expense, and distributed it to those that were in want, as I have related already [*Ant.* 20.49-53]; and besides this, the sons of Judas the Galilean were now slain; I mean of that Judas who caused the people to revolt, when Cyrenius came to take an account of the estates of the Jews, as we have shown in a foregoing book. [*Ant.* 18.4] **The names of those sons were James and Simon, whom Alexander commanded to be crucified.** (*Ant.* 20.101-102) (Emphasis mine)

The names of two of Judas' sons, James and Simon, match up with the list of Jesus' supposed brothers. Most scholars would scoff at this comparison, simply stating that James and Simon were common names. This could be sheer coincidence. But there is much more to this than most scholars could even imagine. First of all, the timing of James' and Simon's deaths occurred at a very pivotal point in Church history. This can be determined by the number of direct and indirect references to the deaths. In Acts 5:36-39, the author of Acts mentioned the death of Judas the Galilean when discussing the fate of the apostles. As discussed earlier, Acts purposely replaced the sons of Judas the Galilean with Judas. This same period of Church history was also detailed in the Slavonic Josephus. There, the authorities questioned how to treat the Jewish Christians. (3) However, the most ingenious hiding place for this crucifixion of James and Simon comes from the Gospels.

Then the mother of Zebedee's sons came to Jesus with her sons and kneeling down, asked a favor of him.
"What is it you want?" he asked.
She said, "Grant that one of these two sons of mine may sit at your right and the other at your left in your kingdom."

"You don't know what you are asking," Jesus said to them. "Can you drink the cup I am going to drink?"

"We can," they answered.

Jesus said to them, "You will indeed drink from my cup, but to sit at my right or left is not for me to grant. These places belong to those for whom they have been prepared by my Father."

When the ten heard about this, they were indignant with the two brothers. (Matt. 20:20-24) (See also Mark 10:35-41).

This supposed exchange between the family of Zebedee and Jesus occurred in Matthew and Mark but was omitted from Luke. It is my contention that Luke/Acts included the crucifixions of Simon and James in Acts 5:36-39 and Acts 12:1-19, while Matthew and Mark masked the real situation in their respective Gospels.

Before attempting to align real historical events to the above passage, it would be instructive to first question the passage as it now stands. Throughout this book, I have emphasized that the followers of "Jesus" during his lifetime included John the Baptist (the Sadduc), his brothers James and John, and a much younger Cephas. If anyone would have been seated at his right or left, it would have been one of these individuals. That is why the verse in Matt. 20.24 rings true, as the followers would have been indignant with the two brothers.

Who, then, were the two brothers? According to the Gospels, these two were James and John, the sons of Zebedee. In another passage, these brothers were called the sons of Thunder. It is safe to say that their father would have been a very powerful man if he were referred to as Thunder. The only knowledge we have of Zebedee comes from Matthew 4:21-22, where the sons left their father in his fishing boat in order to follow Jesus. Note that the lowly Zebedee did not appear to be endowed with such power and that he did not bother to follow Jesus either. He certainly did not warrant the nickname Thunder.

To add insult to injury, Zebedee not only lost his sons to Jesus but his wife as well. In the above passage, Zebedee's wife pleaded with Jesus for her two sons. What was she doing traveling the countryside with this preacher while her husband toiled at home with his nets? Something smells fishy here.

Then there is the wife of Zebedee, the mother of James and John. According to Matthew, she interceded with Jesus on behalf of her two sons. How did this unrelated woman gain such access to Jesus? In that society, it would be very difficult to explain her actions in regards to her husband and her audacity with an unrelated preacher. Certainly, something seems amiss.

And, we must also consider the two sons of Zebedee. According to the above passage, they were to drink the same cup that Jesus was soon to drink, that being crucifixion. According to Acts 12:2, Herod Agrippa put James, the son of Zebedee, to death by the sword. While this was a violent death, it was not crucifixion. John, on the other hand, was not martyred. According to tradition, he lived into his 90's and wrote the Book of Revelation on the island of Patmos, in modern day Turkey. So, neither son of Zebedee was crucified, the very act that the above passage suggests.

If James and John, the sons of Zebedee, were not the brothers referred to above, then who were they? First, we must search the pages of Josephus to find two brothers who endured crucifixion.

...the sons of Judas the Galilean were now slain; I mean of that Judas who caused the people to revolt, when Cyrenius came to take an account of the estates of the Jews, as we have shown in a foregoing book. The names of those sons were James and Simon, whom Alexander commanded to be crucified. (*Ant.* 20.102)

While the above passage about the cup does not make any sense in connection with the sons of Zebedee, it does mesh perfectly with the sons of Judas the Galilean. According to my hypothesis, Judas the Galilean was the Messiah figure upon which the legend of Jesus was built. Consider this scenario: Judas' wife (Mary Magdalene?) came before him with their two sons. She asked her husband to place one of their sons on his right hand and one on his left. This request seems a bit more reasonable than the request of the Zebedee family. But even the request of Judas' own wife would have raised some resentment. In the tradition of the Maccabees, the brothers were to follow in the succession. Jesus (Judas) also had brothers, and they were referred to as the Pillars by Paul. These were the individuals who would follow in the line of command.

It is quite possible that the whole event recorded by Mark and Matthew was a story invented by the early Church to explain the deaths of Simon and James. The importance of James and Simon can be deduced by enumerating their appearances in Acts and in the Slavonic Josephus. Acts chapter 12 simply reworked the arrest and deaths of the brothers while Acts chapter 5 referred to Judas the Galilean in place of the chronologically correct sons of Judas the Galilean. The Slavonic Josephus also referred to this sensitive time in Church history. (4) In short, the sons of Judas the Galilean drank the same cup as their father; they were crucified!

The list of brothers in Matthew included Simon and James, the two sons who were crucified. What about the other two brothers listed in Matthew: Judas and Joseph? There are a few hints of their relationship to "Jesus" in the book of Acts. In Acts 1:23, the author introduced Joseph called Barsabbas and also known as Justus. This Joseph, along with Matthias, supposedly vied for the position of twelfth apostle, vacated by the traitor, Judas Iscariot. (As will be discussed in the next chapter, there was never a traitor named Judas Iscariot. The traitor was actually Paul, the apostle to the Gentiles.) The Acts' narrative replaced the election of James, the brother of Jesus, with this election of Matthias. James replaced the only person who really died, that being Jesus (Judas the Galilean).

Joseph Barsabbas, also known as Justus, was purposely placed into the story as a way to give some credit to James. The two nicknames given to Joseph relate to James. James the Just and Joseph, known as Justus, were closely related. In addition, the nickname Barsabbas means son of the bather, a possible reference to ritual purity, a characteristic also attached to James. It is also possible that this Barsabbas could have been Barrabbas (son of the rabbi) or even Barabbas (son of the father). These nicknames could also have been closely connected with Jesus.

Another Barsabbas can be identified in Acts 15:22. When James made his decision at the Council of Jerusalem, he supposedly dispatched Judas called Barsabbas to Antioch. Again, the Barsabbas figure worked closely with James. This means that the Barsabbas men, Joseph and Judas, were trusted disciples and probably related by blood to James. It should not be surprising that the two Barsabbas individuals were named Joseph and Judas, the very names of the two brothers, or rather, the remaining two sons of Jesus.

It is my conjecture that Joseph and Judas were twin sons of Judas the Galilean (Jesus). It would not have been unusual for a religious figure to name twins Joseph and Judas, as these were the fathers of the Northern and Southern Israelite kingdoms. It should also be noted that the apostle lists suggest that twins were part of the Twelve. Thomas called Didymus was one of the Twelve. (John 20:24) According to John, this Thomas was famous for doubting the resurrection of Jesus. However, the term Didymus may actually be the star of the passage. Didymus means twin. The question is this: who was Thomas? In the Synoptic Gospels, there was a Thomas, a Judas (son of James) and a Thaddaeus. These three distinct names may have been used for just one person or may have represented two separate individuals, Judas and Joseph. Certainly, Judas and Thaddaeus were probably one individual. Josephus also mentioned a Theudas, who was beheaded shortly before the sons of Judas the Galilean were crucified. This Theudas may well have been Thaddaeus or Judas, son of James.

One other possibility exists. In Acts 4:36, another Joseph was mentioned. This Joseph was nicknamed Barnabas, which means son of encouragement. Barnabas was part of the early ministry of Paul but may have been responsible for Paul's eventual removal from the movement. In Galatians, Paul wrote that James sent certain individuals to Antioch who heavily influenced Cephas. He also stated that Barnabas was led astray as well. It is interesting that Paul did not identify the representatives of James. Was this omission purposeful or were the representatives nondescript? Even though the Acts' version of the Antioch affair is historically inaccurate, there may be a few tidbits of truth woven within the story. Acts actually identified the representatives sent by James.

Then the apostles and elders, with the whole church, decided to choose some of their own men and send them to Antioch with Paul and **Barnabas**. They chose **Judas (called Barsabbas)** and Silas, two men who were leaders among the brothers. (Acts 15:22) (Emphasis mine)

Those sent by James included Judas Barsabbas and Barnabas. (To completely confuse matters, Acts also had Paul being sent to confront himself. See Chapter 14, "Acts - Propaganda of the Church," to get an understanding of this whole passage.) It is interesting that the author of Acts had James sending both Judas Barsabbas and Joseph Barnabas to Antioch. This may be one reason why Paul did not identify these individuals to his disciples in Galatia. If Judas Barsabbas and Joseph Barnabas were both sons of Judas the Galilean (Jesus), then the case against Paul would have been insurmountable. How could you defend your Gospel against the brothers of Jesus (represented by James) and the sons of Jesus (represented by Judas Barsabbas and Joseph Barnabas). Instead, Paul hid the identities of his opponents so that his disciples could not easily ascertain the truth.

Acts placed the names of Jesus' sons alongside James, the brother of the Lord. What can explain this relationship between these sons and James? Eisenman argues that James may well have been the disciple whom Jesus loved. (5) If so, then Jesus assigned his mother or more likely, his own wife (Mary) and younger sons (Joseph and Judas) to the care of James. (See John 19:25-27) Most probably, James cared for Jesus' family after the crucifixion.

We have identified the four sons of Judas the Galilean (Jesus). They were named Simon, James, Joseph and Judas. Using my Judas the Galilean timeline, Judas and Mary married around 4 BCE, when Judas was a young man of twenty. From 4 BCE to 6 CE, Judas most likely fathered the four above mentioned sons. Considering that James and Simon were leaders of the movement when they were crucified in 46-48 CE, this would have made them approximately forty to fifty years old. Judas and Joseph were no doubt younger and were employed by James as messengers (Judas Barsabbas) and as monitors (Barnabas). Barnabas worked with Paul but sided with Cephas in the argument at Antioch.

In the early years of Jesus' movement, people may have questioned his claim as Messiah. They would have pointed to his wife and sons, and asked, "Could this man that we know really be the Messiah? He is a fine man, the husband of Mary and the father of James, Simon, Joseph and Judas, but could he be the Messiah as well?" This question was answered as Judas rallied the people to his vision of the "Kingdom of God."

One problem exists with the above scenario: according to Josephus, Judas the Galilean had another son, named Menahem. This Menahem marched to Jerusalem in 66 CE as a Messiah figure after attacking the armory at Masada. (*War* 2.433-434) Why was Menahem left out of the Gospel story? The answer is quite simple: Menahem was born to Judas and Mary well beyond the Census tax revolt. Judas would have already been the apparent Messiah. That is why later children would not be mentioned in an account which questioned Judas' (Jesus') qualifications for being a Messiah. A later date for Menahem's birth can also be deduced from the name itself. Menahem means "comforter", and this may have been the comfort that Mary needed as her husband headed to eventual destruction at the hands of Rome.

If Judas suffered arrest and crucifixion around 19-21 CE, this would have made him approximately forty-three to forty-five years old, assuming he were born in 25 BCE (the Slavonic Josephus' account of the Star of Bethlehem). Menahem could easily have been born in the late first or early second decade of the first century. If Menahem were born in 10 - 15 CE, then he would have been fifty-one to fifty-five years old at his death. This is a reasonable age for a religious leader. Many, including myself (6), have questioned Josephus on this point, thinking Menahem was a grandson and not a son. This doubt is based upon the faulty assumption that Judas was killed in 6 CE, at the Census. The more logical date for his death would have been in the early administration of Pilate, around 19 CE. (See Chapter 1 - "Time Markers", in the section titled "Pontius Pilate.")

Thus, the four brothers could easily have been four sons of Jesus. The addition of Menahem does not disturb this interpretation as noted above. All five sons were integral parts of the Fourth Philosophy: Simon and James were important leaders and were signaled out for crucifixion; Joseph and Judas helped their uncle James as emissaries and Menahem claimed Kingship for a short while during the Jewish War. Just as the brothers of Jesus were downplayed in the Gospels and Acts, the sons were simply expunged. The method for this creative history will be explored in the next chapter entitled, "The Twelve."

CHAPTER 17

JESUS AND THE TWELVE

We have already investigated the passages concerning Jesus' birth and his family. Now, we shall examine the Twelve Apostles, Jesus' closest disciples. I have listed the Twelve as enumerated in the four Gospels and Acts and have also listed the Pillar Apostles written about by Paul around 44 CE. Paul's list is the earliest by at least fifty years, followed by Mark (95-105 CE), Luke, Matthew and Acts (125 CE) and last by John (140 CE). These dates are all approximations as no one will ever prove the exact dates of these documents. (1) Even so, we can discover much by comparing the listings.

	MARK	**MATTHEW**	**LUKE**	**ACTS**	**JOHN**	**PAUL**
	(Mk. 3:16-19)	(Matt. 10:2-4)	(Luke 6:14-16)	(Acts 1:13)	(John - var.)	(Gal. 2:9)
1.	Simon Peter	Simon Peter	Simon Peter	Peter	Simon Cephas	Cephas
2.	James*	James*	James	James	son of Zebedee	James
3.	John*	John*	John	John	son of Zebedee	John
4.	Andrew	Andrew	Andrew	Andrew	Andrew	
5.	Philip	Philip	Philip	Philip	Philip	
6.	Bartholomew	Bartholomew	Bartholomew	Bartholomew		
7.	Matthew	Matthew	Matthew	Matthew	Nathanael	
8.	Thomas	Thomas	Thomas	Thomas	Thomas - Didymus	
9.	James - son of Alphaeus	James - son of Alphaeus	James - son of Alphaeus	James - son of Alphaeus		

10.	Thaddaeus	Thaddaeus	Judas - son of James	Judas - son of James	Judas - not Judas Iscariot	
11.	Simon the Zealot	Simon the Zealot	Simon the Zealot	Simon the Zealot		
12.	Judas Iscariot	Judas Iscariot	Judas Iscariot	Judas (Matthias)**	Judas - the son of Simon Iscariot	

* Also denoted as the sons of Zebedee and the sons of Thunder.
** Matthias replaced Judas Iscariot in the Twelve Apostle scheme after Judas' suicide.

Four of the Twelve Apostles had little to offer the Synoptic Gospel writers. Andrew, Philip, Bartholomew and Matthew appeared in the Synoptic Gospels and Acts, but we only know that Andrew was the brother of Peter and Matthew was a former tax collector. Other than that, these Apostles just fill out the list of Twelve. Only two items can be taken from their names. Andrew was the brother of a great Apostle. This conforms to what we know of the movement; that it was heavily influenced by certain families. The family of Judas the Galilean was represented by Judas' brothers and his sons. It would be likely that Peter also had many brothers and sons participating in the movement.

Second, Matthew was represented as a former tax collector. Once again, this may well confirm my Judas the Galilean hypothesis. The first meeting between Jesus and Matthew occurs in Matt. 9:9-13.

As Jesus went on from there, he saw a man named Matthew sitting at the tax collector's booth. "Follow me," he told him, and Matthew got up and followed him.

While Jesus was having dinner at Matthew's house, many tax collectors and "sinners" came and ate with him and his disciples. When the Pharisees saw this, they asked his disciples, "Why does your teacher eat with tax collectors and 'sinners'?"

On hearing this, Jesus said, "it is not the healthy who need a doctor, but the sick. But go and learn what this means: 'I desire mercy, not sacrifice.' For I have not come to call the righteous, but sinners."

This passage confirms that Jesus absolutely believed that the tax collectors were sinners and needed to stop practicing their profession. This attitude was criticized by the Pharisees, as they did not want to have any contact with these sinners. Jesus did not dispute that these tax collectors were sinners, he just believed that they could be rehabilitated. So, in reality, this action on Jesus' part would have been accepted by the Pharisees, once they understood that it was the sinners who were repenting rather than Jesus being influenced by sinners. However, the Herodian party would have been outraged by Jesus' actions. The Herodians were the tax collectors for Rome. Taking the tax collectors off the streets would have been a financial blow to them and could not be allowed to continue.

Matthew may have been the nickname given to Levi. In Mark 2:13-17 and Luke 5:27-32, the same passage was attributed to Levi and not Matthew, even though Mark and Luke mentioned Matthew and not Levi as one of the Twelve. This may point to the importance of the name Matthew. Matthew means "Gift of God". It is quite probable that Levi became a very vocal supporter of Jesus, as converts often show the most zeal. This zeal would have earned Levi the name of Matthew. It should not be forgotten that Judas the Galilean's co-teacher (and Father?) at the Golden Eagle Temple Cleansing was named Matthias which, also means "Gift of God." So, this nickname would have been a great honor, and it would have been proof positive that God could do anything. Even the Herodian supporters could be rehabilitated.

In the book of John, there was a Nathanael, possibly another name for Matthew. Like Matthew, Nathanael means "Gift of God." Also, this account of Nathanael occurred in the early part of Jesus' ministry, just as the calling of Levi happened before the enumeration of the Twelve. It is quite likely, therefore, that Nathanael was not another Apostle but just a different name for one already listed in the Synoptic Gospels.

Philip may have been just filler. He was not the Philip of Acts 6:5, 8:4-8 and 8:26-40. That Philip was part of the mythical Seven, as detailed in Chapter 14. Philip is a Greek name meaning "the lover of horses". It seems odd that Jesus would have had any Greek names represented in his Twelve Apostle scheme. After all, the Twelve represented the twelve tribes of Israel. Although listed in all the Synoptic Gospels, nothing further was noted about Philip. In the book of John, Philip introduced Jesus to Nathanael, proclaiming that Jesus was the one Moses promised in the Law. (John 1:43-45) Other than that, nothing can be produced concerning this Philip.

Like Philip, Bartholomew was listed in all the Synoptic Gospels. And like Philip, nothing else was written about him. He, too, was filler for the Twelve.

THE SONS OF JESUS

The next four names in the Apostle list have something in common with the supposed list of brothers, as detailed in Matthew 13:55. These names are James, Simon, Joseph and Judas. In the Twelve Apostle scheme, these individuals are named James, the son of Alphaeus, Simon the Zealot, Judas or Thaddaeus, and Thomas.

James and Simon were the two sons of Judas the Galilean. They were arrested by Agrippa I in 43 CE and were subsequently crucified under Tiberius Alexander in 46-48 CE. It is revealing that the Gospel writers designated Simon as the Zealot. Most assume that this Simon was a convert from the Zealot movement, but there is nothing to support this claim. According to Josephus, James and Simon were crucified, drinking the same cup as their father, Jesus (Judas the Galilean). The convergence of the Acts' story concerning the arrest of Simon and Peter by Agrippa I with the actual arrest of the sons of Judas the Galilean has never been fully appreciated. These individuals were leaders in the early movement and their deaths were devastating to that movement. That is one reason why the story of Jesus predicting their deaths by crucifixion was so important. It helped the early movement cope with the loss of two valued leaders. In keeping with Gospel protocol, the two brothers were not totally removed from the story but were rewritten into less important roles.

Judas and Thomas were also sons of Jesus. These two were twins as suggested by their names. Judas was nicknamed Thaddaeus or even Theudas, a combination of Judas and Thomas. (The name Thomas means twin.) There probably also was a son Joseph who was known as Thomas. Thomas and Thaddaeus appear in Acts as Joseph Barsabbas and Judas Barsabbas. They were younger than Simon and James and were utilized as messengers and monitors by James, the brother of Jesus. (See Acts 15:22) Little else is known about the four sons of Jesus as the Gospels and Acts only preserved their names but not their deeds.

THE CENTRAL THREE OR THE PILLARS

The Four Gospels, Acts and Paul wrote of the Central three Apostles. These Three were part of the Twelve and were named Cephas (Peter), James and John. Surely, in outward appearance, the naming of the Three confirms the New Testament's continuity from Paul to the Synoptic Gospels to the Gospel of John. No one can doubt the existence of the Three in relation to Jesus. If Jesus existed, then these Three also existed. But as we have seen, Jesus was really a rewrite of Judas the Galilean. Could there also have been a rewrite of the Three? It appears so!

The first mention of the Three or the Pillar Apostles comes from Paul in his letter to the Galatians. This letter was written around 44 CE and concerns the argument between Cephas and Paul. The same argument was recorded by Josephus in the King Izates conversion. This conflict between Ananias and Eleazar can be positively identified at 44 CE. With knowledge of that date, it becomes possible to work backwards with the time markers given by Paul.

Then after **three years** [of my conversion], I went up to Jerusalem to get acquainted with Peter [Cephas] and stayed with him fifteen days. I saw none of the other apostles - **only James, the Lord's brother**. ...**Fourteen years later** I went up again to Jerusalem, this time with Barnabas. I went in response to a revelation and set before them the gospel that I preached among the Gentiles. But I did this privately to those who seemed to be leaders, for fear that I was running or had run my race in vain. ...**James, Peter [Cephas] and John, those reputed to be Pillars**, gave me and Barnabas the right hand of fellowship when they recognized the grace given to me. ...When Peter came to Antioch, I opposed him to his face, because he was in the wrong. Before certain men came from James, he used to eat with the Gentiles. But when they arrived, he began to draw back and separate himself from the Gentiles because he was afraid of those who belonged to the circumcision group. (Gal. 1:18 - 2:12)

Don't we have the right to take a believing wife along with us, as do the other apostles and the **Lord's brothers and Cephas**? (1 Cor. 9:5) (Emphasis mine)

Paul claimed to have gone off into Arabia after his conversion. Three years later he traveled to Jerusalem and met with Cephas and James, the Lord's brother. Fourteen years later, he once again returned to Jerusalem to meet with the leadership. This leadership was comprised of James, Cephas and John. From the context of his letter, James and John were the brothers of Jesus and not the sons of a Zebedee. This is confirmed by the passage in Corinthians where Paul identified the important apostles as Cephas and the Lord's brothers.

In all, Paul's two visits to Jerusalem covered a span of seventeen years after his conversion. If the letter to the Galatians were written in 44 CE, then the latest possible date for Paul's conversion would have been 27 CE. However, it is probable that a lengthy period of time elapsed between the second visit to Jerusalem and the conflict at Antioch. If this period covered five years, then Paul's conversion can be dated to around 22 CE, give or take a year or so. This would have been shortly after the crucifixion of Jesus as claimed by the *Memoranda*. (2) More importantly, for this discussion, James, the brother of the Lord, was a leader of the movement three years after Paul's conversion or by 25 CE. If so, then where were James and John, the sons of Zebedee?

According to the Gospels, Peter, along with James and John, the sons of Zebedee, were the central Three Apostles. (The brothers of Jesus were severely marginalized and even demonized by the Gospels.) How strange that Paul did not even acknowledge the existence of the sons of Zebedee. Obviously, either Paul or the Gospels told the truth about James and John, but both did not. Even though Paul often shaded the truth to bolster his own arguments, he would have had no reason to replace the sons of Zebedee with the brothers of Jesus. However, the Gospels had a strong motive behind replacing the brothers of Jesus with the sons of Zebedee. The Gospels were designed to separate Jesus from his family: his mother and his brothers as well as his wife and children. Thus, the only logical course would be to accept Paul's word concerning the central Three.

If James and John were the brothers of Jesus (Judas the Galilean), then the sons of Zebedee were pure inventions of the Gospel writers. In fact, the sons of Zebedee were composite figures, representing James and John, the brothers of Jesus and James, the son of Jesus. In the same way, Peter was a composite figure, representing Cephas and Simon (Simon the Zealot), the son of Jesus (Judas the Galilean). The following passages will prove this hypothesis.

John 1:42 - In this passage, the Gospel writer wanted to assure his audience that Peter was simply a translation of Cephas. "'You are Simon son of John. You will be called Cephas' (which when translated is Peter)."

Acts 12:1-18 - Here, Peter and James, the son of Zebedee, were arrested by Agrippa I and imprisoned. In Josephus' writings, Simon and James, the sons of Judas the Galilean were the ones arrested and eventually crucified. Acts simply inserted the composite figures into the roles of Simon and James. Note that Peter could not have been the one arrested by Agrippa I. This arrest occurred near the end of Agrippa's life, approximately 43-44 CE. Those imprisoned were later crucified under Tiberius Alexander in 46-48 CE. (*Ant.* 20.102) In the letter to the Galatians, Paul stated that Cephas was in Antioch in 44 CE. (The Antioch confrontation between Paul and Cephas occurred at the same time as a confrontation between Ananias and Eleazar, as recorded in *Ant.* 20.34-48. The King Izates confrontation occurred in 44 CE.) If Cephas were in Antioch in 44 CE, he could not have been in prison as claimed by Acts.

Matt. 20:20-23 - In this passage, James and John, the sons of Zebedee, replaced James and Simon, the sons of Jesus. The sons of Jesus (Judas the

Galilean) were the only brother combination who suffered crucifixion or drank of the same cup as Jesus.

Acts 12:1-18 - James, the son of Zebedee, had played the role of leader in the Gospels and early chapters of Acts. This was really the role occupied by James, the brother of Jesus. When Acts was forced to introduce James, the brother of Jesus, into the story, it had to eliminate the fictitious James, the son of Zebedee. Acts had this James beheaded. This beheading may have been modeled upon the beheading of Theudas in *Ant.* 20.97, which occurred a few years and just a few verses before the crucifixions of James and Simon, the sons of Judas the Galilean.

JUDAS ISCARIOT

No name in western civilization is as reviled as that of Judas Iscariot, the betrayer of Jesus Christ. But what do we know of this shadowy figure? Was he the one who fingered Jesus to the authorities as claimed by the Gospels or was he an invention of these later writers? But not only the "who" should be answered but the "why" as well. Why would one of the Twelve Apostles, the handpicked disciples of Jesus, betray him to the opposition High Priests and the hated Roman oppressors? Our investigation must begin with the earliest documents and then go forward to the later writings.

The first supposed mention of a betrayal of Jesus comes from the pen of Paul. The dating of Paul's four letters to the Romans, Corinthians and Galatians range from 38-45 CE, at least a generation or two earlier than the Gospels. Per my dating, at least three generations passed. Paul's letter can be dated using the King Izates episode (44 CE) and an earlier Council of Jerusalem, which occurred 17 years after Paul's conversion. This conversion can be calculated to the early 20's, a short time after the crucifixion of Jesus. The Gospels were, no doubt, penned after the writing of *Antiquities* in 93 CE.

This was Paul's only supposed mention of the betrayal:

For I received from the Lord what I passed on to you: The Lord Jesus, on the night he was **betrayed**, took bread, and when he had given thanks, he broke it and said, "This is my body, which is for you; do this in remembrance of me." (1 Cor. 11:23-24) (Emphasis mine)

Note that this information of the betrayal and the Lord's Supper came to Paul from the Risen Christ through revelations. This may comfort some, but it should raise an alarm to others. Most scholars date Corinthians to the

50's while I believe it to be from the late 30's to early 40's. Either way, this is an early date for the recording of a betrayal and for the Last Supper. An early date is usually helpful in determining whether information is reliable. However, there is no evidence that this was handed down to Paul from the Jewish apostles. In fact, in Galatians, Paul was quite vehement in claiming the superiority of his unique gospel over that of the Pillars. He categorically denied human intervention; he did not receive his gospel from any man! If so, then the whole betrayal might have been an invention of a very fertile yet unstable mind.

Just because Paul stated that the betrayal and Last Supper came from the Risen Christ, does not mean that the whole story should be thrown out. Paul's inspiration may have been used in interpreting events that had happened. The body and blood imagery may have been invention on Paul's part, but the Last Supper, a sharing of bread and wine, may have actually occurred. In the same way, the betrayal in Paul's imagination may have had an historical equivalent.

One other objection to the betrayal concerns the translation of betrayal from the Greek. According to the Greek lexicon, this could have been translated "handed over" or "delivered up," slightly different meanings that betrayed. It is very likely that Paul was not even referring to a betrayal, not to mention one committed by Judas Iscariot, one of the Twelve apostles. Paul could have simply meant that Jesus was captured. If so, then all speculation about Judas Iscariot becomes moot.

There are four distinct possibilities concerning this "handing over" process. The first involves the Romans and Pontius Pilate in particular. In Matt. 27:26, Pilate finally accepted the wishes of the crowd. "Then he released Barabbas to them. But he had Jesus flogged, and **handed him over** to be crucified." The same Greek word was used in Pilate **handing over** Jesus to be crucified. But does this tie into Paul's statement about that fateful night? The trial before Pilate occurred the next day, not the night of the Last Supper. Although it is tempting to attach Pilate and Jesus' crucifixion to Paul's description of the "handing over," the timing of events does not perfectly jibe.

The second possibility involves the Chief Priests, Annas and Caiaphas, those Jews aligned with Rome. In John 18:30, the Chief Priests said to Pilate, "If he were not a criminal, we would not have **handed him over** to you." Again, the same Greek word was used in **handing over** Jesus to Pilate. This occurred early in the morning. (John 18:10) This may very well be the answer to the how and why questions. The Chief Priests hated Jesus because he challenged their rule at the Temple. The trial before the Chief Priests occurred during the night and the "handing over" to Pilate happened at the end of the night. All these components are consistent with Paul's description of the Last Supper. Paul may have been referring to the Jews "handing over" Jesus to Pilate in general or to the High Priests in particular. Either way, this may have been the "betrayal" in Paul's mind.

This scenario is supported by the Slavonic Josephus.

The teachers of the Law were envenomed with envy and gave thirty talents to Pilate, in order that he should put him to death. And he, after he had taken [the money], gave them consent that they should themselves carry out their purpose. (3)

This may not be totally historical as it placed the blame for Jesus' crucifixion on the Jews. The only crimes committed by Pilate were greed and corruption. But the following should be noted. It was the Chief Priests and Jewish leaders who paid thirty talents to Pilate as a bribe, enabling them to crucify Jesus. The thirty talents correspond to the thirty pieces of silver supposedly paid to Judas Iscariot. That Judas is not even considered in the above passage is revealing. Obviously, the traditional story of Judas Iscariot was not known by the writer of this section of the Slavonic Josephus.

The third and fourth "betrayal" scenarios are similar in nature. The third involves one of the Twelve, Judas Iscariot. According to the Gospels, Judas "betrayed" Jesus on the night of his arrest. This has always been read into Paul's account, but Paul never mentioned Judas Iscariot or one of the Twelve. The assumed interpretation of the Greek word for "handed over" has been translated as "betrayed" because of the Gospel bias. This act would only be a betrayal if done by a disciple or friend. Pilate and the Chief Priests could not have betrayed Jesus although it could be argued that the Jews could have. Thus, the later interpretation of Judas Iscariot as the "betrayer" rules out the first two explanations for Jesus being "handed over." We will further explore the Judas Iscariot possibility below.

The fourth possibility concerns an unknown disciple "betraying" Jesus. This may explain why Paul did not mention Judas Iscariot. The betrayal may have been well known by Paul's time, but the myth associated with Judas Iscariot may not have been invented yet. This, too, will be further explored near the end of this section. In my opinion, the second and fourth scenarios make the most sense, as they fit into Paul's brief description of the "handing over" process.

But let us assume that a betrayal did occur. This assumption may be quite logical considering Jesus' mode of operation, always careful and on the move. For the Roman authorities to catch Jesus, they may have needed inside information. In the recent attempt to catch Osama Bin Laden, the United States spent tens of millions of dollars in an attempt to gather useful information from Afghan tribal lords. One can argue whether or not this money was well spent, but one point is perfectly clear: to catch an elusive figure is not easy and may require help from unexpected places. Someone in the Jesus camp or on the periphery may have provided some useful information to the High Priests and to the Romans. This information was very valuable, worth much more than the paltry thirty pieces of silver of Gospel lore. Thus, the motive for betrayal may have been primarily financial.

Paul did not mention Judas by name but only said that Jesus was "handed over." The modern reader (and translator) fills in the gap with the name Judas Iscariot, because that is the Gospel story. Yet it seems odd that Paul would not include the name of the betrayer if that person had some intimate connection with Jesus. Another passage by Paul may answer the question of whether an apostle betrayed Jesus.

For what I received I passed onto you as of first importance: that Christ died for your sins according to the Scriptures, that he was buried, that he was raised on the third day according to the Scriptures, and that he appeared to Peter, and then to the **Twelve**. After that, he appeared to more than five hundred of the brothers at the same time, most of whom are still living, though some have fallen asleep. Then he appeared to James, then to all the apostles, and last of all he appeared to me also, as to one abnormally born. (1 Cor. 15:3-8) (Emphasis mine)

Once again, Paul claimed his close ties to the Risen Christ. The beginning of the passage sounds like the Apostles' Creed and refers back to the Scriptures twice. These are the Old Testament Scriptures. Where in the Old Testament was it foretold of the Messiah dying for others' sins and where was the resurrection of Jesus mentioned? Paul's audience was comprised primarily of Gentiles who may not have questioned Paul's supposed knowledge of the Scriptures. It may be argued that Paul referred to the Suffering Servant of Isaiah chapter 53, but to claim this as proof of a new religion took guts, or simply a personal revelation.

Regardless how one views Paul, he does mention one very revealing fact concerning the betrayer. He wrote that Jesus appeared to Cephas and then to the **Twelve**. If this actually came from the pen of Paul, then it blows away the story of Judas Iscariot. According to Mark 16:9-14, Jesus appeared first to Mary Magdalene, then to two disciples as they walked in the countryside and then to the **Eleven**. Note that there are several discrepancies between the Gospel account and that of Paul. If the New Testament documents have been doctored, then some of the problems can be explained. But as they stand, Paul definitely stated that Jesus appeared to **Twelve not Eleven** apostles. If this is true, then no Judas Iscariot ever existed!

By examining the two accounts, one must question part of Paul's order. He never mentioned Mary Magdalene, which may have been his chauvinistic approach to the story. And he uncharacteristically put a definite number on the apostle scheme. Everywhere else in his writings, he speaks of apostles, but always an indefinite number. Thus, it is possible that the Twelve number was added by a later, not too bright, commentator. The 500 disciples also is absent from the Gospel account, but may have been added by Paul to lessen the influence of James. Note that in the Gospels, Jesus appeared to two disciples on the road to Emmaus. These two were probably Cephas and James, the brother of Jesus, the eventual leaders of the Church.

If these possible interpolations are removed from Paul's account, then it is much closer to the Gospel account. And if the Twelve in 1 Corinthians is bogus, then it is possible that Judas Iscariot actually betrayed Jesus. But why would any later church figure adjust this section of Paul's letter? Why would this later writer place the number Twelve into the text? Surely, the story of Judas Iscariot was securely in place by the late first century. But the same questions could be asked concerning Paul's naming of the Pillar Apostles. Why would someone change the sons of Zebedee into the brothers of Jesus? The answer to these questions is obvious. Paul did write that the brothers of Jesus were the Pillars and that Jesus appeared to the Twelve. No one with later knowledge would have made such glaring contradictions to the Gospel story. So, as it stands, Paul's mention of the Twelve may be closer to the truth than the Gospel insistence on the Eleven.

Do any other writings support Paul's claim for the Twelve? One non-canonical Gospel does support the Twelve apostle scenario as reported by our version of 1 Corinthians. The Gospel of Peter said this about the apostles after the death of Jesus, "But we, the **twelve disciples of the Lord**, wept and grieved; and each one returned to his home, grieving for what had happened." (vs. 59) This Gospel was written in the early second century, in the same general time period as Matthew and Luke. Obviously, even by the early second century, some parts of the Christian world had not yet learned of Judas Iscariot and his supposed betrayal. If Judas Iscariot actually existed, then his infamous story would have been known by all Christians. Judas could not have been forgotten by Paul or the churches utilizing the Gospel of Peter. The Gospel of Peter was eventually branded heretical, and as a result, removed from circulation. However, this one mention of the Twelve strongly bolsters Paul's claim for the Twelve. The claim for the Twelve appears solid, so let us examine other aspects of Judas Iscariot.

The name Judas is revealing in that this name approximates Judah or the

Jews. No other name could have been better suited for representing the Jews in general and Judas the Galilean in particular. In Paul's letters, he constantly denigrated the Jewish Christian movement as weak, and at one point wished that they would emasculate themselves (Gal. 5:12). The Synoptic Gospels pitted Jesus against the Jews even though he was a Jewish Messiah figure. And the book of John stated that the Jews were children of the devil (John 8:42-47). This betrayer was conveniently named Judas to condemn a whole nation as well as the individual, Judas the Galilean.

Iscariot is also a very interesting name. If the I and s are reversed, then we are left with sicariot, which approximates Sicarios, or the assassins of the late Fourth Philosophy. Josephus wrote that this group arose in the later 50's or early 60's and was bent on wreaking havoc with Roman authority. These assassins fought Rome with short knives, hidden within their tunics. They were the most fanatical of the Fourth Philosophy, but this splinter group was simply an offshoot of a larger resistance movement against Rome. The Sicarii may very well have been associated with James, the brother of Jesus. In Josephus' account of James' death (*Ant.* 20.200), the Sicarii became extremely active right after the murder. In addition, the youngest son of Judas the Galilean, Menahem, controlled a small group of Sicarii. After Menahem's death, these Sicarii followed Eleazar (grandson of Judas the Galilean) to Masada, where they committed mass suicide. Today, these Sicarii are honored in Israel for their historic opposition to Roman rule.

Placing the blame of the betrayal on Judas Iscariot clearly incriminated the Jews and particularly those Jews who rebelled against Rome. The Gospel writers knew of a betrayal and simply filled in the details, which distanced their cause (Gentile Christianity) from that of the Fourth Philosophy (Jewish Christianity). Thus, the name Judas Iscariot was an invention of the Gospel writers, built upon the scant information provided by Paul and the general negative climate of society towards these revolutionary elements of the Jewish religion.

In John 12:4-6, we learn of Judas' love of money.

But one of his disciples, Judas Iscariot, who was later to betray him, objected, "Why wasn't this perfume sold and the money given to the poor? It was worth a year's wages." He did not say this because he cared about the poor but because he was a thief; as keeper of the money bag, he used to help himself to what was put into it.

According to John, Judas Iscariot was a thief. This is consistent with Josephus' description of members of the Fourth Philosophy, calling them bandits. This whole line of attack upon Judas Iscariot was a backhanded slap at Judas the Galilean, the historical Jesus. The Gospel of John was stating that the bandits were opposed to Jesus, opposed to God. In addition, John asserted that Judas Iscariot was a hypocrite in that he really did not care for the poor. Once again, this ties exactly to Josephus' feelings towards the Fourth Philosophy. Besides all this, one must ask the question: why did Jesus place Judas Iscariot in charge of the money bag? Can you imagine a modern politician placing such a no-good aide in charge of finances? This, in and of itself, would bring down a candidate. It is unbelievable that Jesus would have been so unaware of the situation.

One other sad note should be added concerning the mythical Judas Iscariot. According to the Gospel account, Judas committed suicide after betraying Jesus. In the most famous mass suicide in recorded history, Eleazar, the grandson of Judas the Galilean, led the Sicarii to Masada, where they were surrounded and besieged by the Roman army. After putting up a valiant fight against this mighty army, Eleazar convinced his followers to take their own lives as opposed to letting the Romans slaughter them all. Approximately nine hundred men, women and children took part in the mass suicide. The Gospel story of the mythical Judas Iscariot committing suicide should not surprise us, in that many events of the time were twisted into the Gospels' new and improved history.

If one reads the New Testament as it is written, the betrayer could not have been Judas Iscariot because Paul and the non-canonical Gospel of Peter both stated that Jesus appeared to the Twelve. If the Twelve was a later interpolation in both writings, the story of Judas Iscariot also rings false as this figure clearly represented the revolutionary Jews. One thing is certain: the Gospel writers had no reservations about twisting dates, names and events to their own purposes. This was done in the case of Judas Iscariot as a way of creating a compelling story. And what a story it has been!

Although Judas Iscariot can be disproved from the above, could there have been some sort of betrayal? The later Gospel writers may have inserted the mythical Judas Iscariot into the role of betrayer, replacing someone else. To answer this question, we must go back and understand Jesus' mind-set as he entered Jerusalem.

Rejoice greatly, O Daughter of Zion! Shout Daughter of Jerusalem! See, your king comes to you, righteous and having salvation, gentle and riding on a donkey, on a colt, the foal of a donkey. (Zechariah 9:9)

When Jesus entered Jerusalem, he proudly rode into the city on a donkey, fulfilling the prophecy of Zechariah. We should not be so naive to think that Jesus was unaware of the Scriptures. Jesus knew exactly what he was doing.

The Chief Priests knew as well. This act of fulfilling prophecy was a claim to kingship. The Messiah had arrived!

If Jesus believed himself to be Messiah (he did), then there is reason to believe that Jesus foresaw victory on the Mount of Olives, not arrest and imprisonment. Scholars on the whole have ignored Zechariah chapter 14, where God promised to destroy the nations who dared to fight against Israel.

Then the Lord will go out and fight against those nations as he fights in the day of battle. On that day his feet will stand on the Mount of Olives. …This is the plague with which the Lord will strike all the nations that fought against Jerusalem. Their flesh will rot in their sockets, and their tongues will rot in their mouths. On that day men will be stricken by the Lord with great panic. Each man will seize the hand of another and they will attack each other. Judas too will fight at Jerusalem. (Zechariah 14:3-4; 12-14) (4)

Jesus believed in the prophecy of Zechariah when he rode the donkey into Jerusalem. I am convinced he also believed in Zechariah concerning this battle on the Mount of Olives. Note that God promised to intervene and the enemy would be stricken with great panic. In fact, the enemy was to turn upon itself. All the Jews had to do was start the fight and God would finish it.

According to Luke, at the Last Supper, before heading out to the Mount of Olives, the disciples said, "See Lord, here are two swords." "That is enough," he replied. For Jesus, two swords were plenty. Any fight that they started would end with God on their side, a sure and final victory. So here we have it: Jesus and the disciples were ready to rumble, but it takes two to tango. It was at this point in time that the betrayer story had its genesis.

Although John played the party line in regards to Judas Iscariot, his betrayal scene is curiously different from the other Gospels.

Leaning back against Jesus, he asked him, "Lord, who is it?"

Jesus answered, "It is the one to whom I will give this piece of bread when I have dipped it into the dish." Then, dipping the piece of bread, he gave it to Judas Iscariot, son of Simon. As soon as Judas took the bread, Satan entered into him.

"What you are about to do, do quickly," Jesus told him, but no one at the meal understood why Jesus said this to him. Since Judas had charge of the money, some thought Jesus was telling him to buy what was needed for the Feast, or to give something to the poor. As soon as Judas had taken the bread, he went out. And it was night. (John 13:25-30)

In John's story, Jesus dipped bread and gave it to Judas, who immediately went out to alert the High Priest. If Jesus believed in the prophecy of Zechariah, then the above scene with some follower was necessary in order to arrange an armed confrontation on the Mount of Olives. (This could not have been Judas Iscariot, for Paul knew nothing about such an individual.) Jesus fully expected God to come to the rescue as was promised in Zechariah. Thus, Jesus and his disciples prayed, hoping to prod God into action. When the armed guards of the Chief Priest arrived, Jesus expected to be soon exalted. Instead, he was arrested and imprisoned. God did not honor his promise to Jesus! That is why Jesus groaned these unforgettable words as he hung upon the cross, "My God, My God, why have you forsaken me?"

Later Christians could not bear to accept the fact that Jesus had failed on the Mount of Olives. The original story had to be altered. First, Jesus had to believe that the fight on the Mount of Olives could not be won. Thus, Jesus was made to talk about his impending doom, even though his disciples expected victory. Second, the one sent out to fetch the guards was made to be a betrayer. (This must have been done after Paul because Paul simply stated that Jesus was "handed over" or "delivered up," not betrayed.) This betrayer later took on the name Judas Iscariot as a way to incriminate the Jews in general and the Fourth Philosophy in particular. (Again, Paul stated that the Risen Jesus was seen by the Twelve, proving there was no Judas Iscariot.)

As with most of the Gospels' and Acts' stories, some truth lies hidden beneath the surface. Although Judas Iscariot was invented, there may have been a person sent to alert the High Priest. Unfortunately, historians have accepted the Gospel version, never acknowledging that Jesus may have wanted to win the fight against Rome. The traditional story has to ignore the triumphant entry into Jerusalem and the cleansing of the Temple, for both acts were statements of Jewish kingship. Jesus wanted to be the Messiah, the chosen one of God. He had no desire to offer himself up as a sacrifice.

The above scenario of Jesus' true ambition is probably true, in that no real betrayal occurred. But somewhere along the line, a betrayal event did circulate among the early Church. As has been explained, the Gospels and Acts often took events from history and twisted them into the stories we know today. For example, the Peter and Cornelius meeting (Acts 10) was an attempt to place Paul's theology onto Peter. Thus, the conversion of Cornelius was an act of inclusion into the Church. The parallel version in Josephus concerned Simon and Agrippa, and the thrust of that meeting centered on exclusion from the Temple. The book of Acts turned an exclusionary event into an act of inclusion. This same type of trick may have also occurred with the betrayal.

There was only one Apostle who actually betrayed the Jewish Christian movement. That Apostle was none other than Paul. Paul was a member of the movement for approximately twenty years, and then was removed because of his antinomian teachings. According to Paul, all the Jews turned their backs upon him and his gospel (Galatians). It was at this point that the war between Paul and James (and Cephas) began. The Pseudoclementine literature painted Paul as the "Enemy" of the Church. This was after Paul attacked James and almost killed him in Jerusalem, around the time of the famine (mid to late 40's). This was also the time when the sons of Judas the Galilean (James and Simon) were captured and later crucified. Paul probably had something to do with their capture and eventual execution.

The betrayal of Jesus by Judas Iscariot never occurred. However, a betrayal of the sons of Judas the Galilean (Jesus) probably did happen. And there was only one man who could have perpetrated such an act. That man was Paul. Paul knew the leaders of the Church, and he had a vendetta to settle. The Pseudoclementine literature did not simply make Paul the "Enemy" for any good purpose. Paul threatened the Church with every word he spoke and every letter he wrote. No doubt, the tradition of Paul's betrayal was very deep within the Jewish community. After the demise of Jewish Christianity (post Jewish war, or post 73 CE), the Gentile Church had a monumental restoration project on its hands: how to make Paul the hero and not the villain of Christian history. Obviously, the betrayal of Paul had to be erased or somehow altered. This betrayal label was successfully transferred from Paul to the mythical Judas Iscariot. (Even Paul had never heard of Judas Iscariot!) This bait and switch methodology worked well throughout the Gospels and Acts. It has worked for two thousand years.

MATTHIAS

If Judas Iscariot was mythical, he did not really die. Then it follows that a Matthias did not replace Judas Iscariot. Who really did die? That person was Judas the Galilean, titled Jesus. So, the correct question would be: who replaced Jesus? From various sources already detailed in this book, James, the brother of the Lord, was the person who replaced Jesus in the leadership role within the movement. James then ruled with John the Baptist or the Sadduc. When John was beheaded in 35-36 CE, James became the number one leader in the Jewish Christian movement, and Cephas replaced John as the number two leader.

So, where did this Matthias come from? In Acts 1:23-26, Matthias was chosen over Joseph Barsabbas, known as Justus. First, the nickname Justus or Just was also the nickname for James, the brother of Jesus. Justus or Just means Righteous, and James was known for his righteousness. The author of Acts slighted James, the brother of Jesus, by making him a second place finisher to Matthias. This would have seemed payback to the Gentile Christian Church as James had once hounded Paul, the spiritual founder of the Gentile Church. Second, since Judas the Galilean was being replaced, it must have seemed quite amusing to use Matthias. Judas the Galilean had replaced Matthias as leader of the movement after Matthias' death in 4 BCE, after the Golden Eagle Temple Cleansing. Using Matthias as a name to replace a Judas was a clever move. Only this present study has unmasked this peculiar name game.

CONCLUSION

In reality, the Twelve were much different than the Gospel versions. In the Gospels, these men came from different parts of society and were all non-family members. The current study has determined that the Twelve were all about family. Two members, James and John, were the brothers of Jesus. Four others, Thomas, Judas, Simon and James, were the sons of Jesus. Cephas, who became a later leader within the Church, was also probably related to Jesus. And Judas Iscariot was a rude way to represent the flesh and blood Jesus. This Judas Iscariot was none other than Judas the Galilean. So, the whole family was represented in the Twelve. The only one missing was John the Baptist, a cousin of Jesus. According to Luke 1:36, Elizabeth, the mother of John, was a relative of Mary, the mother of Jesus. The only reason that John the Baptist was omitted from the Twelve was because he had to be written out of the story. This will be detailed in Chapter 18, "Jesus and John the Baptist".

CHAPTER 18

JESUS AND JOHN THE BAPTIST

John the Baptist is the key to unraveling the riddle of the historical Jesus. According to the Gospels, John's life and death had a close proximity to Jesus' life and death. In fact, the dating of John's ministry is crucial in determining the years in which Jesus preached the Kingdom of Heaven. Therefore, it is necessary to investigate everything written about John in the earliest known documents. We will first lay out the traditional viewpoint concerning John, coming straight from the various Gospels. Then, an alternative history will be proposed based upon the Gospels and other early writings, such as Josephus' *Antiquities*, the Slavonic Josephus and the Pseudoclementine *Recognitions*.

THE TRADITIONAL VIEWPOINT

The angel answered, "The Holy Spirit will come upon you, and the power of the Most High will overshadow you. So the holy one to be born will be called the Son of God. Even Elizabeth your relative is going to have a child in her old age, and she who was said to be barren is in her sixth month. For nothing is impossible with God.

...At that time Mary got ready and hurried to a town in the hill country of Judah, where she entered Zechariah's home and greeted Elizabeth. When Elizabeth heard Mary's greeting, the baby [John] leaped in her womb, and Elizabeth was filled with the Holy Spirit. In a loud voice she exclaimed: "Blessed are you among women, and blessed is the child you will bear! But why am I so favored, that the mother of my Lord should come to me? As soon as the sound of your greeting reached my ears, the baby in my womb leaped for joy. Blessed is she who has believed that what the Lord has said to her will be accomplished." …Mary stayed with Elizabeth for about three months and then returned home. (Luke 1:35-56)

The Gospel of Luke has incredible detail concerning the parents of John as well as the reason for naming the child John. The above passage details the relationship between Mary and Elizabeth as well as their soon to be born sons, Jesus and John. Three major points can be gleaned from the above passage and Luke's earlier recorded history of the family. First, John and Jesus were related to one another, ensuring a close relationship between the two families. Second, John was born six months before Jesus, meaning that the two would have started their ministries at the age of thirty (Luke 3:23). Third, both Elizabeth and her fetus were aware that Mary carried the Son of God in her womb. If John believed in Jesus as a fetus, then he would have surely believed in him as an adult!

In the fifteenth year of the reign of Tiberius Caesar - when Pontius Pilate was governor of Judea, Herod tetrarch of Galilee, his brother Philip tetrarch of Iturea and Traconitis, and Lysanias tetrarch of Abilene - during the high priesthood of Annas and Caiaphas, the word of God came to John son of Zechariah in the desert. He went into all the country around the Jordan, preaching a baptism of repentance for the forgiveness of sins.

…John said to the crowds coming out to be baptized by him, "You brood of vipers! Who warned you to flee the coming wrath? Produce fruit in keeping with repentance."

…The people were waiting expectantly and were all wondering in their hearts if John might be the Christ. John answered them all, "I baptize you with water. But one more powerful than I will come, the thongs of whose sandals I am not worthy to untie. He will baptize you with the Holy Spirit and with fire. His winnowing fork is in his hands to clear the threshing floor and to gather the wheat into his barn, but he will burn up the chaff with unquenchable fire." (Luke 3:1-17)

The above passage describes John preparing the way for the Messiah, in fulfillment of Isaiah's prophecy (Isaiah 40:3-5). According to Luke, John's ministry began in the fifteenth year Tiberius' reign. Tiberius came to power in 14 CE, so John's emergence onto the stage can be dated to 28-29 CE. The beginning of Jesus' ministry can also be dated to his own baptism by John, around 29-30 CE (Luke 3:21-23). Since both Jesus and John were thirty years old, their birth dates must have been approximately 2-1 BCE. Unfortunately, Matthew placed Jesus' birth date at around 9-6 BCE while Luke had the birth at 6 CE. No matter how you figure, these dates do not jibe. Something must be wrong!

John's message of repentance was ideal for its purpose, to usher in the day of the Messiah. John was simply preparing the people for Jesus' arrival. Not all people were thrilled by John's message. Those in power were threatened by a new Messiah and were resistant to John's call for repentance. However, John was not sensitive to their reservations. He called them a brood of vipers. This straightforward approach would eventually earn John a place in prison. But one thing is certain: John believed Jesus to be the Messiah. This steadfast belief is consistent with the earlier story of Elizabeth and Mary, where the fetus, John, leaped in Elizabeth's womb. This story, while fanciful, does supply information that Jesus and John were close while young, and that the baptism of Jesus was not the first meeting between the two preachers.

Luke's and Matthew's versions of John's description of the coming Messiah are unusual, as the one to come appears to be a resurrected Messiah with judgment at hand. "His winnowing fork is in his hands to clear his threshing floor and to gather the wheat [the righteous] into his barn, but he will burn up the chaff [the wicked] with unquenchable fire." Thus, it is left open to our guess whether John was ushering in the earthly Messiah or the heavenly (resurrected} Messiah. Most scholars believe John pointed towards the earthly Messiah, but let us keep the heavenly Messiah in our thoughts for further analysis.

The Gospel of Mark did not refer to a judgment scene and added the following colorful description of John:

John wore clothing made of camel's hair, with a leather belt around his waist, and he ate locusts and wild honey. (Mark 1:6)

According to Barclay, the mode of dress surely reminded the people of the great prophets, who lived the simple life apart from life's many luxuries. Elijah wore "a garment of hair and a leather belt around his waist." (2 Kings 1:8) This Spartan attire was either given to John by the author of Mark or was purposely worn by John to evoke the power of the prophets. John was a smart man and no doubt copied the famous prophet of old. The food mentioned in the passage was either actual locusts and honey or carobs and sap from certain trees. (1) Regardless, the diet was simple, as John relied on God to provide from nature.

John the Baptist was indeed an interesting character. He introduced the Messiah to the world and was not afraid to criticize those in positions of power. This unwillingness to live comfortably with the world eventually led John to prison and to his death.

But when Herod heard this [talk of John being raised from the dead] he said, "John, the man I beheaded has been raised from the dead!"

For Herod himself had given orders to have John arrested, and he had him bound and put in prison. He did this because of Herodias, his brother Philip's wife, whom he had married. For John had been saying to Herod, "It is not lawful for you to have your brother's wife." So Herodias nursed a grudge against John and wanted to kill him. But she was not able to, because Herod feared John and protected him, knowing him to be a righteous and holy man. When Herod heard John, he was greatly puzzled, yet he liked to listen to him. (Mark 6:16-20)

After this part of the narrative, where Herod was infatuated with John, we are told of John's death. Herodias tricked her husband, Herod, into granting her daughter a wish after she pleased him with a dance. The girl asked for John the Baptist's head on a platter. In this way, the Gospel writers deflected blame away from Herod and towards his wife, Herodias.

John was doing what he knew best, being a social critic, and those in power hated social critics. Unlike Paul, who entertained Bernice and Agrippa II, those Herodians accused of an incestuous relationship, John never hesitated to criticize actions he deemed inconsistent with the Law of Moses. This criticism enraged Herodias, and she eventually got her way: the death of John the Baptist.

One other passage needs to be examined. This concerns John's attitude towards Jesus while he languished in prison.

When John heard in prison what Christ was doing, he sent his disciples to ask him, "Are you the one who was to come, or should we expect someone else?" (Matt. 11:2-3)

This passage should confuse the reader. Throughout the story of John, he was sure of his own role in history and certain of Jesus, the Messiah. The fetus, John, leaped in his mother's womb upon hearing Mary's words. The man, John, baptized with water but promised that Jesus would baptize with the Holy Spirit. How could it be that John now doubted his role as well as the mission of Jesus? To go one step farther: why did John even have disciples at this point in time? If he truly believed in Jesus, then he would have become part of the Jesus movement. But he did not. John had his own separate movement, one of repentance and water baptism. Why did Jesus and John not work together?

TRADITIONAL TIMELINE

```
|-------|-----|---------|----------------|----------|----------------|----------------|
9       6     2         6                29         30               33               55
BCE           BCE       CE
Jesus         John      Jesus            John       Jesus  John  Jesus      Apollos
Born          and       Born             Begins       is Beheaded  is       Preaches
(Matt.)       Jesus     (Luke)           Ministry   Baptized        Crucified  John's
              Born                                                            Baptism
              (Luke)
```

The following problems emerge when considering the Gospel story of Jesus and John the Baptist.

1. Since Jesus and John were the same age at the beginning of their respective ministries (thirty years old), their birth dates can be calculated to 2-1 BCE. This is inconsistent with the birth narratives related by Matthew and Luke. Matthew's birth of Jesus was between 9-6 BCE while Luke had the birth at 6-7 CE. Either way, these cannot be reconciled to the John the Baptist story. In addition, the Gospel of John had the Jews say that Jesus was not yet fifty years old. (John 8:57) If Jesus preached into his forties, then that again puts the various birth narratives into question.

2. If we accept Matthew's dating for Jesus' birth, then Jesus' ministry would have started in 22-25 CE with his crucifixion occurring between 25-28 CE. (These dates assume a birth date of 9-6 BCE, the beginning of Jesus' ministry at the age of thirty, and the duration of that ministry of three years.) The calculated beginning of Jesus' ministry and his crucifixion both occurred before John the Baptist's ministry as recorded by Luke. Obviously, one or both accounts are false.

3. If John really believed that Jesus was the Messiah, then why did his own movement continue? After baptizing Jesus, and recognizing the Holy Spirit, we would expect both John and his disciples to jump onto the Jesus bandwagon. But they did not. In addition, the Gospels even share that John had his doubts about Jesus. If true, then the earlier stories about John's certainty might have been sheer embellishment.

4. According to the book of Acts, John had disciples into the 50's. (Acts 18:24) This passage stated that Apollos taught about Jesus accurately but knew only the baptism of John. This explanation for Apollos answers the statement

made by Paul in 1 Cor. 3:6, "I planted the seed, Apollos watered it, but God made it grow." If Apollos preached the baptism of John, then we must ask ourselves these questions: did not John die before Jesus, and did not Jesus' apostles baptize in the Holy Spirit after Jesus' death? Put another way, the baptism of John should have been long since forgotten. John was before the resurrection of Jesus and before the baptism of the Holy Spirit. Why would anyone use the baptism of John at this late date? This cannot be explained by the traditional timeline.

5. According to the Gospels, John began baptizing in 28-29 CE, preached a short while and then was beheaded. This beheading occurred before Jesus' arrest and crucifixion. Thus, the traditional date for John's death was some time before 33 CE. However, according to Josephus, John was put to death in 35-36 CE, some years after the supposed crucifixion of Jesus. (*Ant.* 18.116-119) This discrepancy has been overlooked by scholars and church historians because it questions the very Gospel story. Did John outlive Jesus?

WHAT REALLY HAPPENED

From the traditional story, several discrepancies cannot be explained, particularly the dating of events. However, the main thrust of the John the Baptist passages is clear: John came to announce the coming of the Messiah. But was this proclamation by John before the earthly Jesus came onto the scene, or was John proclaiming a return of the resurrected Jesus? From the Gospel accounts, both can be argued. In Mark, John appeared to be ushering in the coming of the earthly Messiah, but Matthew and Luke invoked imagery of the Messiah at judgment, similar to the scenes in the book of Revelation. Is it possible that John the Baptist preached his message of repentance before the earthly Jesus and again after the crucifixion, to prepare his hearers for the return of a conquering Jesus? I believe that is exactly what happened. But if John died **before** Jesus, as tradition claims, then such a proposal is impossible. But what if John died **after** Jesus?

Before we answer the question concerning the death of John, we must make an attempt to pinpoint the beginning date of John's ministry. In the Gospel of Luke, John's ministry began in the fifteenth year of Tiberius' reign, or approximately 29 CE. That is why most scholars have placed Jesus' ministry at 30 CE, even though the birth narratives do not yield such a beginning date. The other three Gospels are silent on the beginning date of John the Baptist's ministry. Josephus also has no direct information concerning the early years of John. Perhaps Josephus underestimated John's importance, or mentioned him under a different title, or maybe such information was expunged from his record. After all, a charismatic character like John would have been very interesting material for Josephus. So we are left with only one source which flat out contradicts Luke's dating, and that source is the Slavonic Josephus.

The Slavonic Josephus was composed in Russia a thousand years after the events, but most scholars believe that it was not an original Russian document, but rather a translation from Greek or Aramaic. Was this entirely from Josephus himself or was some other early Jewish writer involved in the composition? Essentially, this version of Josephus contains the seven books of the *War*, but other "Christian" information is included as well. This information was either part of the original Josephus or from the pen of a first-century Jew. No one will ever know for sure. Either way, the following passage about John the Baptist's beginning is fascinating.

Now at that time a man went about among the Jews in strange garments; for he had put pelts on his body everywhere it was not covered with his own hair; indeed to look at, he was like a wild man. **He came to the Jews and summoned them to freedom,** saying, "God hath sent me, that I may **show you the way of the Law,** wherein ye may **free yourselves from many holders of power.** And there will be **no mortal ruling over you, only the Highest who hath sent me.**" And when the people heard this, they were joyful. And there went after him all Judea, that lies in the region around Jerusalem. And he did nothing else to them save that he plunged them into the stream of the Jordan and dismissed them, instructing them that they should cease from evil works, and [promising] that there would [then] **be given them a ruler who would set them free.**

...And when he had been **brought to Archelaus** and the doctors of the Law had assembled, they asked him who he [was] and where he [had] been until then. And to this he made answer and spoke: "I am pure; [for] the Spirit of God hath led me on, and [I live on] cane and roots and tree-food." But when they threatened to **put him to torture** if he would not cease from those words and deeds, he nevertheless said: "It is meet for you [rather] to cease from your heinous works and cleave unto the Lord your God. (2) (Emphasis mine)

The similarities between this John and the Gospel John include the following items. First, this John covered his whole body in pelts and appeared as a wild man. This description is not quite as dignified as the Gospels, where John dressed like one of the prophets of old. In addition, John's diet of cane, roots and nuts approximates the locusts and honey of the Gospels. According to Barclay, the locusts and honey could have been carobs and sap from certain trees. Regardless, a picture emerges of an unusual preacher, not at all at home with the comforts of this life. In fact, this John's appearance was so unlike others that he must have stood out, like a true prophet.

Also, like the Gospels, John preached repentance to the crowds gathering around the river Jordan, and "plunged them into the stream." The passage goes on to talk about those who disapproved of John. His response to them was similar to the Gospel rebuke of the vipers. In both versions, John promised a ruler who would set them free, an attractive message to the crowd but a dangerous threat to the ruling authorities. In short, this Slavonic Josephus depiction of John has the same charm and power of the Gospels.

However, three points differentiate this John from the Baptist of the Gospels. First, the Slavonic John had a political agenda while the Gospel Baptist was centered strictly on repentance and baptism. The Slavonic John said: "God hath sent me, that I should show you the way of the Law, wherein ye may free yourselves from many holders of power. And there will be no mortal ruling over you, only the Highest who hath sent me." This philosophy to remove the Herodians and Romans in favor of God was identical to the Fourth Philosophy of Judas the Galilean. In the *War* and *Antiquities*, Josephus wrote the following about Judas the Galilean.

...it was that a certain Galilean, whose name was Judas, prevailed with his countrymen to revolt; and said **they were cowards if they would endure to pay a tax to the Romans, and would, after God, submit to mortal men as their lords**. This man was a teacher of a peculiar sect of his own, and was not at all like the rest of those their leaders. (*War* 2.118) (Emphasis mine)

...yet there was one Judas, a Gaulonite, of a city whose name was Gamala, who **taking with him Sadduc, a Pharisee**, became zealous to draw them to a revolt, who **both said** that this taxation was no better than an introduction to slavery, and exhorted the nation to assert their liberty. ...for **Judas and Sadduc, who excited a fourth philosophic sect among us**, and had a great many followers therein, filled our civil government with tumults at present, and laid the foundation of our future miseries. ...But of the fourth sect of Jewish philosophy, Judas the Galilean was the author. These men agree in all things with the Pharisaic notions; but they have an inviolable attachment to liberty; and say that **God is to be their only Ruler and Lord**. (*Ant.* 18.4, 9, 23) (Emphasis mine)

There can be no doubt about it: the Slavonic John the Baptist preached the same philosophy as Judas the Galilean. Since Judas was the leader of the movement, it follows that John was either a disciple of Judas, or more likely, the Sadduc mentioned by Josephus in the above passage. Although Josephus did not directly mention the coming of John the Baptist, he may have introduced him in the Sadduc reference. According to Robert Eisenman, Sadduc or Saddok is a "term linguistically related both to the word 'Sadducee' in Greek and the 'Zaddik' in Hebrew." (3) This Zaddik terminology is associated with the idea of righteousness. It should be noted that Josephus did associate John with the idea of righteousness. (*Ant.* 18.117) Either Josephus referred to John as the Sadduc or later Christians changed the reference of John to Sadduc. The idea of interpolation should not be taken lightly as the one passage about Jesus in *Antiquities* was surely an interpolation, changing the death of Judas the Galilean into the crucifixion of Jesus. (*Ant.* 18.63-64)

By identifying John the Baptist with Judas the Galilean and the Fourth Philosophy (later termed the Zealots), the Slavonic Josephus may help explain a passage from the Gospel of Matthew. "From the days of John the Baptist until now, the kingdom of heaven has been forcefully advancing, and forceful [violent] men lay hold of it." (Matt. 11:12) It is quite likely that Jesus (Judas the Galilean) was referring to the Fourth Philosophy which he and John championed.

The location of the Slavonic passage is after *War* 2.110. The above passage concerning Judas the Galilean is just eight verses later, in *War* 2.118. How interesting that the author of the Slavonic Josephus introduced John right before Judas the Galilean, just as the Gospels introduced John right before Jesus. This reference to John in 6 CE is also supported by the passage itself, where John was brought before Archelaus. This meeting was shortly before Archelaus was summoned to trial for his atrocities against the Jews and Samaritans. In his ninth year (6 CE), he was banished to Vienna, a city in Gaul. (*War* 2.111) This Archelaus was the son of Herod the Great and ruled from 4 BCE to 7 CE. With this mention of Archelaus, it is safe to assign a beginning date to John's ministry at 6 CE, right before the tax revolt of Judas the Galilean. This can only mean that John the Baptist's Messiah was none other than Judas the Galilean.

In support of the Slavonic Josephus passage, the *Recognitions of Clement* stated, "For the people [Israel] was now divided into many parties, ever since the days of John the Baptist." (4) These groups were then denoted as Sadducees, the Samaritans, the scribes and Pharisees, and even some of John's disciples. It should be noted that in *Antiquities* and in the *War*, Josephus wrote of the Jewish sects right after introducing Judas the Galilean, the Sadduc (John?) and the Fourth Philosophy. Josephus mentioned four philosophies: the Sadducees, the Pharisees, the Essenes and the Fourth Philosophy of Judas the Galilean. Is it just coincidence that the *Recognitions* recounted the different Jewish sects right after mentioning John the Baptist? Or is it possible that the *Recognition's* placement of John the Baptist came from a source similar to the Slavonic Josephus? This is clear: both the Slavonic Josephus and the *Recognitions* placed John the Baptist before Judas the Galilean and before the enumeration of the Jewish philosophies.

In addition, one last piece of information connects John to Judas the Galilean. When threatened by torture, John did not flinch but kept on preaching. This, too, was a hallmark of Judas the Galilean's Fourth Philosophy. "They also do not value dying any kind of death, nor indeed do they heed the deaths of their relations and friends, nor can any such fear make them call any man Lord." (*Ant.* 18.23) These followers of Judas did not fear torture and death, just as this John refused to be bullied by the authorities. Such a stance was indeed dangerous, but it played well with the people.

Considering all the other similarities between Judas the Galilean and Jesus of Nazareth, as enumerated in Chapter 13, this John the Baptist revelation may be the smoking gun. Introducing John the Baptist during the reign of Archelaus moves the Jesus movement back to at least 6 CE, to the exact time of Judas the Galilean's tax revolt. Only the most stubborn believer will not recognize that Judas was the Messiah whom John was recommending to the people. My contention throughout this book is that Judas the Galilean and Jesus were two names for the same person. The John passage simply certifies this.

The next mention of John the Baptist outside of the Gospel record comes once again from the Slavonic Josephus. Without being asked, John interpreted a dream by Philip, tetrarch of Trachonitis.

And in those days Philip, while being in his own domain, saw [in] a dream an eagle tear out both his eyes. And he called together all his wise men. And when others were resolving their dreams otherwise, the man we have already described as walking about in animal hair and cleansing people in the streams of the Jordan, **came to Philip suddenly, unsummoned,** and said, "Hear the word of the Lord. The dream you have seen: the eagle is your rapacity, for that bird is violent and rapacious. Such also is the sin; it will pluck out your eyes which are your dominion and your wife." **And when he had spoken thus, Philip passed away by evening and his domain was given to Agrippa. And his wife Herodias was taken by Herod, his brother.** Because of her all those who were learned in the Law detested him but did not dare accuse him to his face. Only the man they call wild, came to him in fury and said, "Since you, lawless one, have taken your brother's wife, just as your brother died a merciless death, so you too will be cut down by heaven's sickle. For divine providence will not remain silent but will be the death of you through grievous afflictions in other lands, for you are not raising seeds for your brother but satisfying your carnal lust and committing adultery, since there are four children of his own."

Hearing this, Herod was enraged and ordered him to be beaten and thrown out. **He, however, did not cease but wherever he encountered Herod, spoke thus [and] accused him until he was put in a dungeon.** (5) (Emphasis mine)

The above passage has four important points to consider. First, John was a social critic. While others refused to comment upon Philip's dream, John appeared on the scene without an invitation to criticize Philip. It is easy to criticize those in power, but how many individuals do this publicly? In the environment in which John lived, this brash act was clearly dangerous. Philip had the power to silence John at any time.

Shortly after John's repudiation of Philip's character, the tetrarch died. This brings us to the second point, which concerns the date of Philip's death. According to Josephus, Philip died in the "twentieth year of the reign of Tiberius", or in 34 CE. (*Ant.* 18.106) This does not jibe with the Gospel account. According to Luke 3:1, John began his ministry in the "fifteenth year of the reign of Tiberius" or around 29 CE. While Jesus was still preaching, John was imprisoned and then beheaded, this occurring within the three year ministry of Jesus. (Matt. 11:1-3 and 14:1-13) Thus, according to the Gospels, John was imprisoned somewhere between 29-32 CE. Since John was still roaming free at the time of Philip's death in 34 CE, John's freedom cannot be reconciled to the Gospel timeline.

Third, according to the passage, when Philip died, his wife was taken by his brother, Herod. This was clearly a mistake made by the Slavonic Josephus' author. It appears as if Philip the Tetrarch was confused with Herod, know as Philip. Philip the Tetrarch died childless (*Ant.* 18.137) while Herod, known as Philip, was married to Herodias. The mistake proves that the author of the Slavonic *War* was very careful in matching his new material to the events in *Antiquities*, but the confusion over the Philips may point to a person not totally familiar with the Jewish history. The claim that John the Baptist was outraged by Herod Antipas' marriage to Herodias was one hundred percent true, but the reason for this outrage was not true. According to the above passage, John was upset because Herod took his dead brother's wife in marriage, out of lust and not to continue the blood line of the brother. However, per the account in *Antiquities*, Antipas took the wife of his stepbrother Herod (Philip) while the stepbrother was still alive. (*Ant.* 18.109-110) This was the act which enraged John and others throughout Jewish society.

The fourth point supports point two, as John was imprisoned and put to death by Herod Antipas in 35-36 CE. This timing for John's death comes well after the traditional date for the death of Jesus. The Slavonic Josephus' story of Herodias and Herod Antipas correlates with a passage from *Antiquities*

18.109-112. It is interesting that the Slavonic version had John hounding Antipas at every turn. This treatment of Antipas is quite different from that of the Gospel of Mark, where Antipas admired John. It might be prudent to list the Gospel accounts of Herod Antipas' feelings for John and compare these inclinations to that of Josephus' account.

So **Herodias** nursed a grudge against John and **wanted to kill him.** But she was not able to, because **Herod feared John and protected him, knowing him to be a righteous and holy man.** When Herod heard John, he was greatly puzzled; yet he liked to listen to him. (Mark 6:19-20) (Emphasis mine)

…John had been saying to him: "It is not lawful for you to have her [Herodias]." **Herod wanted to kill John, but he was afraid of the people, because they considered him a prophet.** (Matt. 14:4-5) (Emphasis mine)

Now, some of the Jews thought that the destruction of Herod's army came from God, and very justly, as a punishment of what he did against John, that was called the Baptist; for **Herod slew him,** who was a good man, and commanded the Jews to exercise virtue, both as to **righteousness** towards one another, and piety towards God, and so to come to baptism; for that the washing [with water] would be acceptable to him, if they made use of it, not in order to the putting away [or the remission] of some sins [only], but for the purification of the body; supposing still that the soul was thoroughly **purified beforehand by righteousness.** Now when [many] others came in crowds about him, for they were greatly moved [or pleased] by hearing his words, **Herod, who feared lest the great influence John had over the people might put it into his power and inclination to raise a rebellion (for they seemed ready to do anything he should advise), thought it best, by putting him to death,** to prevent any mischief he might cause, and not bring himself into difficulties, by sparing a man who might make him repent of it when it should be too late. Accordingly **he was sent a prisoner, out of Herod's suspicious temper,** to Macherus, the castle I before mentioned, and was there put to death. Now the Jews had an opinion that the destruction of this army was sent as a punishment upon Herod, and a mark of God's displeasure against him. (*Ant.* 18.116-119) (Emphasis mine)

Mark placed the blame for John's death upon Herodias and even stated that Herod protected John. No doubt, Herodias would have despised John as he constantly dragged her name through the mud. However, to place the blame upon Herodias is a bit much. On the other hand, Matthew squarely stated that Herod wanted to kill John. Herod was constrained by his fear of the people, who considered John a prophet. So, the Gospel accounts of Herod Antipas are somewhat conflicting.

Josephus painted a much clearer picture of the situation. After describing the Herod and Herodias affair, Josephus wrote that Herod slew John. This was done because Herod feared the great influence that John had over the people. In fact, Herod feared a rebellion. So, it is possible that Herod Antipas arrested John because of John's constant criticisms of his dealings with Herodias, his brother's wife. However, Herod killed John to prevent any chance of rebellion.

When placed together, the dating of this episode (35-36 CE) and Herod's desire to defuse a rebellion led by John, the traditional Christian story becomes unglued. According to the Gospels, John died before Jesus and that his ministry was on the wane. The actual history had John outliving Jesus, with John's power at its zenith. Something must be very wrong with the traditional view!

The Gospel account of John the Baptist also turned the Jews against John, similar to the treatment of Jesus. In Matthew 21:31-32, Jesus supposedly said, "Truly I tell you, the tax collectors and the prostitutes are going into the kingdom of God ahead of you. For John came in the Way of Righteousness and you did not believe him, but the tax collectors and the prostitutes believed him." What an incredible rewrite of history! The Josephus passage said that the people were ready to do anything that John wanted them to, and that it was Herod (the tax collector) and Herodias (the prostitute) who put John to death. In reality, the people did believe in John and his message of repentance and righteousness. John came in the Way of Righteousness, often referred to as the Way. This was the same Way of Righteousness that Jesus also followed.

The Gospels successfully denigrated the Jews in their actions towards Jesus and John. In regards to Jesus, the Jews pressured Pilate into crucifying Jesus, thereby shifting blame from the Romans to the Jews. In the case of John, the Gospels stated that the tax collectors and prostitutes admired him and would surely attain the Kingdom of Heaven before any of the religious Jews. Most scholars have not argued against the Gospel presentation, because it is in line with Paul's relationship with the Jews and with the Herodian hierarchy. The Jews did hate and hound Paul (see Galatians), and his refuge was with Gentiles who believed in his vision of the Risen Christ. Paul was a Herodian (tax collector)! That is the reason why the Gospel story of Jesus and John has been slanted against the Jews in favor of the tax collectors and prostitutes.

Other revealing clues lurk within the above Josephus passage and the various Slavonic Josephus passages. First, the dating of John's death can be positively placed at 35-36 CE. This is five or so years later than the Gospel story and many years **after** the death of the Gospel Jesus. Earlier, we found that the beginning of John's career was in 6 CE, not 29 CE as claimed in the Gospels. This is an interesting find. So, instead of a short two years ministry, John's influence in Judea lasted for thirty years (6-36 CE). Could Jesus' ministry have lasted beyond the three years assigned to him by the Gospels? It would appear so! My Judas the Galilean hypothesis states that Judas' career lasted from 4 BCE to 19-21 CE, and amazing 22-24 years. If John was careful enough to avoid arrest for thirty years, then it is entirely possible for Judas the Galilean (Jesus) as well.

Second, in 35-36 CE, John had a considerable following. His disciples were willing to follow him anywhere. This again poses problems for the Gospel story. According to the Gospels, John introduced Jesus to the world, was imprisoned shortly thereafter and was then put to death by the whims of a wicked woman. In reality, John's rise to stardom began in 6 CE and grew over the next thirty years. In 6 CE, he introduced Judas the Galilean to the world, because he was a member of Judas' Fourth Philosophy. If John were really related to Jesus as claimed by Luke, then this familial connection would have been consistent with the Maccabean movement, where family members were all working together. It is entirely possible that Judas sent his cousin, John, out to proclaim himself (Judas or Jesus) as Messiah. This pre-planning would be no different than Jesus' arrival into Jerusalem on a donkey. Both events could be found in the Old Testament Scriptures, in Isaiah 40:3 and Zechariah 9:9, respectively. To make sure the people understood John's importance, Jesus said, "And if you are willing to accept it, he [John] is the Elijah who was to come." (Matt. 11:14) Jesus also said this, quoting Malachi 3:1, "I will send a messenger ahead of you, who will prepare your way before you." (Luke 7:27) All this talk of John the Baptist was merely a way for Jesus to solidify his Messianic claim. Josephus called Judas the Galilean a clever rabbi, and certainly this use of John the Baptist to support his goals, imbedded in Scripture, was clever.

However, John outlived Judas the Galilean (Jesus). If Judas suffered crucifixion in 19-21 CE, then John's ministry would have lasted another fifteen to seventeen years. During these years, John's influence may have grown to a point of almost rivaling Jesus himself. This may explain the Gospel description of John's message to the crowds. In John's later years, he would have been proclaiming the return of the resurrected Jesus, the Jesus who would judge with a winnowing fork. (Matt 3:11-12) Thus, John's baptism may have been used before the introduction of the earthly Jesus (Judas) in 6 CE and after Jesus' crucifixion, from 19 to 36 CE.

Another possibility exists. According to the *Recognitions*, some of John's disciples separated themselves from the movement and proclaimed John as the Messiah. (6) Since Jesus died in 19-21 CE and John's ministry lasted until 36 CE, it is very possible that some questioned the validity of Jesus' Kingship, as Jesus was dead. This may also explain why John had such a large following. A live Messiah would have been preferable to a dead Messiah in many Jews' minds. Certainly, some of John's disciples believed that he, John, was the Messiah. Josephus claimed that John was put to death because Herod Antipas was afraid of John's influence over his myriad of disciples. Undoubtedly, this was why the New Testament writers expended so much energy in placing John behind Jesus (and Paul) in importance.

This following of John in 36 CE may also explain why Apollos knew of John's baptism. Everyone in this era knew of John's baptism. It also helps date the letters of Paul. If Apollos taught people about Jesus while using John's baptism, then John's influence was still strong. This suggests that the Apollos incident was fairly close to the date of John's death (post 36 CE). Traditionally, the letters to the Romans, Corinthians and Galatians are assigned a date of approximately 55 CE. I believe these letters were written from the late 30's to the mid 40's, much closer to the time of John's death.

From what we have uncovered concerning John's ministry, a startling claim can be made. John supported Jesus (Judas the Galilean) from 6 CE until the crucifixion (19-21 CE). In fact, John would have been the second-in-command to Jesus, just as the Sadduc was co-teacher with Judas the Galilean, according to Josephus. When Jesus was crucified, John became the leader of the movement. It is no coincidence that the Apostles preached water baptism after the death of Jesus. (Acts 2:38) This was the directive from John the Baptist. James, the brother of Jesus, was elected to replace Jesus. So, from 21-36 CE, John led the movement and James was his second-in-command. When John died, James replaced John, and Cephas was elevated to second-in-command.

The Gospels and Acts removed a full generation from the Church's history. Jesus' death was recorded at around 33 CE instead of 19-21 CE while John was written out of the story around 32 CE, instead of 36 CE. By removing this generation, the Gospels could eliminate John the Baptist from the Church leadership. To prove this point, let us go back to the divisions in the Corinthian Church, as reported by Paul.

My brothers, some from Chloe's household have informed me that there are quarrels among you. What I mean is this: One of you says, "I follow Paul", another, "I follow **Apollos**"; another, "I follow **Cephas**"; still another, "I follow **Christ**." (1 Cor. 1:11-12) (Emphasis mine)

I date this passage at around 38 CE. Note that Paul had his own following but the other three factions were disciples of Jesus (Christ), John the Baptist (Apollos) and James (Cephas). These were the first three leaders of the movement. At this early date, the confusion over leadership was causing splits among the disciples. This may be why James called the Council of Jerusalem, in order to establish his own rule over the movement. Regardless, John the Baptist was still highly regarded, even after his death.

Finally, Josephus described John's baptism. John's baptism did not remove sins but was simply a purification of the body, "supposing still that the soul was thoroughly purified beforehand by righteousness." (*Ant.* 18.117) The baptism was a confession before men of an inward change towards God. This was consistent with Deuteronomy chapter 30, where the circumcision of the heart came from a willingness to follow God. This was righteousness before God, the same message as preached by Judas the Galilean and Jesus throughout the Gospels. Josephus stated: "[John] was a good man, and commanded the Jews to exercise virtue, both as to righteousness towards one another, and piety towards God." The two greatest commandments were love thy neighbor as thyself and love God with all your heart, soul and strength. In philosophy, John and Jesus (Judas) were inseparable. However, John's philosophy was quite different from that of Paul. To John, a person could be reconciled to God by righteousness, while Paul insisted that a blood sacrifice was necessary, the death of Christ.

REVISED TIMELINE FOR JOHN THE BAPTIST

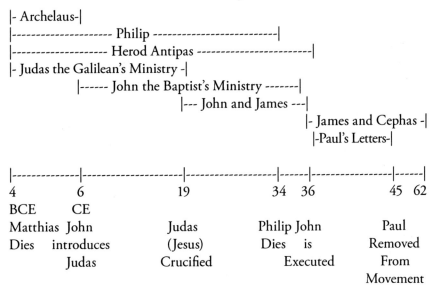

```
|- Archelaus-|
|-------------------- Philip ------------------------|
|-------------------- Herod Antipas ----------------------|
|- Judas the Galilean's Ministry -|
        |------ John the Baptist's Ministry -------|
                    |--- John and James ---|
                              |- James and Cephas -|
                              |-Paul's Letters-|


|-------------|--------------------|------------------|------|----------------|------|
4             6                    19                 34    36                45    62
BCE           CE
Matthias      John                 Judas              Philip John            Paul
Dies          introduces           (Jesus)            Dies   is              Removed
              Judas                Crucified                 Executed        From
                                                                             Movement
```

The above timeline represents all information concerning John the Baptist. The problems associated with the traditional timeline have all been solved.

1. Josephus first mentioned Judas the Galilean in 4 BCE. Judas and his co-teacher, Matthias, raised a rebellion against Herod the Great. They urged their followers to tear down the Golden Eagle, which was a sign of Herod's fealty to Rome. This was known as the Golden Eagle Temple Cleansing. Matthias and Judas were captured. Matthias was executed while Judas escaped death and was eventually released by Archelaus in a Barabbas-style prisoner release. The dual ministry of Matthias and Judas was repeated a decade later by the Judas and Sadduc (John the Baptist) pairing.

2. The traditional dating could not be reconciled to all the other dates given in the New Testament. For example, the birth date of Jesus could have been 9-6 BCE, 2-1 BCE or 6 CE. The revised timeline gives a much more consistent birth date for Judas the Galilean (Jesus) and for John. Both came onto the national scene at the time of the Census of Cyrenius or in 6 CE. (John had the same philosophy as Judas the Galilean and was strategically used to announce the coming of the Messiah, Judas (Jesus)). If they were both approximately thirty years old in 6 CE, then they must have been born around 25 BCE. That is the exact time of the "Star of Bethlehem" story as related by the Slavonic Josephus. (7)

The dating in the New Testament is dependent on the erroneous dating of John the Baptist. The only reason for giving such a late date for the coming of John the Baptist (28-29 CE) was to place Jesus into a later timeframe, closer to 30 CE. By doing this, Jesus was separated from his true historical ties to Judas the Galilean, and John's ministry was cut short, from an amazing thirty years to just a year or two. And this late date also helped hide embarrassing revelations about Paul's relationship with James and Paul's eventual removal from the movement in 44 CE.

3. Even after Judas (Jesus) had died, John continued preaching his message of repentance. However, now it was for the return of the resurrected Jesus. This was unknowingly confirmed by Matthew and Luke, who made the coming Messiah judge the good and evil on the threshing floor of Judgment Day. It should not be missed that **after** the death of Jesus, the Apostles were preaching repentance and water baptism. (Acts 2:38) John's influence was very strong even though the Gospels had eliminated him years before Jesus.

4. John was alive when Philip died (34 CE) and was put to death by Herod

Antipas in 35-36 CE. This was at least five years after John's Gospel death, several years after the Gospel crucifixion of Jesus and fifteen to seventeen years after the actual crucifixion of Jesus (Judas the Galilean).

The historical death of John the Baptist plays havoc with the Gospel story. In reality, John was alive and well many years after Jesus' crucifixion. Thus, many of the Gospel passages about John are placed into an earlier timeframe (30 CE). This was done to overcome the problems of John's great popularity around 35 CE. Therefore, the Gospels presented John and his followers as being disciples of the pre-crucifixion Jesus, right up to the time of John's death.

5. This later death of John in 36 CE makes the reference to Apollos and water in 1 Corinthians more relevant. John had a great following until his death and probably for a short time beyond his death. Therefore, his baptism was probably well known and practiced well into the 40's.

6. This new timeline confirms that Jesus was a title for Judas the Galilean and that the name Sadduc was a title for John the Baptist. John's introduction right before Judas the Galilean in 6 CE seals the debate. In addition, John held the same philosophy as Judas the Galilean. It is beyond belief that John could have prepared the way for Judas the Galilean in 6 CE and for another Messiah (Jesus) in 29 CE. No! Judas and Jesus were one in the same, and John was there at his side.

CHAPTER 19

EVENTS IN THE LIFE OF JESUS

To get a clearer picture of the man behind the Gospel Jesus, some of the more mysterious happenings within the Gospels must be deciphered. In doing this, the 21st century mind will be unleashed, with its knowledge of science. The man of "faith" may object to this methodology, but the intent is to uncover the real meaning of certain events. When these facts are then considered, the picture of Jesus should take a slightly different form, which will allow a proper assessment of his true historical setting.

THE BAPTIZING OF JESUS BY JOHN

According to the Gospels, Jesus was baptized by John the Baptist, even though John baptized with water for repentance. (Matt. 3:11) How could the sinless Jesus be baptized for repentance? The following passage attempts to answer this question:

Then Jesus came from Galilee to the Jordan to be baptized by John. But John tried to deter him, saying, "I need to be baptized by you, and do you come to me?" Jesus replied, "Let it be so now; it is proper for us to do this to fulfill all righteousness." (Matt. 3:13-14)

Where did Jesus come from and where was he going after this meeting with John? According to Matthew, Jesus came from Galilee to be baptized by John (Matt. 3:13) and did not return to Galilee until he heard that John had been put in prison (Matt. 4:12). According to the Gospel of John, Jesus and John were both teaching near the Jordan. Right after John had declared that Jesus would baptize with the Holy Spirit, Jesus went back to Galilee. (John

1:32-33, 43) In addition, John's Gospel did not have Jesus being baptized with a water baptism, or at least it did not explicitly say Jesus was baptized with water. The Synoptic Gospels tried to explain Jesus' water baptism by simply saying that Jesus underwent baptism to fulfill all righteousness. A close relationship between Jesus and John the Baptist was not denied by any of the four Gospel writers, but the baptism of Jesus by John was handled differently.

According to Josephus, John did not baptize with water for the forgiveness of sins but for purification of the body, "supposing still that the soul was thoroughly purified beforehand by righteousness." (*Ant.* 18.117) The baptism of Jesus did not result in forgiveness of any sins, only that Jesus had been purified earlier by the practice of righteousness. That may explain why Jesus said, "Let it be so now, it is proper for us to do this to fulfill all righteousness." This identification with John's movement was quite extraordinary. Jesus supported John at a price: he would be baptized if John would announce the coming of the Messiah. At this point in history, Jesus and John combined their disciples, creating a far more powerful force.

It should not be missed that Judas the Galilean and the Sadduc also combined forces before the Census tax revolt in 6 CE. And as explained earlier in this book, the Slavonic Josephus placed John the Baptist in the exact timeframe as the Sadduc, suggesting that John was the Sadduc and Jesus was Judas the Galilean. Thus, the combination of forces was not only religious in nature but also very political. This combination was designed to help fight Rome and free Israel from bondage. According to the Slavonic Josephus, John said to the Jews: "God has sent me to show you the lawful way, by which you will be rid of [your] many rulers. But there will be no mortal ruling [over you], only the Most High, who hath sent me." (After *War* 2.110) This call for freedom was the call of Judas the Galilean, the historical Jesus.

THE FEEDING OF THE FOUR AND FIVE THOUSAND

No Gospel story can more illustrate the problems associated with the traditional interpretation than the miraculous feeding of the four and five thousand. The feeding of the five thousand can be found in Mark 6:30-44, Matthew 14:13-21 and Luke 9:10-17. The accounts of this miracle are quite similar in that Jesus fed 5,000 men, as well as women and children, from five loaves of bread and two small fish. When the crowd had finished their meal, the disciples gathered scraps totaling twelve basketfuls of broken pieces. This, indeed, was a miracle from God. Jesus had created matter out of thin air, or rather, he had multiplied the existing loaves and fish into a much greater number. This was not a trick seen every day.

The feeding of the four thousand was recorded by just Mark 8:1-21 and Matthew 15:29 - 16:12. The scenario for the four thousand was much similar to that of the five thousand: this time Jesus took seven loaves and some fish and fed the men, women and children. Afterwards, the disciples picked up seven basketfuls of broken pieces. Thus, the miracle had been reproduced, only on a slightly smaller scale.

If Jesus did feed the crowd, how did he do it? Certainly, he did not produce matter out of thin air. That is impossible! What then did he do? A closer investigation of the passages concerning the four thousand may shed some illuminating light. When Jesus saw the crowds, he had compassion for their physical needs. He ordered his disciples to gather their limited resources (seven loaves and a few fish) and to share them with one another and with the crowd. Now, we should ask: If Jesus and his disciples had seven loaves of bread and some fish, would it not be logical that some of the other people had some supplies as well? The example of sharing spurred the crowd to share with one another. Surely, no one went home with a full stomach, but each took what was necessary to sustain himself. Thus, the miracle had nothing to do with hocus-pocus or the magical production of food. The miracle, however, was just as amazing. Jesus convinced a large crowd to share their possessions with others, possibly complete strangers.

This interpretation is bolstered by further commentary by Jesus on the event. The accounts in Matthew and Mark will be reproduced because they do differ slightly.

"You of little faith, why are you talking among yourselves about having no bread? Do you still not understand? Don't you remember the five loaves for the five thousand, and how many basketfuls you gathered? Or the seven loaves for the four thousand, and how many basketfuls you gathered? How is it that you don't understand that I was not talking to you about bread? But be on your guard against the yeast of the Pharisees and the Sadducees." Then they understood that he was not telling them to guard against the yeast used in bread, but **against the teachings of the Pharisees and Sadducees.** (Matt. 16:8-12) (Emphasis mine)

The disciples had forgotten to bring bread, except for one loaf they had with them in the boat. "Be careful," Jesus warned them. "Watch out for the **yeast of the Pharisees and that of Herod.**" (Mark 8:14-15) (Emphasis mine)

Before making his comments about the yeast of the other religious groups, Jesus referred back to the feeding of the five and four thousand. These events should have taught the disciples a very important lesson: material things should be used to help others, not to simply hoard. The yeast of the power structure (the Romans, the Sadducees and the Herodians) was greed. To share was not in their lexicon. The act of sharing was proof of the Kingdom of God, for the kingdoms of this earth had never practiced it.

The Gospels confused the meaning of this message by including the Pharisees in the elite power structure. Surely, a few Pharisees peddled God for a profit, but that should not define the entire lot. According to Josephus, Judas the Galilean and the Sadduc were Pharisees, following the Pharisaic practices with one exception: they also preached nationalism, a cry for liberty from Rome. Josephus did not hide the fact that the movement of Judas pitted the poor against the wealthy. Judas was a champion of the poor. He did not become a champion by upholding the status quo. This, too, could be applied to Jesus in the feeding of the five and four thousand. So, the very thought that Jesus considered the Pharisees equal with the Sadducees and Herodians in their greed is ridiculous.

THE TRANSFIGURATION

The rational man has a good laugh while reading the story of the Transfiguration. On the surface, the events appear to be pure invention, a mad desire to make Jesus other worldly. And of course, this is the case of the matter. To place stock in the literal Transfiguration is akin to believing in Santa Claus. In Mark 9:2-13, Jesus picked Peter, John and James to accompany him onto a mountain to pray, six days after Peter had proclaimed Jesus as the Messiah. As Jesus prayed, a bright light shone upon him, and he conversed with Moses and Elijah. This scene surprised the sleepy Apostle trio, making Peter utter the ridiculous comment of building three shelters, or tabernacles, for Moses, Elijah and Jesus. Just then a cloud enveloped the six figures and God spoke, claiming Jesus as His Son. When the cloud lifted, only Jesus and the Apostles remained.

Could there be any truth behind this ghost story? Hyam Maccoby described this mystical event with perfect clarity as being a Coronation account. The specific six day interval came after the Salutation, where Peter proclaimed Jesus as the Messiah. In Near East coronation rites, a full ceremony would come one week after the Proclamation. In addition, these Near Eastern coronation rites often occurred on a mountain. The tabernacle statement by Peter now makes sense because a tabernacle was used to enthrone the king in these coronation rites. The announcement by God was taken from the Coronation Psalm (Ps. 2) which was recited for every Jewish king. "I have installed my King on Zion, my holy hill. ...You are my Son; today I have become your Father." And the transfiguration itself signified that the king was being reborn. Concerning Saul, the first Jewish King, God said, "The Spirit of the Lord will come upon you in power, and you will prophesy with them; and you will be changed into a different person." (1 Sam. 10:6).

Luke recorded that the seventy-two were sent out after the Transfiguration to announce the coming of the Messiah. The King or Messiah would tour his kingdom after his coronation, but Jesus needed to take care of business in Jerusalem first. After his success there, Jesus planned to make a triumphant tour of his whole kingdom. The fact that Jesus contemplated this makes the crucifixion a surprise and not a planned event as the Gospels declare. (1)

If Jesus did assume the role of Messiah, then this put him on a collision course with Rome. As I have mentioned before, the network built by Judas the Galilean would have had many cells of disciples in every town. The seventy-two went forth to alert these elements and to proclaim the eventual overthrow of Rome. So the Transfiguration and the subsequent sending out of the seventy-two, when stripped of their miraculous overtones, were nothing more than political statements made by Jesus and his closest disciples.

THE WITHERED FIG TREE

Both accounts of the withered fig tree will be reproduced below for comparison.

On the next day as they were leaving Bethany, Jesus was hungry. Seeing in the distance a fig tree in leaf, he went to find out if it had any fruit. When he reached it, he found nothing but leaves, **because it was not the season for figs**. Then he said to the tree, "May no one ever eat fruit from you again." And his disciples heard him say it. …In the morning, as they went along, they saw the fig tree withered from the roots. Peter remembered and said to Jesus, "Rabbi, look! The fig tree you cursed has withered." (Mark 11:12-14 and 11:20-21) (Emphasis mine)

Early in the morning, as he was on his way back to the city, he was hungry. Seeing a fig tree by the road, he went up to it but found nothing on it except leaves. Then he said to it, "May you never bear fruit again!" Immediately the tree withered.

When the disciples saw this, they were amazed. "How did the fig tree wither so quickly?" they asked.

Jesus replied, "I tell you the truth, if you have faith and do not doubt, not only can you do what has been done to the fig tree, but also you can say to the mountain, 'Go, throw yourself into the sea,' and it will be done. If you believe, you will receive whatever you ask for in prayer." (Matt. 21:18-22)

According to Mark, Jesus was hungry and thought that he might partake in a fig from a promising fig tree in leaf. However, Jesus was upset when he found the tree was barren of fruit. How long had Jesus lived in this area? Did he not know that "it was not the season for figs"? Mark's story has three possible explanations. First, Jesus was unaware of the growing season and was a very vengeful man. After all, it was not the fig tree's fault. This scenario does not make much sense as it makes Jesus out to be a bit theatrical. However, this scenario has been endorsed by Matthew. According to Matthew, anything is possible with belief and prayer. If you do not like an inanimate thing, you merely need to pray to change it into something that suits your fancy. This is just a lot of rubbish!

The second scenario concerns the timing of the fig tree episode. If it occurred right before the Passover, then the fig season was not at hand, consistent with Mark's Gospel. However, if it happened before the Feast of Tabernacles, in the fall, then the fig tree should have had ripe fruit. Maccoby makes a good point that the march into Jerusalem may have been before the Feast of Tabernacles. (2) If so, then the fig tree episode at least makes some sense, in that a fig tree at this time of the season would be expected to be laden with fruit. This still does not explain Jesus' incomprehensible cursing of the tree.

The third option also comes from Maccoby. Not only was it the Feast of Tabernacles, in the fall, but Jesus had just been anointed Messiah. In the age of the Messiah, all fruit trees should bear fruit. To Maccoby, the cursing of the tree had more to do with Messianic expectations than with an angry outburst. (3) Jesus was a true believer: if God promised fruit in the day of the Messiah, then Jesus expected fruit.

This seemingly incomprehensible story now has great implications. If Jesus truly believed that he were the Messiah, then he might also have believed that God would deliver Israel from the Romans, and that he, the Messiah, would reign over all Israel. Certainly, Jesus had no doubts about God's power, at least at this time in the story.

THE TRIUMPHAL ENTRY INTO JERUSALEM

Before entering Jerusalem as the Messiah, Jesus did his homework regarding the means of entrance. He rode a donkey into the city to fulfill the prophecy of Zechariah 9:9: "Say to the Daughter of Zion, 'See, your king comes to you, gentle and riding on a donkey, on a colt, the foal of a donkey.'" Per Jesus' orders, the disciples supplied the donkey. (Matt. 21:6) This part of the entry was extremely well orchestrated. But how would the crowd react to such a bold claim?

Concerning these crowds, Matthew wrote the following:

A very large crowd spread their cloaks on the road, while others cut branches from the trees and spread them on the road. The crowds that went ahead of him and those that followed shouted, "Hosanna to the Son of David!" "Blessed is he who comes in the name of the Lord." "Hosanna in the Highest!"

When Jesus entered Jerusalem, the whole city was stirred and asked, "Who is this?"

The crowds answered, "This is Jesus, the prophet from Nazareth in Galilee." (Matt. 21:8-11)

Why was the crowd so excited about Jesus? This question has already been answered by Luke. He plainly stated that Jesus' own disciples were the ones singing his praises. (Luke 19:37-39) Certainly others were caught up in the excitement, but it should not be missed that the crowd reaction to Jesus was also orchestrated by Jesus. Thus, the whole affair was a staged event, not so different from today's political rallies.

The disciples were definitely excited about Jesus' entrance into Jerusalem. They must have had expectations which were expunged from the later Gospels. This snippet comes from the Slavonic Josephus and gives a more realistic view of affairs.

They bade him enter the city, **kill the Roman troops and Pilate and reign over these**. But he did not care [to do so]. Later, when news of this came to the Jewish leaders, they assembled to the chief priests and said, "**We are powerless and [too] weak to oppose the Romans**, like a slackened bow. Let us go and inform Pilate what we have heard; and we shall be free of anxiety; if at some time he shall hear [of this] from others, we shall be deprived of [our] property, ourselves slaughtered and [our] children exiled." (After *War* 2.174)

According to this source, the disciples expected Jesus to rid Jerusalem of the Roman occupiers. Where did the crowd get such an idea? Certainly, this was an integral part of the Messiah's message. Just as Judas Maccabee had reclaimed the Temple for Israel, this Messiah would rid the land of the Roman occupier. Note that the Slavonic Josephus also claimed that the Jewish leaders were afraid of Jesus, thinking he would start a war with Rome, a war the Jews could not possibly win. Of course, after Jesus' arrest, the disciples rewrote history, claiming that Jesus did not really want to engage the Romans.

But if that were really the case, then Jesus would not have entered the city on a donkey.

So, what should be gleaned from this episode in Jesus' life? First, Jesus knew the Scriptures and used them to his advantage. Second, Jesus accepted and encouraged any talk of him being the Messiah. This, in and of itself, was bold. Messiahs or so-called Kings did not usually fare well against the power of Rome. This ride into Jerusalem was putting Rome on notice. A new King had arrived in town. Third, this entry into Jerusalem may have been in the fall and not in the spring, for the crowd placed palm branches on the road. (4) This later timeframe also fits in better with the withered fig story (see above).

The triumphal entry into Jerusalem is missing from Josephus' discussion of Judas the Galilean. Of course, the death of Judas the Galilean is also curiously absent from his records. Does this mean that Judas did not enter Jerusalem as Jesus did? Even though Judas' death has been expunged from the records by the early Church, it may be possible to prove that he did enter Jerusalem as Messiah. In 66 CE, Judas the Galilean's son, Menahem, raided the armory at Masada and then entered Jerusalem as Messiah. (*War* 2.433-435) Judas the Galilean had also raided an armory at Sepphoris before he was proclaimed Messiah. (*Ant.* 17.271-272) It is not unreasonable to conclude that Judas entered Jerusalem as Messiah just as his son had done in emulation of his father.

ONE TEMPLE CLEANSING OR TWO?

Did Jesus cleanse the Temple once or twice in his career? This seems a strange question considering almost all scholars and Church historians have pushed for just a single Temple cleansing. A Temple cleansing represented a challenge to the status quo. The status quo, represented by the Romans, the Herodians and the Chief Priests (Sadducees), would not sit idly by and allow their rule to be threatened. Therefore, any Temple cleansing was extremely serious business. Caiaphas and Annas were High Priests during Jesus' Gospel lifetime, and they had complete support of Rome as long as they maintained order. Their attitude towards Jesus would have been one of contempt and fear. A popular uprising could cost them their lucrative posts. The question is once again raised: could Jesus have challenged this power structure twice?

To answer this question, it is important to understand Jesus' entire career. First, did Jesus spend his entire career in Galilee, only to visit Jerusalem during the last days of his life, or did Jesus spend more time in Jerusalem early in his career before settling in Galilee to raise his army of disciples? In short, did Jesus have the opportunity to cleanse the Temple twice?

The conventional wisdom supports a single Temple cleansing, after Jesus entered Jerusalem as Messiah during the last week of his life. That is the consensus of the Synoptic Gospels.

Jesus entered the Temple area and drove out all who were buying and selling there. He overturned the tables of the money changers and the benches of those selling doves. "It is written," he said to them, "'My house will be called a house of prayer,' but you are making it a 'den of robbers.'" (Matt. 21:12-13)

This cleansing had more importance than just a few moneychangers. By entering Jerusalem as the Messiah, Jesus' first act was to cleanse the Temple of all impurities, and this included all activities sanctioned by the High Priests, Caiaphas and Annas. In effect, Jesus was saying, "Your time is over. Step aside for the new Messiah (King)." Needless to say, this act of Temple cleansing was an act of insurrection, and the ruling elites would deal with it with ruthlessness; they would call in Rome's assistance.

Rome was not an innocent bystander in the Jesus story, even though the Gospels downplayed its importance. Their efficient governing was due to strict discipline. As for religion, Rome generally accepted all kinds of worship, as long as said worship did not threaten the established government. You could teach just about anything as long as you freely paid your taxes to Rome. However, the religion of Jesus was not at all sympathetic to the Roman cause. Remember, **Jesus was crucified** for claiming to be King (Messiah) and for his **refusal to pay taxes to Rome**. Jesus' "Give to Caesar what is Caesar's, and to God what is God's" was a call for the Romans to take their dirty money and leave God's land. So you see, the Temple cleansing pitted Jesus against Rome and its henchmen, led by the Procurator, Pilate, and the High Priests, Caiaphas and Annas, who were also appointed by Roman authority.

One thing is certain: Jesus cleansed the Temple after his arrival in Jerusalem, and this act helped seal his fate, his crucifixion by the Romans. Now the next question is not so easy. Did Jesus cleanse the Temple at the beginning of his career? If he did, then he may have risked the same outcome as suffered under Pilate, that being a certain death. Yet it seems as though Jesus walked away from this earlier Temple cleansing. How could this be?

When it was almost time for the Jewish Passover, Jesus went up to Jerusalem. In the temple courts he found men selling cattle, sheep and doves, and others sitting at tables exchanging money. So he made a whip out of cords, and drove all from the temple area, both sheep and cattle; he scattered the coins of the moneychangers and overturned their tables. To those who sold doves he said, "Get these out of here! How dare you turn my Father's house into a market." (John 2:12-16)

This passage has much in common with the Synoptic Gospels' portrayal of Jesus at the Temple. Note that his actions were the same and the main purpose of the cleansing was to rid the Temple area of the unsavory livestock market. This does not mean that Jesus opposed the selling of sacrifices. However, those that sold animals were doing so for a tidy profit, and it was this greed factor which enraged Jesus. Again, this would have struck home against the High Priests, Caiaphas and Annas.

One thing is completely different when comparing John's account to that of the Synoptic Gospels. The Gospel of John's timing of the Temple cleansing was at the beginning of Jesus' ministry, while John the Baptist was still alive. The Gospel of John kept the overall theme of the Temple cleansing but inexplicably placed the event at the very beginning of Jesus' career. Most scholars have just assumed that this was the same Temple cleansing, thinking that John simply misplaced the event. But what if John knew of an earlier Temple cleansing? Is it possible that John combined the actions of the latter Temple cleansing with a tradition of an earlier Temple cleansing? If so, then there must have been a Temple cleansing at the **beginning** and the **end** of Jesus' career. But could Jesus have escaped the wrath of the ruling authorities after this "first" Temple cleansing?

The answer to this question of whether Jesus cleansed the Temple twice can be found in *Antiquities*. Even though Josephus never wrote about the life of Jesus, he did mention another individual throughout his history of the Jews. Judas the Galilean cleansed the Temple at the **beginning** of his career.

There was one Judas, the son of Saripheus, and Matthias, the son of Margalothus, two of the most eloquent men among the Jews, and the most celebrated interpreters of the Jewish laws, and men well-beloved by the people, because of the education of their youth; for all those that were studious of virtue frequented their lectures every day. ...[Judas and Matthias] excited the young men that they would pull down all those works which the King [Herod the Great] had erected contrary to the law of their fathers. ...So these men persuaded [their scholars] to pull down the golden eagle. (*Ant.* 17.149-152)

At the beginning of Judas the Galilean's career, he and his co-teacher, Matthias, convinced their students to tear down the Golden Eagle which Herod had adorned the Temple. This man-made image was contrary to the law and had to be removed according to the teachers. In addition, the Golden Eagle was a sign of fealty towards Rome, the reason why Herod the Great had erected it in the Temple. To tear it down was consistent with the deeds of the Maccabees, some 160 years earlier. Unfortunately, Herod's men arrested the students and the two popular rabbis. Matthias was put to death by fire while Judas languished in imprison, probably as a way for Herod to maintain control of Judas' followers. Shortly thereafter, Herod died, leaving Judas' fate to Herod's son, Archelaus.

The shaky reign of Archelaus offered a possible escape for Judas. To maintain control over his government, Archelaus acquiesced to the crowd's demand for lower taxes and the release of prisoners. (*Ant.* 17.204-205) Thus, the release of Judas was the result of the death of Herod the Great and the weakness of Herod's son, Archelaus. If Herod had not died, then the story of Judas would have ended much earlier. This whole episode proves that it was possible to cleanse the Temple and survive. Surely, Judas the Galilean performed this act. Could Jesus have performed the same act in a different time and place? That is quite doubtful! My theory simply states that Judas the Galilean was the flesh and blood Jesus. Thus, the escape of Judas was also the escape of Jesus. This is the only rational explanation for the Temple cleansing at the beginning of Jesus' career.

The escape in 4 BCE may have given Judas a false sense of security. He may have felt that God would always answer his prayers. When Jesus entered Jerusalem at the end of his career, he must have known that he was on a collision course with Rome. Could Jesus have believed that God would once again deliver him? In this second Temple cleansing, the Synoptic Gospels clearly stated that Jesus' zeal prompted action from the authorities. The story in *Antiquities* is as follows:

Now, there was about this time Jesus, a wise man, if it be lawful to call him a man, for he was a doer of wonderful works - a teacher of such men as receive the truth with pleasure. He drew over to him both many of the Jews, and many of the Gentiles. He was [the] Christ; and when Pilate, at the suggestion of the principal men amongst us, had condemned him to the cross, those that loved him at the first did not forsake him, for he appeared to them alive again the third day, as the divine prophets had foretold these and ten thousand other wonderful things concerning him; and the tribe of Christians, so named from him, are not extinct at this day. (*Ant.* 18.63-64)

This passage from Josephus is clearly an interpolation, as it even makes Josephus into a secret follower of Jesus. This, of course, is absurd. Note that this passage was inserted among other activities dated at around 19 CE. Possibly someone was crucified in 19 CE, but it was not the Gospel Jesus. Consider the unlikely nature of this passage. Josephus never mentioned a word about Jesus before and now claimed that Jesus was the Christ as foretold by the prophets. Then after this, Josephus never mentioned Jesus or his followers again, until the death of James in 62 CE. It is much more likely that this counterfeit passage was really a replacement passage for the death of Judas the Galilean. Josephus introduced the life of Judas and even traced his Fourth Philosophy in great detail. However, Josephus did not record the death of Judas, even though he recorded the deaths of three of his sons and one grandson. It is my contention that Judas was crucified around 19-21 CE, and this was the original passage in *Antiquities*. In all likelihood, Judas cleansed the Temple like the Gospel Jesus, and was later arrested and crucified. Judas' sense of invincibility may have been caused by the Barabbas-style prisoner release in 4 BCE. He clearly trusted that God would deliver him against any odds.

THE LAST SUPPER

Most Christians believe that Jesus initiated the Gospel version of the Last Supper on the night of his arrest. Matthew's version has been reproduced below:

While they were eating, Jesus took bread, gave thanks and broke it, and gave it to his disciples, saying, "Take and eat; this is my body." Then he took the cup, gave thanks and offered it to them, saying, "Drink from it, all of you. This is my blood of the covenant, which is poured out for many for the forgiveness of sins." (Matt. 26:26-28)

This must have been a very confusing time for the Twelve Apostles, as they believed in Jesus as the Messiah, the King who would install the Kingdom of God. But now Jesus was predicting his own death and inviting his co-workers to dine upon his symbolic flesh and blood, knowing this seeming disaster would ultimately turn to triumph, as his death would lead to the forgiveness of sins for all mankind.

Several huge problems arise from the above account. It was not unusual for the disciples to break bread together as many passages illustrate (Acts 2:42; Luke 24:30), but the pagan symbolism attached to the Last Supper would have been shocking to most Jew. Jesus likened the bread and wine to his body and blood. To the observant Jew, this cannibalism would have been abhorrent, as God officially discontinued human sacrifice with Abraham and Isaac (Gen. 22:1-19), and the prophets railed against the nations for this very practice. In addition, Jesus claimed that this was the new covenant for the forgiveness of sins. In one fell swoop, Jesus replaced God's **Everlasting Covenant** with his own Covenant. Obviously, the word everlasting was not a focal point of the

Gospel Jesus' message. And to top it off, this sacrifice would forgive sins, thus removing this messy job from God. It should be obvious that a good Jew like Jesus would not have said such things. Also, from the above discussions about the Transfiguration, the triumphal entry in Jerusalem and the second Temple cleansing, Jesus strongly believed himself to be the deliverer, the Messiah, the chosen One of God. In reality, Jesus did **not** believe that his mission would end in death and human sacrifice.

If the entire Last Supper dialogue did not come from the mouth of Jesus, then where did it originate? The answer is Paul, the Apostle to the Gentiles.

I want you to know brothers, that the gospel I preached is not something that man made up. I did not receive it from any man, nor was I taught it; rather **I received it by revelation from Jesus Christ**. (Gal. 1:11-12) (Emphasis mine)

Even though Paul had never met Jesus in the flesh, he claimed that the Risen Jesus had given him his own unique gospel, an amazing claim considering the Jewish Apostles were teaching a different gospel, given to them by the earthly Jesus. Paul even admitted that his gospel did not come from any man, whether that was James or Cephas. This mind-set should be considered delusional. So, we must question whether the following passage from Paul actually came from the earthly Jesus. In fact, it came from the Risen Christ, the Jesus of Paul's fertile imagination.

For I [Paul] received from the Lord [through revelations] what I passed on to you: The Lord Jesus, on the night he was betrayed [handed over], took bread, and when he had given thanks, he broke it and said, "This is my body, which is for you; do this in remembrance of me." In the same way, after supper he took the cup, saying, "This cup is the new covenant in my blood; do this, whenever you drink it, in remembrance of me." (1 Cor. 11:23-25)

This revelation has been inserted into the Gospel accounts of the Last Supper. Thus, a long-help sacrament of the Church may be nothing more than a Law-hating Herodian's vision. Such a celebration did not originate with Jesus and was never practiced by his Jewish disciples, including Cephas, James and John, the Pillars of the Jewish Church.

So where did Paul's revelations come from? An early Church writer, Justin Martyr, said this concerning the Christian's Lord's Supper: "The wicked devils have imitated [the Lord's Supper] in the mysteries of Mithra, commanding the same thing to be done." (5) He also stated that the demons anticipated the Christian mysteries [Lord's Supper] and prepared parodies of then beforehand. (6) The Lord's Supper revelation of Paul was simply a borrowing of the Mithraic Lord's Supper. From Mithra, the Gentile Christians also stole the idea of "washed in the blood of the lamb." (7)

After this is understood, the picture of Jesus going willingly to his death must be reassessed. Judas the Galilean had officially been titled "Jesus" at the Coronation (Transfiguration), and he was bent on liberating Israel from Rome, just as Joshua (Jesus) conquered Palestine. The Last Supper may have been filled with prayer but those were confident prayers. God would not forsake them.

One other element which supposedly occurred during the Last Supper was the foretelling of Judas Iscariot's betrayal and the denial by Peter. As members of the 21st century, we should question the veracity of these stories, as prophecy is unscientific and cannot be proved with empirical data. It is quite possible that a betrayal did occur (Paul betrayed the Jewish Church) and that Cephas denied Jesus after the arrest, but the prediction by Jesus may have been placed upon his lips by later authors. Most likely, these stories were circulated by Jesus' later disciples, for the sole purpose of excusing Jesus' and Cephas' failures. We have already detailed that Judas Iscariot was an invented character to help shift blame from the Romans to the Jews. This we can be certain: Jesus did not predict a betrayal by Judas Iscariot. As for Cephas (Peter), he may have denied Jesus three times. The prediction of Cephas' denial by Jesus helped insulate Cephas from criticism after Cephas had disassociated himself from Jesus right after the arrest. Certainly, Cephas may have saved his own skin by denying his allegiance to Jesus. From what we know of the Fourth Philosophy, this was extremely unusual. A good disciple would have died with his master. But the denial by Cephas may have been **ordered by Jesus beforehand**, in order to help keep the movement going in case of the unthinkable, arrest and crucifixion.

THE ARREST ON THE MOUNT OF OLIVES

When the Last Supper had ended, Jesus and the disciples prepared to leave for the Garden of Gethsemane. "The disciples said, 'See Lord, here are two swords.' 'That is enough,' he said." (Luke 22:38) Now it seems astonishing that Jesus planned to confront the Roman soldiers with only two swords in hand. Surely, he could have mustered quite an army of followers, equipped with all types of weapons. Why then did he choose to have only two swords? The traditional view claims that Jesus had accepted the fact that he was to die for the sins of humanity. But if that were the case, then why take any swords?

After leaving the house, Jesus took Peter, James and John to the Garden of Gethsemane for a prayer vigil. Again, if the game had already been decided, then why was there a need for constant prayer? Perhaps this vigil was a final push to gain access to the power of God. Remember that the disciples had taken two swords to the Garden. Jesus and his few disciples were to start the battle and God would finish it. Jesus had plenty of Biblical precedents to support this foolhardy idea. Gideon was asked to fight the Midianites even though his clan was the weakest in Manasseh, and he was least in his clan. Even so, Gideon raised an army of 30,000 men. God unilaterally decided that the number was too great, for if Gideon defeated the Midianites with such a large army, then Israel might boast of its own strength and not the strength of their God. So Gideon sent 20,000 able bodied men home and proceeded with 10,000. Still, God said that there were far too many soldiers.

So Gideon took the men down to the water. There the Lord told him, "Separate those who lap with their tongues like a dog from those who kneel down to drink." Three hundred men lapped with their hands to their mouths. All the rest got down on their knees to drink. The Lord said to Gideon, "With the three hundred men that lapped I will save you and give the Midianites into your hands." (Judges 7:5-7)

At first, Gideon believed his 30,000 men would not suffice, but God led him to victory with only 300 men. As Jesus saw it, this miracle would be reproduced on an even greater scale on the Mount of Olives, with God leading the way. In fact, the battle and the results had already been prophesied.

When Jesus entered Jerusalem, newly anointed Messiah or King of Israel, he rode into the city on a donkey, as prophesied by Zechariah.

Rejoice greatly, O Daughter of Zion! Shout, Daughter of Jerusalem! See, your king comes to you, righteous and having salvation, gentle and riding on a donkey, on a colt, the foal of a donkey. (Zech. 9:9)

Surely, Jesus and his advisors knew of this passage as they prepared to enter Jerusalem. Like any competent politician, Jesus used the Scriptures to his advantage. Jesus was placed on a donkey to fulfill this prophecy. Now this is not to say that Jesus and his disciples did not believe that Jesus was really the Messiah. They just knew that the Messiah would perform certain tasks, and the fulfillment of this prophecy was one of these tasks. So, if they all believed that Jesus was fulfilling the prophecy regarding the triumphal entry into Jerusalem, then why would they ignore the great Oracle by Zechariah?

Then the Lord will go out and fight against those nations as he fights in the day of battle. On that day his feet will stand on the Mount of Olives. ...

This is the plague with which the Lord will strike all the nations that fought against Jerusalem: Their flesh will rot while they are standing on their feet, their eyes will rot in their sockets, and their tongues will rot in their mouths. On that day men will be stricken by the Lord with great panic. Each man will seize the hand of another, and they will attack each other. Judah too will fight at Jerusalem. (Zech. 14:3-4, 12-14) (8)

From this passage, one can sense why Jesus believed two swords were enough. All they had to do was initiate the fight on the Mount of Olives and the enemies would turn upon themselves. Jesus was an apocalyptical preacher; he believed the word of the Lord literally. If God said that the victory would be his, who was he to argue.

The prayer in the Garden of Gethsemane was designed to access the power of God. For God to intervene, Jesus and his disciples had to believe fully in the word of God. Listen to the words of James, the brother of the Lord:

Elijah was a man just like us. He prayed earnestly that it would not rain, and it did not rain on the land for three and a half years. Again, he prayed, and the heavens gave rain, and the earth produced its crops. (James 5:17-18)

If the prayers of men could change the course of Mother Nature, then these prayers could also defeat Rome. So why did the prayers of Jesus go unanswered? Reading the passage in Matthew 26:36-46, we note that although Jesus prayed with fervor, his favorite three disciples (James, Peter and John) could not help themselves; they napped through the entire prayer vigil. On the night of God's deliverance of Rome into their hands, these three (the Pillars) could not stay awake. This would be like running for President and not staying up for the election results. Such an idea is fantastic, but was absolutely necessary in order to retain the Messianic fervor for Jesus. You see, the arrest was not Jesus' fault but that of the Three Apostles. (9)

All this appears ridiculous to our 21st century conception of sane behavior. But this happened two thousand years ago, when miracles were commonplace. All acts of nature and events of chance, which could not be easily explained, were attributed to God or the gods: from floods, to earthquakes, to plagues to dreams and visions. And one thing is certain: Jesus was well versed in Scripture. He believed in the prophecy of Zechariah so much that common sense would appear as an affront to God. That is why only two swords were taken to confront the Roman soldiers. It should not be missed that Judas the Galilean had already participated in a disastrous conflict with the authorities, in the Golden Eagle Temple Cleansing, during the reign of Herod the Great. In that Temple cleansing, the followers of Judas were no more prepared than the followers of Jesus. Judas was also well acquainted with Scripture, being called a wise man by Josephus, well respected by the people for his knowledge of the Law. (*Ant.* 17.149) So, in this blind, almost foolhardy devotion to God, Judas the Galilean and Jesus were inseparable. In fact, the earlier arrest of Judas (4 BCE) had made him a much more careful preacher. He carried on the Census rebellion in 6 CE but was never caught. His luck ended with his march into Jerusalem and this final conflict with Rome.

The rush to confront Rome may have been precipitated by Pilate's first acts as procurator in 18 CE. Judas (Jesus) had been careful in avoiding the long arm of the law, having evaded Herod, Archelaus and Pilate's predecessors since 4 BCE. In fact, the last time Judas had been in Jerusalem was during the Golden Eagle Temple Cleansing in 4 BCE. That sedition ended tragically with the deaths of Matthias and many of the young students. But a funny thing happened as a result of this debacle: the movement grew. The blood of the martyrs fueled a great expansion. This lesson was not lost upon Judas. Although he believed mightily in the power of God to defeat Rome, he nevertheless had a fall-back position. I believe that Judas (Jesus) and his core advisors (Cephas, James and John) had already worked out the Suffering Servant scenario based upon Isaiah 53. If Judas (Jesus) were captured and killed like Matthias, then his death would serve the movement as well.

The ability to fashion Scripture was an important element of the evolving Fourth Philosophy. Judas (Jesus) had become the Righteous Teacher and now assumed the role of Suffering Servant. This was absolutely necessary to connect the Fourth Philosophy with God's ultimate plans. If Jesus had succeeded on the Mount of Olives, such an interpretation would have been unnecessary. In the Gospel story, this alternative plan was put into Jesus' own words **before** he entered Jerusalem. Jesus clearly told his disciples that he had to suffer and die. Note that his disciples had trouble understanding this message. That is because it was not reality. This was only a secondary plan, one to be used in case of failure on the Mount of Olives. But the Gospel story was meant to make Jesus all knowing. It is more comforting to think that Jesus understood what he was doing as opposed to failing miserably. This treatment of Jesus' own failure on the Mount of Olives was repeated when Jesus' own sons were also captured and crucified. In the Gospel story, Jesus predicted that two brothers (James and John) were to drink of the same cup as he, namely crucifixion. The two sons of Judas the Galilean suffered crucifixion, not the sons of Zebedee. This could have been a crushing blow to the movement, but instead was turned into a prediction by Jesus. So, even in defeat, the movement claimed victory. These guys had a future in marketing!

THE TRIAL BEFORE ANNAS AND CAIAPHAS

After the arrest in the Garden of Gethsemane, Jesus was taken to see the High Priests, Annas and Caiaphas. This trial occurred at night so that a guilty sentence could be passed before the disciples could organize themselves in opposition. Before examining the evidence against Jesus, it would be useful to outline the backgrounds of the High Priests, those responsible for capturing and convicting Jesus.

Annas became High Priest in 6 CE, right after Judas the Galilean's tax revolt. According to Josephus, Annas was appointed by Cyrenius to replace Joazar, a High Priest appointed under Herod the Great. (*Ant.* 18.26) Thus, Annas became the first High Priest to be appointed under **direct** Roman rule. This is important because it describes the type of man who now held the High Priesthood. Annas was responsible for keeping the masses in line while Rome continued to raise revenues through onerous taxation. It should not be missed that Annas' greatest thorn in the flesh was Judas the Galilean, the rebel who opposed Roman taxation. According to Josephus, Annas remained High Priest until the rule of Gratus (15 CE) and was replaced by a series of High Priests, ending with his son-in-law, Caiaphas, in 18 CE. (*Ant.* 18.33-35) (John 18:13) We also know that five of Annas' sons also served as High Priests, until the year 62 CE. (*Ant.* 20.198) It could easily be argued that Annas was the real power behind the capture of Jesus, as he surely controlled the High Priesthood through his family ties for over a half century (6-62 CE). This power can also be seen in two passages from the New Testament. Luke's timeline had John the Baptist coming in 28-29 CE, during the High Priesthood of Annas and Caiaphas. (Luke 3:2) In addition, Acts had Peter and John tried before Annas, the High Priest, along with members of his family, including Caiaphas, John and Alexander. (Acts 4:5-6)

Caiaphas, the son-in-law of Annas, was appointed High Priest in 18 CE by Gratus. He served in that position until 37 CE, the same year that Pilate was removed as Governor. (I have argued that Pilate also came to office in 18 CE as the text in *Antiquities* suggests. (See Chapter 1.)) The close relationship between Annas and Caiaphas should not be dismissed as unimportant. Just as Annas protected the Roman government, so did Caiaphas.

The Gospel of Matthew had Jesus being brought to Caiaphas after the arrest. (Matt. 26:57) Mark had Jesus being brought before the High Priests, the elders and the Sanhedrin, not designating either Annas or Caiaphas. Likewise, Luke also omitted the names of Annas and Caiaphas, although he did mention them in Luke 3:2 and Acts 4:5-6. However, the Gospel of John gave these two High Priests a larger role in the drama. Why was there such divergence in the treatment of the High Priests? The answer is obvious: in the very early Gentile Church, it may have been the practice to hide the true origin of Jesus. Any mention of Annas brought the reader back in time to the Census of Cyrenius and the tax revolt of Judas the Galilean. Therefore, the Synoptic Gospels downplayed both Annas and Caiaphas. (10) By the time John was written (mid second century), the fear of identification was no longer an issue. The traditions of Annas and Caiaphas were more clearly defined in his Gospel.

The Gospel of John stated that Caiaphas had prophesied that Jesus must die for the nation. (John 11:49-53) John also mentioned that Caiaphas was High Priest **that year** (John 11:51). We know that Caiaphas served as High Priest from 18-37 CE, so what does John mean by **that year**? Under Gratus, the High Priesthood was changed yearly from 15-18 CE. Caiaphas would have been High Priest starting in 18 CE. Therefore, his first year was 18-19 CE, the very time when Jesus (Judas) was arrested. This is consistent with the rest of Josephus' chronology in *Antiquities* 18:4-84 and the *Memoranda*, which stated that Jesus died in 21 CE. This may also explain why Annas was still so powerful and active in Jewish affairs. He, most likely, was calling the shots, with his sons and son-in-law, Caiaphas, simply following orders.

After the arrest, Jesus was taken from the Garden of Gethsemane directly to Annas. According to John, the questioning of Jesus was performed by Annas, and when all questions were answered, either by silence or guile, Annas sent Jesus to Caiaphas. (John 18:12-24) John simply stated that the Jews then led Jesus from Caiaphas to Pilate. (John 18:28) In short, the one responsible for the actual arrest and questioning was Annas.

This obsession by Annas with Jesus and his followers is very important in our search for the historical Jesus. There were two individuals whose legacies dominated first century Judea: Annas and Judas the Galilean. Annas became High Priest while Judas was fomenting his tax revolt in 6-7 CE. He later presided over the arrest and questioning of Jesus. In Acts 4:5-6, Annas also led the charge against Peter and John, after the crucifixion of Jesus. His son, Jonathan, was murdered by the Sicarii, a later designation of the Fourth Philosophy of Judas the Galilean. (*War* 2.254-257) And finally, another son, Ananus, was responsible for the stoning of James the Just, the brother of the Lord. (*Ant.* 20.197-200) After this murder of James, the Sicarii began kidnapping members of Ananus' family. Thus, it appears as if the history of Annas' family was tied closely together with the movement of Judas the Galilean.

THE TRIAL BEFORE PILATE

The High Priests, Annas and Caiaphas, were closely aligned with the Roman Governor, Pontius Pilate. When they had finished questioning Jesus, they handed him over to Pilate for sentencing. As already noted, the timeframe for Annas' and Caiaphas' role in the Jesus arrest was approximately 18-19 CE. Traditionally, Pilate has been assumed to have been Governor from 26-37 CE. However, per Chapter 1, it was determined that Pilate fit into the 18-19 CE timeframe, per the events related by Josephus.

Pilate was a vicious man, as noted by both Josephus and Philo. (11) He would not have cringed from ordering a crucifixion or two. Rome had used crucifixion as a political punishment since the first century BCE. The most famous political prisoner crucified was Spartacus (died 71 BCE), who led a slave revolt of 70,000. The 1960 movie starring Kirk Douglas shows the crushing power of mass crucifixions, where six-thousand tortured souls rotted in the sun for up to three months, for all to witness. Such an execution was meant to send a message to the living: follow Rome or follow these poor creatures to the cross.

So the question is this: what crime would warrant the sentence of crucifixion? The orthodox answer is that Jesus spoke and acted against the Jewish Law (like Paul) and the Jews **forced** Pilate to crucify him. The Gospels claimed that Jesus supported Roman taxation (like Paul) and did not proclaim an earthly kingdom for himself. At this, Pilate could see no need to crucify an innocent man. However, the Jews blackmailed Pilate, and he was forced to "wash his hands" of the whole affair. That is the Gospel portrayal of Roman justice. The Slavonic Josephus adds a bit to this picture. According to the main passage about Jesus, the Chief Priests bribed Pilate with thirty talents so that Jesus would be killed. (12) This source also blamed the Jews more than Pilate, although this section of the passage was no doubt reworked by later Christian editing. Note also that the thirty talents was substituted for the thirty pieces of silver, suggesting that the story of Judas Iscariot had not yet been invented when this was originally written.

That Pilate "washed his hands" of the whole affair does not ring true. After all, it was his job to keep peace in the name of Caesar. Beyond this, Pilate supposedly offered a prisoner release to the Jewish mob. Only an incompetent ruler, unsure of himself and his supporters, would have released a dangerous prisoner in such a manner. Remember, Pilate had the power of Rome behind him. So this was **not** Roman justice, but elements of this story did occur during the lifetime of Judas the Galilean. At the Golden Eagle Temple Cleansing, the High Priest stepped down because of a dream where he had sexual relations with his wife. (*Ant.* 17.166) In the Gospels, Pilate was much troubled by a dream his wife had concerning Jesus (Matt. 27:19), causing him to step down or to "wash his hands". Also, after the Golden Eagle Temple Cleansing and the death of Herod the Great (4 BCE), Archelaus did release prisoners to the mob, with the most important prisoner being Judas the Galilean. He did this to appease the people. Thus, our story of Pilate's hand washing and his release of Barabbas really came from the 4 BCE story of Judas the Galilean. (*War* 2.4)

In reality, Rome accepted all types of religions as long as those religions were not opposed to Roman rule. For instance, the religion of Paul would have been perfectly fine with the Roman authorities.

Everyone must submit himself to the governing authorities, for there is no authority except which God has established. The authorities that exist have been established by God. ...He [ruler] is God's servant, an angel of wrath to bring punishment on the wrongdoer. Therefore, it is necessary to submit to the authorities, not only because of possible punishment but also because of conscience. That is why you pay taxes, for the authorities are God's servants, who give their full time to governing. (Romans 13:1-7)

It is no wonder that Gentile Christianity thrived in Roman lands, eventually capturing the government as well. We can take Paul's reasoning here even further, to the absurd: God condoned Hitler and his massacre of the Jews. Therefore, all men should have submitted to Hitler's desires as he was established by God. Remember that Paul wrote Romans in the late 30's by my calculation and in the mid 50's by traditional dating. In the late 30's, Caligula ruled the Roman Empire. This Caligula threatened the Jewish nation with the greatest threat since the days of Judas Maccabee: he ordered a statue of himself erected in the Temple in Jerusalem. Only Caligula's assassination stopped this blasphemy. In the mid 50's, Nero was Emperor. Nero killed his own wife and unborn child as well as his evil mother. In 64 CE, Nero presided over the torture and execution of "Jewish Christians" after the Great Fire of Rome. In either case, Paul supported a lunatic and claimed that God empowered this lunatic to by his angel of wrath. Can this Pauline dribble be considered anything but utter nonsense? And by the way, Caligula and Nero were as mad as Adolf Hitler.

Paul showed good political sense by sucking up to the ruling elites. Paul did have a Herodian background and probably worked for his cousin, Agrippa I (See Chapter 10). Certainly, the Jewish Christians or Fourth Philosophy had a much different viewpoint. They had no sympathy for Rome or for any other occupying power (remember Judas Maccabee and the Greeks). So the idea of Pilate intervening in purely Jewish affairs cannot be supported by the facts. However, Pilate and the other Roman procurators did have a stake in squashing dissent. No doubt, Pilate viewed Jesus as a real threat to the government and its tax collecting machine.

Two charges were leveled against Jesus that would have earned him a crucifixion penalty: his crusade against paying taxes to Rome and his claim of Kingship. The Gospel of Luke succinctly stated, "We have found this man [Jesus] subverting our nation. He opposes payment of taxes to Caesar and claims to be Messiah, a king." (Luke 23:2) These two charges were supported by Jesus' popular arrival in Jerusalem. (Matt. 21:6-11) The people would support a Messiah who could free them from foreign occupation and taxation. What type of Messiah would support the Roman tax system?

On the tax issue, both Jesus and Judas the Galilean strongly opposed foreign taxation. The Fourth Philosophy coalesced around the tax issue during the Census of Cyrenius (6 CE). On the side of Roman taxation stood the Herodians and the appointed High Priests, the most important being Annas (6-15 CE). Annas supported the taxation and would have been the archenemy of Judas the Galilean. As noted earlier, Annas and his son-in-law, Caiaphas, were in charge of the trial which accused Jesus of opposing Roman taxation. (It should be once again noted that Paul would have sided with Annas and Caiaphas regarding the tax issue.) In reality, the tax issue brought Jesus to the cross. Anyone standing in the way of revenue collection would be crucified as an example for others.

The second charge of being Messiah, a King, would also have brought swift retribution. Judas the Galilean's disciples would never have accepted Roman rule since God was their only master. (*Ant.* 18.23) The introduction of Pilate and his overt confrontational style must have maddened the Fourth Philosophy. Not only did Pilate bring effigies into the Temple courts, but he siphoned off Temple funds for his own building projects. Each of these acts goaded the Fourth Philosophy into action, and it is at this point that Judas accepted his role as Messiah of all Jews. He would cleanse the Temple as he and Matthias had done some twenty-three years earlier (4 BCE). Judas may have been hailed as Messiah as early as 4 BCE, but this nationwide fight had brought the movement to new heights. By fighting the greatest power in the world, Judas (Jesus) would be a savior to all Jews throughout the world.

THE TRIAL BEFORE HEROD ANTIPAS

The trial before Herod Antipas was only reported by the Gospel of Luke. (Luke 23:6-15) It seems strange that this trial would be reported by only one of the four Gospels. Perhaps this event did not really occur or did not occur at the end of Jesus' life. The argument against the Herod trial has much to do with Pontius Pilate. If Jesus were really a rebel leader, then would Pilate relinquish his role in the affair? Pilate would not have sent Jesus to Herod as even Luke admitted that the two were enemies at this time. (Luke 23:12) So where did this story originate?

I have no doubt that the Herod story had its origin in Judas the Galilean's rich history. Thus, Luke did not invent the story; he merely twisted some facts about the movement's founder. At the Golden Eagle Temple Cleansing, Judas and Matthias were arrested and brought before Herod the Great (4 BCE). After they had explained their actions to Herod in Jerusalem, he sent the two preachers to Jericho, where he (Herod) questioned the preachers in front of other religious leaders. (*Ant.* 17.157-161) This shifting of locales and the name Herod were simply employed by Luke in his account of the trial before Pilate.

THE BARABBAS PRISONER RELEASE

No story is as questionable as that of Jesus and Barabbas. The New Testament pits Jesus against Barabbas (the son of the Father), in a popularity contest among the Jews. In fact, in many early manuscripts, Barabbas' first name was Jesus. So, we have a good Jesus (son of the Father) versus a bad Jesus (son of the Father). And of course, the Jews opted for the bad Jesus. This unfortunate choice shifted the blame for Jesus' crucifixion from Rome to the Jews. This shift of blame alone should warn of us some historical shenanigans. When Pilate washed his hands of all responsibility, the Jews said, "Let his blood be on us and on our children." (Matt. 27:25) This blood has been the excuse for countless persecutions against the Jews over the subsequent centuries.

The connection between Jesus and Barabbas may have been conveyed in an early Christian story, as it is reported in all four Gospels. This story was probably about an actual prisoner release, and Barabbas was simply a literary device, invented by the Gospel writers, to shift blame from Rome to the Jews. A representative passage from Matthew is as follows:

Now it was the **governor's custom at the Feast to release a prisoner chosen by the crowd**. At that time they had a **notorious [distinguished]** prisoner, called Barabbas. So when the crowd had gathered, Pilate asked them, "Which one do you want me to release to you: Barabbas, or Jesus who is called Christ?" For he knew it was out of envy that they had handed Jesus over to him.

While Pilate was sitting on the judge's seat, his wife sent him this message:

"Don't have anything to do with that innocent man, for I have suffered a great deal today in a dream because of him."

But the chief priests and elders persuaded the crowd to ask for Barabbas and to have Jesus executed.

"Which of the two do you want me to release to you?" asked the governor.

"Barabbas," they answered.

"What shall I do then, with Jesus who is called Christ?" Pilate asked.

They all answered, "Crucify him!" (Matt. 27:15-22) (Emphasis mine)

In Mark and Luke, Barabbas had also been imprisoned for insurrection and for murder. Undoubtedly, Barabbas was a bad character, at least to the ruling authorities. In Matthew, Barabbas was given the description of a "distinguished prisoner," translated as notorious in the quoted version. (13) From the Roman standpoint and from Josephus' writings, this Barabbas was a revolutionary, designated as a bandit. It should not be missed that Jesus was crucified between two bandits! Hyam Maccoby wrote this concerning Barabbas: "As a leader and distinguished man, Barabbas was probably a Rabbi like the Zealot leaders, Judas the Galilean and Zadok." (14) And according to Josephus, Judas and his former partner, Matthias, were known as the "most eloquent men among the Jews…and men well-beloved by the people." (*Ant.* 17.149) This tie between Barabbas and Judas the Galilean makes perfect sense as the Fourth Philosophy was intent on fomenting revolution. It also answers why the crowd asked for Barabbas: his movement was a popular one among the masses. Such a figure as Barabbas may have been a hero to some, but not to the Romans. That is why placing a member of the Fourth Philosophy in a bad light was standard fare for the Gospel writers and Josephus. They were writing to a Roman audience and hoped to gain their favor.

This Barabbas, whether real or invented, had a huge problem: an uprising or revolt against Rome was punishable by death, death by crucifixion. The Romans had used crucifixion as a deterrent for years. Spartacus, the ex-gladiator, led a slave revolt in 73 BCE. He threatened the status quo in Rome and was crucified along with 6,000 of his followers. This method of punishment was inhumane as the victim often lived on for days. But the greatest deterrent was for the living. Rome's message was this: misbehave and you, too, may someday hang from a cross. It was a ruthless but extremely efficient tool for keeping order. Any bandit like Barabbas knew that such an ending was likely, for the Romans did not coddle revolutionaries.

If Rome's attitude towards insurrectionists was set in stone, then why did Pilate release Barabbas to the crowd? Was Pilate a soft-hearted man? From what is known through the writings of Josephus, Pilate was anything but kind. In fact, he was recalled to Rome because of his brutality. Did the tradition of releasing prisoners trump Pilate's hatred of the Jews? This is doubtful as nowhere in the Roman Empire did the Romans practice this supposed ritual of releasing a prisoner to the crowd. In addition, Matthew wrote that the prisoner release was the governor's custom to grant to the crowd at Passover while Mark 15:6 stated it was the custom at **every** Feast. (Josephus never mentioned any prisoner release custom. For example, Herod the Great would have been as ruthless as the Roman governors, and he did not release prisoners.) Regardless of whose custom it was, or how often it was supposedly practiced, following such a ritual would defy logic for Pilate. Why would the Romans expend resources in capturing revolutionaries only to release them once again into the population?

Think of it this way: if the United States captured Bin Laden, would there be any chance of releasing him to the Arab crowds? Of course not! Just imagine the outrage that this action would create in the streets of America. Congress and the President would be summarily thrown out of office and replaced with hardcore opponents to terrorism. The same held true for the efficient Roman government. They would not have released Barabbas if he had truly been an insurrectionist. And considering that Pilate was not bribed, he had absolutely nothing to gain from this action. Thus, the traditional view of the Barabbas event has this one insurmountable problem: Rome's efficiency and mercy did not mix.

Hyam Maccoby argued that the Barabbas story was simply a purposeful garbling of a Jesus legend. Perhaps Jesus was imprisoned by the Romans for insurrection. (Jesus did enter Jerusalem as a Messiah and did cleanse the temple, thus challenging the status quo. It should also be remembered that Jesus was later crucified for claiming to be King and for his refusal to pay taxes to Rome.) While in prison, his followers clamored for the release of Jesus, son of the father. This chant could have also been phrased as the release of Jesus Barabbas! Jesus was known to have called God Abba, or Father. Jesus may have been the only prisoner with Pilate, and this Jesus was the one accused of insurrection against Rome. (15) This explanation makes more sense than the Gospel version because Pilate would have never released a dangerous revolutionary to the crowd. But if this scenario were true, then no prisoner release actually occurred under Pilate. In this, Maccoby was on the right track: **there was no Barabbas prisoner release during the governorship of Pilate.** The supposed release of a dangerous revolutionary was simply a way to shift blame from the Romans to the Jews. Note that the Jews preferred a revolutionary figure over the peace-loving Jesus. This appears absurd considering the Jews had hailed Jesus as Messiah just a few days earlier. By accepting Jesus as Messiah, the Jewish crowds were honoring a revolutionary figure. The Jews never really believed that Jesus was a peace-loving preacher. Just the opposite was true: he was the Messiah, the one who would rid the land of its foreign oppressors. So, does this mean that there was never a prisoner release? After all, this Barabbas prisoner release may have been an early legend about Jesus. There may have been some truth to the story.

The only other explanation to the Barabbas question involves another character from the pages of Josephus, namely Judas the Galilean. In 4 BCE, Judas and his co-teacher, Matthias, led an insurrection in Jerusalem. They instructed their followers to tear down Herod the Great's Golden Eagle, which adorned the Temple. This Golden Eagle was Herod's homage to Rome, but it was seen as a graven image and a symbol of an occupying power, Rome. To Judas and Matthias, this removal of the Golden Eagle was a cleansing of the Temple, in the same way that Judas Maccabee (167 BCE) cleansed the Temple when Antiochus Epiphanes polluted it with idols and unholy sacrifices. The result of Judas' and Matthias' cleansing was arrest and imprisonment for the two teachers as well as for their students.

Herod had Matthias put to death by the flame. Judas the Galilean was kept in prison for a special event. Herod was nearing the end of his life, and he had serious mental problems. He knew that the people of Judea hated him with a passion, and no one throughout the land would mourn his death. Therefore, the demented mind of Herod arrived at a solution to his unpopularity: arrest and imprison notable people throughout the kingdom and kill them on the day of his own death. In that way, all of Israel would mourn on the day of Herod's death. (*Ant.* 17.175-181)

After Herod's death, his advisors canceled this mass execution. To this act of sanity, Judas owed his life. However, Judas still languished in prison. This continued to be the case as Herod's son, Archelaus, tried to win support from the people. Archelaus' power base was weak, so he tried to sway the peoples' opinions by granting their requests. Concerning the aftermath of Herod's death in 4 BCE, Josephus reported the following:

Whereupon the multitude, as it is usual with them, supposed that the first days of those that enter upon such governments, declare the intentions of those that accept them; and so by how much Archelaus spoke the more gently and civilly to them, by so much did they more highly commend him, and made application to him for the grant of what they desired. Some made a clamor that he would ease them of some of their annual payments; **but others desired him to release those who were put in prison by Herod, who were many and had been put there at several times**; others of them required that he would take away those taxes which had been severely laid upon what was publicly sold and bought. **So Archelaus contradicted them in nothing**, since he pretended to do all things so as to get the good will of the multitude to him, as looking upon that good will to be a great step towards the **preservation of the government**. (*Ant.* 17.204-205) (Emphasis mine)

Unlike Pilate, Archelaus had reason to listen to the crowd. He needed the goodwill of the masses. Pilate had the power of Rome and cared little for the wishes of those he governed. The Jewish crowd asked three favors of Archelaus: the easing of their annual payments, the release of prisoners and the removal of a sales tax. In addition to the obvious prisoner release request, the crowd asked for the reduction or elimination of two taxes. This hatred of taxation ran throughout the ministry of Judas the Galilean and was also present in the charge against Jesus, as related by Luke 23:2.

After the prisoners were released, Judas escaped to Galilee and began building his forces. His dual messages of equality and tax relief were popular and drew the poor to his cause. The poor were a majority in Judea, so there was always a sympathetic ear to hear his preaching. This same dynamic can also be argued for Jesus. Traveling among the small villages in Galilee, Judas the Galilean (Jesus) became Messiah, and later he would take his mission back to Jerusalem, to confront Rome and their hirelings on the Mount of Olives.

Was this 4 BCE prisoner release the framework for the Barabbas prisoner release? Judas was a revered rabbi just as Jesus was reported to be. Judas had just lost his co-teacher, or perhaps his father, to the flames of Herod the Great. Could Barabbas mean son of the father, or rather, Judas, the son of Matthias? Note that Judas Maccabee was the son of a Mattathias.

In addition, the prisoner release makes sense only in the timeframe of Archelaus and definitely not in the governorship of Pilate. Pilate would never have released a dangerous revolutionary, but Archelaus performed this very act as a way of gaining popular support from the masses.

The Slavonic Josephus offers a few insights into the Barabbas affair which support my hypothesis. According to this tradition, the miracle worker (Jesus) was captured by Pilate's guard at the insistence of the Jewish leaders. When Pilate questioned Jesus, he found him innocent of all crimes and summarily released him. This enraged the Jewish leaders, who then bribed Pilate with thirty talents to arrest Jesus again. With money in hand, Pilate gave the Jewish leaders authority to have Jesus crucified. (16) Note that the Slavonic Josephus denied the existence of both Judas Iscariot (the thirty talents) and Barabbas (the actual release of Jesus).

It must be understood that this particular Slavonic Josephus passage has been altered or greatly influenced by an early **Gentile** Christian, not unlike the Gospel presentation. The Romans were not totally innocent in the whole affair. In the process of capturing Jesus, Pilate killed many of the disciples, and

Pilate did accept a bribe which resulted in Jesus' crucifixion. But the treatment of the Romans was quite friendly in relation to the author's portrayal of the Jews. The Jewish leaders were selfish, unscrupulous and blood thirsty in this account. Surely, this particular part of the Slavonic Josephus was slanted against the Jews by a Gentile hand. No early Jewish Christian would have painted such a picture of events. To the early Jewish Christians, Rome was the enemy. After all, Rome crucified Jesus!

If this came from an early Gentile Christian, then one would expect an orthodox interpretation of Jesus' last days. But that is not the case! The Slavonic Josephus states that Pilate released Jesus, not Barabbas. This release of Jesus is consistent with my contention that Judas was released by Archelaus. The difference being that that Slavonic Josephus placed Jesus' release at the hands of Pilate, an unlikely event. This telescoping of Judas the Galilean's life into a few short years necessitated placing all events into the last days of the ministry. The release of Judas in 4 BCE was too good of a story to be omitted. The Gospels and the Slavonic Josephus both shifted this event to the timeframe of Pilate.

In the early Gentile Church, the release of Jesus was still being preached. Note that a Barabbas was not even mentioned; he had not yet been invented by the Gospel writers. Although this Slavonic Josephus passage has been plainly altered by a sympathetic Gentile Christian, the details do not support the traditional Barabbas story. One thing is clear: the tradition of Jesus' release was strong, and the author of this passage was relating the truth as he understood it.

The traditional story of Barabbas is not true, as determined by common sense and supported by the Slavonic Josephus. The Roman procurator, Pilate, would not have acted in such an irresponsible manner. Thus, this story is merely a twisted version of an earlier event in the life of Judas the Galilean. Maccoby wrote that Barabbas was probably a rabbi like Judas the Galilean. But Maccoby did not realize that Judas was part of the prisoner release story. This Judas was nicknamed Jesus, a name meaning salvation. The chants of the Jewish crowd for Jesus Barabbas was real, a part of history. What was lost was the actual man of history, Judas the Galilean.

THE CRUCIFIXION

Paul claimed that righteousness was gained through the death of Jesus on the cross, not in the vain act of following the Law.

I have been crucified with Christ and I no longer live, but Christ lives in me. The life I live in the body, I live by faith in the Son of God, who loved me and gave himself for me. I do not set aside the grace of God, for if righteousness could be gained through the Law, Christ died for nothing. (Gal. 2:20-21)

This is the same letter where Paul claimed personal revelations from God, a gospel obviously different than that of the Jewish apostles. (Gal. 1:11-12) These personal revelations had much to do with the pagan religions of the time. Paul absorbed these into his subconsciousness and injected the practices and beliefs of Mithraism into his vision of Jesus. In Mithraism, "the doctrine was that resurrection and eternal life were secured by drenching or sprinkling with the actual blood of a sacrificial bull or ram … or lamb." (17) To be "washed in the blood of the lamb" was the same for the followers of Mithra, Paul and most Christians today. (18) So the Crucifixion to Paul was not only necessary but a good thing as well. For outside of this blood of Christ, there could be no forgiveness. This belief stood in stark contrast to that of John the Baptist, who preached that the soul could be purified through righteousness. (*Ant.* 18.117) To John and the early Jewish Christians, no blood sacrifice could purify the soul.

We have already discovered that Jesus had no intention of being a blood sacrifice for the forgiveness of sins. Such an idea of human sacrifice had long since been discredited by the story of Abraham and Isaac (Gen. 22) and by God's words to Moses: "Any Israelite or any alien living in Israel who sacrifices any of his children to Molech must be put to death. The people of the community are to stone him." (Lev. 20:2) According to the traditional Christian view, God himself sacrificed his one and only son. If God did sacrifice Jesus, then he purposely broke his own commandment. This inconsistency cannot be right. The Crucifixion of Jesus was not a God-ordained sacrifice but rather a cruel punishment, ordained by the power of Rome.

Rome had used crucifixion as a punishment for political crimes since the first century BCE. The most famous political prisoner crucified was Spartacus (died 71 BCE), who led a slave revolt of 70,000. The 1960 movie, starring Kirk Douglas, showed the crushing power of mass crucifixions, where 6,000 men rotted in the sun for three months for all to witness in horror. Such an execution was meant to send a message to the *living*: follow Rome or follow these poor creatures to the cross. Jesus himself warned his disciples of the cost of following his message. He stated: "Anyone who does not carry his cross and follow me cannot be my disciple." (Luke 14:27) Surely, one had to weigh the cost (possible crucifixion) with the benefit (being a disciple of the Messiah).

Jesus was crucified with the main charge against him posted upon a placard above his head. "This is Jesus, the king of the Jews." (Matt. 27:37) Crucified on each side of him were "robbers." From the writings of Josephus, robbers and innovators were derogatory designations for Judas the Galilean's followers. So in reality, Jesus was crucified amongst his own captured followers. (Cephas (Peter) was careful to escape, using the Golden Eagle Temple Cleansing as an example. In that Temple cleansing, both leaders, Judas and Matthias, were captured. Peter was probably following Judas' orders and staying clear of trouble.). The Gospels put a new slant on the three crucified men. "In the same way, the chief priests, the teachers of the law and the elders mocked him. ... In the same way the robbers who were crucified with him also heaped insults on him." (Matt. 27:41-44) It is understandable that Jesus' enemies would insult him. This was their hour to gloat. The enemies consisted of the Romans and those who enjoyed Rome's privileges: the Herodians, the chief priests and those sympathetic to the upper class. But fellow rebels would not have heaped abuse on Jesus. Josephus stated that the followers of Judas the Galilean would suffer all types of tortures without cursing God or without betraying their compatriots. (*Ant.* 18.23) It is hard to believe that these bandits were so atypical. In fact, Luke made one of the bandits defend Jesus to the other bandit, a good bandit versus a bad bandit. (Luke 23:39-41) In reality, the two bandits would have mourned for Jesus as did the disciples.

When Jesus had time to reflect upon the whole situation, and the failure that had overtaken him, he cried out, "My God, my God, why have you forsaken me?" On the Mount of Olives, Jesus was assured, by his faith in God, that Israel would be rescued from the invaders as foretold by Zechariah. But now the realization of defeat brought uncontrollable despair. Why had God forsaken him? Had he not followed the words of the prophets and the oracle of Zechariah? Orthodox Christians believe that this cry of despair was simply the moment when Jesus was separated from his Father. But I think the explanation is much simpler: Jesus was petitioning the only One who could possibly know the answer to his question. And as he died, his followers looked on in horror, doubting if God would ever answer their prayers.

One other point should be made. The Gospels claimed, "At that moment [the ninth hour] the curtain of the temple was torn in two from top to bottom." Josephus also described an event which happened at the ninth hour.

At the ninth hour of the night, so great a light shone around the altar and the Temple, that it appeared to be the brightness of midday. This light continued for half an hour ... and was interpreted by the sacred Scribes as a portent of events that immediately followed upon it. (*War* 6.290-291) (19)

The Gospel writers took the ninth hour theme from Josephus and made their version say that Judaism was forever changed with the death of Jesus.

Josephus wrote that the sign meant that God was leaving the Temple, and that it was to be destroyed by the Romans. This event occurred in 70 CE, not at the time of Jesus' death. Once again, the Gospel writers "borrowed" an idea from Josephus and applied it to their "Jesus."

THE RESURRECTION

The disciples must have been crushed at the loss of their leader. The words, "My God, my God, why have you forsaken me?" must have terrified and even paralyzed many of them. It was out of this despair that the idea of resurrection occurred to the remaining leadership. (Perhaps Jesus had already planted the idea of resurrection in their minds as a fall-back position.) Without a resurrection, the Fourth Philosophy would be seriously damaged. After all, would you be attracted to a political party whose king or Messiah had already been defeated in grand fashion? The answer is a resounding no! Only with the resurrection could the movement go forward.

Those credited with the resurrection were Cephas and James, the brother of the Lord. Paul grudgingly gave them preeminence in the first sightings of Jesus after his death (1 Cor. 15:3-8) and Luke's account of the sighting of Jesus by two disciples on the road to Emmaus was undoubtedly referring to Cephas and James. (Luke 24:13-35) Thus, the purpose of the resurrection was twofold: it maintained the cohesion of the Fourth Philosophy behind an undefeated and powerful Messiah and was used as a recruitment tool in the fight against Rome. As already noted, Jesus no doubt had a fall-back position in the case of failure. This "clever rabbi" (a designation given to Judas the Galilean by Josephus in *War* 2.433) may have instructed his inner circle to preach the Suffering Servant of Isaiah chapter 53 as well as the resurrection. In this way, confrontation with the Romans on the Mount of Olives was a win-win proposition.

The Gospels omitted any mention of John the Baptist at this time as he was supposedly put to death before Jesus. As we have seen, John was the Sadduc, the second-in-command to Jesus. He may not have played a role in the Jerusalem uprising, as his ministry was focused upon baptizing at the Jordan or preparing the way for the Messiah. However, John's influence over the movement was evident after Jesus' death. John preached the resurrection along with his call for baptism and repentance. Note that the apostles in Jerusalem also preached a baptism dependent on repentance. (Acts 2:38) In the garbled Gospel account, John the Baptist stated:

"I baptize you with water for repentance. But after me will come one who is more powerful than I, whose sandals I am not fit to carry. He will baptize you with the Holy Spirit and with fire. His winnowing fork is in his hand, and he will clear his threshing floor, gathering the wheat into his barn and burning up the chaff with unquenchable fire." (Matt. 3:11-12)

John was pointing to a resurrected Jesus who would judge the good from the bad. That John would have preached this message is not in doubt, but after the crucifixion and resurrection, not before as claimed by the Gospels. We must trust Josephus on this matter. He claimed that John was alive well after the death of Jesus (Judas the Galilean). As such, John's words only make sense if he were predicting the coming of the resurrected Jesus. (This will be examined further in Chapter 20, concerning passages from the book of Revelation.).

The resurrection was viewed differently by Paul. As a later convert, Paul did not personally meet the living or physically resurrected Jesus. His only meetings with Jesus came through visions and dreams of the Risen Christ. Not surprisingly, his interpretation of the resurrection was much different from the Jerusalem Apostles. In fact, the resurrection was the cornerstone of his faith.

If there is no resurrection of the dead, then not even Christ has been raised. And if Christ has not been raised, our preaching is useless and so is your faith. ...And if Christ has not been raised, your faith is futile: you are still in your sins. (1 Cor. 15:13-17)

To Paul, everything was useless without the resurrection; without resurrection there could be no forgiveness of sins. On the other hand, Jews had the Law (a purpose), and they already believed that God could and would forgive sins. John the Baptist preached that the soul was purified through righteousness, not through a blood sacrifice and a miraculous resurrection. (*Ant.* 18.117) So, the viewpoints of resurrection were wildly different between the Jewish Christians of John the Baptist, James and Cephas and the Gentile Christians who followed the teachings of Paul. Today, traditional Christianity follows the interpretation of Paul. Thus, we are left with a religion which proclaims forgiveness of sins through identification with a dead and resurrected god. Today's Christianity is simply a repackaged pagan mystery religion.

CHAPTER 20

OTHER PASSAGES OF INTEREST

In our search for the historical Jesus, we have examined similarities between Judas the Galilean and Jesus and have also reviewed the Church's history in great detail. So much of the four Gospels and the book of Acts have been interpreted in light of my thesis. However, there are many passages within the Gospels and in the book of Revelation which have not yet been fully explored, and these passages may shed even more light upon the true nature of earliest Christianity.

THE WAR WITH ROME

Throughout this book, I have emphasized the Fourth Philosophy's main message of liberty, to be freed of all human interference, to be freed from Rome. The New Testament's book of Revelation also recounted a war with Rome, this time on a cosmic scale. I believe that much of Revelation came from the nearly devastated Zealot movement. It was written at least a decade after the Jewish war with Rome, which ended with the suicide at Masada in 73 CE. This new war with Rome, headed by the cosmic Christ, was meant to give the struggling movement hope.

Revelation's war was meant to explain away the disastrous ending to the Jewish war with Rome. This type of revisionism had been used before to explain away failure. When the two sons of Judas the Galilean were crucified, the movement concocted a story which stated that "Jesus" foretold their deaths. Their crucifixions, like his own, were part of God's overall plan. (Matt. 20:20-23) Likewise, this new cosmic war against Rome was really the end game, not the actual Jewish war which ended in utter defeat.

In Revelation 6:9-10 and 19:11-16, Jesus was seen as the avenging agent of God.

When he opened the fifth seal, I saw under the altar the souls of those who had been slain because of the word of God and the testimony they had maintained. They called out in a loud voice, "How long, Sovereign Lord, holy and true, until you judge the inhabitants of the earth and avenge our blood?" …I saw heaven standing open and there before me was a white horse, whose rider is called Faithful and True. With justice he judges and makes war. His eyes are like blazing fire, and on his head are many crowns. He has a name written on him that no one but he himself knows. He is dressed in a robe dipped in blood, and his name is the Word of God. The armies of heaven were following him, riding on white horses and dressed in fine linen, white and clean. Out of his mouth comes a sharp sword with which to strike down the nations. "He will rule them with an iron scepter." [Psalm 2:9] He treads the winepress of the fury of the wrath of God Almighty. On his robe and on his thigh he has this name written: King of Kings and Lord of Lords.

This message of heavenly power was designed to give hope to those still being persecuted for their beliefs. Note that the saints who had experienced martyrdom were clamoring for vengeance. How long could God wait before He would come to their rescue? Those still living could definitely be somewhat comforted by the pleas of those who had gone before. At least there was a presence in heaven which represented their viewpoint.

So we have the avenging Messiah. But who was the Messiah going to fight? The answer from Revelation is clear: the enemy of God was Rome. In chapter 13, several passages point to Rome. The Beast of the Sea stood for the Roman Empire while the Beast of the Earth represented Emperor worship. The Beast was assigned a number, that being 666. Which historical figure of the time had earned that number?

According to William Barclay, the number 666 belonged to Nero. In Latin, each letter in a name can be assigned a numerical value. Let us take Nero and Neron as examples.

N = 50	N = 50
E = 6	E = 6
R = 500	R = 500
O = 60	O = 60
N = 50	
─────	─────
616	666

Neron equals 666 while Nero equals 616. Many of the early manuscripts had the number at 616. If Nero were the man with the number 666, then what does that mean? Simply put, Nero was the embodiment of everything opposed to God. He was the anti-Christ. (1) Earlier, in Revelation chapter 13, the Beast of the Land had seven heads, one of which had been fatally wounded but was now healed. The fatally wounded head represented Nero, who had died in 67 CE. A Nero redivivus legend had arisen, where the spirit of Nero would return. This reborn Nero was the head which had been healed.

In chapter 17, there are more clues in our identification concerning Nero and Rome.

"Come, I will show you the punishment of the great prostitute, who sits on many waters. With her the kings of the earth committed adultery and the inhabitants of the earth were intoxicated with the wine of her adulteries." Then the angel carried me away in the Spirit into a desert. There I saw a woman sitting on a scarlet beast that was covered with blasphemous names and had seven heads and ten horns. ..."This calls for a mind with wisdom. The **seven heads are seven hills** on which the woman sits. They are also seven kings. **Five have fallen, one is, the other has not yet come**; but when he does come, he must remain for a little while. **The beast who once was, and now is not, is an eighth king.**" (Emphasis mine)

The seven heads represented seven hills and seven kings. The seven hills obviously referred to Rome, the city that sits upon seven hills. The seven kings were the Roman Emperors. A list of these Emperors is as follows:

Julius Caesar	60-44 BCE
Mark Antony and Octavius	43-31 BCE
Octavius (Augustus)	27 BCE - 14 CE
Tiberius	14-37 CE
Caligula	37-41
Claudius	41-54
Nero	54-68
Galba	68-69
Otho	69
Vitellius	69
Vespasian	69-79
Titus	79-81
Domitian	81-96

Barclay explains the situation as well as anyone. The seven Emperors began with Octavius (Augustus). This may well be the case as Emperor worship had its origin with the latter reign of Augustus. Thus, the first five emperors were Augustus, Tiberius, Caligula, Claudius and Nero. These were the five that had fallen. The one currently ruling was Vespasian and the one who would rule for a short while was Titus (just two years). These were the seven heads or kings. (Galba, Otho and Vitellius were generals who ruled for a very short period and not considered Emperors per this study.) Note that these seven also ruled during Judas the Galilean's movement, which began in 4 BCE, during the reign of Augustus. (Galba, Otho and Vitellius were short-lived leaders, not counted among the Emperors.)

The focus of Revelation concerns Emperor worship. The fatally wounded head was Nero, the monster who raised Emperor worship to its zenith. With his death in 68 CE, the world was spared the spectacle of this insane worship. Vespasian and Titus were generals, responsible for the downfall of Jerusalem. However, they did not restore Nero's reign of terror. That role would be reserved for Domitian.

Revelation stated: "The beast who once was, and now is not, is an eighth king. He belongs to the seven and is going to his destruction." This eighth king embodied the return of Nero's spirit. Domitian first made Emperor worship compulsory. Tertullian called Domitian "a man of Nero's type of cruelty." (2)

Thus, the writer of Revelation was merely trying to explain the current situation facing Christians. This was placed into an historical context. The Jewish Christian movement had always fought against Rome. They were even blamed by Nero for setting Rome ablaze. And certainly, Judas the Galilean had battled the inroads of Roman culture and influence in Judea. Revelation was a last ditch effort for the Jews to conquer Rome. Just as the Jews had lost the earthly war with Rome, so too did they fail in this cosmic battle. Jesus did not return!

CLASS WARFARE

In today's political climate, anytime a Democrat proposes a tax on the wealthiest one percent, Republicans cry "Class Warfare", the pitting of poor versus rich. Republicans believe that such a tax would not only be unfair, but would also single out just one group, the rich. On the other hand, Democrats argue that the only ones who could possibly afford a tax would be the rich. The questions remains: where do we get the money to run the government?

A similar argument appears throughout the pages of the Gospels. Jesus and his followers were constantly advocating for the poor, asking the rich to share their wealth. This was the ultimate in "Class Warfare". I will list the passages where Jesus either condemned the rich or sided with the poor.

Luke 6:20-24 - "Blessed are you who are poor, for yours is the kingdom of God. …But woe to you who are rich, for you have already received your comfort."

Matt. 6:19-24 - "Do not store up for yourselves treasures on earth, where moth and rust destroy, and where thieves break in and steal. But store up for yourselves treasure in heaven, where moth and rust do not destroy, and where thieves do not break in and steal. For where your treasure is, there your heart will be also. …No one can serve two masters. Either he will hate the one and love the other, or he will be devoted to the one and despise the other. You cannot serve both God and Money."

Matt. 13:22 - "What was sown among the thorns is the man who hears the word, but the worries of this life and the deceitfulness of wealth choke it, making it unfruitful."

Matt. 13:45-46 - "Again, the kingdom of heaven is like a merchant looking for fine pearls. When he found one of great value, he went away and sold everything he had and bought it."

Matt. 25:31-46 - "Then he will say to those on his left, 'Depart from me, you who are cursed, into the eternal fire prepared for the devil and his angels. For I was hungry and you gave me nothing to eat, I was thirsty and you gave me nothing to drink, I was a stranger and you did not invite me in, I needed clothes and you did not clothe me, I was sick and in prison and you did not look after me.' "They also will answer, 'Lord, when did we see you hungry or thirsty or a stranger or needing clothes or sick or in prison, and did not help you?' "He will reply, 'I tell you the truth, whatever you did not do for one of the least of these, you did not do for me.' "Then they will go away to eternal punishment, but the righteous to eternal life."

Matt. 19:16-24 - Jesus answered, "If you want to be perfect, go, sell your possessions and give to the poor, and you will have treasure in heaven. Then come, follow me." When the young man heard this, he went away sad, because he had great wealth. Then Jesus said to his disciples, "I tell you the truth, it is hard for a rich man to enter the kingdom of heaven. Again, I tell you, it is easier for a camel to go through the eye of a needle than for a rich man to enter the kingdom of God."

Jesus' diatribe against the wealthy was repeated by James, his brother.

Now listen, you rich people, weep and wail because of the misery that is coming upon you. Your wealth has rotted, and moths have eaten your clothes.

Your gold and silver are corroded. Their corrosion will testify against you and eat your flesh like fire. You have hoarded wealth in the last days. Look! The wages you failed to pay the workmen who mowed your fields are crying out against you. The cries of the harvesters have reached the ears of the Lord Almighty. You have lived on earth in luxury and self-indulgence. You have fattened yourselves in the day of slaughter. You have condemned and murdered innocent men, who were not opposing you. (James 5:1-6)

Finally, a short description of Jesus' earliest Jewish followers tells us about their relationships with one another, vis-a-vis wealth. "All the believers were together and had everything in common. Selling their possessions and goods, they gave to anyone as he had need." (Acts 2:44-45) Obviously, the Church has changed since those early days. In fact, in the United States, a so-called Christian nation, the top one percent hoards as much wealth as the bottom ninety-five percent. Jesus would have been labeled a Socialist or a Communist and would have been a fringe element of our society.

The Gospel Jesus' message on wealth is clear, although this message has been effectively diminished by the greed of succeeding preachers and interpreters of Scripture. How did Jesus' "Class Warfare" compare to that of Judas the Galilean's Fourth Philosophy?

Josephus wrote that the later followers of Judas the Galilean were robbers and that these robberies were "done in pretense for the public welfare, but in reality for the hopes of gain to themselves." (*Ant.* 18.7) Josephus clearly stated that the Zealots took from the rich and gave to the poor. His own personal beliefs could not be hidden. He strongly believed that this sharing was just a cover for their own greed.

Two other passages by Josephus may strengthen my claim that Jesus' teachings on "Class Warfare" and pure communism were exactly like that of the Fourth Philosophy.

In the first passage, the Sicarii destroyed the debt records, so that the poor would no longer be indebted to the rich. The second passage recalls the Zealots' practice of sharing property. Both acts were firmly denounced by Josephus, a defender of the status quo.

...their opponents [Eleazar and the Sicarii] rushed in and burnt down the house of Ananias the high priest and the palace of Agrippa and Bernice; then they took their fire to the Record Office, eager to destroy the money-lenders bonds and so make impossible the recovery of debts, in order to secure the support of an army of debtors and enable the poor to rise with impunity against the rich. (*War* 2.426-427)

The dregs, the scum of the whole country [Zealots], they have squandered their own property and practiced their lunacy upon the towns and villages around, and finally have poured in a stealthy stream into the Holy City. (*War* 4.241)

To share one's property with the poor may seem ridiculous to us today, but these Jewish Christians believed that they would be rewarded in heaven. They also believed that Jesus would come and rescue them. What happened was much different. They ran out of money and were eventually slaughtered by the Romans.

THE LAW

Most Christians believe that Jesus fought against the Jewish establishment, hoping to replace the Law with the new covenant of Grace. This concept of Jesus comes from the Pauline interpretation of Jesus. However, the following passages make it quite clear that Jesus himself was firmly behind the Law of God. He taught a righteousness based upon following God's Law.

Matt. 5:17-20 - "Do not think that I have come to abolish the Law or the Prophets; I have not come to abolish them but to fulfill them. I tell you the truth, until heaven and earth disappear, not the smallest letter, not the least stoke of a pen, will by any means disappear from the Law until everything is accomplished. Anyone who breaks one of the least of these commandments and teaches others to do the same will be called least in the kingdom of heaven, but whoever practices and teaches these commands will be called great in the kingdom of heaven. For I tell you that unless your righteousness surpasses that of the Pharisees and the teachers of the law, you will certainly not enter the kingdom of heaven.

Jesus preached that righteousness was earned not only through the outward obedience to the law but the inward obedience as well. This is what made him different from the other teachers of the law. He was not a hypocrite. Jesus also stated that the Law would not pass away until the earth and heavens disappeared or until everything was accomplished. Christians have been taught that the crucifixion and resurrection satisfied this stipulation. But is that true? In our above study of Revelation, Jewish Christians did not believe that all had been accomplished: they believed that Jesus would return again to save them from the devil, or the Roman Empire. This did not happen. So, in effect, the Law should still be followed by the disciples of Jesus.

Matt. 15:1-20 - Then some Pharisees and teachers of the law came to Jesus from Jerusalem and asked, "Why do your disciples break the tradition of the elders? They don't wash their hands before they eat!" Jesus replied, "And why do you break the command of God for the sake of your tradition? For God said, 'Honor your father and mother' [Exodus 20:12] and 'Anyone who curses his father or mother must be put to death.' [Exodus 21:17] But you say that if a man says to his father or mother, 'Whatever help you might otherwise have received from me is a gift devoted to God,' he is not to 'honor his father' with it. Thus you nullify the word of God for the sake of your tradition. ...For out of the heart come evil thoughts, murder, adultery, sexual immorality, theft, false testimony, slander. These are what make a man 'unclean'; **but eating with unwashed hands does not make a man 'unclean.'**" (Emphasis mine)

Jesus was clearly defending the Law against the traditions of man. Nowhere did Jesus say that the dietary laws were no longer in effect. In fact, he was defending all the laws of God, including the dietary laws. In Mark 7:19, this encounter was interpreted by the later Gentile Church as follows: "In saying this, Jesus declared all foods 'clean.'" Jesus never said this! He simply said that the tradition of eating with washed hands does not make one clean.

The folly of Mark's interpretation can be illustrated by Peter's vision in Acts chapter 10. (As already noted, Acts chapter 10 was a rewrite of Simon's clash with Agrippa I.) Long after Jesus' death, Peter still followed the dietary laws. Peter supposedly said, "I have never eaten anything impure or unclean." Obviously, Peter did not believe that Jesus had declared all foods clean.

The author of Acts inadvertently shared information about James' followers in Acts 21:20. "You see, brother, how many thousands of Jews have believed, and all of them are zealous for the law." A full generation after Jesus' crucifixion, the Jewish Christians were zealously following the law. I submit to you that Jesus also zealously followed the law, just as was attributed to Judas the Galilean and the Fourth Philosophy.

SENDING OF THE TWELVE

Two important passages must be addressed concerning Jesus sending out the Twelve, as reported by Matt. 10:1-42.

These twelve Jesus sent out with the following instructions: "Do not go among the Gentiles or enter any town of the Samaritans. Go rather to the lost sheep of Israel. As you go, preach this message: 'The kingdom of heaven is near.'" (Matt. 10:5-7)

"Do not be afraid of those who kill the body but cannot kill the soul. Rather, be afraid of the one who can destroy both soul and body in hell." (Matt. 10:28)

The first passage may relate to early instructions from Jesus. He claimed to be Messiah or King of Israel. His subjects, therefore, were the lost sheep of Israel. Jesus was simply trying to galvanize his movement amongst the Jews. If he could not gain the support of his own people, how could he gain support from outsiders? Remember, Jesus preached a message which could only appeal to the poor Jewish population.

The second passage brings to mind the statements made by Judas and Matthias concerning the Golden Eagle Temple Cleansing.

So these wise men persuaded [their scholars] to pull down the golden eagle; alleging, that although they should incur any danger which might bring them to their deaths, the virtue of the action now proposed to them would appear much more advantageous to them than the pleasures of life; since they would die for the preservation and observation of the law of their fathers. (*Ant.* 17.152)

"...and it ought not to be wondered at, if we esteem those laws which Moses had suggested to him, and were taught him by God, and which he wrote and left behind him, more worthy of observation than thy [Herod the Great's] commands. Accordingly we will undergo death, and all sorts of punishments which thou can inflict upon us, with pleasure, since we are conscious to ourselves that we shall die, not for any unrighteous actions, but for our love to religion." (*Ant.* 17.159)

Judas and Matthias taught their followers to place the commands of God before the commands of men, just as Jesus had taught his disciples. In fact, both Judas and Jesus stressed the difference between dying for God and dying for man. This belief that they were dying for God made them much more willing to die. They would die with pleasure. This fanaticism belonged to the Fourth Philosophy and to Jesus as well. It also belongs to the religious fanatics of our own time.

ONE RULER

Jesus stated: "Do not swear at all; either by heaven, for it is God's throne; or by the earth, for it is his footstool; or by Jerusalem, for it is the city of the Great King." (Matt. 5:34-35)

But the fourth sect of Jewish philosophy, Judas the Galilean was the author. These men agree in all other things with the Pharisaic notions; but they have an inviolable attachment to liberty; and say that God is to be their only Ruler and Lord. (*Ant.* 18.23)

Jesus certainly did not give Rome any credit for ruling Jerusalem. To Jesus, the heavens, the earth and Jerusalem belonged to God. Judas the Galilean also preached against Roman occupation, saying that God was their only ruler. This attachment to liberty was the reason why Jesus underwent crucifixion, the penalty for political crimes against Rome.

WIVES

Most biblical students assume that Jesus was not married. After all, there are no passages within the Gospels which talk of a Mrs. Jesus. This concept of a celibate preacher has been pitched to the masses for over 2,000 years. However, one passage may help answer the question concerning celibacy. In Matt. 8:14-17, Jesus entered Peter's house, only to find Peter's mother-in-law in bed with a fever. He healed her, and she then began to wait on him. If Peter had a mother-in-law, he also had a wife. (Remember, the Roman Catholics claim Peter as the first Pope.) This short encounter contains the only information about the disciples' personal lives. This leads to an important question: Were any of the other Apostles married?

Paul answered that question in 1 Cor. 9:5: "Don't we have the right to take a believing wife along with us, as do the other apostles and the Lord's brothers and Cephas?" According to Paul, all the Jewish apostles had believing wives, including the Lord's own brothers. If the apostles all had wives, then it seems logical that Jesus did as well. However, this will never be answered with 100 percent certainty.

Judas the Galilean had a wife and many children, including two sons who died from crucifixion, one son who marched into Jerusalem as Messiah and a grandson who led the last band of resistance against Rome at Masada. The Fourth Philosophy married and had children, consistent with the early Jewish Christians. In fact, the Essenes were the only sect which did not marry. Therefore, the Jewish Christians were more in line with the Fourth Philosophy than with the Essenes.

THE DROWNING PIGS

In his book *Caesar's Messiah*, Joseph Atwill claims that the events described in Matt. 8:28-34 involved a rewrite of a battle waged by Rome against the Jewish insurgents. (3) The passages are as follows:

Some distance from them [two demon possessed men of Gadara] a large herd of pigs was feeding. The demons begged Jesus, "If you drive us out, send us into the herd of pigs." He said to them, "Go!" So they came out and went into the pigs, and the whole herd rushed down the steep bank into the lake and died in the water. (Matt. 8:28-34)

[Certain men of Gadara, referred to as] "the wildest of wild beasts" [were chased by the Romans to the swollen Jordan] "where they were stopped by the current." [The insurgents were cut down] "at which fight, hand to hand, fifteen thousand of them were slain, while the number of those that were unwillingly forced to leap into Jordan was prodigious. ...the lake Asphaltitis was also full of dead bodies, that were carried down to it by the river." (*War* 4.425-439)

The similarities between the two stories include the town (Gadara) and dead bodies in a lake. In Matthew, the dead bodies were demon possessed pigs while Josephus wrote of Jews who were "the wildest of wild beasts." Note that the Gospel writer replaced the Jewish insurgents with pigs, unclean animals. If nothing else, this is an interesting coincidence.

THE KINGDOM OF HEAVEN

Perhaps one of the least understood passages in the New Testament concerns the Kingdom of Heaven.

"From the days of John the Baptist until now, the kingdom of heaven has been forcefully advancing and forceful men lay hold of it." (Matt. 11:12)

The Greek word translated as forceful should actually be translated as violent. Is it possible that this passage escaped the censorship of Matthew? Did "Jesus" equate the kingdom of God with violent men? We know that Judas the Galilean was a rabbi, but his methods and his later disciples' methods may have been quite violent. The Sicarii were trained assassins. But we must remember that they were fighting an insurgent war against Rome. In the Second World War, French resistance fighters certainly killed many Nazis. We view the French with admiration but Judas the Galilean with scorn. We have merely been conditioned to believe what the authorities want us to believe.

THE SABBATH

Was Jesus' attitude about the Sabbath different from all other Jewish leaders? In the Gospels, we are led to believe that Jesus did not follow the Sabbath guidelines and was therefore opposed to the Law of Moses. A passage in Matthew may help change this perception.

He said to them, "If any of you has a sheep and it falls into a pit on the Sabbath, will you not take hold of it and lift it out? How much more valuable is a man than a sheep! Therefore it is lawful to do good on the Sabbath." (Matt. 12:11-12)

If this is read closely, it proves that Jesus supported observance of the Sabbath. He just questioned the religious community's interpretation of the Sabbath requirements. He said, "It is lawful to do good on the Sabbath." Doing good trumps doing nothing! This seems like good common sense.

Was Jesus the first to make this type of statement concerning the Sabbath? The answer is no! Judas Maccabee and his father, Mattathias, insisted that it was proper to defend oneself on the Sabbath.

And they avoided to defend themselves on that day, because they were not willing to break in upon the honor they owed the Sabbath, even in such distresses; for our law requires that we rest upon that day. There were about a thousand, with their wives and children, who were smothered and died in these caves; but many of those that escaped joined themselves to Mattathias, and appointed him to be their ruler, who taught them to fight even on the Sabbath day; and told them that unless they would do so, they would become their own enemies, by observing the law [so rigorously], while their adversaries would still assault them on this day, and they would not then defend themselves; and that nothing could then hinder but they must all perish without fighting. This speech persuaded them; and this rule continues among us to this day, that if there be a necessity, we may fight on Sabbath days. (*Ant.* 12:274-277)

This common sense approach to warfare on the Sabbath was applied to doing good on the Sabbath by Jesus. Note that **Mattathias** and **Judas** Maccabee were the archetypes of the Fourth Philosophy, coincidentally headed by **Matthias** and **Judas** the Galilean. In regards to the Sabbath,

Jesus' interpretation was no different than the Maccabees and no different than the Fourth Philosophy.

GALILEANS

Now there were some present at that time who told Jesus about the Galileans whose blood Pilate had mixed with their sacrifices. Jesus answered, "Do not think that these Galileans were worse sinners than all the other Galileans because they suffered this way." (Luke 13:1-4)

Who were these Galileans? According to Brandon, "there is even some evidence that the Zealots were sometimes called Galileans." (4) If Pilate attacked these Galileans, they most likely were members of the Fourth Philosophy. It should also be noted that all of Jesus' Apostles were Galileans. Jesus was also accused of being from Galilee (John 7:41-52) and unfit for the role of Messiah.

THE ABOMINATION THAT CAUSES DESOLATION

This designation was originally assigned to Antiochus Epiphanes, who despoiled the Temple by setting up an altar to Zeus. (5) Judas Maccabee gained great fame for cleansing the Temple of these abominations. Jesus supposedly referred to the "abomination that causes desolation" in the following passage.

"When you see 'the abomination that causes desolation' standing where it does not belong - **let the reader understand** - then let those who are in Judea flee to the mountains. Let no one on the roof of his house go down or enter the house to take anything out. Let no one in the field go back to get his cloak. How dreadful will it be in those days for pregnant women and nursing mothers! **Pray that this will not take place in winter,** because those will be days of distress unequaled from the beginning, when God created the world, until now - and never to be equaled again. If the Lord had not cut short these days, no one would survive. But for the sake of the elect, whom he has chosen, **he has shortened them.**" (Mark 13:14-20)

Only twice was the Temple threatened with this type of abomination, during the reign of Caligula (37-41 CE) and the eventual destruction of the Temple by Titus in 70 CE. According to Brandon, this warning was written so that the reader would understand about the destruction under Titus in 70 CE. However, the original passage related to the Caligula affair. Brandon claimed that two elements of this passage pointed to Caligula. First, in the winter,

Petronius had his forces ready to attack Jerusalem. That is why the passage said, "Pray that this will not take place in winter." Second, the calamity was avoided when Caligula was assassinated. (6)

The Zealots may have originally warned their followers to flee when Caligula's forces invaded. They would have then instructed their members to set up a guerrilla war from their hideouts. This inclusion in the Gospel story suggests that the Jewish Christian movement was just another name for the Fourth Philosophy.

CHAPTER 21

JESUS OF NAZARETH - A COMPOSITE

I have attempted to prove that Jesus of Nazareth was not an historical figure, but rather a combination of the life and deeds of Judas the Galilean mixed together with an anti-Jewish Pauline tilt. Judas the Galilean provided many elements which were incorporated into the Gospel Jesus. Judas cleansed the Temple, was released in a prisoner release reminiscent of the Barabbas release, was proclaimed Messiah, led a tax revolt against Rome, and he founded a new philosophy. These elements were incorporated into the Gospel Jesus story. Yet the Gospels and Acts did not recognize Judas for his accomplishments. Instead, Jesus was imbued with Judas' history and Judas was purposely downplayed and forgotten as a failure (Acts 5:37).

The teachings of Paul, the Apostle to the Gentiles, were rejected by the Pillar Apostles, yet these teachings became incorporated into the Gospel Jesus' framework. As such, Jesus was pitted against the Jewish nation and all the religious authorities. While Judas the Galilean was part of the Pharisaic movement, Jesus was constantly hounded by these Pharisees. Certainly, this opposition from the Pharisees did not occur in the lifetime of Judas the Galilean but was part of Paul's experience.

The melding of Judas the Galilean's life with Paul's outlook has left us with the Gospel Jesus, a man (or god) who never made it into the history of Josephus. How could Josephus have missed out on this fabulous story of Jesus, the wonder-worker and great Messiah? Only one explanation makes sense: Jesus of Nazareth never existed! Josephus could not have written about someone who was invented in the latter part of the first century. He could have known nothing about this literary character. So, Jesus of Nazareth was a late first-century invention. But why was he invented? Why did the Gospel writers remove the historical Judas the Galilean in favor of the invented Jesus of Nazareth?

Judas the Galilean's movement (the Fourth Philosophy or Jewish Christianity) spread throughout the Roman world but was centered in Judea and Galilee. The Fourth Philosophy had preached revolution against Rome which led to expulsions from Rome and eventually to the Jewish war against Rome. By 73 CE, this movement had been smashed, the remnants no longer influential throughout the Empire. This vacuum gave the Gentile Christian movement (founded by Paul) a chance to reinvent itself. Unfortunately, the Gentile Church had to explain its relationship to a Jewish Messiah figure. This crucified Messiah had to be explained in terms of Paul's philosophy as opposed to the Jewish political truths. Thus, the crucified Messiah had to become a redeemer to the whole world, not just to the Jews.

The Gospel writers had their work cut out for them. They had to incorporate much of Judas the Galilean's original story, yet somehow divorce him from Jewish political concerns. The greatest sleight-of-hand concerned the coming of John the Baptist. The Slavonic Josephus reported that John came baptizing in 6 CE, right before Judas the Galilean's tax revolt. This makes historical sense as Josephus wrote extensively about Judas and his movement. To distance the Gospel Jesus from Judas the Galilean, the Gospel of Luke moved John the Baptist's arrival to 28-29 CE, a good generation later that the actual events. This, in turn, shifted all other events in the traditional timeline by a generation. Thus, nothing in the Gospels and Acts can be reconciled to Josephus' history. However, much can be reconciled if we ignore this bogus date of 28-29 CE for John. The following revised timeline will help summarize all the findings within this book.

THE THREE MESSIAH TIMELINE
THE FIRST MESSIAH - JUDAS THE GALILEAN

36-25 BCE	Judas was born in Gamala, near Galilee.
25	The Star of Bethlehem was reported by the Slavonic Josephus.
35-24	James the Just, the brother of Jesus (Judas) was born.
25	An assassination attempt on Herod the Great failed.
4	Matthias and Judas led the Golden Eagle Temple Cleansing.
4	Herod burned Matthias but imprisoned Judas.
4	Herod the Great died.
4	Judas was released by Archelaus to the Jewish crowd - Barabbas story.
4-3	Judas raided the armory at Sepphoris.

4-2	Judas was proclaimed Messiah in Galilee.
4 – 73 CE	The Dead Sea Scrolls were appropriated by the Fourth Philosophy.
6 CE	John the Baptist introduced Judas right before the Census revolt.
6	Judas the Galilean led a nationwide tax revolt against Rome.
6-15	Annas named High Priest.
18-37	Caiaphas named High Priest.
18-37	Pilate named Procurator.
19	Judas the Galilean (Jesus) was arrested on the Mount of Olives.
19	An unnamed Jew (Paul) swindled Jewish converts in Rome.
21	Per the Memoranda, Jesus was crucified under Pilate.
21-36	John the Baptists led the movement, with James as his second.
22	Saul, a Herodian, converted to Jewish Christianity.
22-25	Paul studied with the Pharisees for three years.
25	Paul made his first post-conversion trip to Jerusalem.
35-36	John the Baptist was beheaded by Herod Antipas.
36-62	James became the leader with Cephas as his second.
38-39	The Council of Jerusalem dealt with the Gentile issue and factions.
38-39	Paul attended the Council, seventeen years after his conversion.
40-41	Caligula ordered the desecration of the Temple.
41	Caligula was assassinated. Agrippa I may have been involved.
41	Claudius became Emperor with the help and counsel of Agrippa I.
41	Claudius and Agrippa I expelled the Jewish Christians from Rome.
41-44	Agrippa I was seen as a Messiah figure.
43	Agrippa I interrogated Simon for excluding him from the Temple.
43	James and Simon, the sons of Judas the Galilean, were imprisoned.
44	Agrippa I was assassinated by the Fourth Philosophy or by Claudius.

THE SECOND MESSIAH – CHRIST JESUS

39-44	Paul taught his new gospel of grace and wrote Romans and 1 Cor.
39-44	Paul's gospel meshed with Agrippa's goal of converting Gentile kings.
39-44	Paul became known as the "Liar", due to his teachings.
44	King Izates converted to Judaism, choosing Eleazar over Ananias.
44	Paul and Cephas also argued about the Law. Cephas won.
44	Paul was removed from the movement, prompting Barnabas' defection.
44	Paul wrote Galatians and 2 Corinthians.

44-67	Paul now became known as the "Enemy".
44-48	A famine spread throughout Israel.
44-48	Paul came to Jerusalem with famine relief, and kept the money.
44-48	The "Enemy" attacked James at the Temple.
44-46	Theudas was beheaded.
46-48	James and Simon, the sons of Judas the Galilean, were crucified.
62	James the Just was stoned to death, the original "Stephen" story.
62	After the stoning, Saul persecuted the movement.
62	By now, Saul was also known as the "Traitor".
64	The Jewish Christians were persecuted by Nero after the Great Fire.
66	Menahem, Judas the Galilean's son, cleansed the Temple as Messiah.
66	Menahem was stoned by his adversaries.
66	Saul met with Agrippa II to petition for an army to fight the insurgents.
66-70	War with Rome ended in defeat for the Jews.
67	Saul met with Nero to focus blame for the war on someone else.
70	The Temple was destroyed by Titus.
73	Eleazar, grandson of Judas the Galilean, led the Sicarii in mass suicide.

THE THIRD MESSIAH – JESUS OF NAZARETH

75	Josephus wrote the War.
85-95	The Jewish portion of Revelation was penned.
93	Josephus wrote Antiquities.
100	The Gospel of Mark made its debut.
120-140	Luke, Matthew and Acts were written.
130-150	Recognitions of Clement was written
140	The Gospel of John was written.

THE MYTHICIST ARGUMENT

In their book, *The Jesus Mysteries*, Timothy Freke and Peter Gandy summarized the intersection of the Pagan mystery religions with the Gospel Jesus. These authors represent the Mythicist viewpoint, which denies the historicity of the Gospel Jesus. Not all Mythicists believe the same things. Some believe that Jesus was a myth but that Paul existed. Others believe that both Jesus and Paul were inventions. I, too, am a Mythicist of sorts. I believe that historical people were used as the frameworks for both Jesus and Paul. The Gospels twisted Judas the Galilean into Jesus while Acts shaped Saul, the Herodian, into Paul, the Apostle to the Gentiles.

It may be beneficial to list some of Freke's and Gandy's arguments. (1)

1. Son of God – This title given to Jesus was also given to many of the Pagan redeemers. For example, Dionysus was the "Son of Zeus."

2. Virgin Birth – Like Attis, Adonis, Dionysus, and Hercules, Jesus was born to a human virgin mother and fathered by a God. It should be noted that this virgin birth was not included in the writings of Paul or in Mark, the earliest Gospel. As the real Jesus (Judas the Galilean) became less recognizable, due to the passage of time, such additions to the "record" made Jesus more like the competing mystery gods.

3. The Nativity – Both Jesus and Mithra were born in caves and the births were witnessed by shepherds. Mithra's birth date was celebrated on December 25th.

4. The Lord's Supper – Just as the later Gentile Christians partook in the body and blood of Christ, so too did the followers of Mithra venerate their God. This mimicry of the Pagan religions can be attributed to Paul. Paul's interpretation of the Last Supper was dependent on his revelations from the Risen Christ. Surely, Paul incorporated the rites of Mithra into his Gentile Christian community's celebration of the Lord's Supper. This identification with the body and blood of Jesus would not have been part of the original Jewish religion.

5. The Death and Resurrection – Like many of the Pagan redeemers, Jesus was put to death and then resurrected. The Gentile Christian Church was taught by Paul to identify with this death and resurrection, in the same way that the Pagan religions identified with their resurrected deities. However, the Jewish resurrected Messiah would return to conquer Rome, a task the human Messiah failed to accomplish.

6. The Lamb of God – Jesus had become a sacrifice for the sins of the world similar to other Pagan redeemers. However, John the Baptist actually preached that sins were forgiven through the practice of righteousness.

This list is but a barebones treatment of the subject. To fully grasp the extent of the mimicry of Pagan rituals and teaching, please read *The Jesus Mysteries*.

The authors summed up their position concerning the historical Jesus as follows:

The first possibility we considered was that the true biography of Jesus had been overlaid with Pagan mythology at a later date. This is a common idea often advanced to account for those aspects of the Jesus story that seem obviously mythical, such as the virgin birth. But we have found so many resemblances between the myths of Osiris-Dionysus and the supposed biography of Jesus that this theory seemed inadequate. If *all* the elements of the Jesus story that had been prefigured by Pagan myths were later accretions, what would be left of the "real" Jesus? **If this theory is true then the Jesus we know is a myth and the historical man has been completely eclipsed.** (2) (Emphasis mine)

Freke and Gandy came to the conclusion that the Gospel Jesus was so imbued with the Pagan mystery religions that the actual man, if he really existed, would have been totally "eclipsed". In short, could the Gospel Jesus have really existed? After all, this Gospel Jesus was not part of Josephus' Jewish history. In the authors' opinion, any historical person could no longer even be recognized after the extreme Gospel makeover.

My hypothesis concerning Judas the Galilean fits in quite well with this opinion by Freke and Gandy. The Gospel Jesus has not been associated with Judas the Galilean for the following two reasons. First, the timeframe was distorted, placing the Gospel Jesus in a later period, where no corroboration from Josephus can be found. And second, the Gospel Jesus was changed so much by his identification with the Pagan redeemers that it is hard to image any person actually being the historical Jesus.

Even though it may be hard to see the revolutionary Judas the Galilean as the Gospel Jesus, we must look first to our historical sources. Josephus never wrote about the Gospel Jesus, because the Gospel Jesus was not part of Jewish history. He never existed. However, Judas the Galilean's life can be seen as a framework for this Gospel Jesus. Judas had a history, one well chronicled by Josephus. The Pauline gospel was then woven throughout this framework, giving us a man who no longer represented the revolutionary Jews. And the later identification with the Pagan religions, through the virgin birth, the water into wine episode, and the death and resurrection, helped create a character so unlike any human being. It is understandable that Freke and Gandy do not recognize Judas the Galilean as the Gospel Jesus. The Gospel writers did their job well. They have hidden the historical Jesus for two thousand years. In Judas the Galilean's stead, the Gospel Jesus was brought forth, a composite which has helped shape the Western world, for good or for evil.

BIBLIOGRAPHY

Baigent, Michael and Leigh, Richard. *The Dead Sea Scrolls Deception*. New York: Summit Books, 1991.

Barclay, William. *The Daily Study Bible*. Philadelphia: The Westminster Press, 1978.

Bettenson, Henry. *Documents of the Christian Church*. New York: Oxford University Press, 1979.

Brandon, S.G.F.. *Jesus and the Zealots*. New York: Charles Scribner's Sons, 1967.

Brandon, S.G.F.. *The Trial of Jesus of Nazareth*. New York: Dorset Press, 1968.

Crossan, John Dominic and Reed, Jonathan L.. *Excavating Jesus*. San Francisco: Harper San Francisco, 2001.

Ehrman Bart D.. *Lost Scriptures*. New York: Oxford University Press, 2003.

Eisenman, Robert. *James the Brother of Jesus*. New York: Penguin Books, 1997.

Ellegard, Alvar. *Jesus One Hundred Years Before Christ*. New York: The Overlook Press, 1999.

Eusebius. *The History of the Church*. Translated by G. A. Williamson. United States: Dorset Press, 1984.

Freke, Timothy and Gandy, Peter. *The Jesus Mysteries*, New York: Harmony Books, 1999.

Gibbon, Edward. *The History of the Decline and Fall of the Roman Empire - Volume 1*. New York: Penguin Books, 1994.

Grant, Michael. *The History of Ancient Israel*. New York: Charles Scribner's Sons, 1984.

Johnson, Paul. *Civilizations of the Holy Land*. Atheneum, New York: 1979.

Leeming, H. and Leeming K.. *Josephus' Jewish War and its Slavonic Version*. Leiden: Brill 2003.

Maccoby, Hyam. *Revolution in Judaea*. New York: Taplinger Publishing Company, 1980.

Maccoby, Hyam. *The Mythmaker*. New York: Harper and Row Publishers, 1986.

Philo. *The Works of Philo*. Translated by C. D. Yonge. United States: Hendrickson Publishers, Inc., 2002.

Robertson, J. M.. *Pagan Christs*. New York: Dorset Press, 1987.

sacred-texts.com. Slavonic Josephus.

Suetonius. *The Twelve Caesars*. London: Penguin Books, 1979. Translated by Robert Graves; Revised by Michael Grant.

Tacitus, *The Annals and The Histories*. Chicago: Encyclopedia Britannica, Inc., 1952. Translated by Alfred John Church and William Jackson Brodribb.

Unterbrink, Daniel T.. *Judas the Galilean - the Flesh and Blood Jesus*. New York: iUniverse, Inc., 2004.

Unterbrink, Daniel T.. *New Testament Lies - The Greatest Challenge to Traditional Christianity*. New York: iUniverse, Inc., 2006.

Vermes, Geza. *The Complete Dead Sea Scrolls in English*. New York: Allen Lane, The Penguin Press, 1997.

Whiston, William. *The Works of Josephus*. Mass: Hendrickson Publishers, 1984.

Williamson, G. A.. *Josephus The Jewish War*. New York: Penguin Books, 1981.

Wise, Michael and Abegg, Martin, Jr. and Cook, Edward. *The Dead Sea Scrolls - A New Translation*. New York: HarperSanFrancisco, 1996.

NOTES

INTRODUCTION

1. S. G. F. Brandon, *Jesus and the Zealots*, p. 217.

2. Hyam Maccoby, *Revolution in Judaea* and *The Mythmaker*.

CHAPTER 1

1. Daniel T. Unterbrink, *New Testament Lies*, pp. 31-37.

2. Slavonic Josephus, After *War* 2.168.

3. *Ibid.*, After *War* 2.168.

4. *Ibid.*, After *War* 2.110.

5. Daniel T. Unterbrink, *Judas the Galilean*, p. 7. Also see *Ant.* 18.63-64.

6. Slavonic Josephus, After *War* 1.400.

7. Eusebius, *The History of the Church*, Christ and His Contemporaries, Book 1.9.

8. Suetonius, *The Twelve Caesars*, Claudius 25.

9. Tacitus, *The Annals,* xii. 54.

10. Dio Cassius 60.6.6-7.

CHAPTER 2

1. Slavonic Josephus, After *War* 2.222.

2. Eusebius, *The History of the Church*, Tiberius to Nero, Book 2.11-12.

3. *Ibid.*, Christ and His Contemporaries, Book 1.5.

4. Henry Bettenson, *Documents of the Christian Church*, p. 5; Justin, *Apology*, I. xlvi. 1-4.

5. *Ibid.*, pp. 1-2, Tacitus, *The Annals*, xv. 44.

6. *Ibid.*, pp. 3-4, Pliny, *Epp. X (ad Traj.)*, xcvi.

7. Pseudoclementine *Recognitions*, 1.70-71.

CHAPTER 3

1. Tacitus, *The Annals*, ii. 42.

2. Hyam Maccoby, *Revolution in Judaea*, p. 136.

3. Robert Eisenman, *James the Brother of Jesus*, p. 252.

4. Slavonic Josephus, After *War* 1.650.

CHAPTER 4

1. Suetonius, *The Twelve Caesars*, Claudius 25.

2. Robert Eisenman, *James the Brother of Jesus*, p. 17.

3. *Ibid.*, p. 133.

4. Eusebius, *The History of the Church*, Tiberius to Nero, Book 2.23.4.

5. *Ibid.*, Book 2.1.3.

6. Daniel T. Unterbrink, *Judas the Galilean*, p. 83.

7. Robert Eisenman, *James the Brother of Jesus*, pp. 154-184.

8. Ibid., p. 467. Eisenman quotes Epiphanius (Haeres 78.13.2 and 14.5) and notes that the death of Jesus would be 38 CE, the approximate year of John the Baptist's death, per Josephus. Eisenman has not recognized the relationship between John and the Sadduc and therefore is a bit misdirected on the year of "Jesus'" death.

CHAPTER 5

1. Robert Eisenman, *James the Brother of Jesus*, pp. 154-184.

CHAPTER 6

1. Karl Marx and Friedrich Engles with introduction by A.J.P. Taylor, *The Communist Manifesto*, pp. 37-38.

2. Michael Wise, Martin Abegg, Jr., and Edward Cook, *The Dead Sea Scrolls, a New Translation*, p. 24.

3. *Ibid.*, p. 25.

4. *Ibid.*, p. 26.

5. *Ibid.*, p. 32.

6. Daniel T. Unterbrink, *Judas the Galilean*, The Dead Sea Scrolls, pp. 82-97.

7. Michael Wise, Martin Abegg, Jr., and Edward Cook, *The Dead Sea Scrolls, a New Translation*, p. 33.

8. *Ibid.*, p. 33.

9. *Ibid.*, p. 25.

10. Eusebius, *The History of the Church*, Christ and His Contemporaries, Book 1.9.

11. Tacitus, *The Histories*, v. 9.

12. Suetonius, *The Twelve Caesars*, Claudius 25.

13. Robert Eisenman, *James the Brother of Jesus*, p. 870.

14. Suetonius, *The Twelve Caesars*, Claudius 28.

15. Tacitus, *The Histories*, v. 9.

16. Alvar Ellegard, *Jesus One Hundred Years Before Christ*, p. 85.

17. In the *War* 6.300-309, a prophet named Jesus was tried before Albinus. This Jesus cried out, "Woe to Jerusalem" for seven years and five months. It is possible that this Jesus was also molded into the Jesus of Nazareth composite.

18. William Whiston, *The Works of Josephus*, p. 815.

19. S.G.F. Brandon, *Jesus and the Zealots*, p. XX.

20. Tacitus, *The Annals*, xv. 38.

21. *Ibid.*, xv. 44.

22. *Ibid.*, xv. 44.

23. Suetonius, *The Twelve Caesars*, Nero 16.

24. Edward Gibbon, *The History of the Decline and Fall of the Roman Empire*, Vol. 1, chapter 16, pp. 530-531.

25. Eusebius, *The History of the Church*, Book 2, Tiberius to Nero, 25.

26. Henry Bettenson, *Documents of the Christian Church*, p. 37, Irenaeus, *Adv. haer.* I. xxvi. I, 2.

CHAPTER 7

1. Robert Eisenman, *James the Brother of Jesus*, chapter 14, pp. 411-465.

CHAPTER 8

1. Eisenman, *James the Brother of Jesus*, p. 52.

2. Hyam Maccoby, *The Mythmaker*, p. 65.

3. *Ibid.*, p. 67.

CHAPTER 9

1. www.ccel.org., *Recognitions of Clement* 1.70.

CHAPTER 10

1. *Ant.* 18.130-142; Robert Eisenman, *James the Brother of Jesus*, pp. 968-969.

2. Robert Graves, *Claudius the God*, pp. 282-283.

3. Why did Josephus omit Agrippa's role in the initial telling of the assassination? Maybe Josephus was uncomfortable writing about the assassination of a Caesar by a Jewish King. This would have put the Jews in an even worse light.

4. Suetonius, *The Twelve Caesars*, Claudius 25.

5. Robert Graves, *Claudius the God*, p. 324.

CHAPTER 11

1. Romans 1:1; 3:24; 6:3; 6:11; 8:1 (twice); 8:34; 15:5; 15:16; 15:17 and 16:3.

2. Romans 6:23 and 8:39.

3. Romans 1:6; 1:8; 2:16; 3:22; 5:15; 5:17; 16:25 and 16:27.

4. Romans 1:4; 1:7; 5:1; 5:11; 5:21; 7:25; 13:14; 15:6 and 15:30.

5. Romans 3:26 and 8:11.

6. Romans 4:24; 10:9; 14:14 and 16:20.

7. Romans 14:5-10 (seven times); 16:2; 16:8; 16:11; 16:12 (twice); 16:13 and 16:22.

8. Romans 5:6; 5:8; 6:4; 6:8; 6:9; 7:4; 8:10; 8:11; 8:17; 8:35; 9:1; 9:3; 9:5; 10:4; 10:7; 12:5; 14:18; 15:3; 15:7; 15:8; 15:18; 15:19; 15:20; 15:29; 16:5; 16:7; 16:9; 16:10 and 16:16.

9. Romans 14:9 and 16:18.

10. Romans 8:9.

11. Henry Bettenson, *Documents of the Christian Church*, p. 37, Irenaeus, *Adv. haer.* I. xxvii. 2-3.

12. *Ibid.*

13. *Ibid.*

CHAPTER 12

1. Suetonius, *The Twelve Caesars*, Claudius, 25.

2. Tacitus, *The Annals*, xv. 44.

3. *Ibid.*

4. Daniel T. Unterbrink, *Judas the Galilean*, Appendix 4, pp. 219-228.

5. Josephus, *Antiquities* 18.85-89 and Philo, *On the Embassy to Gaius*, 299-305.

CHAPTER 13

1. Edward Gibbon, *The History of the Decline and Fall of the Roman Empire*, Vol. 1, Chapter 16, pp. 530-531.

2. Slavonic Josephus, After *War* 1.400.

3. Ibid., After *War* 2.110

4. Ibid., After *War* 2.110

5. Pseudoclementine *Recognitions* 1.53-54.

6. John Dominic Crossan and Jonathan L. Reed, *Excavating Jesus*, p. 18.

7. Slavonic Josephus, After *War* 1.650.

8. Hyam Maccoby, *Revolution in Judaea*, p. 19 and p. 222 (note 3).

9. G. A. Williamson and E. Mary Smallwood, *The Jewish War*, Appendix A, p. 461.

10. John Dominic Crossan and Jonathan L. Reed, *Excavating Jesus*, p. 174.

CHAPTER 14

1. Daniel T. Unterbrink, *Judas the Galilean*, Appendix 4, pp. 219-228.

2. Pseudoclementine *Recognitions*, 1.54.

3. Tacitus, *The Annals,* xv. 44.

4. William Barclay, *The Daily Study Bible*, Revelation.

5. Josephus, *The Life of Flavius Josephus*, pp. 14-15.

6. William Barclay, *The Daily Study Bible*, Acts.

CHAPTER 15

1. John Dominic Crossan and Jonathan L. Reed, *Excavating Jesus*, p. 18.

CHAPTER 16

1. Bart D. Ehrman, *Lost Scriptures*, The Gospel of Philip.

2. *Ibid.*, p. 38.

3. Slavonic Josephus, After *War* 2.220.

4. *Ibid.*, After *War* 2.220.

5. Robert Eisenman, *James, the Brother of Jesus*, pp. 592-597.

6. Daniel T. Unterbrink, *Judas the Galilean*, p. 153.

CHAPTER 17

1. Daniel T. Unterbrink, *Judas the Galilean*, Appendix 4, pp. 219-228.

2. Eusebius, *The History of the Church*, Christ and His Contemporaries, Book 1.9.

3. Slavonic Josephus, After *War* 2.174.

4. Hyam Maccoby, *Revolution in Judaea*, pp. 143-144.

CHAPTER 18

1. William Barclay, *The Daily Study Bible*, Mark p. 16.

2. Slavonic Josephus, After *War* 2.110.

3. Robert Eisenman, *James the Brother of Jesus*, p. 17.

4. Pseudoclementine *Recognitions*, 1.53-54.

5. Slavonic Josephus, After *War* 2.168.

6. Pseudoclementine *Recognitions*, 1.54.

7. Slavonic Josephus, After *War* 1.400.

CHAPTER 19

1. Hyam Maccoby, *Revolution in Judaea*, pp. 127-128.

2. *Ibid.*, pp. 133-134.

3. *Ibid.*, p. 133.

4. *Ibid.*, pp. 132-133.

5. J. M. Robertson, *Pagan Christs*, p. 112.

6. *Ibid.*, p. 118.

7. *Ibid.*, p. 110.

8. Hyam Maccoby, *Revolution in Judaea*, pp. 143-144.

9. *Ibid.*, pp. 147-149.

10. Luke always supplied more information concerning the real events. He mentioned Annas and Caiaphas twice (Luke 3:2 and Acts 4:5-6) and each time gave preeminence to Annas.

11. *Ant.* 18.55-59 and 18:85-89 and Philo, *On the Embassy to Gaius*, vs. 299-305.

12. Slavonic Josephus, After *War* 2.174.

13. Hyam Maccoby, *Revolution in Judaea*, p. 160.

14. *Ibid.*, p. 160.

15. *Ibid.*, pp. 164-165.

16. Slavonic Josephus, After *War* 2.174.

17. J. M. Robertson, *Pagan Christs*, p. 110.

18. *Ibid.*, p. 110.

19. Robert Eisenman, *James the Brother of Jesus*, p. 581.

CHAPTER 20

1. William Barclay, *The Daily Study Bible*, Revelation Volume 2.

2. *Ibid.*

3. www.caesarmessiah.com/summary.html.

4. S. G. F. Brandon, *Jesus and the Zealots*, p. 54.

5. *Ibid.*, p. 88.

6. *Ibid.*, pp. 88-90.

CHAPTER 21

1. Timothy Freke and Peter Gandy, *The Jesus Mysteries*, pp. 27-61.

2. *Ibid.* pp. 61-62.

Lightning Source UK Ltd.
Milton Keynes UK
172660UK00002B/18/P